ADULT EDUCATION AND LIFELONG LEARNING

This is the third edition of Peter Jarvis' classic textbook *Adult and Continuing Education*, which established itself as the most widely used and respected book about education for adults today. In this new edition, the author has made extensive revisions and included substantial additional material to take account of the many changes that have occurred in the field of the education of adults.

Additional and updated material in this much anticipated new edition includes:

- a discussion on both globalization and Europeanization – indicating the pressures that have been exerted on the educational system to change;
- a greater emphasis on lifelong education, lifelong learning and society;
- an extended discussion on the theorists of distance education, and introductory material on e-learning and on-line learning;
- an updated look at changes in UK policy and European policy documents;
- new material on the relationship between research, learning and the changing approaches to knowledge, with more emphasis placed on action learning and research.

Students of education for adults will find this an invaluable course companion, whilst practitioners and researchers in adult and lifelong learning will find the new edition even more of a fixture than the last.

Peter Jarvis is Professor of Continuing Education at the University of Surrey and has published extensively in the field of the education of adults.

ADULT EDUCATION AND LIFELONG LEARNING

3rd edition

Theory and Practice

Peter Jarvis

 RoutledgeFalmer
Taylor & Francis Group

LONDON AND NEW YORK

First edition published 1983
by Croom Helm

Second edition published 1995
by Routledge

This edition published 2004
by RoutledgeFalmer
11 New Fetter Lane, London EC4P 4EE

Simultaneously published in the USA and Canada
by RoutledgeFalmer
29 West 35th Street, New York, NY 10001

RoutledgeFalmer is an imprint of the Taylor & Francis Group

© 1983, 1995, 2004 Peter Jarvis

Typeset in New Baskerville by Wearset Ltd, Boldon, Tyne and Wear
Printed and bound in Great Britain by TJ International, Padstow,
Cornwall

British Library Cataloguing in Publication Data
A catalogue record for this book is available from the British Library

Library of Congress Cataloging in Publication Data
A catalog record for this book has been requested

ISBN 0-415-31492-5 (HB)
ISBN 0-415-31493-3 (PB)

In memory of Mother, Father and Jack in gratitude

CONTENTS

CONTENTS

FIGURES

TABLES

ACKNOWLEDGEMENTS

Few books can be written without the encouragement, inspiration and, even, provocation of friends and colleagues. This book has all of these origins and without them it would have been the poorer. There are, however, some who deserve especial mention and to whom I am greatly indebted: Miss Sheila Gibson, Dr Alan Chadwick and Dr Cohn Griffin have read all or part of the book in draft form and their comments have enriched the text considerably; the postgraduate students in the Department of Education Studies at the University of Surrey have continued to help me to clarify some of my ideas in our teaching and learning sessions; Mrs Hilarie Hall has undertaken the responsibility of transforming my handwritten draft into a typescript with expertise and efficiency.

I would like to express my gratitude to those who have given me permission to quote or reproduce from other writings: the Cambridge Book Company, New York, to quote Roby Kidd's 'Ten Commandments'; Dr Cohn Griffin, to summarize most of the points he raised in his paper on continuing and recurrent education in Table 9.3; Holt, Rinehart and Winston, to reproduce Professor Dennis Child's diagram of Maslow's hierarchy of needs and Professor Robert Gagné's diagram of the relation between phases of learning and events of instruction; Jossey Bass, to reproduce two diagrams from Professor C. Houle's *The Design of Education*.

Once again, I must gratefully acknowledge the help and support of my wife, Maureen, and children, Frazer and Kierra, who have encouraged me to write, even though it has resulted in them undertaking additional family responsibilities.

Many people have helped me to produce this text but, like every writer, the final responsibility for what has been produced must rest with me.

INTRODUCTION TO THE
FIRST EDITION

The study of adult education is growing in significance as the training of educators of adults is being undertaken more frequently in the United Kingdom and elsewhere. But there are few textbooks that seek to introduce students to a broad sweep of the field, and so this text has been prepared with this aim in view. It is hoped that students of the education of adults on ACSET I, II and III, Certificate, Diploma and Degree courses might find it a useful volume. In addition, it is hoped that other practitioners in the field of adult and continuing education will find much in this book that is relevant to their work.

With this aim in mind, the book has been very fully referenced so that readers can follow up any of the points that interest them and can also refer to the original sources. Further reading suggestions for each chapter are at the end of book, so that ideas from each chapter might be developed by interested readers. The contents of the book are wide enough to introduce students and practitioners to a variety of contemporary issues in the study of the education of adults. The aspects discussed in this book reflect the purpose for which it has been written, so that a great deal of it is devoted to the teaching and learning transaction. These have been divided into different chapters in the book for reasons of clarity but in reality such a division is frequently artificial.

The text attempts to combine the theoretical with the practical and it is hoped that those who read it will find it informative, relevant and, above all, useful.

INTRODUCTION TO THE
REVISED EDITION

This book was originally written as a textbook for the first year MSc course in Adult Education which I taught at the University of Surrey, a course which has subsequently been modularized in line with many of the other changes that are discussed in this revised edition. Adult educators are only too well aware of all the changes that have happened and, no doubt, like me they are not happy with all the things that they have been forced to do, despite many of the changes having been anticipated in one form or another for a number of years. But there have been so many changes that the latter part of this book has required considerable rewriting so that much of it is new. I hope that I have captured the changes without changing the nature of the book too greatly.

Not only have there been considerable changes in the fields of study, but over the period I have changed some of my views and also have published a number of other pieces about adult and continuing education. Where I have written something since the original version of this book was published, I have tried to make reference to it, so that readers of this revised version will see how much of my own development has occurred.

In addition, the original version was written using the pronoun 'he' in the impersonal sense, and I was rightly taken to task about this soon after the publication of this book. I hope that I have rectified this throughout this present study, although I acknowledge that it has made the revision even more complex than it would have been had only the changes referred to above been incorporated.

I am most grateful to Routledge, and especially to Helen Fairlie for asking me to revise the book, and for awaiting a slightly delayed manuscript, although the reasons for this have been due to events beyond my control. I am also most grateful to those who edited and typeset this revised version for taking the original book and all my alterations and making it into a comprehensive and comprehensible volume.

I would also like to thank those readers who made comments to the publishers about additions that they considered I should make to update this book. I hope that I have done justice to their comments, although, like every other author, I cannot blame anybody but myself for what I have written!

Over the years some people have been kind enough to tell me that they have found the original version of this book useful and I can only hope that this revised edition might also prove useful to some who use it.

INTRODUCTION TO THE
THIRD EDITION

It is a rare privilege for any author to have his work in print for as long as this has been – it is now 20 years since the first edition appeared. When I revised the book in the 1990s I thought that the revisions were extensive but I never dreamed that, if a third edition was to appear, it would almost be a new book. Indeed, when the proposal for this edition was read, some of the reviewers suggested that I should actually write it as a new book. At the time I thought that my proposals were sufficient, but having now completed this edition I realize that the reviewers were not wrong; there are so many changes, including the title, that I might have written a new book. However, I have tried to retain as much of the second edition as possible, and in one or two places I have retained some of the material in order to provide a full overview of the way that things developed.

The last ten years have seen massive changes to our field and it is now becoming more complex than ever. This complexity is reflected in the book's new title – adult education and lifelong learning. Lifelong learning is probably the more popular title for the field in UK at the moment, but as I travel around the world I still meet the term adult education as frequently as ever. The effects of globalization are rather like the ripples on a pond when a stone is thrown into the water. In Western Europe we are seeing rapid changes, while adult education is developing more slowly in some others. I have wanted to try and catch this diversity in the title and in the content of the book. Additionally, I was tempted to change the order of terms Theory and Practice to Practice and Theory – but, in the end, I retained them because this was the way that they appeared in the original book.

Over the years, people have been kind enough to tell me that this book has been useful to their understanding of the education of adults and it has also been translated into other languages. I am grateful for this and it has been this encouragement that inspired me to undertake this edition. I can only hope that this edition will also be useful to other people working on our field, and perhaps to some who have honoured me by reading the earlier editions.

I would like to recall the way that the first edition was written because I think that it is a lesson, for many of us have, or are expected by validating bodies to, become so much more instrumental and didactic about the way that we view education – often I think to its detriment. In the first edition, I recorded my thanks to the students with whom I worked on the Master's degree at Surrey at the time. That was a collaborative exercise – the students, all teachers of adults and part-time students chose the topics that they wanted to study throughout the year and we ordered them logically. We then decided which individual would lead which session – I did not lead many. However, each week during the year I wrote a paper on the same topic as the students, so that I could contribute to the discussion. My papers formed the basis of the first edition of this book, enriched by the discussions that occurred each week. Probably the book has survived for so long because they, practising educators of adults, chose the subjects because they were what interested them in their professional practice. It was certainly one of the most enriching groups with whom I have had the privilege of working, and if any of them read this book I hope that they will recall that time as fondly as me.

I wish to thank the unknown reviewers of my proposal for this edition for their many excellent suggestions and I hope that if they do me the privilege of reading this they will see that I have responded quite fully to their points. All the chapters have been rewritten, some quite extensively, one chapter has been subdivided – although I considered it for at least two others (Chapters 3 and 5), and some of the later chapters have been re-ordered so that there is a reasonable progression through them. Finally, I would like to thank everybody who has worked with the Publisher – which has also changed over the years – who over the years have ensured that this book should remain in print.

Peter Jarvis
Thatcham, Berks
August 2003

1

TOWARDS A RATIONALE FOR THE PROVISION OF LEARNING OPPORTUNITIES FOR ADULTS

When the first edition of this book was published, it was important to argue a strong case for the education of adults since it was still something that we did not take for granted, but it was also the start of the most rapid period of social change that we have witnessed, which has transformed our understanding of both education and learning. Now we take it for granted that adults should continue to be educated throughout their lifetime. Now we no longer have to argue a case for this education to be provided, but it is still important to understand the changes that have occurred to help us understand education in our present society.

It will also have been noted that the title of this book has been changed, since when the first edition of the book appeared we were watching the development of continuing education amongst the professions and the rearguard action that liberal adult education was taking place to ensure its survival. Now continuing education, while still a term frequently used, is less common than lifelong learning, which is itself an ambiguous term which will be discussed more fully below. At the same time, the term adult education still retains considerable currency around the world and so it has been retained. However, the title to this chapter in the earlier editions was about 'the education of adults', a term that I started using in the early 1980s rather than 'adult education' in order to seek to combine the ideas underlying continuing professional education and adult education. Now the chapter is about the provision of learning opportunities for adults, which seeks to capture something of the ambiguity of the term lifelong learning.

The chapter has four major sections: the first is about the changing nature of society in which these learning opportunities are provided; the second is about the nature of the individual; the third is about human beings as lifelong learners; and the final section is about the nature of the human being as having a need to learn.

The nature of contemporary society

Any discussion on the nature of society inevitably assumes certain theoretical perspectives and in contemporary society there are certain concepts

1

that we do need to grasp. For instance, the terms globalization, knowledge society, learning society, and so on are buzz words today but they all indicate in their different ways how education has been forced to respond to contemporary social forces. In order to understand this relationship, it is necessary to discuss each of these processes from the outset, starting with globalization, and see their relationship to education and learning.

Globalization

There are a variety of different ways of looking at the concept of globalization, e.g. economic, sociological and social, amongst others. Indeed, for some people it is also about the global rather than the processes of globalization. However, this book is not a study of the processes of globalization *per se* (see Castells, 1996; Held *et al.*, 1999), but we will treat it here as a socio-economic phenomenon that has profound political and cultural implications for education.

From an over-simplistic perspective, it can be understood by thinking of the *world* as having a substructure and a superstructure, whereas the simple Marxist model of society was that each *society* had a substructure and a superstructure. For Marx, the substructure was the economic institution and the superstructure everything else in social and cultural life – including the state, education, and so on. In Marx's analysis those who owned the capital, and therefore the means of production, were able to exercise power throughout the whole of their society. But over the years ownership has changed to control, the capital has become intellectual as well as financial and the boundaries between the states have been lowered – Europeanization is a good illustration of this. However, a major weakness of Marx's model is its determinism. But there is a sense in which globalization still acts rather like the rudiments of Marx's model of society – now this substructure has become global rather than societal, but it does not determine the shape of the global superstructure, only influence it in the same way in different societies of the world. This process of globalization has two main drivers (which we could see as the global substructure): the economic institution and information technology.

Now those who have control of the substructure in the countries of the dominant West have been enabled to extend their influence over the substructures of all the other countries in the world. The effects that these substructural changes are having on the superstructure of each society mean that the common substructure exerts similar forces on each people and society despite each having different histories, cultures, languages, and so on.

The other driving force in the globalization process is information technology. The tremendously rapid changes that have occurred in this have facilitated the global processes and have also contributed to the development of rapidly changing knowledge. Significantly, the widespread use of information technology almost makes state boundaries redundant in respect to the flow of information across the globe. Consequently we can see that the forces of globalization exercise standardizing pressures, but a variety of peoples and societies resist this by endeavouring, to differing extents, to retain their uniqueness and independence. Robertson (1995) refers to the processes whereby societies retain their unique cultures whilst still functioning within the wider globalization process as glocalization.

The global superstructure is now more like a lattice work in which the various parts are fluid and changing as some lose their distinctness within the sea of change, whilst others fight to retain their uniqueness. Each state apparatus, for instance, has endeavoured to retain some of its own sovereign power but this is at the time when those who have power at the substructural level operate on a global playing field, so that individual governments are now almost incapable of regulating the global market or its substructure. We can all think of cases of large corporations who could, and we have seen how they should have been regulated by governments but they have appeared to be almost independent of them. Beck (2000:11) actually suggests that globalization is 'the *processes* through which sovereign national states are criss-crossed and undermined by transnational actors with varying prospects of power, orientations, identities and networks' (italics in original).

The process of globalization, as we know it today, began in the West (USA followed by Western Europe) in the early 1970s. There were a number of contributory factors at this time that exacerbated this process, such as:

- the oil crisis in the 1970s, which dented the confidence of the West;
- the demise of the Bretton Woods Agreement, that eventually enabled both free trade and the flow of financial capital to develop throughout the world;
- the development of sophisticated information technology, initially through the star wars programme, through which the information technology revolution took off, with one development leading to another, as Castells (1996:51f.) demonstrates. He (1996:52) makes the point that 'to some extent, the availability of new technologies constituted as a system in the 1970s was a fundamental basis for the process of socio-economic restructuring in the 1980s';
- the economic competition from Japan, which challenged the West;
- the use of scientific knowledge in the production of commodities in the global market;
- the fall of the Berlin Wall – the democratization of the Eastern Bloc – for, from the time it occurred, there has literally been 'no alternative' (Bauman, 1992) to global capitalism and so it reinforced the process.

It was at this same period in the 1970s that theorists, recognizing these processes, first began to suggest that there was actually a world economy (Wallerstein, 1974, *inter alia*) based on the capitalist system of exchange. His approach was questioned in part by Robertson (1995), amongst others. Castells (1996 – vol. 1) has also argued that the state still has a place to play in a not-completely free but extremely competitive global market. Nevertheless, corporations began to relocate manufacturing and to transfer capital around the world from about the early 1970s, seeking the cheapest places and the most efficient means to manufacture, and the best markets in which to sell their products so that an international division of labour has been created and a competitive international market generated. Additionally, the corporations have been able to locate themselves in countries where they have to pay fewer taxes, so that they underplay their responsibility to the world (see Cohen, 2002 for a recent example), although some of them seek to persuade the world that they are exercising social responsibility by establishing charitable foundations or contributing some financial and intellectual assistance to under-privileged peoples, or to other needy causes. Somewhere, I think, Reinhart Niebuhr called this paternalistic.

However, as manufacturing has been relocated, new knowledge-based industries have taken their place in the West, and this has had a phenomenal effect on the nature of education and learning.

While this is a brief outline of the globalization processes, we want to focus on two aspects here in order to develop our argument: power, and inequality and social exclusion. But before we do so, it is necessary to remind ourselves that Europeanization is also helping to penetrate the boundaries of all the member states and bring about some forms of standardization. It is paradoxical that this process should act in a similar manner to economic globalization. Other outcomes of these processes will be discussed during the remainder of the chapter [see Held *et al.* (1999) for a full discussion of global transformations].

Power

The law of global society is the law of the global market in which transnational corporations are the major players, whereas the laws of the states are still apparently controlled by the democratic (or not so democratic) governments, although the extent to which the national governments are sovereign is much more questionable (see Korten, 1995; Monbiot, 2000). Certainly the laws of the market have simply by-passed the laws of the states and the corporations are now able to exert tremendous pressures on national and local governments in order to pursue their own policies. These processes have made the nation states far less powerful than ever before in their history, so that politicians now call for partnerships between the public and private sector. But politicians are only willing to do this and to cooperate with these powerful institutions because they are realists and recognize where the power lies – it is at least shared, if not lost! But as Bauman (1999:156) noted:

> Once the state recognizes the priority and superiority of the laws of the market over the laws of the *polis*, the citizen is transmuted into the consumer, and a 'consumer demands more and more protection while accepting less and less the need to participate' in the running of the state.
>
> (*italics* in original)

We are nearly all aware of the way in which education, even state-supported education, has become a commodity to be sold on the learning market rather than a state provision for the good of its population, and some of the points discussed below will refer to this.

However, it might be claimed that the tragic events of 11th September 2001 and the allegations about the way that a few leading corporations, especially in the USA, have illegally mislead the world might actually have called into question their socio-economic power because they do not have the control of legitimate force and they can still be brought to courts of justice, so that politicians conceivably have the opportunity to act independently of the corporations – although their willingness to do so might sometimes be questioned. But as we have suggested already, if the states are part of the superstructure, then those who control the substructures will continue to exercise very strong influence over them and get them to defend the corporations' interests.

Inequality and social exclusion

The global market always favours the rich – since the market is never free – so that its operation is actually a function of power. Very few people who have had power have not used it in some way to become rich – even very rich (fat cats)! Countries also have made themselves much more wealthy by the same process. Those countries that have developed a knowledge economy have continued in their growth, others like Zambia are virtually excluded from the market. Similarly, those people who are employable can – if they wish – play an active part (to greater or lesser extent) in being citizens, but those who have no job are socially excluded. Bauman (1999:5–6) summarizes a United Nations' Development report, which illustrates these points:

- consumption has multiplied by a factor of six since 1950, but one billion people cannot even satisfy their most elementary needs;
- 60 per cent of residents in developing countries have no basic social

infrastructures, 33 per cent no access to drinking water, 25 per cent no accommodation worthy of the name and 20 per cent no sanitary or medical services;
- the average income of 120 million people is less than $1 per day;
- in the world's richest country (USA), 16.5 per cent live in poverty, 20 per cent of the adult population are illiterate; 13 per cent have a life expectancy of shorter than 60 years;
- the world's three richest men have private assets greater than the combined national products of the 48 poorest countries;
- the fortunes of the 15 richest men exceed the total produce of the whole of sub-Saharan Africa;
- 4 per cent of the wealth of the world's richest 225 men would offer the poor of the world access to elementary medical and educational amenities as well as adequate nutrition.

While the lack of welfare provision, or little genuine concern for the poor, is not a precondition of globalization, it certainly helps global capitalism expand its profitability because corporations can, and do, pay lower wages when there is a surplus of labour both nationally and internationally. The poor are excluded socially and economically from both local and global society. The division between the north and the south, for instance, is one of inclusion and exclusion. In those countries that are excluded, whilst they may aspire after lifelong learning policies, for example Nepal has a policy, they may not be quite so exposed to the driving forces of capital and information technology to have changed their ways of life nor forced upon them the necessity of lifelong learning. In these countries we find that the education of adults is still in its infancy and, even if there were to be cultural changes, it is doubtful whether they would have the finance to introduce it, so that they borrow from the West, for example the World Bank, and put themselves permanently in its debt. However, in this new economy it is not only poverty that leads to social exclusion, it is also the lack of the requisite knowledge to get work; we will discuss the nature of knowledge in the following section.

The changing nature of knowledge and the knowledge society

In order to understand the nature of social change and its effects on education, it is necessary to understand the way that our conceptions of knowledge, and even knowledge itself, have changed.

Knowledge

There are at least seven ways in which these changes have occurred: the legitimation of knowledge, the social construction of knowledge, its relativity, the types of knowledge, the nature of practical knowledge, the integrated nature of knowledge itself and Mode 1 to Mode 2 knowledge. We shall discuss these briefly and then show the relevance of the discussion to what we commonly call the knowledge society.

LEGITIMATION OF KNOWLEDGE

When I was young, knowledge was considered to be something that was factual and true and even when I started my academic life we still regarded research as a gathering of facts. But even then we were aware that knowledge was legitimated as fact by at least three different processes:

- *Rational* – we start with a premise (a priori) and argue a case; if the premise is accepted then it is only the rationality of the argument that can be disputed – we find this approach in philosophy, pure mathematics, and so on.
- *Empirical* – something is factual because it can be verified by empirical measurement and sense experience. For many people this is the main type of knowledge. For something to be true it has to be measurable, as we see in the constant endeavours to measure learning outcomes. However, not all measurement of phenomena is actually empirical and we do well to remember at this point that no fact has meaning – facts still need to be interpreted.
- *Pragmatic* – Pragmatism has been a significant part of the intellectual history of the United States for much longer than it has in Europe. Basically, pragmatism suggests that knowledge is legitimate if it is practical (see Rorty, 1982:160–175 for a discussion on James and Dewey). In more recent times, Lyotard (1984) has used the word performativity to argue that this is a major means of legitimating knowledge in a capitalist, market-orientated society in which it is important to know in order to do.

Habermas (1972) would list a slightly different three:

- empirical, incorporating a technical cognitive interest and coming from the analytical sciences;
- historical-hermeneutic, incorporating a practical interest;
- emancipatory, which comes from the critically orientated social sciences.

Knowledge, then, can be legitimated in a number of different ways, but there are other ways of looking at knowledge.

THE SOCIAL CONSTRUCTION OF KNOWLEDGE

Different scholars have, at different times, recognized that knowledge is subjective and socially constructed. Berger and Luckmann (1966) brought this to the attention of a wide audience and yet, from an entirely different perspective, Marx and Engels made a similar point many years before:

> The ideas of the ruling class are the ruling ideas: i.e. the class which is the dominant force in society is at the same time its dominant intellectual force.
>
> (cited from Bottomore and Rubel, 1963:93)

Marx and Engels were not so concerned about the epistemological questions as about why certain forms of knowledge dominated society. Gramsci (Joll, 1977) called this control of knowledge, which is often unrecognized, hegemony. Thus we can see why thinkers from the critical theory school, such as Habermas, were concerned to highlight the significance of emancipatory knowledge. Foucault also related dominant ideas to power, but he was concerned to illustrate that knowledge also legitimizes the exercise of power:

> ... at one point in history power could be understood quite simply in terms of a king or queen having a divine right to exercise it (they more or less stood in for God, so you could not really argue with them, from the seventeenth century on the guarantor of power – God – was replaced by something else – truth and knowledge.
>
> (Danaher *et al.*, 2000:25)

While these analyses differ from each other, they all point to the idea that knowledge is constructed and in some way it is related to the exercise of power in society which, as we have suggested, lies with those who control the economic institutions and information technology.

RELATIVITY OF KNOWLEDGE

In 1926, Max Scheler (1980:76) began to isolate the issues of the relativity of knowledge and he suggested that there are seven types of knowledge based upon their speed of change:

- myth and legend – undifferentiated religious, metaphysical, natural and historical;
- knowledge implicit in everyday language – as opposed to learned, poetic or technical;
- religious – from pious to dogmatic;

- mystical;
- philosophic-metaphysical;
- positive knowledge – mathematics, the natural sciences and the humanities;
- technological.

Scheler regarded his final two forms of knowledge as artificial because they changed so rapidly, whereas the other five are embedded in culture. Whilst his analysis was a little over-simple, he does make the point clearly that positive and technological knowledge change rapidly – he suggested 'hour by hour' – but that was in 1926! Not all scientific knowledge changes rapidly – the speed of light, for instance, has not changed, whereas our understanding of the nature of light has changed. Hence, Scheler's typology, whilst useful for our discussion only represents some aspects of our understanding of the complex nature of knowledge itself. We might also dispute with Scheler that the humanities should be coupled with mathematics and the natural sciences – indeed, I would place them in the same category as philosophical and metaphysical knowledge. While Scheler was not totally correct, his artificial forms of knowledge are related to the driving forces of globalization.

Whilst we have talked here about the relativity of knowledge, it must be pointed out that relativism in the philosophical sense not only accepts the idea that knowledge changes but also that no one form of knowledge is better than any other. But we have already clearly made the point that dominant knowledge, even if it is relative, is related to the power structures of society and consequently to those forms of knowledge useful to those who exercise power in society.

TYPES OF KNOWLEDGE

In *The Practitioner Researcher* (Jarvis, 1999a) I distinguished between knowledge and information but here I want to suggest that there are four types of knowledge important to our thinking about knowledge: data, information, knowledge and wisdom.

Data These are collected during research and fact-finding. They are about facts, but we do have to recognize that 'facts' have to be qualified and interpreted. They do not have intrinsic meaning; it is a construction of meaning, and data are therefore open to control and to being relative.

Information This is objective and transmitted to people through teaching, literature or the media. It is what is frequently referred to as objective knowledge. Information is usually written down and it is, therefore, unchanging. Both cultural and artificial knowledge should be seen as information when they are written. All forms of theory should also be treated as information that has been constructed and selected for transmission. Once information has been learned by individuals it becomes knowledge that can be transmitted to other people as information for them to consider.

Knowledge This is information that is learned and accepted – although it is not necessarily true, or fact. In this sense knowledge is always personal – but many people can learn the same information and that gives it the impression that it is objective. In fact, it is often inter-subjective which gives it the appearance of objectivity, and this commonness helps to bind individuals together – but as society becomes more open, there are more choices in learning, more opportunities to reflect and even more opportunities of creating one's own individual knowledge. However, the inter-subjectivity and the similarity of some individual knowledge between individuals is reflected in networks and communities of practice.

Wisdom This is a concept that has, until recent times, fallen into disfavour because there has been a greater emphasis on young people and rapidly changing knowledge. Consequently, the idea of the wisdom of the fathers has been something of an anachronism, although it seems to be regaining some of its credibility (Jarvis, 2001a). However, wisdom is knowledge gained through a great deal of experience, knowledge gained through repeated action and thought/contemplation. The idea of practical wisdom can be found in the writings of Aristotle, who claimed that this is a form of knowledge to be found amongst adults. He emphasized that:

> What has been said is confirmed by the fact that while young men become geometricians and mathematicians and wise in matters like these, it is thought that a young man of practical wisdom cannot be found. The cause is that such wisdom is concerned not only with universals but with particulars, which become familiar from experience, but a young man has no experience, for it is length of time that gives experience . . .
>
> (Aristotle, VI. 8:148)

He also noted that the possessor of practical wisdom must be able to deliberate about the reasons for acting accordingly, and amongst the reasons should be that of producing ends which are 'just and noble and good' (Book VI. 12:154) for humankind. Wisdom is usually regarded as a cognitive phenomenon but Aristotle was concerned with practical wisdom and this suggests that there is another element – expertise.

PRACTICAL KNOWLEDGE

Rather than distinguish knowledge from skills since we do not perform skills mindlessly, I want to combine them and to consider the combination as practical knowledge. This personal, practical knowledge has at least six dimensions which interact with each other in an integrated fashion when we act in any way:

- content knowledge – prepositional and theoretical (in some instances) knowledge;
- process knowledge – knowledge of the 'how' to do it;
- everyday knowledge – the experience which we bring to the learning/ action situation, which includes my understanding gained through the senses, such as smell and taste (Heller, 1984; Schutz, 1967 [1972]);
- attitudes, beliefs, values and emotions;
- tacit knowledge – that which enables me to function without apparent thought and to presume upon situations for whatever reason (Polanyi, 1967; Schutz and Luckmann, 1974);
- skill – the ability to do something.

Naturally, this formulation raises fundamental questions about the relationship between theory and practice (Jarvis, 1999a), and we shall return to this apparent problem later in the book, but we can see here why, not only wisdom, but also expertise are being re-established as part of the acceptable vocabulary and we can also see why Aristotle thought that practical wisdom is an adult characteristic.

However, expertise is also a form of wisdom since it involves practical knowledge; experts are usually knowledgeable about what they do even though they sometimes find it difficult to explain it.

INTEGRATED KNOWLEDGE

Knowledge has been divided into its academic disciplines and we have been accustomed both to teach and learn individual disciplines and sub-disciplines. However, when we act in almost any capacity we do not divide our practical knowledge into a little bit of philosophy, a little bit of sociology, and so on; we assume it to be totally integrated. It is important to distinguish here between multi-disciplinary knowledge and integrated knowledge; the former is about looking at a phenomenon from more than one perspective whereas integrated knowledge does not divide knowledge into disciplines – so that educational knowledge, nursing knowledge, and so on, are integrated practical knowledges. Now this does not mean that disciplinary knowledge is of no value – we still need it in order

11

to analyse and interpret phenomena. Both a knowledge of the academic disciplines and of practical knowledge are important to the expert practitioner and to our understanding of the nature of knowledge and the knowledge society.

MODE 1–MODE 2 KNOWLEDGE

These terms have come to the fore as a result of the book by Gibbons *et al.* (1994) in which they suggest that:

> in Mode 1 problems are set and solved in a context governed by the, largely, academic interests of a specific community. By contrast, Mode 2 knowledge is carried out in the context of application. Mode 1 is disciplinary, while Mode 2 is transdisciplinary. Mode 1 is characterised by homogeneity, Mode 2 by heterogeneity. Organisationally, Mode 1 is hierarchical and tends to preserve its form, while Mode 2 is more heterarchical and transient.
>
> (Gibbons *et al.*, 1994:3)

It will be seen from the above discussion that this distinction only achieves the types of changes that have been discussed already and, in a way, it over-simplifies that complexity of the ways in which knowledge has changed. At the same time, it does capture what we have discussed in a straightforward manner.

Our conception of knowledge has, therefore, undergone quite profound changes over recent years, but it is not difficult to see that these have major implications for teaching and learning; we shall consider these throughout the following chapters. Before we undertake this, however, it is important that we relate this understanding of knowledge to the concept of the knowledge society.

The knowledge society

Stehr (1994) suggested that the knowledge society is based, not on all forms of knowledge, but on scientific knowledge – that is, in Scheler's terms, on artificial or relative knowledge. But this knowledge has grown in volume and changes rapidly, so that Senge (1990:69) makes a significant point that perhaps for the first time in human history humankind now produces more knowledge than people can absorb.

Sociologists have always studied the structures of society although in recent years the survival of society itself is being questioned (Bauman, 2002), but one thesis, relevant to our thinking that attracted considerable attention in the 1960s and 1970s when society was a taken-for-granted concept, was that of the logic of industrialization. This was first published at the beginning of the 1960s in *Industrialism and Industrial Man* (Kerr *et al.*, 1973). Like Marx, but from an entirely different viewpoint, these authors implied that each society has a substructure and a superstructure. They argued that the substructural driving force of change was the industrialization process itself. However, it was the identification of this substructural force that was to prove a major weakness in their thesis; they did not foresee the changes that were to occur in the 1970s with the processes of globalization and the introduction of information technology that was to alter the faces of the industry and commerce. I have explored this elsewhere (Jarvis, 2001b) and so I do not want to pursue it here.

But another aspect of their argument that is important is that they regarded higher education as part of the social superstructure – as the handmaiden of industrialism:

> The higher educational system of the industrial society stresses the natural sciences, engineering, medicine, managerial training – whether private or public – and administrative law. It must steadily adapt to new disciplines and fields of specialization. There is a relatively smaller place for the humanities and the arts, while the social sciences are strongly related to the training of the managerial groups and technicians for the enterprise and for government. The increased leisure time, however, can afford a broader public appreciation of the humanities and the arts.
>
> (Kerr *et al.*, 1973:47)

They claimed that the higher educational system would have to expand to meet the needs of industrialization, and this would create an increasing level of education for all citizens, albeit with a greater emphasis on those subjects relevant to the substructural demands. But it is not only higher education that has been affected in this way, it is the education of adults – especially what is now termed lifelong learning. Whilst Kerr and his colleagues misread the driving forces of change, they actually had focused on precisely the direction that education would be forced to take. They recognized that certain forms of knowledge would become prevalent in the higher education of the latter part of the twentieth century; these were the sciences, law and relevant social sciences. Basically, they were saying that in the knowledge society, the dominant form of knowledge by which all other knowledge is assessed, is based on rapidly changing scientific and technological – especially, information technological – knowledge. This dominant form is now prevalent and the holders of power place far less value upon Scheler's cultural forms of knowledge, because apparently they are not wealth producing, than they do on scientific and artificial knowledge. Individuals in the work force are expected to keep

13

abreast with all the technological changes that occur in their place of work. This point was made as early as 1982:

> In recent years the obsolescence of knowledge has been most marked in the professions. Many professional bodies now encourage, and sometimes require, their members to undertake regular courses of continuing education and professional development. The need for regular updating will broaden across much more of the working population.
>
> (ACACE, 1982b:9)

By this time, continuing education had become a reality in the professions (see Houle, 1980) and by the mid-1990s it had become lifelong learning. Over this period some more traditional occupations have declined while others have disappeared leaving many to seek new forms of employment and industrial training, while many more new occupations have appeared, especially in knowledge-based industries. Government retraining schemes have now become relatively common in the United Kingdom and many forms of vocational education have increased and expanded. Indeed, Woodhall (1980:22) estimated that in 1978–9, in the United Kingdom, a figure of £3,000 million was spent on all forms of vocational training, equivalent to one-third of the total expenditure on education and equal to about 3 per cent of all wages and salaries. In 1988:83f. she repeated these figures whilst arguing that it is tremendously difficult to calculate the real cost of part-time education, although it had been clear for years that the amount of investment in education was growing.

What was also actually growing tremendously rapidly was corporate investment in education. Companies in Germany in the 1990s, for instance, invested some 27 billion DM annually in further training, which is nearly 40 per cent of the total amount spent on all forms of continuing education in Germany in 1994 (Dohman, 1996:15). Employers are regarded as good if they invest in people – but the reality is that unless they do so they will not survive in today's knowledge society.

In America, Eurich (1985:6), citing Harold Hodgkinson who was formerly the director of the Professional Institute of American Management Associations, suggested that the cost of training in 1981 came close to the total cost of running the whole of America's higher education system, which in that year amounted to $55 billion. But by 1990, Carnivale *et al.* (1990a:xi) were suggesting a figure closer to $210 billion on formal and informal job training. The growth was not to stop here, however, and by 2002 Morrison and Meister anticipated that the corporate budget in America for e-learning alone in 2003 would be $11.5 billion (Morrison and Meister, 2002:1). The cost of providing education for the work force is, therefore, not a small addendum to the total expenditure on education each year, a point to which we shall return in the final chapter of this book. Technological innovation has also led to structural unemployment, which calls for retraining and this also costs countries a great deal in financial support that has to be included in any final calculations about the cost of providing vocational education.

With the rapidly changing knowledge being at the heart of what we regard as the knowledge society, we can see how the focus of education and learning has moved much more to be responsive to the demands of the global substructural forces and away from its traditional humanistic orientation – although this move has not occurred without considerable resistance, as we shall see later in this book, but it is also hardly surprising that we now also have the concept of the learning society.

The learning society

The learning society is both a confused and a confusing idea that requires some explication here, but in this instance the learning society is associated with social change. The more prevalent or profound the changes that occur in a society, the greater the likelihood that it will be regarded as a learning society. Change is now endemic but the speed of change is different in different countries, and it is slower in the socially excluded south where behaviour is more patterned and repetitive giving the society a sense of permanence and people can take their behaviour for granted, so that there is little new learning in later life. In other words, for societies to exist their members must repeat certain fundamental processes, like language and behaviour patterns, but in many societies of rapid social change these patterns are at a minimal level and so taken-for-grantedness cannot always be assumed, and more learning occurs (Jarvis, 1987 *inter alia*). Consequently, we may think of modern society being threatened by the rapidity of social change – but even in the West not everything is changing; there is still a degree of stability and permanence. There must be both learning and non-learning in social living. However, Coffield (2000:28) suggests that, as a result of the research projects for the learning society programme in the UK for which he was the ESRC co-ordinator, 'all talk of *the* learning society will have to be abandoned rather than refined' (*italics* in original). He says that there are simply too many modern and post-modern readings of the term for any general agreement on one approach or model to be possible. He highlights ten different approaches to teaching and learning that can be detected in the various research projects on which he (p.8) reports, which are:

- skills growth;
- personal development;
- social learning;

- a learning market;
- local learning societies;
- social control;
- self-evaluation;
- centrality of learning;
- a reformed system of education;
- structural change.

A number of things emerge from these: first, that they are not different models of society but merely different aspects of learning in the society being studied; second, they may be describing something of the fragmentation of contemporary post-modern society; third, they have neither a sophisticated nor an agreed model of learning on which to base the analysis which prevents genuine comparison of the fourteen projects; this is something about which Coffield is acutely aware.

Since all the ESRC projects were conducted in the United Kingdom, I want to argue that these projects have actually demonstrated that learning, in a variety of different forms, is becoming embedded in the culture of society – but whether there is enough evidence to say that fourteen projects are sufficient to indicate changes in the whole of society is debatable.

Coffield's ten approaches indicate that the forces of change do not produce standardized responses, but we should not expect this unless we have a deterministic model of society. Nevertheless, we can see that it is possible to reduce his number of categories to four:

- *personal development* – personal development, self-evaluation, centrality of learning;
- *utopian vision* – social learning, structural change;
- *planned development* – social control, skills growth, reformed system of education, local learning societies;
- *market* – learning market.

The personal development issues occur naturally in any learning process and so they are not distinctive to the learning society, but if the development is controlled and directed then it involves planning and falls into the category of planned development, or strategy. The other two, vision and market, are distinctly different from each other.

However, one aspect of a learning society not touched upon in Coffield's report is that of everyday learning, which occurs in what Beck (1992) calls reflexive modernity. Coffield (2000:22) makes an implicit reference to this when he claims that the phrase 'We're all learning all the time' is anodyne. The fact that we are being forced to learn all the time is actually the very basis of a learning society, rather than an educative one, something that underlies many of the projects in this programme. Society is changing so rapidly that many of the traditional educative organizations are not able to keep abreast with the new demands and so individuals are forced to learn outside of the education system. Much of this is either unplanned or uncontrolled, or both, but it is an aspect crucial to contemporary society – for the learning society is also reflexive. This form of everyday learning is a crucial dimension of the learning society but it is one that cannot be controlled, something that is very important when we consider the complex nature of teaching. Only those who have disengaged from society are not really being forced to learn a great deal, and even they are still exposed to some of the forces of change. I suggest, therefore, that there are four other dimensions to a learning society: vision, planning, reflexivity and market; the order in which we shall now examine them.

Vision

Early writers about the learning society, Hutchins (1968:133) for instance, started with an educational vision that everybody would have access to part-time adult education throughout the whole of their lives, but it would also be a society which had 'succeeded in transforming its values in such a way that learning, fulfilment, becoming human, had become its aims and that all its institutions would be directed to this end'. For him, the learning society would be the fulfilment of Athens, made possible not by slavery but by modern machinery.

It was the realization of the computer revolution that led Husen (1974:238) to very similar conclusions when he argued that '*educated ability* will be democracy's replacement for passed-on social prerogatives'. He recognized that the knowledge explosion would be fostered by a combination of computers and reprographics and he (p.240) foresaw the possibility of '*equal opportunities* for all to receive as much education as they are thought capable of absorbing'. Despite Sweden's long history of adult education, Husen still regarded the learning society as being educational and based on an extension of the school system.

There are reflections here of Dewey's (1916:51) claim that

> It is commonplace to say that education should not cease when one leaves school. The point of this commonplace is that the purpose of school education is to insure the continuance of education by organizing the powers that insure growth. The inclination to learn from life itself and to make the conditions of life such that all will learn in the process of living is the finest product of schooling.

In a sense these are all variations on an educative society concept, but in a more recent book on the learning society, Ranson (1994:106) has suggested:

There is the need for the creation of the learning society as a constitutive condition of a new moral and political order. It is only when the values and processes of learning are placed at the centre of polity that the conditions can be established for all individuals to develop their capacities, and that institutions can respond openly and imaginatively to a period of change.

The vision of these authors, and others who have written on this topic, is of a 'good society' that is both democratic and egalitarian; one in which individuals can fulfil their own potential throughout the whole of their lives through education and learning, for which school is but a preparatory mechanism. The question that arises is: is this what those in power are planning?

Planning

There have been many policy documents published by European governments in recent years, all illustrating the strategies that they regard as important in the development of the learning society. It is unnecessary to make reference to many of these here, but they all recognize the significance of the knowledge economy and, as we pointed out above, influence societies to become more standardized despite the doctrine of subsidiarity, and so these forces act in the same direction as globalization.

In the introduction to the OECD report (1996:13), the following occurs:

Success in realising lifelong learning – from early childhood education to active learning retirement – will be an important factor in promoting employment, economic development, democracy and social cohesion in the years ahead.

The OECD reports have been quite influential beyond the confines of the European Union and many of the countries that aspire to modernize cite these OECD documents. Nevertheless, the European Union White Paper (1995:18) made a similar claim:

The crucial problem of employment in a permanently changing economy compels the education and training system to change. The design of appropriate education and training strategies to address work and employment issues is, therefore, a crucial preoccupation.

This idea has developed in Europe, but it is also prevalent in some other societies of the world, such as Hong Kong and Singapore. But in the

British government report *The Learning Age* (DfEE, 1998:13) it is clearly stated that the learning society is something still to be created, rather than something emerging out of structural changes, and that it will be educative and vocational in nature:

> In the Learning Age we will need a workforce with imagination and confidence, and the skills required will be diverse: teachers and trainers to help us acquire these skills. All of these occupations ... demand different types of knowledge and understanding and the skills to apply them. That is what we mean by skills, and it is through learning – with the help of those who teach us – that we acquire them.

However, there is just one place where *The Learning Age* (p.7) makes a totally different reference:

> As well as securing our economic future, learning has a wide contribution. It helps make ours a civilised society, develops the spiritual side of our lives and promotes active citizenship.

The recognition that lifelong learning is more than economic is also to be found in recent European documents (EC, 2001a). But despite the rhetoric about learning enriching our humanity, even our spirituality and the democratic society, the main emphasis of planning in all of these documents is that the end-result of learning will be employability, since the new welfare state will be built around it. In a world where global capitalism exercises such influence, it is perhaps not unrealistic to see why the concerns of the planners are orientated towards employability, but the concept of lifelong learning has been usurped by those who use it to define work-life learning. Work is something that is clearly essential both to our human development and to the good of society, but with the rapid social change we must recognize that work is no longer a permanent phenomenon for many people so that they are compelled to keep abreast with employable knowledge.

But the other main concern of the planners has been active citizenship. Knowledgeable people, it has been argued, are much more able to play a part in the wider life of society, and democracies need people who are not only able to think but who are also knowledgeable about areas of social and political life. Only by having a thinking and educated populace can a democratic society be achieved; and even if the ideal of democracy is only an ideal, it is still a goal to strive towards (Jarvis, 1993a)! Lengrand, one of the most influential writers on lifelong education, suggested that modern democracy

> in its political, social, economic and cultural aspects can only rest on solid foundations if a country has at its disposal increasing

numbers of responsible leaders at all levels, capable of giving life
and concrete substance to theoretical structures of society.

(Lengrand, 1975:30)

It is hardly surprising, therefore, that one of the other central aims of lifelong learning for the European Union (see EC, 2000 *inter alia*), and elsewhere, has been to create active citizens, although it is doubtful whether
there are sufficiently innovative forms of education being provided to
create *active* citizens. Such events as the huge peace rallies around the
world on 15th February 2003 suggest that it might be an issue or a sense of
injustice created by the issues that generate active citizens rather than lifelong learning.

Reflexivity

Change is endemic and rapid. This is a risk society (Beck, 1992), one in
which the complexities of the contemporary world make decisions based
on certainty impossible, and uncertainty is introduced into an instrument-
ally rational world. There are now hardly any points of decision in individual or social life that do not offer alternative viable solutions. Every
decision and subsequent action involves a risk, which demands monitoring, or reflexivity:

> Let us call the autonomous, undesired and unseen, transition
> from industrial to risk society *reflexivity* (to differentiate it from
> and contrast it with reflection). Then 'reflexive modernization'
> means self-confrontation with the effects of risk society that
> cannot be dealt with and assimilated in the system of industrial
> society – as measured by the latter's institutionalised standards.
> The fact that this very constellation may later, in a second stage,
> in turn become the object of (public, political and scientific)
> reflection must not obscure the unreflected, quasi-autonomous
> mechanism of the transition: it is precisely abstraction which pro-
> duces and gives reality to risk society.
>
> (Beck, 1994:6 – *italics* in the original)

That society has emerged in the way that it has means that its leaders take
risks when they implement 'solutions' to its problems because there is no
necessarily proven answer. Consequently, there is always a need for society
to confront itself about the outcomes of the decisions it makes, or fails to
make. Individuals are also forced to take risks, to learn and reflect upon
their decisions, so that Beck's distinction between reflexivity and reflection seems rather forced. Therefore, people must decide for themselves,
adjust to social changes and keep on learning, either by doing and reflect-

ing upon the outcomes or thinking and planning before the action takes place. As Beck (1994:13) suggests, individuals 'must produce, stage and cobble together their biographies themselves'. In this society, individuals begin to ask questions about their own identity and about the meaning of life.

Market

Contemporary society is also a consumer society and the history of consumerism can be traced back to the romantic period in the eighteenth century (Campbell, 1987), when pleasure became the crucial means of realizing that ideal truth and beauty which imagination had revealed. Significantly, this Romantic Movement 'assisted crucially at the birth of modern consumerism' (Campbell, 1987:206), so that a longing to enjoy those creations of the mind becomes the basis for consuming new phenomena. The market transforms individual members of society into individuals and consumers who endeavour to satisfy their desires. In other words, there can be no market economy unless there are consumers who want to purchase the products that are being produced. Advertising creates these consumers and the learning market underlies the learning society.

Advertising plays on imaginary pleasure, indeed, it might actually distort desire. However, once further learning is separated from education, learning becomes fun! It has become a more popular thing to do in the United Kingdom, especially since the creation of the British Open University. It marketed learning packages as commodities, and other organizations have followed suit. Now it is possible to learn all the things people want to know – by purchasing their own multi-media personal computers and surfing the web, watching the television learning zone programmes, buying their own 'teach yourself' books and magazines and, even, purchasing their own self-directed learning courses. Increasingly people across the world are being exposed to global events, as information technology penetrates more countries and more cultures.

Consequently, it may be seen that education is a form of production whereas learning is a form of consumption – the learning society is a consumer market. This has tremendous implications for our understanding of teaching since the social milieu in which we teach has changed, people of all ages are exposed to much more information and are free to, and do, learn a wide variety of things. Now teachers can no longer have the authority of being the possessors of knowledge that their students lack, nor can they assume that they know more about their topics than do their students: the nature of teaching is being changed by the learning society.

Two other elements of the learning society need to be looked at here: learning towns and cities, and learning organizations.

Learning towns and cities

The idea of 'educating cities' was developed as early as the 1970s, and it was about this time that the first books pointing in this direction were published (Illich, 1973a; Schon, 1973). But the first international congress of educating cities was held in Barcelona in 1990, and the second in Gothenburg in 1992. It is significant that the term 'educating' was still being used, but by the mid-1990s the concept of the 'Learning City' had emerged. This might be defined as:

> one which strives to learn how to renew itself in a period of extra-ordinary global change. The rapid spread of new technologies presents considerable opportunities for countries and regions to benefit from the transfer of new knowledge and new ideas across national boundaries. At the same time shifts in global capital flows and production are creating uncertainties and risk in managing national and local economies.
>
> (Learning City Toolkit)

The emphasis, once again, in this document is economic and the definition itself reflects the argument of the previous pages. A more simple definition is that provided by the European Lifelong Learning Initiative:

> A Learning Community is a City, Town, or Region which mobilizes all its resources in every sector to develop and enrich all of its human potential for the fostering of personal growth, the maintenance of social cohesion, and the creation of prosperity.
>
> (cited from Longworth, 1999:109)

While this definition does not contextualize the learning city in quite the same way as does the former one, it does overcome the weakness of over-emphasis on the economic factor. The European Lifelong Learning Initiative has also developed a charter for learning cities (Longworth, 1999:205–206). Learning cities, illustrating the standardizing tendencies in the global economy, have developed in all parts of the world. In the UK, there is a Learning City Network eNews, which held its conference in Milton Keynes in 1998; in Australia there was a first national conference in 2000 in Albury/Wodonga (Adult Learning Australia); in the OECD (2001) report the learning regions cited come from different European counties. Ireland has proclaimed that it is to become a nation of learning cities and counties (Press Release – November, 2002). Learning regions are developing elsewhere in the world and research on the learning cities is also ongoing in Korea.

Learning cities try to create partnerships and involve as many sectors of society as possible in the planning and organising of their activities, and the national UK survey (HMSO, 1998) illustrates this. Norwich, for instance, had amongst its partners, the City Council, the Norfolk County Council, the tertiary education college, the university, the local Training and Enterprise Council, the Chamber of Commerce, the voluntary services, the schools, the media, the careers service and the employment service. The Learning City committee, which I attended on one occasion, in Albury/Wodonga had the mayor as its chair, rather than an educationalist – even though the driving force behind it was an adult educator, and the local military establishment was also a member. The task of these committees is to plan the wide range of provision of learning opportunities for the local population. It is interesting to note that in Norwich the schools were included in the partnership, whereas the schools are often omitted from lifelong learning opportunities and, significantly, the education of adults is hardly mentioned in the *Teaching and Learning in Cities* report (Learmouth, 1993), despite the fact that one of the reports was focused on partnerships. (Many of these reports and newsletters are available on the World Wide Web.)

Learning organizations

In the same way as the ideas of learning cities were being pointed to in the 1970s, so was the idea of learning organizations (Argyris and Schon, 1978). This was part of their larger studies in theory, action and learning. However, it was the 1990s before the term learning organization gained currency, Senge (1990) being in the vanguard. The questions that he asked in this book were reminiscent of my own work on organizations in the 1970s, from a sociological perspective (Jarvis, 1977) when I discovered that the practitioners (ministers of religion) having a professional orientation towards their work were more likely to have low job satisfaction working in bureaucratic organizations, such as the churches. Senge (1990:17ff.) asked whether an organization has a learning disability, in other words does it have a tendency to be bureaucratic? He (1990:69) recognized that for the first time in history humankind has the capacity to create more information that the human mind can learn, but with systems thinking people can be seen as active participants in shaping their reality. His was a book for management that pointed the way beyond sending single individuals for continuing education, to introducing the new learning to the whole organization or to a relevant section of it. Pedler *et al.* (1997:3) define the learning company as 'an organization that facilitates the learning of all of its members and *consciously* transforms itself *and its context*' (*emphasis* in original).

Throughout the studies there is an idea that teams learn (see also Watkins and Marsick, 1993) and while this conveys the idea of a group of people all learning the same thing together, it is quite misleading. Only individuals learn, but within a team there is a great deal of inter-subjectivity, so that exposed to the same pressures different individuals might reach similar conclusions and decide together on a plan of action. The learning organization metaphor reflects the reality that individuality has been over-emphasized in contemporary society and that we need to learn to collaborate a great deal more.

In a real sense, the learning organization is the antithesis of bureaucracy; it is more democratic and much flatter. It accepts that individuals can learn and contribute to the good of the whole, provided that the organizational structures (and management itself) are open to change. It is easy to see how this approach to learning has achieved the degree of popularity that it has, since it is both outcomes based and measurable.

This first section has illustrated how the global processes have generated both the knowledge and the learning societies and has begun to indicate how the education of adults and lifelong learning fits. We shall explore this to a greater extent in later chapters, but now we need to see how individuals fit into this form of society, moulded as they are by the forces being exerted upon them as they seek to discover a place for themselves in society. However, human beings are not merely the passive recipients of social pressures acting upon them, they are also able to act back upon their world and become agents who contribute to the processes of social change.

The social nature of the individual

The nature of humankind has occupied the minds of philosophers and theologians for centuries and it is not the purpose of this section to encroach upon their deliberations, nor even to attempt to summarize their arguments. It is intended, however, to suggest that human beings are active participants in the learning process throughout the whole of life and that the reason for this lies both in their nature and in their relationship with the wider society (Jarvis and Walters, 1993).

Traditionally, every society has produced its own culture, which is carried by human beings and transmitted both through social interaction and through the educational system. Culture, in this context, refers to the sum totality of knowledge, values, beliefs, etc. of a social group. It is in the process of socialization that individuals learn their local culture. There is a sense in which some facets of education may be regarded as part of the process of socialization, although the former is usually viewed as a more formal process than the latter. Consequently, it is possible to understand precisely how Lawton (1973:21) could regard the curriculum as a selection from culture. Obviously, the process of acquiring local culture is very significant during childhood, both through socialization and education.

However, sociologists regard socialization as a lifetime process having at least two aspects: primary socialization is 'the first socialization an individual undergoes ... through which he (*sic*) becomes a member of society. Secondary socialization is any subsequent process that inducts an already socialized individual into new sectors of the objective world of his society' (Berger and Luckmann, 1966:150). However, in this global society, individuals are exposed to many more local cultures – it is as if each was a subculture of a more global culture. Yet, as we have already pointed out there is resistance to this process and local cultures are seeking to retain something of their difference. Being exposed to other local cultures is now a lifetime process – a process of lifelong learning. Similarly, education may be regarded as a lifelong process and further reference will be made to the concepts of lifelong learning and lifelong education below.

It is not difficult, however, to realize that in a society where the rate of social change is very slow, such as pre-industrial Europe or a primitive tribe, it would be feasible for individuals to learn most of the cultural knowledge necessary for them to assume their place in that society in childhood. In such societies it was, and still is, only the elite (e.g. Plato's philosopher-kings, the priesthood) who continued to study esoteric knowledge during adulthood, while the remainder of the populace are regarded as having completed their education. Consequently, it is not hard to understand why a front-end model of education emerged, although it is equally obvious that such a model has little relevance to a society whose culture is changing rapidly.

From the onset of the Industrial Revolution, with the introduction of more sophisticated technology, the rate of social change increased. Indeed, change is endemic to technological societies. This means that the learning process should not cease at early adulthood. New knowledge, new ideas, new values and new practices all have to be confronted. Hence, a growth of educational provision occurred in the eighteenth and nineteenth centuries and the people were encouraged to learn more. Both children and adults were provided with additional educational opportunities, Sunday Schools and other educational institutions emerged to respond to this need, and it is frequently claimed that the reason for this new emphasis on education was because a need existed to produce a competent and literate workforce. Clearly this was so. Yet education, once introduced, had functions of a non-educational kind; we might today say that these are amongst 'the hidden benefits of learning'! Quoting one of Her Majesty's Inspectors for Education in London during the late nineteenth century, Kumar writes: 'If it were not for her 500 elementary schools London would be overrun by a hoarde of young savages' (1978:248f.) Perhaps education is still being used to keep people 'off the streets', but now the subjects are a little older – and maybe unemployed!

Education has many purposes, but, clearly, it is an important agency in assisting individuals to respond to the rapid social change that is occurring. Because it is so rapid, it is necessary for individuals to keep learning, so that they should not become alienated from the culture that engulfs them, but we can also understand that this is a way in which individualization emerges. The more technologically based the society, the more easy it is for individuals to become alienated unless they keep on learning, but as they learn they will individualize, and we note, for example, that more people are choosing to live alone as they develop their own individuality. All are affected by the changes in technology, as evidenced by the introduction of the pocket calculator, the digital watch, the micro-computer, and so on. Hence individuals need to learn new knowledge to prevent the onset of alienation or anomie, and lifelong learning – even lifelong education – helps them to adjust to the cultural changes prevalent in their society, but, paradoxically, the more that they learn the more likelihood that they become individualized and perhaps alienated. (Given the fact that all people are born with their unique genetic inheritance, individualization is exacerbated by lifelong learning).

But, more recently, with the advent of globalization and the networked society it is much more difficult to think of any society having a single culture. Every society is affected by innumerable cultures since they are also being transmitted by all forms of information technology, as well as by people with whom we interact. Because of its apparent commonality among members of a society, culture seems to be a phenomenon external to the individual and objective. Actually this objectivity is more apparent than real since individuals have internalized a great deal of their own local culture and shared it through social interaction. It is the fact that individuals do share it that provides the impression that it is actually objective and residing outside them. Consequently, culture should be regarded as 'objectified' rather than objective, and the manner by which infants acquire culture having been born into a society is illustrated in Figure 1.1. In the earlier editions of this book I referred to this culture into which

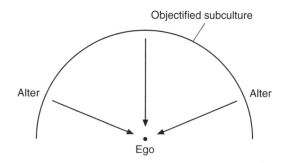

Figure 1.1 The process of internalization of 'objectified' local culture.

children were socialized as 'objectified culture', but it is now more accurate to regard it as 'objectified local culture'.

All individuals have the culture of their local society transmitted to them through interaction with others. The arrows in Figure 1.1 suggest that both children or other recipients of this objectified local culture are passive, that is, they are passive learners – and while this may be true in the very early days of life, it is not so for very long as the following figure (Figure 1.2.) indicates: it is an interaction between 'ego' and 'alter' that actually occurs in a two-way transmission of individually internalized subcultures. Human beings rarely merely process ideas that they receive, they are frequently proactive in the pursuit of the knowledge, ideas, values, beliefs enshrined in their objectified culture, which is also indicated in the double arrow (see Jarvis, 1987, 1992 for a much more extensive discussion of this).

Since we live in an information society we are the recipients of a great deal of information (see the discussion on information above) and so some of the arrows are still one-way whereas the others are two-way illustrating the fact that our society is one in which we gain a great deal of information through interaction, when we can also influence others.

In these situations, it is easy to understand how people can feel secure supported by like-minded people within a community setting. Individuals knew who they were within the dominant site of their daily existence. However, as society has become more complex and we now live in a multicultural society, the arc illustrating objectified local culture is too simple since we are recipients of a variety of local cultures and so we could depict this situation in which ego is at the centre of a number of different subcultures, as Figure 1.3 illustrates.

In this figure we can see how individuals are involved in a variety of local subcultures, each of which affects the roles that they play in different situations, so that they might see their role in one subculture as being totally different to that in another. Not only might they play their roles

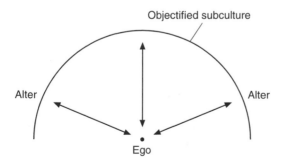

Figure 1.2 The process of internalization and externalization of 'objectified' local culture.

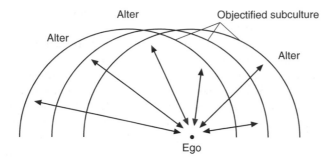

Figure 1.3 The process of internalization and externalization of
'objectified' local cultures.

differently, they may actually be perceived and/or see themselves differently. O'Neill (2003) has studied the way in which young males acquire their identities in a residential school and he has shown quite clearly that their self-identity is often not acquired through the culture of the school, but their social identity is acquitted through the culture of the school. Consequently, we can see the process whereby people acquire multi-identities, and we shall return to this shortly.

In multicultural society individuals are exposed to more than one culture, or a number of subcultures, as Figure 1.3 depicts. However since the subcultures are undergoing change, it would be possible to redraw the diagram with ego having moved further along the base axis to mark the change in time and then all the overlapping subcultures would need to be redrawn to illustrate that they had also changed. This would be too cumbersome here, although we can see that since people are exposed to different subcultures and that they process their learning differently, each person rapidly becomes individualized and distinct. But, as we noted earlier, some cultures change more rapidly than others and so we have to try to imagine them changing at different speeds. However, we can begin to understand the complexity of individuals' life-world from these simple diagrams.

It is clear from the above that many individuals have lost the security of a single dominant local subculture, which helped provide them both with a sense of membership of a community and an identity. For some people this new situation is at the heart of identity crises, which Giddens (1991) refers to as 'existential anxiety'. He also notes how personal counselling has mushroomed as a result of these changes.

However, there are additional reasons why lifelong learning opportunities should be provided in society; there is a growing body of evidence that there are hidden benefits to learning and, at the time of writing, the Department of Learning and Skills is funding research into these, such as having better health – including mental health (Grossman and Kaestner,

1997); self-fulfilment (Cox and Pascall, 1994); sense of belonging (Jarvis and Walker, 1997); and so on. In addition, the National Institute of Adult Continuing Education has been running a major campaign about education and the elderly *Older and Bolder* (Carlton and Soulsby, 1999). Over the coming years the evidence for the social benefits of learning will no doubt grow a great deal stronger.

Individuals do not just receive passively all of these changes but they process and change them as part of the process of cultural change. Hence, human beings are not only born into a changing culture, but they are part of the process of change. Their adaptation to this ever-changing society is itself a learning process, and all forms of education assist people processing and adapting to these changes throughout the whole of their lives. In this sense human beings are lifelong learners, and in the remainder of this chapter it will be shown that they are also seeking meaning for their existence. This endeavour of human beings to understand themselves, their society and their universe lies at the root of the learning process. Finally, it is concluded that the provision of education for people of all ages is essential because it helps to facilitate this quest to understand, which is at the heart of humanity itself.

Individuals as lifelong learners

Lifelong education is not a new concept (Yeaxlee, 1929) but the rapidly changing social conditions of contemporary society have provided impetus for a wider acceptance of the idea. In recent years the stimulus has been strengthened by a considerable number of publications and an increasing amount of research has also been devoted to the topic. Organizations such as UNESCO and the European Union (1995 *inter alia*) have adopted it and have thereby brought it into the political arena. However, adult educators have, generally, been a major force in drawing attention to the practice of lifelong learning. One of the earlier writers to popularize the idea was Ronald Gross (1977) who recorded some of the stories of lifelong learners. Quoting from one of these, Cornelius Hirschberg, he wrote:

> I am stuck in the city, that's all I have. I am stuck in business and routine and tedium. But I give up only as much as I must; for the rest I live my life at its best, with art, music, poetry, literature, science, philosophy and thought. I shall know the keener people of the world, think the keener thoughts, and taste the keener pleasures as long as I can and as much as I can.
>
> (Gross, 1977:27)

In case this sounds too idealistic to be practical, Hirschberg read on the subway to and from work each day, and during his lunchtime, for most of his business life. He estimated that he had undertaken some ten hours of serious reading each week for about 2,000 weeks – enough reading time to get at least five college degrees! His university was the world of books and the opportunity to think about the ideas he acquired from them.

Consequently, there are many sources and sites of learning. We have already indicated that work has become a significant one and we shall return to this later in the book. But libraries and museums are also important adjuncts to human learning. Their existence is an indication that people seek to learn from numerous sources. Adult educators have taken considerable cognizance of their significance to lifelong education and a number of studies have been published in this field, such as Chadwick, 1980; Dadswell, 1978; Dale, 1980; Surridge and Bowen, 1977. Additional learning facilities are provided by the media. Groombridge (1972:27ff.) regarded television as a liberal educator because it makes people aware of what lies beyond their milieu, it helps them to understand each other and it provides a rich diet of imaginative experience. As long as it is recognized that what is seen and heard is actually a distillation of reality through the media, then these claims are valid. Indeed, the British Broadcasting Corporation's charter specifically states that one of its functions is to educate. In a totally different context, Moemeka suggested that in African countries local radio can 'provide a continuous flow of educational information and messages on all aspects and endeavours that affect the lives of rural communities, and so arouse their awareness and stimulate them' (1981:104). Travel is another medium through which individuals learn, so that the European Union has introduced many opportunities for educators to get to know and understand how colleagues in other countries work, through Erasmus, Grundtvig, Socrates and other programmes. Perhaps these educational programmes will be extended as greater cooperation between the European Union and the Asian countries on lifelong learning begins to emerge, as a result of the first conference and six-month project on the first half of 2002 (ASEM, 2002).

In addition, many adult education institutions, schools and colleges organize visits and study tours both in the United Kingdom and abroad as part of their programme of learning activities. The arts, museums, libraries, radio and television all cater, in one way or another, for something in human beings which drives them to learn more about the universe in which they live and about other people with whom they inhabit this planet.

Not only have technological innovations led to unemployment but recent monetarist policies in Western Europe, especially the United Kingdom, and in the United States have resulted in increased unemployment and also in a gradual lowering of the age of retirement. Indeed, it could well be argued that the capitalist system which needs a lean workforce that is paid the lowest possible wage actually creates unemployment – 'regrettable lay offs' – and so education has become important to help the unemployed learn new knowledge and skills in order to get them back into the workforce, and also to help them consider the meaning of their lives.

This process has resulted in more leisure time, even though it is enforced and often unwanted. In a society dominated by a work ethic, in which it has been regarded as good to work but evil to be idle, leisure has always been regarded as a mixed blessing. Consequently, it is being recognized that values about leisure will have to adapt or they will be changed, which, incidentally, illustrates a way by which values respond to social pressure. But some people have to learn how to use their leisure time and Parker (1976) drew a useful distinction between education for leisure and education as leisure.

That some people have to learn how to use this leisure may appear to be surprising initially, but it is less surprising when it is realized that many who are now entering enforced unemployment at an earlier stage of their lives than they originally anticipated were brought up with the expectation that they would work until they approached the end of their lives and that not to work was regarded as malingering. Hence, the expectation of having to work for the greater part of their lives has meant that many people have not really learned how to use non-work time as constructively as they might. Yet it may actually be wrong to tell people what to do with their leisure, but correct and beneficial to provide them with the opportunity to consider how they employ creatively the additional freedom that technological changes and specific economic policies have produced. One aspect of preparation for unemployment that has occurred has been pre-retirement education (see Coleman, 1982; Glendenning and Percy, 1990, *inter alia*; Jarvis, 1980, 1983b) in which programme time is frequently devoted to the use of leisure. Indeed, there is now a *Pre-Retirement Association of Great Britain* which devotes much of its time to mid-life planning, pre-retirement education and other aspects of education for retirement.

By contrast, education as leisure has traditionally been undertaken by more educated people because many, especially those from the working classes who were unsuccessful during their initial education, have tended to shun the formal provision of leisure time education once they had completed their initial and, perhaps, their vocational education. The history of liberal adult education is a long and honourable one being enshrined in the university extension movement and other types of provision, such as the Workers Educational Association, and the demand for it appears to be unabating (ACACE, 1982b). This may be demonstrated by the many people who attend the university extension classes, local education authority classes, and courses organized by other commercial and voluntary

31

agencies. Additionally, the creation of the Open University demonstrated the tremendous attraction that academic study has for many people who do not possess the traditional, formal qualifications for university entry. Similar movements exist in many parts of the world (Rumble and Harry, 1982) and in America with its Free Universities movement (Draves, 1980) and the provision of part-time degree education throughout the lifespan. More recently, education and the elderly has assumed increasing significance: in America, there are the elderhostels (Zimmerman, 1979:10, 22) and the 'université du troisième age' began in France and spread throughout Europe, so that it is now to be found throughout the world and has its own international meeting. Many of these new educational movements have already shown that leisure time education does not necessarily result in any lowering of academic standards; indeed, the academic standards may be lifted in some instances. Hence it is more than hobby-type education, which is often belittled. Yet the provision of this latter form of education is also of great importance since it provides opportunity for life enrichment and reflects a positive attitude on behalf of the learner to the acquisition of new knowledge and skills. Parker (1976:99) quotes Jary with approval when he concludes that 'the leisure centredness of liberal adult education ought not to be hidden or apologised for. It should be recognised and its gratifications elaborated. It should be seen as a highly distinctive form of leisure.'

If adult education can help people to relate more easily to contemporary culture, if it can help them to use their leisure time in a creative manner, if it can enrich the lives of many who undertake it, then it would appear to be quite ludicrous to relegate it to the margins of the world of education; and, clearly, its provision will become even more important since more people are living longer and hence have more actual time in their lives to learn things. 'But what is the use of learning new things when a person is old?' is a question frequently posed. Yet if learning is life enriching, as it is for many people, then the elderly have as much right as anyone else to enjoy the fruits of learning. Dewey wrote that since

> life means growth, a living creature lives as truly and positively at one stage as another, with the same intrinsic fullness and the same absolute claims. Hence education means the enterprise of supplying the conditions which insure growth, or adequacy of life, irrespective of age.
>
> (Dewey, 1916:51)

Indeed, people of all ages are realizing that they either want, or need, to continue learning all their lives. This has led to the growth of other important spheres of education, such as ACCESS and return to study courses. ACCESS courses began in order to help disadvantaged adults to gain access to professional preparation but they soon evolved to offer opportunity to prepare individuals of all backgrounds to enter higher education. Some of these also began to offer fresh horizons for women who felt that they had been disadvantaged earlier in their lives (see Hutchinson and Hutchinson, 1978). In addition, there has been a growth in courses teaching people the skills of studying, such as Richardson (1979) and Gibbs (1981).

There is considerable evidence that a large proportion of the British population have returned to study. Sargant et al. (1997:vi) reported that 40 per cent of the adult population had taken a course of study over the past three years from the time of the survey, whereas the National Learning Survey (Beinart and Smith, 1997:35) found that 74 per cent of those surveyed had taken part in a learning activity over the previous three years. It should be noted that the latter statistic refers to learning activities rather than courses of study. Nevertheless, both of these figures are higher than that which Sargant (1990) found only a few years earlier, when she suggested that one-tenth of the adult population were engaged in education and that a further 16 per cent had undertaken some form of study within the previous three years. In addition, she found that a further 10 per cent were engaged in self-directed learning, which suggested that over one-third of the adult population are undertaking some form of planned learning exercises. Obtaining accurate statistics about the participation rate of adults in education is a very complicated undertaking and, therefore, in the end an estimate is all that may be obtained.

The same is true in the United States. For instance, Johnstone and Rivera (1965:33) calculated that between June 1961 and June 1962 there were at least 2,650,000 adults in full-time education, 17,160,000 in adult classes and some 8,960,000 undertaking self-education, but they recognized that these totals were no more than approximations. Nevertheless, their research highlighted the prevalence of the autodidact and they wrote that 'the incidence of self-education throughout the adult population is much greater than we anticipated' (Johnstone and Rivera, 1965:37). They had discovered millions of lifelong learners who were not using the educational services, people who wanted to learn and understand under their own direction. Not long after Johnstone and Rivera published their monumental study another seminal research report highlighting the lifelong learner appeared. Allen Tough (1979) reported research into adults' self-directed learning projects and he suggested that self-directed education is even more common than Johnstone and Rivera indicated. He wrote that it 'is common for a man or woman to spend 700 hours a year on learning projects. Some people spend less than 100 hours, but others spend more than 2000 hours in episodes in which the person's interest to learn or to change is clearly his primary motivation' (1979:1). Tough was not concerned merely to count the odd hours of enquiry in which an individual might indulge, since he considered that these could not be described as learning projects. Rather he defined a learning project as 'a series of related episodes, adding up to at least seven hours' (1979:6). Tough, and his fellow researchers, interviewed 66 people in depth in their initial research and discovered that all but one of them had undertaken at least one learning project during the year prior to the interview, that the median number of projects was eight and that the mean time spent on learning projects was 816 hours. A participation rate of 98 per cent was discovered – far higher than Johnstone and Rivera would have anticipated from their research. But Tough and his colleagues employed a more intensive interview technique than Johnstone and Rivera and this method of research was one reason for the higher statistics. Additionally, Tough acknowledged that his sample was not random, so that it is not technically correct to claim that 98 per cent of the population of Canada, nor even of Ontario (where the research was conducted), undertake at least one seven-hour learning project per annum. Indeed, his statistics may be a considerable overestimation, although they might actually be correct, but they do suggest that people have a need to learn, know and understand.

These various research statistics may all indicate that the human being has a basic need to learn, a need that may be as basic as any of the needs identified by Maslow in his well-known 'hierarchy' of needs.

The human being and the need to learn

Maslow's 'hierarchy' of needs is usually represented as in Figure 1.4. D. Child (1977:40) suggested that the need to know comes at the top of the hierarchy, but in the third edition of his text he (1981:43) has adapted this slightly and omitted the highest stratum. At the same time he has continued to highlight the significance of knowledge and understanding. Maslow (1968:60) certainly considered the need to know but claimed that knowledge has a certain ambiguity about it, specifying that in most individuals there is both a need to know and a fear of knowing. However, the fear of knowing may be the result of social experiences rather than being basic to the person. The need to know may be fundamental, even if the consequences of that knowledge may be dangerous. If this is the case, then Child's suggestion does require further consideration. Does the need to know actually occur at the apex of the hierarchy? Is there a progression through the hierarchy which occurs only when the more preponderant needs are satisfied? Is it even a hierarchy? Argyle (1974:961) suggested that the main supporting evidence for the hierarchy comes from the lower end but that there 'is not such clear evidence about the upper part of the hierarchy'. Houston *et al.* (1979:297) claimed that the order of needs is itself arbitrary and that the exact order is not particularly important. If the

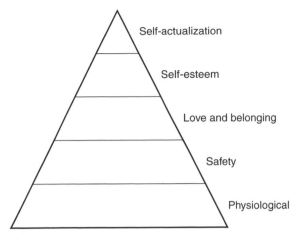

Figure 1.4 Maslow's 'hierarchy' of needs.

Source: Maslow (1968).

order is unimportant, then both Maslow's and Child's construction of a needs hierarchy is open to reconsideration.

Child may be correct when he suggested that the intellectual pursuit of knowledge is a higher order need, but this may only be true for the academic pursuit of knowledge. But the fact that Tough (1979) has suggested that many people undertake learning projects implies that the need to learn may be quite fundamental to the human being. Indeed, this need may be better understood as being one to learn rather than to know and understand since individuals need to learn in order to comprehend the world in which they live and to adapt themselves to it. If this is the case, then the need to learn is quite basic and should perhaps occur lower in Maslow's hierarchy because the individual is conscious of the need to learn from very early in life, as is manifest in children from the time that they acquire the facility of language (and ask the question 'why?') and during the process of the formation of the self.

Elsewhere (Jarvis, 1983c:20–23) this theme has been expanded a little in the context of the religious development of the individual. Without seeking to rehearse that argument, some of its conclusions are summarized here because of their significance to this discussion. It is suggested that the processes of the formation of the self and of beginning to make sense of the objective world occur simultaneously during early childhood. Indeed, Luckmann maintains that a human organism becomes a self, constructing with others an 'objective and moral universe of meaning' (1967:50). Prior to the construction of this universe of meaning, however, it must be recognized that every individual poses many questions of meaning. This process of focusing upon the 'unknowns' of human experiences begins in childhood and appears fundamental to humanity. Nearly every parent has experienced that period during which their child persistently asks questions about every aspect of its experience. Initially these questions appear to be restricted to its immediate experience but as the child's universe expands its questions of meaning change. Answers, however, demand different types of knowledge: empirical, rational, pragmatic, belief, and so on. Hence, learning initially progresses, unfettered by the boundaries of the disciplines, as a result of a process of questioning at the parameters of children's experiences. As the questions are answered children acquire a body of knowledge, so the learning need receives some satisfaction. During early childhood these questions are overt and the learning experience explicit. When children attend school, however, teachers (and other adults) sometimes attempt to provide information that bears little or no relation to the questions being posed at that time and, therefore, the knowledge being transmitted may appear irrelevant to the recipient. Unless the teacher is able to demonstrate its relevance and create a questioning attitude there may be little internal stimulus to learn what is being transmitted. (This does not mean that children do not want or need to learn, only that they may not want to learn what is being transmitted.) However, by the time children mature, answers to many of the questions may have been discovered and the adults socialized into the objectified culture(s) of society. The adult appears to ask fewer questions. But during periods of rapid social change the questioning process is evoked. During traumatic experiences the accepted internalized body of knowledge may not be able to cope with the situation and the questioning process is reactivated. Schutz and Luckmann write: 'I only become aware of the deficient tone of my stock of knowledge if a novel experience does not fit into what has, up to now, been taken as a taken-for-granted valid reference scheme' (1974:8).

In other words, when individuals' biographies and their current experience are not in harmony, a situation is produced whereby they recommence their quest for meaning and understanding. It is this disjuncture that underlies the need to learn and this has been developed much more thoroughly in other works (Jarvis, 1987, 1992). While the need to learn occurs continuously throughout most of the lifespan, the religious questions are raised intermittently throughout life, so that the process is never really complete. Perhaps, as Tough has implied, questions are asked much more frequently than adult educators have generally assumed, so that the learning need is ever prevalent.

Before progressing further with this discussion it is necessary to recall Maslow's original 'hierarchy' of needs and Child's adaptation of it. Maslow suggested that there are five basic areas of need: physiological, safety, love and belonging, self-esteem and self-actualization. Child suggested that understanding and knowledge should be added to the pinnacle of the hierarchy. But it was suggested that the needs do not actually form a hierarchy and it has been argued here that the need to learn is quite fundamental to humanity and that it manifests itself during the process of the formation of the self, so that in any formulation of human needs the learning need should be specified. Hence, it is suggested that Maslow's hierarchy should be adapted and seen as a taxonomy (see Figure 1.5). This is clearly not a hierarchy but a process through which a child passes during early maturation. All the needs exist in individuals and, wherever possible, human beings seek to satisfy them. Hence the provision of education throughout the whole of the lifespan may help the learner to satisfy a basic human need, especially in a rapidly changing world in which the individual may be posing many questions of meaning. More recently, I (Jarvis, 2002b) have argued that learning is actually an existential phenomenon and so I want to revise Child's adaptation of Maslow's famous diagram even further.

It might be objected that if human beings have a basic need to learn, there is no need to provide education since they will seek to satisfy their learning needs in any case. However, this argument contains no substance because education, the provision of libraries, museums, and so on, have all emerged as means by which individuals may learn answers to their questions of meaning. Yet it must be recognized that education *per se* is only one of a number of ways through which the learning need can be satisfied. Another answer to the objection may be posited in the form of an analogy: if safety is a need that is always going to be satisfied then there would be no reason for legislation about health and safety at work, and yet today there are probably very few people who would dispute the need for the existence of such an Act of Parliament.

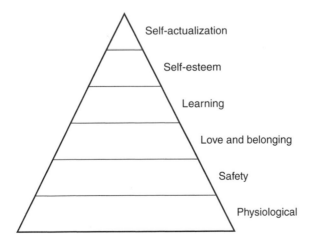

Figure 1.5 A taxonomy of human needs.

Summary

In this chapter it has been argued that the provision of education for adults is necessary because of the nature of contemporary society and the nature of humanity. It was suggested that there are various features in society that have to be taken into consideration, including: globalization and the knowledge society resulting in the need for individuals working with such knowledge to keep abreast of developments; an increase in the amount of leisure time and an increasing number of people living into old age; the need to work towards a democratic society. Additionally, it has been suggested that human beings have a basic need to learn and that they are lifelong learners and that the provision of education across the lifespan is one way by which people can satisfy this basic need.

However, it was recognized at the outset that these two aspects are not discrete entities but that there is an inter-relationship between the individual and society, and that this division is made only for ease of analysis. One approach without the other is to present a false picture of reality, so a rationale for the provision of education for adults must always contain a combination of both sets of reasons proposed here.

Thus far the concepts employed have gone undefined and undiscussed, so it is now necessary to explore some of the many concepts that are discussed in the literature about the education of adults.

2

FROM ADULT EDUCATION TO LIFELONG LEARNING

A conceptual framework

Many concepts were mentioned in the opening chapter without any being rigorously defined; it is now necessary to examine some of them. The concept of education will be analysed first and this will form the base for examining some of the terms in contemporary usage that relate in some way to the education of adults, during which the underlying philosophies will become more apparent. The chapter has nine sections. While the chapter title implies something of a historical sequence, it should more accurately be read as a conceptual continuum. In addition, it will become clear that the same terms are employed in different ways, while, on occasions, different terms are used to convey the same meaning!

The changing concept of education

In the opening chapter, reference was made to the way in which knowledge changes rapidly and consequently the so-called 'front-end' model of education, which was appropriate for less technological societies, is no longer relevant to contemporary society. However, this requires further discussion, and perhaps the simplest way to illustrate the concept is diagrammatically and an adaptation of Boyle's diagram is used for this purpose (see Figure 2.1).

This clearly demonstrates the idea that education was regarded as occurring only during the formative years and that when social maturity,

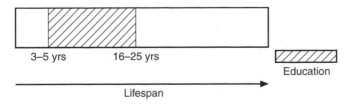

Figure 2.1 The front-end model of education.

Source: Boyle (1982:8).

or adulthood, was achieved then education ceases. This approach may be found in many early writers on the subject of education. John Stuart Mill, for instance, claimed that the content of education was to be found in 'the culture which each generation purposely gives to those who are to be their successors' (cited in Lester-Smith, 1966:9). Emile Durkheim, a French sociologist and educationalist, regarded education in a similar manner: for him it was 'the influence exercised by adult generations on those who are not yet ready for social life' (1956:71). But by the beginning of the twentieth century, it was becoming more apparent in the West that an inter-generational perspective was not adequate to describe the educational process. John Dewey (1916:8), for instance, was forced to add the prefix *formal* to the term *education* in order to express the same sentiments as those specified by Mill and Durkheim if society was to transmit all its achievements from one generation to the subsequent one. Today, formal education both refers to institutionalized learning and a teaching method – to the structure and the process. In addition, it is the term most likely to be used to convey the same idea is *initial education*. This has been described as:

> going to school, including nursery school, but it could go on full or part-time into the mid-20s. After compulsory schooling, 'initial' education takes a wide variety of forms: full-time study in sixth form, university, college, polytechnic, medical school, military academy and so on; part-time day release, evening classes and correspondence courses; on the job training in the factory.
>
> (ACACE, 1979a:9–10)

In a similar manner, Coombs and Ahmed sought to distinguish formal education from informal and non-formal education. They define it as: 'the highly institutionalized chronologically graded and hierarchically structured "education system" spanning lower primary school and upper reaches of the university' (1974:8). Their intention was to distinguish this initial formal system from other forms of lifelong education occurring throughout the world. The idea underlying initial education is that at a given stage in the lifespan individuals have stored away sufficient knowledge and skill to serve them for the remainder of their lives, so that their education is then complete.

Such a model of education is also implicit in the writings of the well-known English philosopher of education, R.S. Peters, who made a clear distinction between education and the educated man (a term which Peters used without gender bias). Peters (1972:9) regarded being educated as a state that individuals achieve, whilst education is a family of processes that lead to this state. However, it might be advantageous to enquire whether the educated person is an end-state without being the end of the journey. Peters' writings tend to suggest that he considers it as such, for he claims that education 'was not thought of (previously) explicitly as a family of processes which have as their outcome the development of an educated man in the way in which it is now' (1972:7). While this seems to imply that Peters considered that the educated person is an end-state, it is possible to regard it as a social status in contrast to the uneducated person. Yet even if it is an achievement, is it possible for the educated person to undertake more education? Of course it is – but to where does the additional process lead? If it is regarded as a status, then that status remains unchanged. Peters rightly claimed that to be an educated person is not to have arrived but to travel with a different view during life. Hence, for him, the educated person is both educated and being educated throughout the whole of his life. Indeed, if the state were achieved then the process must continue or else it would be lost. Hence it is maintained here that the process is significant, perhaps more significant than the state or the end-product. Therefore, no initial or intergeneration aspect may be considered intrinsic to the concept of education, since the educated person should always be in the process of being educated.

It may, therefore, be concluded that education is an institutionalized learning process and, as such, it may be seen as the way in which societies respond to the basic learning need in humankind, which was discussed previously. However, not all learning is educational. Few people would deny, for instance, that indoctrination is a learning process but they would almost certainly deny that it is an educational one, so that specific criteria need to be adduced in order to ascertain whether any learning process is educational. Elsewhere (Jarvis, 1983a), this has been worked out in some detail, so that it would be repetitive to do more than summarize that discussion here.

Peters (1966:23ff.), following Wittgenstein, claimed that the concept of education is too complex to define and so he suggested that there is a family of similar phenomena that may be regarded as education, as we pointed out above. He put forward three sets of criteria for consideration as a basis for education, but they were not regarded as totally satisfactory, so that other criteria were suggested. For him education must involve: a learning process which is institutionalized; the learning process should not be a single event; the process should be planned rather than haphazard; an essentially humanistic process because knowledge is humanistic and because the process involves human beings as learners and, also, maybe as teachers; learning has to involve understanding, which is essentially a quality of critical awareness. Before a definition is offered it is necessary to examine the term 'humanistic' here. Dewey claimed that knowledge is essentially 'humanistic in quality not because it is about human products in the past, but because of what it *does* in liberating human intelligence and human sympathy' (1916:230 – *italics* in original). It is this human element that was reflected in the discussion in the

41

opening chapter when knowledge was separated from information. He went on to suggest that any specific matter that does this is essentially humane, so that in this context humanistic has two facets: it is concerned about the welfare and humanity of the participants and it is humane. Hence this implies that the educational process is normative and idealistic. Education may now be defined as 'any institutionalized and planned series of incidents, having a humanistic basis, directed towards the participants learning and understanding'. This definition is very broad since it is the common factor in the multitudinous branches of education, and it is possible to modify and adapt it, so that the definition may reflect the meaning added to the basic idea when a prefix is placed before the term education, for example lifelong education requires only that 'and which may occur at any stage in the lifespan' be added to the above definition. Hence it may be seen that this basic definition of education does not restrict education to any specific learning process; to any time in life; to any specific location; to any specific purpose. The front-end model of education, depicted in Figure 2.1, is, therefore, only one branch of education rather than being the total educational process. It has been difficult to change people's attitudes towards education and this front-end model of initial education has been equated with education *per se* in people's minds. This would also be true in many other countries throughout the world. Consequently, the education of adults is still often viewed by some as an optional extra added after initial education has actually been completed, so that it has remained marginal to the institution of education in society.

In the following sections we shall examine some of the prefixes that describe the various branches of education that are relevant to the education of adults; but, prior to embarking upon this, it is necessary to clarify the relationship between teaching, learning and education.

Teaching, learning and education

Tough (1979), among others, demonstrated that many of the adults' learning projects are completely self-directed and that neither a teacher nor an educational institution is necessary to their successful implementation. Yet it would be difficult to claim that many of these projects were not educational, since they are intended and planned. It might be more true to claim that the more self-directed the project the greater the likelihood that learners can respond to their own learning needs and also self-actualize in the process, thus demonstrating the humanistic nature of education and learning itself. Consequently, it may be seen that while the learner is an essential element in the learning process, the teacher is not. Learning may, and often does, occur without teaching, but the extent to which teaching can occur without learners and learning is much more debatable. A teacher may claim to have taught a subject and say that nobody learned anything – but would the claim actually be correct? If nobody had learned, had the teacher actually taught or only tried to teach but not succeeded? Teaching is dependent upon the learners being present – either actually or virtually, but not that they learn. Teaching may be regarded as the intention to bring about learning (Hirst and Peters, 1970:78), but if it is unsuccessful it may be viewed as unsuccessful teaching rather than as an unsuccessful attempt to teach. Unsuccessful teaching may also occur when some learning has resulted from the teaching but when all the intentions have not been achieved.

It can be seen that this form of argument is one of the reasons why, in contemporary society, the concept of education has been seen as inadequate and more recently the term learning has assumed a greater prominence for what might previously have been seen as educational. Learning is often defined in behavioural terms; Hilgard and Atkinson, for instance, define it as 'any more or less permanent change in behaviour which is the result of experience' (1967:270). However, the acquisition of new knowledge need not result in behavioural change, but learning has occurred. Hence this definition is too narrow. It will be recalled from the last chapter that learning was put into the context of the acquisition of culture and it is, therefore, proposed to regard one aspect of learning as any process of receiving and assessing any aspect, or aspects, of culture. It has been defined elsewhere as the process of transforming experience into knowledge, skills, attitudes, values, emotions, and so on (Jarvis, 1987, 1992), but more recently I have reconsidered this definition and it will be discussed further in the following chapters.

Many different learning processes occur during the human lifespan, but not all of them may be considered educational, since any definition necessarily excludes as well as includes. Some forms of teaching and learning, such as indoctrination, may be seen as a learning process but not an educational one. Self-directed learning, for instance, may be considered to be educational but it is not necessarily part of institutionalized education unless it is used as a teaching method. Additionally, there are some teaching techniques that rarely allow for the learner's own humanity and experience to surface, and when these techniques are employed, some questions must be raised about the extent to which the learning process is educational (see Jarvis, 1983a:80–93 for further analysis). Since education is regarded here as a humanistic process, teaching must be seen to be a moral activity and teaching and learning as a moral interaction (Jarvis, 1997).

From this brief discussion it may be seen that because education is regarded here as an institutionalized and humanistic process, it is seen as one in which the value of the human being and the quality of interaction between teachers and learner are recognized (see Jarvis, 1997). Where these high ideals are not manifest in the learning process then the extent to which it is educational is open to doubt.

Adult education and the education of adults

At first sight the terms adult education and the education of adults appear to mean precisely the same thing, and many writers seem to employ them synonymously (see Hostler, 1977:58), and to some extent this can still be discovered in the adult education literature in the United States; but, because of the history of the former term, there is a considerable difference between the two in the UK.

The term 'adult education' carries specific connotations in the United Kingdom, which imply that it is specifically liberal education, which has been stereotyped as a middle-class leisure time pursuit. Underlying this implication is the idea that the adult's education has been completed and, during leisure time, the adult improves or broadens existing knowledge, skills or hobbies. Hence, these implications reflect a conception of a front-end model of education and, perhaps because of the prevalence of this perception of education, it is hardly surprising that adult education was regarded as marginal. Obviously much adult education, especially that provided by Local Education Authorities, University Extension, etc., continues to occur during leisure time, but leisure need not be equated with the pursuit of only the creative arts or physical or domestic skills. Leisure time activities do not preclude any form of learning, whether aesthetic, athletic or academic, although they may have been undertaken for the sheer enjoyment of learning rather than for a vocational purpose. Hostler rightly stated that 'one quite common error is to imagine that because liberal education is not undertaken for the sake of results, it does not *have* any results' (1977:134; emphasis in original). Clearly it often does have results, as contemporary research into the hidden benefits of learning is revealing. The existence of the Open University in the United Kingdom, and similar institutions in other parts of the world, also bear witness to the fact that leisure time education for adults can and does produce results. Indeed, we have seen a tremendous increase in academically accredited leisure time education in the past decade, and even people undertaking research projects for higher degrees.

In the first instance, then, it must be recognized that the term 'adult education' has a social definition as being a form of liberal education undertaken by those people who are regarded as adults. Nevertheless, it must also be recognized that this distinction is not quite so firm in other parts of the world, including the USA. Even so, it should be noted that this is a social rather than a conceptual definition and this is why it is important to distinguish between adult education and the education of adults. However, the definition of adult still complicates this discussion.

A number of major differences occur in the analysis of the term adult and it is necessary to summarize them here. Wiltshire (1976) suggested that adult education might also be understood as an educational process

44

conducted in an adult manner. Taken to its logical extreme this interpretation would allow for children in schools to be regarded as participating in adult education if the process in which they were engaged is conducted in an adult fashion. However, Wiltshire was aware of this possible interpretation and so quite arbitrarily suggested that an adult also has to be mature, experienced and over twenty years of age. Even though it is possible to agree with Wiltshire that adulthood also implies maturity and experience, it is harder to accept that these are either absolute or discrete, or that they occur at a specific biological age. Hence, it is necessary to pursue this discussion about adulthood a little further here and then to return to the adult learning environment in a subsequent chapter.

Paterson (1979) discussed the concepts of adult, education and adult education, but since he regarded education as the process of developing learners as persons, he was a little restricted in his analysis of adult education. Nevertheless, he viewed adulthood as a status, involving certain responsibilities, entered into at a specific age. He (1979:1) claimed that people are deemed to be adults because of their age but, although they are not necessarily mature, they are expected to behave in an adult manner. Adult education is, therefore, different from other forms of education because of the nature of its students and this may be an answer to Legge's (1982:3) question about whether there is a need to have a sharp dividing line between child and adult and clearly the concept of lifelong responds to this point. That the term is still employed is an even more significant reason why it requires analysis. By contrast to Paterson, Knowles (1980a:24) suggested that the basis for treating people as adults is that they behave as adults and that they perceive themselves to be adults. Like Legge, he did not regard the distinction between adulthood and childhood to be absolute, recognizing that during the individual's lifespan the process of transition is both gradual and continuing, although while he acknowledged this conceptually he did appear to find it much harder to accept emotionally. However, he suggested that andragogical techniques could be used with children and pedagogical ones with adults. Nevertheless, it might be objected that Knowles' subjective approach is tautologous, and to some extent it is since he defines 'adult' by 'adult'. Adulthood is regarded here as having reached a level of social maturity in which individuals can assume a responsible position in society and only then may they be regarded as an adult. Knowles, reflecting the same type of discussion we had when we looked at the concept of education claimed that clarification of the term 'adult education' was more difficult because it is used with at least three different meanings: the process of adults learning; a set of organized activities carried out by a variety of institutions to achieve specific educational objectives; a field of social practice. He described the last of these three, a combination of the other two, as bringing 'together in a discrete social system all the individuals,

45

institutions and associations concerned with the education of adults' (1980a:25).

It is clear from this brief discussion that in any analysis of the terms 'adult education' and 'education of adults' the definition of the term 'adult' is deceptively difficult. In a sense, it might be easier to employ the term 'post-compulsory education' to overcome this problem, but this term does not convey the same wealth of meanings as does the word adult. However, the terms post-initial education and post-compulsory education overcome some of these conceptual problems.

At this stage it is possible to draw some conclusions about the two terms under discussion. In the United Kingdom, but not in the United States, 'adult education' is used within a liberal education framework, sometimes carrying with it implications of a front-end model of education. For these reasons, it was more desirable to employ the term 'education of adults' because this refers to any educational process undertaken by adults, whether liberal, general or vocational, and located in the spheres of adult, further or higher education or outside the institutional framework entirely. This term also implies that education is not completed at any stage in the lifespan and, indeed, that the education of adults may begin in the period of initial education and, for some people, it continues into post-initial and post-compulsory sectors. Additionally, the concept has some overlap with the idea of continuing education, which will be referred to in the next section. However, the term 'education of adults' is a broad term that encourages the development of a separate sphere of study within education. Clearly this latter usage is very similar to the American use of the term 'adult education', so that the different implications in the terminology should be borne in mind when reading the literature from either nation. While these differences are unfortunate, they reflect the differing historical traditions of the two nations.

Continuing education

As the education of adults began to develop, there was considerable confusion and overlap between the different terms. For instance, a symposium organized by Jessup in 1969 was published as 'Lifelong Learning – a symposium in Continuing Education' and the discussion paper published by the Advisory Council for Adult and Continuing Education stated: 'Continuing education has long been a popular idea among some people concerned with the education of adults. It has gone under a variety of names in different countries: education permanente, lifelong education, recurrent education' (ACACE, 1979a:7). This report was clear that continuing education should not be regarded as further education in the manner in which this currently exists in the United Kingdom. This confusion has not gone away; indeed, it still exists, especially in the European

Union where the distinction between lifelong learning, higher education and education and training is still drawn (Directorate General, Education and Culture, EC, 2002:14).

The debate in the late 1970s and early 1980s, when this book was first written, illustrates that even then there was no agreed definition of continuing education. Venables, for instance, defined continuing education as 'all learning opportunities which can be taken up after full-time compulsory schooling has ceased. They can be full-time or part-time and will include both vocational and non-vocational study' (1976:19). But McIntosh (1979:3) [now Sargant] disagreed with the definition, suggesting rather that continuing education refers to post-initial rather than post-compulsory education. The logic of this suggestion is quite clear from the previous discussion on the education of adults: initial education may continue for longer than compulsory education, so if continuing education followed compulsory education it might actually commence during initial education for many people. Hence, it may be concluded that continuing education is post-initial education (which could include higher education), but that it is not synonymous with lifelong education. Lifelong education should make no distinction between initial and post-initial education whereas continuing education refers only to the latter part of lifelong education. While the intricacies of this debate are of little significance, those of the European Union are more so, with an academic from one of the countries seeking entry to the Union in the next expansion saying that they found the EU documents quite confusing in policy terms.

Briefly, to return to the concept of continuing education, Figure 2.2 shows how it can take different forms. A suggests some form of continuous part-time education and is less frequent than other forms; B suggests that continuous education can be both full-time and part-time, this is even rarer than A; C is the most realistic as it implies that continuing education is intermittent rather than continuous. This is where the confusion in terms shows itself again since C is recurrent education, and will be discussed below.

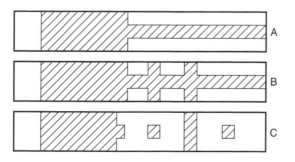

Figure 2.2 Models of continuing education.

Continuing education, however, is not the same as further education for a number of reasons: further education may be post-compulsory but not necessarily post-initial; further education tends to imply a specific level of study whereas continuing education does not; further education is pre-vocational, vocational or academic while, conceptually, continuing education need not be directed towards any course assessment or award.

From this discussion it is clear that the concept of continuing education differs slightly in its conceptualization from any of the previous terms that have been thus far elaborated upon. Yet the national organization for the UK is The National Institute of Adult Continuing Education (NIACE), following the Advisory Council, which linked together adult and continuing education in the period of rapid social change in the 1970s and 1980s – this also occurs in a number of other national organizations, such as the American Association of Adult and Continuing Education. It must be pointed out, however, that NIACE omitted the 'and' so that it sought to combine the concepts of adult education and continuing education and, as we shall see below, the practices of both leisure and vocational education – perhaps if it renamed itself again it would call itself something like the National Institute for Lifelong Learning.

How then does continuing education differ from adult education? It was pointed out earlier that adult education has connotations of hobbies and skills in part-time leisure education and that this is much narrower and more specific than the education of adults. Continuing education embraces aspects of personal, social, economic, vocational and social education (Venables, 1976:23–24). While this debate may now appear nit-picking and quite irrelevant, it does reflect the rapidity of change that was forced upon the educational system and, with it, the considerable lack of conceptual agreement that existed, and as we have seen – still exists.

However, the implications of McIntosh's definition include the fact that the concept appears to be politically neutral, neither making reference to or criticizing the initial education system nor implying any form of evaluation of the total educational system. Its apparent neutrality means that it has a conservative bias, which made it a politically acceptable term and it is for this reason that it gained a lot of support in the 1980s and the British government financed a great deal of continuing vocational education, and even pre-vocational learning. This was done through a number of differing agencies, such as the Manpower Services Commission, PICKUP, the local TECS (Training and Enterprise Councils). Now it is the Learning and Skills Councils that control the larger part of the budget. Indeed, government policy towards education might be summarized by a claim made initially in the 1960s by Clark Kerr and his colleagues:

> Industrialization requires an educational system functionally related to the skills and professions imperative to its technology.

Such an educational system is not primarily concerned with con-
serving traditional values or perpetuating the classics; it does not
adopt a static view of society, and it does not place great emphasis
on training in the traditional law. The higher educational system
of the industrial society stresses the natural sciences, engineering,
medicine, management training – whether private or public – and
administrative law. It must readily adapt to new disciplines and
fields of specialization. There is a relatively smaller place for the
humanities and the arts, while the social sciences are strongly
related to the training of managerial groups and technicians for
the enterprise and the government. The increased leisure time of
industrialism, however, can afford a broader public appreciation
of the humanities and the arts.

(Kerr *et al.*, 1973:47)

While the analysis of society contained in this quotation is dated in the
light of globalization and the philosophy underlying this claim might be
questioned by many adult educators, it is clear that it correctly predicted a
great deal of government policy in the United Kingdom and elsewhere in
the world which has supported continuing education that has a vocational
bias whilst expecting liberal adult education to be more self-financing.
However, in recent years there has been an acknowledgement that this
was a rather extreme policy and in the UK, government is now making
funds available for award-bearing liberal adult education.

Significantly, the professions used the term *continuing professional education* (CPE) and this became widely accepted for all forms of in-service
training, although Houle (1980) referred to this as continuing learning.
Cervero (1988), in the USA, however, regarded continuing professional
education as a significant area of educational activity, introducing educators to those forms of continuing education that occurred in a number
of different professions. In the USA, continuing professional education
was defined by the Accrediting Commission of the Continuing Education
Council of the United States as:

the further development of human abilities after entrance into
employment or voluntary activities. It includes in-service, upgrading and updating education. It may be occupational education or
training which furthers careers or personal development.
Continuing education includes that study made necessary by
advances in knowledge. It *excludes* most general education and
training for job entry. Continuing education is concerned primarily with broad personal and professional development. It includes
leadership training and the improvement of the ability to manage
personal, financial, material and human resources. Most of the

subject matter is at the professional, technical and leadership training levels or the equivalent.

(Apps, 1979; 68f. emphasis added)

In 1988, I (Jarvis, 1988) explored the continuing education developments in the United Kingdom for an American audience, and with the rapid changes that have occurred in the British system a similar study is called for again. Indeed, I have recently been asked by an American academic, who is teaching adult education courses, if there is such a study available. Certainly the Americans continued to emphasize the idea of continuing education for the professions longer than we did in the UK, but that was because the term lifelong learning has not had the same currency in the USA as it has had in the UK.

Professions provided their members with many updating programmes in continuing education and there has been considerable debate over the past twenty years as to the extent to which continuing education should become mandatory for registration as a member of a professional occupation. Additionally, universities, polytechnics, colleges of further and higher education, business schools and the professions themselves are all offering continuing education provision for the professions, so that unless a national policy is actually drawn up and implemented, problems and disputes might occur. Alford (1980) highlights how some of these problems – of competition between educational providers; of finance; of the political nature of accreditations – are occurring in America. These are all issues that have to be confronted in the United Kingdom, unless the 'law of the jungle' is to become manifest in continuing education (see Stephens, 1981:138). The policy of the Conservative government in the United Kingdom throughout the 1980s was to treat education as a commodity to be marketed, so that Stephens' 'law of the jungle' could have been written more aptly as the 'law of the market', and as we argued in the first chapter the learning market has become an intrinsic characteristic of the learning society. This approach to education, and the whole of culture in late modern society, has been nicely summarized by Bauman (1992:17):

> Literature, visual arts, music – indeed the whole of the humanities – was . . . set inside market-led consumption as entertainment. More and more the culture of consumer society was subordinated to the function of producing and reproducing skilful and eager consumers; . . . in its new role, it had to conform to the needs and rules as defined, in practice if not in theory, by the consumer market.

Yet there is a danger that a national policy might restrict innovations, so that too tight a control might be as damaging as no control at all to the development of continuing education. Continuing education may, therefore, be seen to be a prolongation of the educational provision beyond initial education, especially in the vocational sphere, and it is also a concept that implies no criticism of the present system.

Whilst it was the professions that emphasized continuing education in the first instance, paradoxically globalization led to the corporations being much more effective in introducing it not only for their knowledge workers but also to all their employees. This process began to emerge in the 1980s with Eurich's (1985) book, *The Corporate Classroom*, being one of the earliest studies. Other studies were to follow quite rapidly (e.g. Castner-Lotto, 1989). At this stage it was recognized that the corporations, working with knowledge and changing rapidly to respond to the wider social forces, had to become learning organizations and in both the UK (Pedler *et al.*, 1997) and the USA (Senge, 1990; Watkins and Marsick, 1993) focusing on these. Thereafter, there followed one innovative outcome: the corporations founded their own universities (Jarvis, 2001b; Meister, 1998) and the idea of corporate knowledge was developed (Tuomi, 1999). We have already discussed the learning organization in the first chapter, but the significant factor is that it was not the professions but the corporations that were the main forces behind continuing education because they had to compete in a very competitive global market.

Since, continuing education offered no criticism of the current structure of education, it actually served to reinforce the status quo, so that it is inherently conservative. No such claims may be legitimately made about the next form of education strategy to be discussed in this chapter, for recurrent education has certainly had some radical claims made on its behalf.

Recurrent education

This was the concept espoused most frequently by the Organization for Economic Cooperation and Development (OCED) until the 1980s, when the term appeared to fall into disfavour. Brought to the attention of a wider audience in the late 1960s by Olaf Palme, it gained currency through the OECD publications and, in the United Kingdom from the mid-1970s, through the publications of the Association of Recurrent Education. There was some agreement about the definition of the term, which is perhaps summarized by the following, rather tautologous, suggestion that recurrent education is 'the distribution of education over the lifespan of the individual in a recurring way' (OECD, 1973:7). This is a little broader than an earlier definition proposed by the OECD that recurrent education 'is formal, and preferably full-time education for adults who want to resume their education, interrupted earlier for a variety of reasons' (OECD, 1971, cited by Kallen, 1979). These two definitions have been selected because they indicate two conceptions of recurrent education, which may be illustrated in the manner shown in Figure 2.3. In (a) it may be seen that the education is full-time, but in (b) it is either full-time or part-time, and it may be recalled that continuing education might also assume a full-time or a part-time form, so that it would be legitimate to ask whether these two terms were actually synonymous.

One of the most significant features of recurrent education was the belief that individuals should have a right to a specified amount of full-time formal education beyond compulsory schooling, and this need not have been taken during their formative years. Indeed, Gould (1979) not only regarded this as a moral argument about the equality of educational opportunity but he also related it to a wider perspective of equality of occupational opportunity. Therefore some of its exponents saw this as a radical, moral strategy for lifelong education. Unlike continuing education, which appeared to occur in a piecemeal manner in response to expressed or perceived needs, etc., recurrent educationalists regarded their approach to be a 'comprehensive alternative strategy for what are at present three unrelated sectors: (a) the conventional post-compulsory educational system ... (b) on-the-job training of all kinds (c) adult education' (OECD, 1973:25).

Houghton (1974:6) actually claimed that recurrent education 'was the first new idea in education this century ... It represents one of those very rare shifts in the framework of thinking which Kuhn has described. Its emergence marks the beginning of the end of the dominant apprenticeship paradigm in education'. Clearly this is a massive claim but, at the

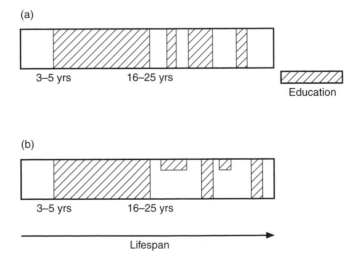

Figure 2.3 Alternative models of recurrent education.
Source: Boyle (1982:8).

same time, recurrent education did offer a radical alternative system, one that its exponents claimed to be realistic in the light of contemporary society (e.g. Flude and Parrott, 1979). Others may have viewed recurrent education as a reaction to the technological innovations in society rather than a radical alternative idea. However, not all exponents of recurrent education actually expected the whole education system to be radically changed, as Cantor (1974:6–7) indicated when he described its emergence in the United Kingdom.

> It is hardly surprising therefore to discover that recurrent education is not at all systematically organized in the United Kingdom; indeed many of its critics would argue that there is as yet little official recognition of the need to make systematic provision for it. However, education in the United Kingdom does contain elements of recurrent education upon which to erect a more systematic provision.

Obviously Cantor thought that a system would emerge, perhaps with a few policy decisions to aid it on its way. Indeed, this type of presentation reflects a less radical approach to recurrent education and seems to coincide with a continuing education perspective; it is also reflected in some of the later OECD publications (e.g. OECD, 1977).

Since some exponents of recurrent education presented it as a more radical approach to education and others have embraced the more moderate continuing education perspective, it was not surprising that some theorists have extended this distinction to other aspects of the curriculum. Griffin (1978), for instance, focused upon the main aspects of teaching and learning in the curriculum: aims, content and method. He suggested that recurrent educationalists tend to be more student-centred, have a more integrated approach to content and generally have a more romantic curriculum perspective, while those who had adopted a continuing education approach had a more classical perspective on curriculum issues. While he polarized continuing and recurrent education, he admitted that he had undertaken a tentative exercise. However, he raised many valuable points about these two forms of education, and this might have been even more insightful had he also sought to incorporate some of the other philosophical issues espoused by many adult educators.

One of the main practical features in recurrent education was the idea that full-time education may be embarked upon later in life by some people. Having a right to full-time education later in life is both inconvenient and expensive to employers and governments and so it is hardly surprising that with the economic stringency of the 1980s and the advent of 'new right' politics that the idea of recurrent education disappeared from the political and educational agendas. Indeed, it even fell into disfavour with the OECD, and the Association of Recurrent Education in the United Kingdom also adopted a new name – the Association of Lifelong Learning.

One aspect of recurrent education which has survived, however, is the idea of paid educational leave. This was recognized in some of the early OECD literature (OECD, 1973:70–72), where discussion occurred about the extent to which paid educational leave should be a statutory right or whether it should be the result of negotiations between employers and employees. By the time that the OECD had actually published this document, France had already introduced legislation which allowed for up to 2 per cent of a firm's labour force to take leave of absence at any one time and for 1 per cent of the wage bill, rising to 2 per cent by 1976, to be spent on employee education (OECD, 1975:35).

Other European countries were also introducing similar legislation and the International Labour Organization called for each member state to formulate and apply a policy of paid educational leave (Convention 140:1974). Killeen and Bird (1981) investigated the extent to which paid educational leave existed in England and Wales during this period and concluded that between 15 and 20 per cent of the total workforce received some paid, or assisted, educational leave in the year of the study, 1976–7, which approximated to six days per person for courses organized by the employing organization and twelve days per person attending courses mounted by other organizations. They noted that this educational leave was not evenly distributed, younger workers being more likely to be released than older ones, and that the courses tended to be vocationally based and had a qualification as one of their end products. Bryant (1983) reported a similar research project in Scotland in which he recorded a similar picture to that discovered in England and Wales. Mace and Yarnit (1987) also recorded a number of examples of paid educational leave, including developments in London (Workbase), Sheffield (Take Ten – a day off to study each week for ten weeks) and Liverpool (Second Chance to Learn): this book was an important one since it sought to address the issue of why low paid and disadvantaged groups get fewer opportunities for educational development than do the more advantaged groups. In addition, the book reported on the 150-hour programme in Italy, which is an exemplar of what can be done with careful planning. Paid educational leave is still very important since corporations realize that it is crucial that their employees keep abreast with developments in their own field. However, the concerns of the 1970s and 1980s were recorded here as one of the examples of how rapidly our attitudes towards education policy have changed with the advent of globalization. A new version of paid educational leave, however, was promulgated at the UNESCO World Adult Education Conference in Hamburg in 1997, which was 'one hour a day of learning'.

One writer who continued to use the term recurrent education was

Tuijnman (1989), whose use of the data from the 50-year longitudinal study of men in Malmo, Sweden, has shown how significantly adult education and occupation are related. He demonstrated, for instance, that adult education has significant positive effects on occupation and career development. Tuijnman suggests that 'men who participate in adult education tended to view their lives as more "full," "worthwhile," "rich," and "interesting" than those who did not take part in such activities' (1989:228). Tuijnman's research was only with men so that, while it might be postulated that the same would be true for women, he did not produce data to demonstrate it. This research is a forerunner of the current concerns in the UK towards the hidden benefits of learning.

Recurrent education, then, had two major stands: a more radical one that regards it as a strategy for the reform of the whole education system and perhaps also the wider society, while the more conservative stand was less ambitious in its claims, preferring rather to regard it as a reformist approach to implementing lifelong education. There is a marked difference in the philosophy of the two stands and yet they both recognize that while education may not be continuous after initial education it should be lifelong, a right that all people should receive and that sufficient provision should be made for them to do so.

Human resource development

As we noted in the section on continuing education, the corporations began to develop their own education and training during this time. However, there was another conceptual shift just a little earlier when Schultz (1961) introduced the term *human capital*. He pointed out that economists shied away from the use of this term because, while individuals actually invested in themselves, they might find it offensive to think of themselves in this manner. He (1961) wrote:

> Our values and beliefs might inhibit us from looking upon human beings as capital goods, except in slavery, which we abhor. We are not unaffected by the long struggle to society on indentured service and to evolve political and legal institutions to keep men free from bondage. These are achievements we prize highly. Hence, to treat human beings as wealth that can be augmented by investment runs counter to deeply held values.
> (cited from Jarvis with Griffin, 2003, vol. 5:246)

However, it was not long before the idea of human capital development arose, and corporations opened their own human resource development (HRD) departments, some of which eventually turned into the corporate universities. HRD seeks to enhance the personal and work-related knowledge and skills of individuals, helping them to achieve their full potential. In more recent years competency-based training, and National Vocational Qualifications (NVQ), have been introduced, which involve work-based learning and with it systems of mentoring have also been introduced. Training officers, and even some personnel and welfare officers, have become human resource managers and trainers and gradually HRD has assumed its own place in the learning society (see Brinkerhoff, 1987; Jayagopal, 1990; Hargreaves and Jarvis, 2000 *inter alia*). In 1993 the Academy of Human Resource Development was founded in the United States by adult educators who had undertaken a great deal of their research in organizational settings, and human resource development became a separate profession. The Academy runs its own conferences and publishes its own books (see Redmann, 2000).

In the United Kingdom the system has been extended to the level of Masters' degree and gradually some employers are beginning to expect their managers and senior personnel to undertake NVQs rather than releasing them to attend university courses, which are often regarded as not sufficiently work orientated. At the same time, universities and colleges have assumed a significant HRD role.

It was also recognized that HRD training could have effects more widely, so that workers could take what they learned and use it in the community (Dovey and Onyx, 2001), and a number of analysts developed the concept of social capital (see Coleman, 1990; Putnam, 2000 *inter alia*).

Community education

Occasionally a word appears in the English language that becomes ideologically acceptable for a period of time. 'Community' is such a word becoming widely accepted in the United Kingdom in the 1960s and 1970s as something intrinsically good and right. Now sociologists talk about idealized communities, which is the extension of this. Perhaps this is because a certain nostalgia exists for a world that is past, one we imagine, or which we would like to see re-emerge. Hence the idea of community education appeared to have been accepted with almost the same uncritical appraisal as the term *community*. This process was aided and abetted by the fact that it is a confused and multifarious concept. In order to begin to appreciate some of these facets it is necessary to understand the use of the word community.

In sociology the main meaning of the word stems from the work of the German sociologist Toennies (1957), who wrote in the nineteenth century about social change. He recognized that a change in the type of human relationships was occurring, from one that may be seen as personal and long lasting (community) to one that was formed by personal interaction (association). Hence, the term 'community' assumed a distinctive meaning in sociology referring both to personal relationships and to the fact that they should be established within a specific locality. Toennies actually considered that these personal, long lasting relationships were disappearing as society became more urban and its members more mobile. Thus it is not surprising that the term assumed an ideological significance in an increasingly impersonal and individualized society. Durkheim (1933) also discussed this phenomenon, distinguishing between organic and mechanical solidarity as the structures of society changed. Now, clearly the societies in the West, especially, have become even more individualized and even the idea of society questioned.

A second, but quite similar, use of the term refers to those groups of people who live together in a specific place, such as a monastery, and where the value of the community life is extolled. Here people interact in a personal manner in a specific locality but the boundaries of the community are even more tightly drawn. Third, the word is sometimes used without reference to the personal relationships, when it refers only to the locality, for example the people of such-and-such a community. This is perhaps the most common use of the word, although there is one other that is employed very frequently; in this instance it refers to 'extramural' in its widest sense, so that community nurses, for instance, care for their patients outside the walls of the hospital, etc.

Consequently, it is easy to understand how ambiguous is the term 'community education', since all of these meanings of community are interrelated and confused in the diverse educational processes that are often classified as being a part of it. Therefore, it is not surprising that an analytical philosopher, such as Lawson (1977), should have pointed out this conceptual confusion and raised doubts about the idea of community education. However, other adult educators, such as Kirkwood (1978), considered that Lawson's approach, while valuable, was rather conservative and not entirely correct. Perhaps it would be true to say that new forms of adult education arise in response to expressed needs or demands and that in their initial stages they are not classified in any manner, so that Lawson's analytical approach was a necessary reflection on the innovations that were occurring in the education of adults.

Traditionally, Scotland has always used the term community education, even when adult education was used in England, and the term embraced both adult education and other forms of education in the community.

However, it is possible to distinguish at least three different types of education that might be called community education: education for action and/or development; education in the community; extramural forms of education. Lovett et al. (1983:36ff.) also sought to distinguish between different forms of community education and they suggested four types: community organization/education; community development/education; community action/education; social action/education. However, for the purposes of this analysis the three types of community education distinguished here will now be briefly discussed.

Education for community action and/or development

Perhaps the most well-known exponent of this position was Paulo Freire, who maintained that education can never be neutral. He formulated his ideas in Latin America, against a background of illiteracy and poverty, and his thinking was a synthesis of Christian theology, existentialism and Marxism – one that underlay liberation theology. While his ideas developed in a Third World context, they are relevant to the United Kingdom and America, as Kirkwood and Kirkwood (1989) showed (see also London, 1973). Even though much of Freire's work was written in Portuguese, it is widely available in English (see bibliography), and even his posthumous works are widely available (see, for instance, Freire, 1996, 1997, 1998). He emphasized that education should make the learners critically aware of their false consciousness and of their social condition. In becoming aware, they should reject many of the myths erected by the ruling elite that inhibit them (the learners) from having a clear perception of their own social reality. Having undergone a process of consciencization, learners should act upon the world to endeavour to create a better society. Clearly Freire's radical, but moral, approach is one that has been criticized, especially by those who for varying reasons wish to see education as a neutral process, but over the years his stature has grown and his thinking has been much admired throughout the educational world.

Freire was not alone with this perception of education, although few other writers have formulated it in such a sophisticated manner. Among those in the United Kingdom whose approach to education is similar to Freire's is Lovett (1975, 1980) who worked both in inner-city Liverpool and in Belfast in Northern Ireland. Lovett suggested that some adult educators see 'the role of adult education in community action . . . as . . . providing the working class with an effective educational service so that they can take full advantage of the educational service *and* make the best use of their individual talents and abilities' (1975:155 – emphasis in original). In his work in Northern Ireland, Lovett (Lovett *et al.*, 1983) continued to work out these ideas and subsequently offered a model of different types of community education. While Lovett worked his own ideas, Kirkwood and Kirkwood (1989) were applying Freire's ideas in a community education project in inner-city Edinburgh. They recorded how they adapted his educational techniques to their own situation, although the project was certainly less radical than some of Freire's own ideas.

In America, perhaps the most well-known institution organizing radical adult education is Highlander, which was founded by Myles Horton in

Tennessee, and worked with labour unions and citizenship groups. It played a significant role in the civil rights movement in the United States and its work is becoming increasingly well documented (Horton, 1990). In 1987, Horton and Freire came together at Highlander to 'talk a book' (Horton and Freire, 1990) in which they exchanged their understanding of radical adult education and produced a most insightful understanding of the place education might play in community development.

One of the clear distinguishing features about the education being described here is that these are not formalized educational systems, but that they are non-formal and occur beyond the boundaries of the traditional formal, bureaucratic educational system that exists in many societies in the world.

But should adult educators be involved in the action in the community? Newman suggested that there are conditions under which the adult educator 'should not try to stop short of involvement in community action' (1973:26), but by contrast, a few adult educators considered that while they should be prepared to teach activists what to do, they should not actually be involved in the action (Flude, 1978:163). This latter position was a minority view that has had little currency of late, since it has now been widely recognized that no education is neutral and that a great deal of formal education is culturally and socially reproductive.

It is clear that education is an essential tool in the process of community development and an early project carried out in UK was undertaken by Fordham *et al.* (1979) from the University of Southampton, in which they sought to establish and strengthen adult education provision in an informal educational setting in a working-class housing estate in Havant. Here the educators were concerned to develop adult education for the sake of the whole area rather than as a response to the demands of potential students. It would be quite possible to record a multitude of community development projects in which adult education has played a major role, but perhaps it is wiser to note here that the journals of the International Council of Adult Education, *Convergence,* and the Institute for International Co-operation of the German Adult Education Association (DVV) *Adult Education for Development* usually carry reports of many of these enterprises from developing countries and, recently, *The International Journal of Lifelong Education* has also published similar studies.

Education in the community

Perhaps the earliest formal education of this type stemmed from the work of Henry Morris, who was responsible for the establishment of community colleges in Cambridgeshire before the Second World War (see Jennings, n.d.), and whose ideas were influential in their introduction in Leicestershire shortly afterwards (Fairbairn, 1978). From these beginnings have grown the larger urban educational and social complexes, such as the Abraham Moss Centre in Manchester and the Sutton Centre in Nottinghamshire. One of the central ideas of these schemes is that the school should be the focal point of the community, in a similar manner to that of the parish church in medieval times, and that adults, as well as children, should be able to attend classes in these centres. As a result of his work in Liverpool, Midwinter (1975:99) concluded that:

> Education must no longer be open to caricature as a few hours at school for a few years in ... pre-adult life. It must be viewed as a total, lifelong experience, with the home and the neighbourhood playing important parts, and everybody contributing to and drawing on this educative dimension of the community.

However, he did not specify all the advantages of comprehensive schools including adults among their learners, but Mary Hughes (1977:226–232) saw many advantages in allowing adults to attend community schools at the same time as children, not the least being that it is education on the cheap. These large urban educational complexes have also been introduced in other parts of the United Kingdom, and a similar community school complex established in the suburbs of Grenoble, in France, was also influenced by these developments. Clearly educational innovation is occurring throughout the world and much of it could be discussed under this sub-heading. Poster and Kruger (1990), for instance, brought together a number of examples from different countries in the Western world, highlighting some of the ways in which educationalists are reaching out into the community. More recently Mark Smith (1994) dropped the term community and introduced the idea of local education to describe some of these developments. In America, the community college concept has also been implemented and comprehensive programmes are offered for younger and older students who wish to study (Yarrington, 1979:86–94).

Adult education beyond the walls

Extra-mural adult education is a term usually restricted to university adult education extension classes where academic staff from the universities teach in the community, or the universities employ part-time staff to teach liberal adult education classes under their auspices in the wider community. Recently, the term has assumed some significance with other educational institutions organizing educational classes in their local communities. However, these forms of educational outreach are rarely regarded as community education, even though they are examples of education 'beyond the walls' of the educational institution.

With the growing emphasis on practical knowledge, we have also seen the development of educational courses based in the home, the community, the work place, and so on. These opportunities to learn might have been regarded as community education, extra-mural or placements within a more traditional course whereby learners could learn to apply theory to practice. Now this has changed, and even the idea of applying theory to practice has been thoroughly questioned (Jarvis, 1999a). Hence we shall deal with each of these approaches to learning in future pages in this study.

Fletcher (1980a, 1980b) suggested that there are three premises in community education:

- the community has its needs and common causes and is the maker of its own culture;
- educational resources are to be dedicated to the articulation of needs and common causes;
- education is an activity in which there is an alternative between the roles of student, teacher and person.

He argued that certain implications follow from this in terms of centre or periphery activities, formality and informality and democratic control. This, in turn, resulted in active and reactive processes. However, perhaps Fletcher was guilty of reification of the concept of community in the first of these premises, but his second one – groups and categories of persons in the locality who have common causes – is increasingly significant, even more so as the United Kingdom becomes the host society for many refugees and migrants. The philosophy underlying this approach to community education is one of responding to certain forms of social inequality in order to produce a more equal society in which more people interact on an interpersonal basis, so that the locality begins to generate its own community ethos. It would, therefore, be a matter of social policy and educational commitment to divert educational resources to the underprivileged and, as such, it would reflect the philosophy that led to the creation of educational priority areas in initial education.

Lifelong education

Once the front-end model of education is rejected the way is open to formulate other approaches to the subject, one being that the process of education begins in childhood and continues throughout the lifespan. One of the first influential definitions of lifelong education was that of Dave who regarded lifelong education as 'a process of accomplishing personal, social and professional development throughout the lifespan of individuals in order to enhance the quality of life of both individuals and their collectivities' (1976:34). Lawson tried to show that such a wide conception of education 'fails to distinguish between the general mass of formative influence that shapes us or between the general learning which an intelligent being undergoes in adapting to circumstances' (1982:103). He pleaded for a more careful analysis of the claims that are made on behalf of lifelong education. While Lawson was clearly right to criticize Dave's approach since it offered no definition of education, Lawson himself did not offer an alternative. Even so, Lawson seemed to be in danger of including the content of what is taught and learned in the educational process, rather than regarding the actual content as incidental to the process. Fundamentally, this debate reflected the confusion that has existed since there have been few clear definitions of learning and education, and as we shall show below with the advent of the term lifelong learning, this confusion has been exacerbated.

Once education is regarded as institutionalized learning, we can discuss the variety of providers of education for adults at all ages that have emerged in recent years, but this does not mean that we have, or should have, a national state-provided lifelong educational system. Lifelong education is every institutionalized learning opportunity, having a humanistic basis, directed towards the participant's development that may occur at any stage in the lifespan. This development might refer to knowledge, skills, attitudes, values, emotions, beliefs and the senses – the whole person.

While lifelong education as an ideal has been adopted by the United Nations Educational, Scientific and Cultural Organization (UNESCO) it was not really a new concept:

> It is common place to say that education should not cease when one leaves school. The point of this common place is that the purpose of school organization is to insure the continuance of education by organizing the powers that insure growth. The inclination to learn from life itself and to make the condition of life such that all will learn in the process of living is the finest product of schooling.
>
> (Dewey, 1916:51)

While not everyone would agree with Dewey's understanding of the purpose of the school organization, they may well agree with the sentiments expressed in the remainder of the quotation:

> Since life means growth, a living creature lives as truly and positively at one stage as at another, with the same intrinsic fullness and the same absolute claims. Hence education means the enterprise of supplying the conditions which insure growth, or adequacy of life, irrespective of age.

For Dewey, education is one of the major foundations of a rich life, but it is also one that need not be laid at the beginnings of life or in childhood; it may be laid at any stage of life and then built upon. However, in the light of our current understanding, Dewey might actually have used the term learning rather than education to make his point more clearly. While he has not been overtly influential to a great deal of adult education in the United Kingdom, his influence has been far greater in the United States. Among his disciples was Lindeman, author of *The Meaning of Adult Education* (1961, first published 1926), who became a major influence on Malcolm Knowles and other influential practitioners in the field.

Soon after Dewey's influential book, from which these quotations have been drawn, appeared in America, an important document about adult education was published in Britain. A.L. Smith, chairman of the committee that produced the famous 1919 Report, wrote:

> That the necessary condition is that adult education must not be regarded as a luxury for the few exceptional persons here and there, nor as a thing which concerns only a short span of early manhood, but that adult education is a permanent national necessity, an inseparable aspect of citizenship, and therefore should be both universal and lifelong.
>
> (Smith, 1919: Introductory letter para xi: 5)

This far-sighted statement, like many others in the Report, was loudly acclaimed but never implemented, so that the idea of lifelong education remained an ideal. Yeaxlee (1929:31), who served on the committee that drafted the 1919 Report, returned to the subject in the very first book about lifelong education and claimed that:

> the case for lifelong education rests ultimately upon the nature and needs of the human personality in such a way that no individual can rightly be regarded as outside its scope, the social reasons for fostering it are as powerful as the personal.

Here, then, lies an argument for lifelong education, very similar in substance to that produced earlier in this study; yet this case was made in the United Kingdom three-quarters of a century ago.

It was not until after the Second World War that the term gained prominence and this was because organizations such as UNESCO adopted it, influenced by such individuals as Lengrand (1975). Thereafter many publications, emanating from UNESCO, developed and expounded the concept. The Faure Report (1972) advocated that education should be both universal and lifelong, claiming that education precedes economic development and prepares individuals for a society that does not exist but which may do so within their lifetime. The Report claimed that education is essential for human beings and their development and that, therefore, the whole concept of education needs to be reconsidered. The sentiments of this report were echoed by the Delors Report (1996) in which it was claimed that learning has four pillars – learning: to know; to do; to live together; to be.

In 1976, lifelong education appeared to have 'come of age' when the Lifelong Learning Act was passed into law in the United States, which authorized the expenditure of $40 million annually between 1977 and 1982 on lifelong education (Peterson *et al.*, 1979:295). However, Peterson and his associates were forced to conclude that while 'lifelong education and learning policies are gaining favour in numerous foreign countries, notably Scandinavia, there are at the moment signs of slackening progress [in America]' (1979:423). Despite this rather gloomy assessment lifelong education has now been thoroughly established in the USA, although probably not in the same form as was intended by the Mondale Act.

Higher education was also gradually changing its direction and beginning to practise policies of lifelong education, although this process has been extremely slow. Knapper and Cropley (1985) traced the implications of the idea of lifelong learning for higher education and Kulich (1982) documented how Canadian universities are moving in this direction. Williams (1977) actually claimed that lifelong education was the new role for institutions of higher education. While this assertion is supported here, it is recognized that some universities have found it very difficult to adapt to these demands and some of them have actively resisted such changes. Nevertheless, with the gradual growth in part-time higher education and the introduction of schemes of accreditation of prior learning and credit transfer changes are occurring, which might result in higher education institutions regarding themselves as institutions providing opportunities for education throughout the lifespan. However, the European Commission has distinguished higher education from lifelong learning, which has added to the conceptual confusion. As we shall see in the next section this exists because the distinction between lifelong education and lifelong learning has not been clearly made. One of the reasons for this is because there was never a clear point in the current development of lifelong learning when the educational policies were specifically directed towards lifelong education *per se*, as they were with continuing education. And by the mid-1990s there had been a clear movement away from discussions about continuing education to those about lifelong learning.

Lifelong learning

The concept of lifelong learning is extremely confusing since it combines individual learning and institutionalized learning. Learning can be understood as an individual process which continues throughout the whole of life – lifelong learning. But learning can also be considered as institutionalized and formalized: in other words the educational system. It has been widely acknowledged that many learning opportunities have to be provided by the non-educational sectors of society, such as the corporations, and that there need to be partnerships between education and those other providers of learning opportunities. Consequently, lifelong learning embraces the socially institutionalized learning that occurs in the educational system, that which occurs beyond it, and that individual learning throughout the lifespan, which is publicly recognized and accredited (Jarvis, 1996). In this sense, it is impossible to create a fully institutionalized system of lifelong learning although the networks of learning opportunities have to be recognized. These different meanings of lifelong learning confuse the concept and while the emphasis is on institutionalized learning it undermines the learning processes themselves. Indeed, it is impossible to have a policy for individual lifelong learning, although there can be one which either makes the facilities for learning available to people throughout their life times (ACCESS), or which accredits the learning that occurs privately if the learner so desires it (APEL), but it is possible to have one for the institutional interpretation of lifelong learning. These are essential for those societies that aspire to be learning societies, as we highlighted in the previous chapter, but which Boshier (1980:1–2) claimed could not emerge through additional learning programmes being grafted on to existing provision, rather it required a deliberate policy and definite changes in curriculum aims, especially in initial education.

Summary

This chapter has sought to illustrate some of the philosophies and concepts that were prevalent during this period of rapid social and educational change. Initially, the front-end model of education was discussed, but such an approach is not particularly relevant for education in contemporary society. A humanistic definition was then offered, i.e. that education is any planned series of incidents, having a humanistic basis, directed towards the participants' learning and understanding. Education is seen, therefore, as an idealistic process in which the humanity of the participants is paramount.

The education of adults was regarded as any process directed towards the participants' learning and understanding, where the participants regarded themselves and were treated by others as socially mature. The reasons for the use of the term education of adults revolve around the fact that the concept of adult education carries liberal education connotations, while a great deal of educational provision is vocational in nature. However, liberal adult education provision must lie at the heart of the learning society in which education is seen as a lifelong process of learning and developing – which is an ideal at which to aim.

Three strategies for implementing lifelong education were discussed: the reasons why continuing education gained wide acceptance were highlighted since it is a conservative concept that casts no aspersions on the present system. In addition, recurrent education ideas have been incorporated into the continuing education system and its more radical implications have been only partially recognized in such phenomena as paid educational leave, but those which imply that the current system needs radical reform so that everybody may receive an equal entitlement of education at some stage during their life have little currency. Community education was also shown to be a rather confused concept. Kulich (1982) documented how Canadian universities are moving in this direction and use their learning to improve the quality of life in a specific locality, while other forms of education generally classified under this heading might be better regarded as other innovations in lifelong education. Finally the ideas of lifelong education and lifelong learning were discussed. While there is a certain logical progression through these as the concept of lifelong learning emerged, this progression is not inevitable in other countries of the world and so this is better regarded as a taxonomy. Now it is necessary to examine the adult learner and adult learning, subjects that form the bases for the next two chapters.

3

THE ADULT LEARNER AND
ADULT LEARNING

Earlier in this book it has been argued that learning is an existential phenomenon, processes that occur in most people throughout most of their lives. Hence, it is maintained that lifelong education – or now, lifelong learning – should be regarded both as a human right and as a fundamental necessity in any civilized society so that all people can respond to their learning needs, fulfil their potential and discover a place in the wider society. For too long education was regarded as 'something done to children', continued in adolescence, and then for the most part it had no further place in their lives. Now things have changed, but there are still many who may never again darken the doors of an educational institution after their schooling. However, this does not mean that they have ceased to learn and some may also continue the process of self-education, even if the learning that they provide for themselves might not always be quite as enriching (but certainly not necessarily so) as they may have received had they availed themselves of the wider educational provision. Much of this learning may have been covert and, despite the work of Candy and similar research projects (see Candy, 1991 for a bibliography and analysis), the actual amount of learning per adult remains unknown and probably unquantifiable. However, over the years since the first edition of this book an increasing emphasis has been placed upon adult learners and their learning, with studies appearing to which some reference has already been made. Consequently, this chapter focuses upon these aspects and contains two main sections: the adult learner and adult learning. In the following chapter some of the writers about adult learning are examined.

The adult learner

Adulthood is reached when individuals are treated by others as if they are socially mature and when they consider themselves to have achieved this status. However, such an approach does not really enrich the debate about the adult learner, nor does it contribute much to the theory of adult learning, or learning in general, so that it is necessary to pursue this discussion a little further and discuss the nature of personhood.

Personhood

The person is, in a sense, an embodied self, or as we shall suggest below – embodied selves. We have only one body, located in space and time and yet complex beyond our understanding, but we do almost certainly have multiple selves. We will include two brief sections here: the body and the self, although psychologists and sociologists have pursued this subject in far great depth (Harre, 1998; McAdams, 2001 *inter alia*).

The body

There has been considerable recent research about the nature of the body (Shilling, 1993 *inter alia*), and much of which lies beyond the focus of this study. Nevertheless, the body is a fundamental element in the person and cannot be omitted in any discussion about learning. We all know, for instance, how the body can be programmed by constant repetition of an action – by a pianist, for instance, so that the sequence of music learned can be played almost automatically. We do the same when driving a car. At birth, the body is already the subject of evolutionary processes, carrying with it our genetic structures, and so on. But the body also contains a brain – not a mind but a brain – which, as Gardner (1983) points out, processes different bits of information in different parts and, as Greenfield (1999) shows, responds to experiences in a physical manner and she (1999:112) defines consciousness, for instance, as 'an emergent property of non-specialised groups of neurons ... that are continuously variable with respect to an epicentre'. We shall return to the idea of conscious awareness later in this chapter. In addition, our construction and perception of our body influences our self-identity, which itself is a learned phenomenon. Gardner (1999) also illustrates how brain damage affects specific parts of the brain which in turn relates to different human abilities, and so on. In addition, we are aware that the ageing processes do affect our bodies and, consequently, our learning abilities in different ways. It is clear, therefore, that new developments in learning theory might well come from neuroscience and biology – even from chemistry, if we were to think about the drugs that affect our brain functioning.

Adult educators have been the only educationalists, until very recently, who have considered the ageing body within the educational processes. The physical capabilities of the adult do decline after they have reached a peak in late adolescence or in early adulthood. Verner (1964:18) summarized these as including: 'sensory decline; loss in strength; lengthening of reaction time; decline in sexual capacity; changes in skin texture, muscle tone and hair colour; and a gradual decline in overall energy'. He suggested that there are some physiological losses that are very significant in the process of adult learning: loss in visual acuity, loss in audio acuity, loss of energy and the problems of homeostatic adjustment. Since these all affect adult learning and, therefore, adult teaching, they need to be taken into consideration. However, these physiological changes may induce adults to underestimate their powers to learn and so reinforce the perception that education is something that occurs early in life. In addition, recent research has suggested that older people can continue to learn both physical and mental fitness (Cussack, 1996). At the same time, learning can be used as a therapy and, in a more recent book, I (Jarvis, 2001a) have argued for the creation of an occupation of learning therapists who can assist the confused elderly re-develop some of their faculties. But the person is more than body – mind and, therefore, self are constituent elements.

The self

It was noted in the first chapter that the self-concept is central to learning theory. Jarvis (1987, 1992), following George Herbert Mead, has argued that the mind and the self are learned phenomena. The brain stores memories of experiences, almost certainly from the time that the baby is still in the womb and certainly from the time of birth, from which emerge the mind and then the self. Luckmann (1967:48–49) argues that during the early years the individual self becomes detached from its immediate experience in the interaction with other persons. This detachment leads to individuation of consciousness and permits the construction of schemes of meaning that responds to the learning needs that the evolving self develops. We can see this in children as they first use their own names to refer to themselves, then they use 'me' and, finally, they employ 'I' – they have become a self. This, in turn, results in the person integrating the meanings that have evolved in response to the learning questions that have arisen from previous experience. Hence, ultimately, a self is formed that integrates the 'past, present and future in a socially defined, morally relevant biography' (Luckmann, 1967:48–49). There is, therefore, a sense in which the self transcends its biological body, reaching out to the socio-cultural environment and responding to pressures from it in a dialectical relationship in order to create a sense of meaning, as was illustrated in the opening chapter.

Yet we are all aware that the sense of self-identity is much more complex than just a single 'self identity'. We know that we have a personal identity and a social identity – and we are aware that in different social situations we might assume more than one social identity. Harre (1998:4) makes the point that:

To have a sense of self is to have a sense of one's location as a person, in each of several arrays of other beings, relevant to personhood.

But this, he suggests is Self 1, whereas Self 2 is the awareness that we possess different characteristics from others and Self 3 is the impression that the personal characteristics of a person has on others. Yet there is still a singular self to be found within the one body, individual and unique. Following Apter (1989:75), he agrees that the person has a sense of personal distinctiveness, personal continuity and personal autonomy, the acquisition of which are learned. The debate about the complexity of the sense of self would take us far beyond the intention of this book – but we can see from this discussion that the acquisition and development of Apter's three characteristics constitute the processes whereby we learn and construct our own biographies.

Thus it may be seen that every new experience is interpreted by the mind and has a personal meaning given to it, which is then integrated into the meanings of past experiences already stored in the brain, which gives us a greater understanding of how we, as individuals, can behave. This ultimately results in a system of meaning or a body of knowledge that helps us interpret 'reality'. This enables us to understand the ideas underlying wisdom and expertise. But what if the physical body and even the brain itself begin to deteriorate during adulthood? Does it not affect the ability of the self to process these experiences in a meaningful way? Luckmann might respond in the negative to this, at least until such time as the brain ceases to function efficiently. In recent years, psychologists have tended to support this conclusion.

Until fairly recently, however, it was thought that when human beings achieved biological maturity they reached a plateau on which they remained for a few years, before they began to deteriorate. Thorndike (1928), for instance, concluded that the ability to learn 'rises until about twenty, and then, perhaps after a stationary period of some years, slowly declines' (cited in Yeaxlee, 1929:41). However, this argument has now come under considerable criticism and Allman (1982) summarized some of these research findings as early as 1982. She recorded how Horn suggested that there are two forms of intelligence: fluid, which stems from the biological base, and crystallized, which is capable of growth through the major part of life since it is influenced by the social processes that the individual experiences. More recently, however, Gardner (1983, 1999 *inter alia*) has argued for even more and different forms of intelligence. In the same paper, Allman (1982:47) pointed to Birran's 'discontinuity hypothesis' which states that 'the biological base ceases to be the primary influence on behaviour after physical maturation is complete and as long as the biological base does not enter into a hypothesized critical range of pathology, it will not regain supremacy of influence'.

From these and other studies, she concluded that since adulthood is not the end-product of childhood and adolescence; lifelong education becomes a means of facilitating future adult development. In a similar fashion, one of the foremost investigators of education and ageing, Gisela Labouvie-Vief, concluded nearly a quarter of a century ago that 'much of what we now know about the educability of adults is in need of revision' (1978:249). Therefore, the old adage that 'you can't teach an old dog new tricks' is not only misleading, it is also entirely wrong. We continue to construct our biography, our personhood, throughout the greater part of our lives. Irrespective of the condition of the physical body, the individual self continues to interact with others within the same socio-cultural milieu enabling the person to continue to construct a universe of meaning. If there are no other people with whom to interact then the dynamic tension between the self and the wider society, which is at the heart of learning, disappears and people may begin to doubt themselves, suffer anomie, etc.

But do adults always learn when they are interacting with other people? Clearly many situations are familiar so that individuals do not have an experience in every interaction and the amount of new knowledge gained may be minimal and it may merely reinforce that which is already known. On other occasions the discrepancy between what individuals know and the meaning that they give to their experiences is greater and then the learning experience becomes more explicit. Schutz and Luckmann state:

> In the natural attitude, I only become aware of the deficient tone of my stock of knowledge if a novel experience does not fit into what has up until now been taken as a taken-for-granted valid reference scheme.
>
> (Schutz and Luckmann, 1974:8)

Thus it may be argued that given specific social and new situations every adult is a learner, whereas in familiar experiences the knowledge gained may merely reinforce that which the individual already has. Yet there is a sense in which this argument suggests that the motivating force for learning is a discordant experience between the biography and the understanding of the socio-cultural environment. This I have called 'disjuncture', but it would be unwise to suggest that this is the only reason for undertaking such an activity. Tough (1979:44–62), who studied those people who had undertaken an educational project, showed how complex the reasons for undertaking a learning episode are and it would not do the sophistication of his argument justice to attempt to reproduce it here; suffice to note that amongst the reasons he discussed were pleasure, esteem, desire to employ what is learned, satisfying curiosity, enjoyment gained from the content of what is learned, completing unfinished learning, and social benefits.

Characteristics of the adult learner

It may thus be asked, who is the adult learner? From my argument thus far the response must be – everybody. But not everyone is a self-directed learner, nor does everybody enrol in an educational course or take up other learning opportunities. It was the equation made between learning and enrolling in an educational course that led to many people assuming that most adults were non-learners, but Tough's (1979) finding showed that 98 per cent of his sample were involved in self-directed learning. During the same period as Tough worked, Peters and Gorden (1974) discovered that 91 per cent of their sample of 466 had also conducted learning projects. Other research has supported these findings, and so it gradually had been recognized that it was false to equate education with learning. Recent research into the learning processes have helped change our perception of learning itself, as we shall discuss in the second part of this chapter. Consequently, it is now necessary to discuss motivations to learn, who actually learns and what benefits they get from learning.

Motivation

Wlodkowski (1985) suggested that there are six major factors that affect motivation, a concept that he conceded is most difficult to define, but which relates to the reasons why people behave in the manner that they do. These factors are: attitudes, needs, stimulation, emotion, competence and reinforcement. His concern, however, was much more specifically on the motivation to learn rather than on the motivation to enrol on a course of study, i.e. on participation. We briefly mentioned Tough's (1979) research into self-directed learning and the number of reasons that he gave for undertaking individual learning projects.

But most of the research into motivation to learn is actually based on the motivation to enrol on an educational programme, although as Courtney (1981) claimed, quite correctly, research in this area had been rather sporadic in Britain at the time he wrote. There were, however, two very early pieces – Hoy (1933) and Williams and Heath (1936). The National Institute of Adult Education's report *Adequacy of Provision* records that 'the two main reasons for going to classes were "work" and "know more about the subject/learn the correct way"' (Hutchinson, 1970:59). The Advisory Council research discovered that:

> Men attach more importance to the idea that education is a
> means to getting on in the world: women give rather less

emphasis to it. Such a difference is not large – a matter of 7 per cent less agreement in the case of women – but it confirms what has been said elsewhere in this report about the contrast between the male and female view of continuing education.

(ACACE, 1982b:41–42)

By the end of the 1980s, however, studies in why adults enrolled in educational courses had became more frequent. Both Woodley *et al.* (1987) and Sargant (1990), for instance, confirmed the ACACE finding that men tend to have a slightly more instrumental attitude towards education than do women. In Beinart's and Smith's (1998) 1997 survey, they had five clusters of reasons why people enrolled on courses, and in their report demographic data are provided for each cluster.

- Connected with work, and in nearly half the cases the learning had been required by the employer, sometimes provided, and often paid for, by the employer.
- With future work in mind, and in the majority of cases, people in this category either wished to develop their career or find new employment.
- With voluntary work in mind, but the main reason for learning was to improve the learner's knowledge or skill.
- With no initial connection with work, but having a potential impact on working life. Once more the reasons revolve around knowledge and skill, but a considerable number just wanted to do something interesting.
- With no work connection – the main reasons were the same as above.

One of the interesting motivations that this research records is that for many one of the reasons why they enrol on educational programmes is to meet other people. This is clearly an important social function of a great deal of adult education, one that might be undermined by distance education provision. Most of the other surveys conducted recently also include this social function of adult learning.

In contrast to this, the research in the United States began much earlier (see Courtney, 1981; Cross, 1981; Houle, 1979). Cross (1981) indicated that four main methods had been employed to investigate this phenomenon: in-depth interviews, motivation scales, questionnaires and, what she called, hypothesis testing. Space forbids a full account of all the work published but a brief résumé of some of the findings is included here. Houle (1979:31–32) drew the general conclusion that participation in any type of educational activity is usually undertaken for a variety of motives rather than a single one, and that these usually reinforce each other. Houle (1961) himself formulated an early and useful typology within which to classify these motives: goal-orientated learners, activity-orientated learners and those whose main orientation is learning for its own sake. Within each of these classifications a number of different motives can be specified. And if we examine Sternberg's (1997) styles of thinking (see below) we can begin to see the type of person who is likely to be a self-directed learner. Houle's typology has formed the basis of a number of analyses and there have been many studies on self-directed learning (see Long and assoc, 1988, 1993, 1997, 1998 *inter alia*).

Johnstone and Rivera (1965:46) classified the motives of their sample in the following manner: prepare for a new job; help with the present job; become better informed; spare-time enjoyment; home-centred tasks; other everyday tasks; meet new people; escape from daily routine; other or none – a miscellany of unclassifiable responses. This classification is very close to the one developed by Beinart and Smith (1998) and developed above. They went on to show how motives to participate vary with different subjects studied and with the age, sex and socio-economic position of each respondent. They concluded that: there are very pronounced ways in which the uses of adult education differ across the range of social classes, with the lower socio-economic levels using adult education primarily to learn skills necessary for coping with everyday life.

> As one moves up the social class ... they shift ... to getting ahead
> ... In general, there is an overall shift away from learning for the
> purpose of basic life adjustment ... [to] enrichment of spare
> time.
>
> (Johnstone and Rivera, 1965:159–160)

Other research projects have subsequently employed different typologies to these and yet the overall findings do not differ greatly. Burgess (1974), for instance, identified seven basic orientations to adult education, which were a desire: to know; to reach a personal, social or religious goal; to take part in a social activity; to escape; to comply with formal requirements. Morstain and Smart (1974) highlighted six clusters of reasons: social relationships; external expectations; social welfare; professional advancement; escape stimulation; cognitive interest. In a later piece of research, Aslanian and Brickell (1980) interviewed 744 adult learners by telephone and discovered that 83 per cent of them specified a life transition as the motivating factor that caused them to start learning, for example a change in employment. While their research method might have biased their response, it does point to the significance of analysing the life-world of learners in order to understand both their motivation and their approach to learning, and this finding fits precisely into the phenomenological approach adopted by Schutz and Luckmann (1974).

It is quite clear from all of these research findings that most of the main reasons for participating in adult education classes lie in a cluster of orientations that are quite similar, despite the fact that different researchers employ their own terminology and that the research cited here was conducted both in the UK and USA. Recent research has merely tended to reinforce this, although it must be emphasized that there have been significant changes in the reasons for returning to study by women since the nature of work and the types of knowledge required for work have changed. This has resulted in more opportunities for lifelong learning and, consequently, more opportunities, for women returners. At the same time, more women still enrol on educational courses for non-work reasons as Table 3.1, taken from Beinart and Smith (1998:176) shows.

Thus we can see that whilst a greater proportion of men learn because of their work, a greater proportion of women have future, or potential, work in mind when they return to studying. Clearly the other two categories are ones that fit the more traditional pattern, although a greater proportion of men have a voluntary work rationale than might have been expected and while it might have been assumed that this figure reflected the number of people taking early retirement, Beinart and Smith (1998:131) found that 59 per cent of these were in employment when they began their studies.

The reason for participation does not always lie with learners alone, but in the dynamic tension that exists between learners and their socio-cultural world. There are, therefore, barriers to enrolling on courses. In the USA, Carp, Peterson and Roelfs (1974), for instance, suggested three sets of factors which inhibit participation: situational barriers, institutional barriers and dispositional barriers. They suggested that cost and time are the major hurdles, and this is in accord with Charnley et al. (1980:37) who also focused upon fees as a major issue preventing leisure time education, but who also suggested other factors, such as a lack of flexibility in the adult education service prevented some people from attending. Sargant et al. (1997) also indicate that finance is a major issue especially amongst younger adults. Additionally, they also point to lack of childcare as being a major barrier in returning to learning.

Table 3.1 Adult learners – by gender

Reason for learning	%Male	%Female
Taught learning – connected with job	54	46
Taught learning – future work in mind	46	54
Taught learning – voluntary work	43	57
Taught learning – no initial work connection but having a potential impact on work	47	53
Taught learning – no work connection	37	63

McGivney (1990:79) also recorded the most frequently mentioned deterrents to participation, which are:

- lack of time – cited most frequently by unskilled workers and young mothers;
- negative effect of school experience – from both the unemployed and the unskilled;
- lack of money – cited by unemployed and by women and older people;
- lack of confidence – cited by the black groups;
- distance from classes – elderly, women with dependent children and ethnic minority groups all mentioned this;
- lack of childcare – mentioned by mothers with dependent children;
- lack of day-time opportunities – mentioned by women and older adults;
- education is regarded as irrelevant by unskilled people;
- lack of transport – cited by mothers with dependent children, older adults and ethnic minority groups;
- reluctance to go out at night – mentioned by women and elderly adults.

These ten deterrents provide a wide variety of reasons why these groups of adults do not participate in learning opportunities, and if education and learning is to attract them it needs to continue to address some of the problems. Beinart and Smith (1998:227) list some some eighteen reasons, with being otherwise occupied as being the greatest barrier to learning, but lack of finance also being quite prevalent. Without financial support from the Government, it is clear that the adult education service cannot reduce fees a great deal but, despite the change in orientation of the UK government, education is still expected to be a wealth producer rather than a welfare provision. Indeed, it might be argued that courses with high overheads, many work-based courses therefore, cannot be offered by the education service and need to be offered by corporations and businesses themselves. Thus we have seen the growth of learning opportunities being offered by the corporations and the emergence of corporate universities (Meister, 1998) many of which are not actually offering university level courses (Jarvis, 2001b).

Perhaps one of the attractions of the University of the Third Age (U3A) is that it has fewer overheads because of its non-formal approach. However, the fact that it has high levels of membership and relatively low membership fees means that it has been regarded by some adult educators as a threat to the liberal adult education service. Now there are over 500 universities of the third age in the United Kingdom and thousands more abroad. Not all U3As throughout the world have the same structure.

In the United Kingdom, for instance, they are non-governmental organizations with no specific ties to their local universities (this is also true for Australia), whereas in continental Europe many of the U3As are affiliated in some way with their local university. Having such an affiliation almost certainly inhibits organizational flexibility.

Adult learners

Adults who learn through enrolling on a course at an educational institution may be of specific types. But it is clear that this figure is increasing slightly. Charnley *et al.* (1980:7) suggested that about 16 per cent of the adult population of England and Wales attended post-secondary education in any one year. However, their statistics for vocational education appear to be incomplete, so that this figure was probably an underestimate. Sargant (1990:69) suggested that 17 per cent of the population were trying to teach themselves informally, while 10 per cent actually enrolled on a course. In all, she suggests that 36 per cent of the population have enrolled on a course or have studied informally over the three years prior to her research. By 1997, this figure had increased slightly to 40 per cent (Sargant *et al.*, 1997:11). By contrast, Beinart and Smith (1998:13) found that 74 per cent of their sample had taken part in learning in the three years prior to their survey. They discovered that 52 per cent of their learners, while 42 per cent of their non-learners, were male; 85 per cent of the age group 20–29 years were learners and this figure declined with every ten years, with 67 per cent of those between 50 and 59 years and only 47 per cent of the 60–69 year age group being learners. In addition, the majority of non-manual workers were learners, but those from the manual occupations were less likely to study. It is perhaps significant that since adult learning has become much more prevalent, the above findings do not differ a great deal from those some twenty years ago, as for instance Sidwell (1980:309–317) and Jarvis (1982b) discovered. Sidwell conducted a survey of 63 evening and nine day classes in modern languages for adults in Leicestershire between November 1978 and May 1979. In all 1,139 students were sent a questionnaire and a response rate of 41.7 per cent was achieved. Women outnumbered men, over 75 per cent of the respondents could be classified as coming from the non-manual socio-economic classes, and 71.5 per cent had already studied a language during their initial education. The modal age group was between 30 and 34 years. Jarvis studied a small adult education centre in a Surrey village during the academic year 1979–80 in which 477 students registered. Of the remainder, the great majority were from non-manual backgrounds, 62 per cent were in the age group 22–45 years and only 5.7 per cent of the respondents were over 65 years. The one major difference in Jarvis' findings was that of the 368 respondents to a questionnaire, 87.8 per cent were women and many classified themselves as housewives, but this might be accounted for because the village studied was a rural location.

These figures merely demonstrate the validity of McGivney's (1990:66–118) research in which she isolated five groups who are under-represented in liberal adult education: unskilled/semi-skilled manual workers; unemployed people; women with dependent children; older adults; ethnic minority groups. In addition to these five groups, McGivney also noted the fact that those adults with basic education needs are another category which are inhibited from participating because of their insecurity, distrust, low aspirations, limited time, dependence, negative attitudes towards education and shame at the low level of their own achievement. Each of these reasons reinforces the recognition that already having some schooling is an important precursor to returning to learning. Cross (1981) concluded that it is the one variable most significantly correlated to educational interest and participation in adulthood, which is in agreement with the phenomenological argument of Schutz and Luckmann (1974), who wrote that individuals are likely to repeat their past successful acts because it enables them to act upon the world in a confident manner. Bourdieu (1973) called this cultural capital. Support for such a position would also come from behavioural psychology since repetition of past successful acts may be interpreted as a reinforcing action.

It is difficult to compare adult learner statistics over time since the opportunities that now exist for returning to study and further learning are so much greater than they have ever been before. In addition, there are many more opportunities to take courses leading to academic qualifications. What is perhaps more significant is to see how pioneer adult educators led the way in education in order to get the educational institution to change, but it did not occur until the economic and technological conditions in the wider society demanded these changes. That adults have now returned to study in great numbers is naturally a reason to rejoice, although Kett (1994:xviii) made a very insightful comment about this present position in the United States, but one which is also valid for the UK and elsewhere in the world:

> Today no one can plausibly describe adult education as a marginal activity, but professional adult educators have become increasingly marginal to the education of adults.

Kett's warning is probably much more valid for formal education than for non-formal, and in the UK especially there is still a wide take-up for leisure time courses. The point is, however, that universities and colleges have been forced to expand their provision to meet the demands of the knowledge society and they have, naturally, used subject specialists – many of whom were poorly trained, if trained at all, in the art of teaching adults. This has meant that in many situations, there has been a slow 're-invention of the wheel' when it comes to teaching adults, as almost any perusal of papers on teaching and learning in higher education reveals (see, for example, Wang *et al.*, 2000, 2002).

Research into those who join tutor-less discussion groups or who attend voluntary organizations in order to learn is still in its infancy and it might be unwise to estimate numbers, although Beinart and Smith (1998:200) discovered some 57 per cent of their sample had undertaken some non-taught learning in the three years before their survey, including a high proportion who studies for an qualification. Many years ago, Verner (1964) suggested that the same type of people participate in community life as those who participate in adult education, but this might not be the case now since adult education is no longer a voluntary leisure time pursuit.

Few mature people enter the field of higher education as full-time students although many more study part-time, especially with the Open University. Hopper and Osborn (1975) investigated mature students in three universities and one polytechnic and discovered that there were more men than women and that they had, on the whole, received more than the basic minimum education and that many of these students had been socially downwardly mobile since leaving school, so that they re-entered the educational system classified as socio-economic class III (non-manual). By contrast, those who had been upwardly socially mobile tended to enter it from socio-economic class II. They also noted that many of the students had a low sense of personal self-esteem and that they tended to experience a sense of marginality. Roderick *et al.* (1981) conducted a similar study in Sheffield and they also discovered that more men than women were mature students but that the median age of male students was lower than that of the female students. However, they also noted that a surprising number of the mature students were either separated or divorced, suggesting that 'in cases where marriages run into difficulties, some women become alarmed at their lack of qualifications and consequent inability to earn enough to support themselves and their children' (1981:53) and so they returned to full-time education. However, it would be a feasible interpretation to suggest that the marriage breakdown also frees some people to return to full-time education. They also recorded data from 520 mature students who applied to one of the universities of Birmingham, Leeds, Liverpool, Manchester and Sheffield for the years 1977 and 1978:69 per cent were men, 49 per cent were under 30 years of age and only 11 per cent were over 40 years; 48 per cent were married but only 6 per cent were separated or divorced; 25 per cent were already in the professions and a further 20 per cent were in clerical employment.

Tight (1991) undertook research into part-time higher education and he pointed out, quite correctly, that there was little government policy on this subject, although this has changed a little in the past decade. He characterized the part-time student in higher education thus:

> Part-time students are different from full-time students, and they form a more diverse group. They tend to be older ... with the majority in their twenties and thirties. The older part-time students naturally tend to be married, and to have children. Most part-time students are male, although this pattern is rapidly changing ... they are overwhelmingly middle class – but part-time students show greater evidence of upward mobility.
>
> (Tight, 1991:106)

He pointed out that many of them did not do well at school and that they gained entry qualifications through part-time study. He also recorded that there is a disproportionate number in London and the south-east, and that many of them travelled considerable distances in order to continue their studies. As universities and colleges are being forced into the market to recruit more students, they are being forced to innovate and more part-time courses are beginning to emerge. This is certainly true with part-time vocationally orientated Masters degree courses. In the market-orientated learning society, one of the new niches in the market has been for higher degrees in vocational courses and, one suspects, that as more knowledge-based workers retire there might be a greater demand for both under-graduate and postgraduate leisure time education.

Since its foundation in 1969, the Open University has enabled many mature students to study part-time for a degree whilst remaining at home and continuing in their employment. Throughout the period of its establishment it has maintained and published full statistical reports about its students. McIntosh (now Sargant) (1974) noted that in the early years of its establishment there was a downward shift in the age of those who registered, that school teachers predominated amongst the first students although there was an increasing number of students without any formal educational qualifications.

However, she (1974:59) pointed out that only 8 per cent were objectively working class, although 15 per cent classified themselves as such, and she considered that many Open University students were socially upwardly mobile. Rumble (1982) recorded how the proportion of school teachers studying in the Open University declined as teaching in the United Kingdom has moved towards an all-graduate entry. He showed how each year between 1970 and 1980 more men than women have applied to study but that the overall trend has been for an increasing number of women to apply. However, the male applicants classified as either in a skilled trade or other manual occupations had never exceeded

10 per cent of the total number of applications nor had the number having no formal education qualifications ever exceeded 12 per cent. The majority of those applying for the Open University were under 40 years of age, with less than 1 per cent of the total number being over the age of 65 years. However, as the traditional universities are being forced to expand and the new universities – which were polytechnics when many of the surveys were conducted – endeavour to recruit younger adults into part-time education, this picture is beginning to change a little and, significantly for the Open University, they become its rivals in the learning market.

Benefits of learning

From the above discussion it is clear that one of the major reasons for returning to learning is vocational – but, it might be asked, are there not other benefits? In Beinart's and Smith's (1998) survey, those who returned to learning for vocational reasons only assessed the benefits in vocational terms (1998:108), but for those whose return was with future work in mind:

> For about half the episodes (47%), the learner made new friends or met new people as a result, and for a slightly smaller proportion (41%), the learning had boosted the respondent's confidence. For three in ten (31%) ... the respondent's knowledge or skills had been refreshed; and for a similar proportion (31%) the learner had been encouraged to do further learning or training.
> (Beinart and Smith, 1998:128)

With the less vocationally-oriented learning, other benefits, such as enjoyment and interest, new friends, and increased confidence and encouragement to further study were among the benefits.

In 1999, a Centre for Research into the Wider Benefits of Learning was funded by, what was then, the Department for Education and Employment to:

i produce and apply methods for measuring and analyzing the contribution that learning makes to wider goals including (but not limited to) social cohesion, active citizenship, active ageing and improved health;

ii devise and apply improved methods for measuring the value and contribution of forms of learning including (but not limited to) community-based adult learning where the outcomes are not necessarily standards ones such as qualifications;

81

iii develop an overall framework to evaluate the impact of the lifelong learning strategy being put in place to 2002 and beyond to realize the vision set out in the former DfEE's Green Paper 'the Learning Age' (CM3700) February 1998, covering both economic and non-economic outcomes.

(Schuler *et al.*, 2002:5)

In the first of their reports, Preston and Hammond (2002:9) asked tutors what they perceived were the benefits learners gained from their course and they reported that 'FE practitioners are most likely to agree that students benefit in terms of improved self-esteem, development of social networks, and in the control and management of their lives'. They also noted students are more aware of their rights and responsibilities and tolerance suggesting that the key benefits relate to 'notions of identity capital and social capital'. However, it must be pointed out that the researchers preset the answers in the research instrument.

Brassett-Grundy (2002) found that family learning, especially amongst disadvantaged and underrepresented groups, was also beneficial. Blackwell and Bynner (2002:26) discovered learning is a rich resource for family life, while Feinstein (2002a) suggests that learning can help lower crime, although this claim has to be treated with caution, and Feinstein (2002b) also begins to ask questions about the cost-benefits of learning on depression, and mental health. However, at present there is little evidence that learning can lower the incidence of obesity.

It is clear that learning can have many benefits to the person because it is itself an existential phenomenon, and this will be the focus of the next section of this chapter.

Adult learning

Theories of adult learning have been implicit in much of the previous discussion but it is now necessary to make these explicit. It will be recalled from the opening chapter that learners were located within their socio-cultural framework and that it was suggested that both the learners and their socio-cultural milieu have to be taken into consideration when endeavouring to construct a theory of adult learning. The socio-cultural milieu may itself be divided into three distinct elements: the objectified subculture of a local society, the learners' position in that community and the means by which whatever to be learned is transmitted to individuals. But the individual may also be regarded as a duality of the self and the physical body. Hence, there are at least five factors that need to be taken into consideration when framing any theory of learning, three of which – body, self and subculture have already been discussed. The agencies of transmission will be discussed in chapters 5 and 7 on teaching and distance education and the remainder will be discussed in the following pages. We shall first of all examine the relationship between learning and the wider world; second, we shall examine briefly some of the theories of learning; third, an existential theory of learning will be introduced; fourth we shall look at types of learning; and finally, we shall examine styles of learning and thinking.

Learning and the wider society – a learning cycle

The significance of each of these five factors to the process of adult education and learning is apparent from the above discussion and each of these will be referred to frequently in this and subsequent chapters. However, everybody's experience is unique and as individuals grow older so their uniqueness is even more apparent. This is not to deny each child is unique but merely to state that since adults have had more experience of life they are more likely to grow and develop in different directions. Hence generalizations only seek to convey a sense of the norm rather than specific situations.

The processes of learning appear in interaction between people, and between individuals and experiences. The wider world affects the individual and these changes in the individual in turn affect the wider society. This could be depicted in the form of a cyclic relationship between individuals and the wider world as learners both process and internalize the objectified culture of the wider society and, thereafter, externalize their learning through social interaction. Hence, it is now possible to develop a learning cycle (see Figure 3.1). However, it must be emphasized that the learning cycle represents only one episode of learning and this repeats itself like a spiral, even like a double/triple helix, through the process of time as various attributes of the person – knowledge, skills, attitudes, values, emotions, beliefs and senses – are recipients of experiences from the wider global/local culture, which for the purposes of simplicity we have called data/information.

Thus learning may be regarded initially as a process of receiving and processing any element of culture, by whatever means it is transmitted. This is only an operational definition and a much more precise one will be discussed later in the chapter. But even this definition is much wider than those frequently cited by learning theorists: learning is a relatively permanent change in behaviour that occurs as a result of practice' (Hilgard and Atkinson, 1967:270) or learning is 'any more or less permanent change in behaviour which is the result of experience' (Borger and Seaborne, 1966:14). Both of these definitions emphasize a change in behaviour as being the main focus of learning, but this is too restrictive because it necessitates the exclusion of the acquisition of new cognitive knowledge unless it resulted in behavioural change. The definition offered by Brundage and Mackeracher is much closer to that suggested

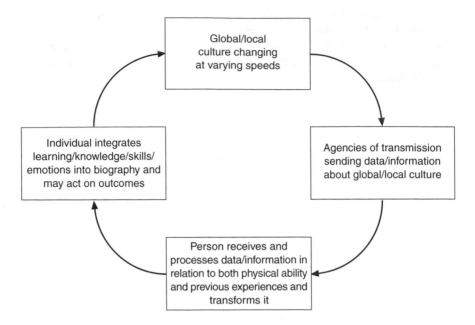

Figure 3.1 A learning cycle.

here: they state that adult learning 'refers both to the process which individuals go through as they attempt to change or enrich their knowledge, values, skills or strategies and to the resulting knowledge, values, skill, strategies and behaviour possessed by each individual' (1980:5). However, this is a rather cumbersome definition, which while conveying many of the main ideas suggested in this section does not actually capture the totality of the argument. These definitions each emphasize the orientations of the theorists concerned and in order to criticize their definitions it is necessary to understand their understanding of human learning itself.

Basic theories of learning

Merriam and Caffarella (1991) have typified the variety of learning theories: behaviourist, cognitive, humanist and social. In many ways this is a useful framework within which to examine the theories that have been produced over the years, although it has to be recognized that these are not discrete and that considerable overlap exists between them and, indeed, the latter two coincide in many of the ideas presented in this book. At the same time, it may be seen that there are ideological underpinnings to the different theories and, most certainly, there are implicit statements of the human condition to be discovered in each. The significance of this is that no theory is value free so that the theory cannot be divorced from the wider world of ideology and belief. In this section, behaviourist and cognitive theories will first be discussed and then experientialist theories will be examined, which are both social and humanistic.

Behaviourist theories

Two forms of behaviourist theory are discussed here: connectionism and conditioning.

CONNECTIONISM

This was perhaps the first theory to gain recognition as 'trial and error' learning. This was first propounded by Thorndike (1928) towards the end of the last century, and as a result of his research with animals he expounded three laws, that of:

- readiness, which relates to the circumstances under which the learner is satisfied, annoyed, etc.
- exercise, which refers to the process of strengthening the connection discovered between stimulus and response by practice
- effect, which relates to the process of strengthening, or breaking, any connection as a result of the consequences of any action.

Basically, this theory focuses on a quite fundamental way of behaving: that if the learner discovers some act or explanation to be effective or valid it will be repeated until such time as the consequences of the action no longer produce the desired or expected results. By virtue of starting with the learner it is hardly surprising that Thorndike was able to pursue his work into adult learning.

CONDITIONING

In contrast to Thorndike's thinking, this begins with the teacher. There are two basic theories. Perhaps the most well-known of all psychological research into learning is that of Pavlov (1927), who proposed the theory of classical conditioning. Briefly stated, this asserts that the learner learns (is conditioned) to associate the presentation of a reward with a stimulus that occurs fractionally prior to it. Thus Pavlov's dogs salivated at the sound of a bell since they had been fed when this had been rung on previous occasions. Operant conditioning, however, occurs when the response is shaped by the reward, so that after every action that approaches, approximates or achieves the desired behaviour the learner receives a reward. This form of conditioning was expounded by Skinner (1951), who later argued that 'man is a machine in the sense that he is a complex system behaving in lawful ways, but the complexity is extraordinary' (Skinner, 1971:197). Throughout this latter book, Skinner suggested that conditioning can explain all learning and that the exciting possibilities for the future lie in what human beings will create of humankind. He grappled with the philosophical problems of behaviourism but was not be able to convince everyone that his perspective was quite so all-embracing as he suggested. Even so, there is a great deal of research evidence to support many of the claims of the behaviourists.

There are also a number of problems with the behaviourist approach, two of which are briefly discussed here. First, the definition is conceptually confusing: Hilgard and Atkinson suggest that learning 'is a relatively permanent change in behaviour that occurs as the result of prior experience' (1979:217). However, the change of behaviour is a product whilst learning is the process that occurs before the change: process and product cannot be the same thing. Second, much of the behaviourist research into learning has been conducted on animals, so it has not been possible to research the thought processes that occur during learning, and thus the research methodology is suspect for the claims that are made about the findings. This does not deny that there are behavioural changes as a result of learning, only that learning is the change.

Not all conditioning may be intentional, nor is it all conscious, but it certainly occurs during the process of the education of adults. Lovell (1980:35), for instance, suggested that classical conditioning occurred when students chose an evening class or a subject because the tutor had created a warm, friendly atmosphere. By contrast, the process of grading assignments, or praising a reticent student for contributing to a group discussion, are both aspects of operant conditioning.

Cognitive theories

Perhaps the most influential learning theorist in the West has been Piaget (1929, *inter alia*), who postulated a number of stages in the process of cognitive development which he related to the process of biological development during childhood:

Stage 1 Sensori-motor, when infants learn to differentiate between themselves and objects in the external world, and this occurs during the first two years of life.

Stage 2 Pre-operational thought, children classify external objects by single salient features, and this spans the period from about two to four years.

Stage 3 Intuitive, when children think in classificatory terms without necessarily being conscious of them, a stage that stretches from pre-operational thought to about seven years of age.

Stage 4   Concrete operations, between seven and eleven, when children begin to think using logical operations.

Stage 5   Formal operational thinking, when children take early steps in abstract conceptual thought.

Piaget's work has been very influential in education and it also provided a basis for two other well-known thinkers in this area, Kohlberg (1981), who has written about moral development, and Fowler (1981), who has concentrated on faith development.

However, Piaget's final stage was reached before adulthood, so his theories have not been influential amongst adult educators. Allman (1984), however, pointed to a number of pieces of psychological research that suggest that adult thought processes continue and change and develop during the lifespan. She concentrated on Riegel's (1979) idea of dialectic logic, which demands the ability to tolerate contradictions and which enables the tensions within them to generate new ideas.

Kohlberg's (1981) work on moral judgement is amongst the most well-known developments of the Piagetian approach; he demonstrated how moral theorizing develops in stages with age and his work has become increasingly significant as people are beginning to ask the ethical questions once again, including those surrounding adult education and life-long learning. The basic premise is that learning is constructivist and that the knowledge gained through the process can be analysed thereafter, but that it is only at different stages in human development that the meaning of the moral concepts can be grasped and operationalized. Hence, younger children have a simpler conceptual understanding of moral knowledge than do those who have developed through a number of previous stages. But, like Piaget, most of Kohlberg's work has thus far been applied to children although its significance for the education of adults must be noted here.

In Eastern Europe, Vygotsky (1978, 1986) has had a similar influence, one that is beginning to spread to Western Europe and the USA. Like Piaget his (1978) book focuses on children's development but his concerns are slightly different. While he acknowledges the debt psychology has to Piaget, he (1986:112–157) offers an extended analysis of his work. But, unlike Western thinkers who were more concerned with stage in development Vygotsky was concerned with potential, although he is clear that developmental processes do not coincide with learning processes. For him (1978:90) 'the developmental process lags behind the learning process'. He postulated that there is a level of actual development and also a zone of proximal development: the former he (1978:85–86) defines as 'the level of development of a child's mental functions that has been established as a result of already *completed* developmental cycles' (*italics* in original) whereas the latter is 'the distance between the actual developmental level as determined by independent problem solving and the level of potential development as determined by problem solving under adult guidance or in collaboration with more capable peers'. Thus we see an important factor in Vygotsky's work: he did not isolate the individual but recognized that development is dependent upon relationship and collaboration. However, Illeris (2002:51) argues that Vygotsky's approach does open itself to the adult controlling the process of development and, therefore, to teacher-centred education.

Basing some of his thinking on Vygotsky's work, Engestrom (1987) regards the zone of proximal development as a space for creativity and this he applies to all forms of activity and learning, both adult and children. Engestrom (1990) has also developed his work with specific reference to activity theory in organizational settings and in this latter book there are 12 very carefully researched and analysed case studies.

Cognitivist theories also have another basis, and this is to be found in the work of the Gestalt theorists, and they, like the behaviourists, based their understanding on research with animals. The word Gestalt actually means shape or form, and as early as 1912 Max Wertheimer postulated that the individual did not perceive the constituent elements of a phenomenon but that they were perceived as a totality. He formulated the 'Law of Prägnanz' in which there are four aspects of perception: similarity, proximity, continuity and closure. Similarity refers to the fact that people group phenomena by their similar salient features rather than by their differences; proximity refers to the fact that individuals group phenomena by their closeness to each other rather than by their distance from one another; continuity refers to the fact that objects are often perceived in relation to the pattern or shape that they constitute in their totality; closure refers to the fact that there is a tendency to complete an incomplete representation so that the whole is perceived rather than the incomplete parts (see Child, 1981:73–74). From the holistic perspective Köhler (1947) suggested that solutions to problems appear to come abruptly, as by a flash of insight, and that they are achieved because the insight emerges from the perception of the relationship between the different factors rather than in response to separate stimuli. Whilst this theory has a number of attractive features, especially since it is recognized that some people are holistic learners, the idea of insight or intuition almost demands that it should be rooted in an earlier process, either socialization or an earlier learning experience, so that it would be unwise to regard all learning in such an inspirational manner.

There have been many other cognitive approaches to learning, such as Gagné, Ausubel and Bruner. Gagné (1977) proposed an eight phase model of learning, which may be summarized as follows:

• Motivation – expectancy;
• Apprehending – attention: selective perception;

- Acquisition – coding: storage entry;
- Retention – memory storage;
- Recall – retrieval;
- Generalization – transfer;
- Performance – responding;
- Feedback – reinforcement.

This model has certain attractions in terms of its logical progression. However, it is that logic which seems to oversimplify the process slightly, as will be seen later in this chapter. Other aspects of Gagné's work are discussed more fully in the next chapter.

Gagné focuses upon memory in this model and Child (1981:112–134) depicts the information-processing model of memory quite clearly when he suggests that learning begins with a stimulus which is partially picked up by a sensory register and processed through selective perception to the short-term memory. This memory has a limited capacity, so some of the information is retained but some is lost at this stage. He then suggests that what is retained is coded and stored in the long-term memory from where it can be recalled or rehearsed. Child's emphasis on memory loss here points to the fact that there is a sharp decline in what is remembered immediately after the event: with only 58 per cent being retained after 20 minutes, according to Ebbinghaus, 44 per cent being retained after an hour and only 33 per cent after a day (Child, 1981:119). The loss of memory in this manner indicates that rehearsing that which is stored soon after a learning event will almost certainly add to the amount of material that is remembered and that systematic repetition thereafter continues to aid recall.

As will be pointed out in the following chapter, Gagné also postulated that there are different types of learning, so he was not just concerned with recall of facts, etc. Another theorist who emphasized the distinction between rote learning and meaningful learning is Ausubel *et al.* (1978). For him, learning is a process of constructing new meaning. This is a feature that Mezirow (1991) has also focused on perspective transformation, to which further reference is made below. Dahlgren actually defines learning this way: 'To learn is to strive for meaning, and to have learned something is to have grasped its meaning' (1984:23–24).

The final theorist to be examined here is Bruner (1979), whose work is almost exclusively about the education of children. However, his work on discovery echoes that discussed above. He suggested that:

> the degree that one is able to approach learning as a task of discovering something rather than 'learning about' it, to that degree there will be a tendency for the child to work with the autonomy of self-reward or, more properly, be rewarded by discovery itself.
>
> (Bruner, 1979:88)

Naturally, this points self-directed learning theorists in the direction of a cognitive strategy that underlies the motivation of some self-directed learners. Bruner also suggests that the main problem that individuals have is in memorizing what they have learned and he, echoing the early Gestalt theorists, suggests that the way that the material is organized is related to the amount that can be recalled.

It would be possible to review other theorists who have written about learning from a cognitive framework, but this introduction points to the fact that learning is viewed as a complex set of processes having different outcomes. Other theorists have adopted different approaches although, naturally, their analyses overlap in some ways.

Social learning

Vygotsky clearly recognized the social nature of learning and we are all well aware of learning through imitation, the adoption of role models, 'sitting by Nellie', and so on. Social learning theory emphasizes behavioural learning, and clearly relies on certain forms of reinforcement, but it is necessary to focus briefly on those researchers who have seen learning from a social perspective. The main theorist of social learning has been Bandura (1969, 1973 *inter alia*) who has shown through numerous experiments that many of the behavioural patterns that we exhibit have been acquired though observing and copying others. Indeed, we are probably all aware that we do it, especially when we enter new situations and we are unsure about how to behave. We watch others and imitate their behaviour in order to feel safe in the strange environment. Bandura showed that children acquire aggressive behaviour in the same way, and so it seems strange to hear people putting forward arguments that children are not affected by the aggression that they observe on television!

'Sitting by Nellie', watching the expert perform, gained a bad reputation in the days when practical knowledge was not emphasized. But this is perhaps because we tended to assume that it would result in unconsidered behaviour or ignorant practice; today we know that, while we might not acquire all the theory when we watch the expert, we rarely act mindlessly as a result of imitation.

Experience and learning

Experiential learning theory has become quite central in recent years to a great deal of thinking about learning in the education of adults. This is not surprising in the light of the fact that adult education itself has become quite learner-centred and that a great deal of vocational education has emphasized work experience, and even learning in the workplace (Marsick, 1987). But it is quite significant that the concept of experience

90

itself remains largely unexplored by those learning theorists who write about it. However, experiential learning consists of a number of different approaches: Weil and McGill (1989:4), for instance, suggest that there are four 'villages', that is the 'different meanings and purposes for experiential learning'. Their (1989:4–19) four villages are:

- The assessment and accreditation of 'prior' experiential learning.
- Experiential learning and change in post-school education and training.
- Experiential learning and social change.
- Personal growth and development.

Unfortunately, the idea of practical experience (internship) is missing from this categorization, but in professional education it is a most important form of learning. Significantly, there may be a reason for this, or it might even be included in the second village, and that is because the practical experience is not regarded by them so much as learning but as the application, or transfer, of previous classroom learning into practice.

However, the practice situation is actually one in which potential learning experiences do occur. Indeed, transfer is a misleading idea, since when students enter the practical situation for the first time, they are entering a new learning situation and this is true irrespective of how much learning has occurred in the classroom before that new experience happened – they are now having for the first time a primary, rather than a secondary, experience about practice and they experience it differently. However, they are experiencing a new learning situation, so that the more that they have learned form previous experiences, the more likely they are to have some knowledge which they can use in the present situation.

Weil and McGill endeavoured to provide a descriptive framework whereby it becomes possible to grasp the multitude of meanings that the term has acquired rather than providing theoretical perspectives to enrich our understanding of the learning processes. Boud and Miller (1996:9–10) suggest five propositions upon which learning is based:

- Experience is the foundation of, and stimulus for, learning.
- Learners actively construct their own experience.
- Learning is holistic.
- Learning is socially and culturally constructed.
- Learning is influenced by the socio-emotional context in which it occurs.

Whilst these points are written for animators of experiential learning, they do provide a framework within which it can be understood more widely.

Many writers have focused on experience as a basis for human learning over the years, but it has been Kolb's (1984) work that has become its popular focus, although one of his main aims was building a theory based on the thinking of those who preceded him. We shall return to Kolb's work below, but before we do, it is necessary to ask what we mean by experience. Perhaps it is a word that educators have taken for granted and so have not endeavoured to explore the concept in the same manner as have philosophers, such as Dewey (1938, 1958), Husserl (1973) and Oakeshott (1933). Oakeshott does make the point, however, that experience 'of all the words in the philosophic vocabulary, is the most difficult to manage' (1933:9). Consequently, the concept of experience needs discussion here before it is possible to understand experiential learning. There are at least two distinct forms of experience and that learning is different in both the learning processes relates to both the classroom and practical learning.

The concept of experience

Life might be described as a passage through time, so time must be the starting point of any discussion of experience. Human existence is situated within time and emerges through it, and it has been argued elsewhere that learning is the process through which the human, as opposed to the biological, being grows and develops (Jarvis, 1992). In a simplistic sense time is experienced as past, present and future. But the present is always problematic because immediately people try to conceptualize their present it becomes a past event, so that more realistically people think about time as a matter of past and future, although the act of experiencing is itself something that occurs at their intersection. Indeed, it is possible to argue that for the most part people live almost unconscious of the passing of time: they act in a taken-for-granted manner. Bergson (Lacey, 1989) called this 'duration', which is the almost unconscious passing of time. However, he was clear that there is still a consciousness of the passing of time even when people act in an almost taken-for-granted manner, but it is at a low level. This taken-for-grantedness lies in the fact that people are in harmony with their socio-cultural environment, they do not have to think too deeply before they act because, almost instinctively, they seem to know how to act in those particular circumstances. It is not, however, intuitive but the result of previous learning experiences. They are bringing their past learning to bear upon a present situation and they experience it in a meaningful manner, and thus appearing to act instinctively. In many situations, however, we do act almost unconsciously – we are aware that we actually do have 'to think on our feet' and having understood the situation, we act accordingly. This points to the fact that we actually construct our experiences.

This experience of time is an important factor in the adult's learning process and one that is often forgotten in discussions about learning, but it helps construct the way in which we interpret an experience. Brundage and Mackeracher note a significant point when they state that children and young adults 'tend to measure time as "time from birth"; adults past 40 tend to measure time as "until death"' (1980:35–36). Hence, as time becomes shorter, so the learning needs focus more acutely upon the problems of the immediate present and previous experience becomes increasingly important to the older person. It may be, therefore, that certain subjects are more appropriate to the psychological orientations of different age groups: history, for instance, may be a more popular study for those whose orientation is already towards their past experiences than would be mathematics. However, more research is required to investigate the extent to which there is any correlation between preferred 'learning' topics, age and orientation towards time.

However, another significant point about this is when people cannot act in such a manner, when they have to stop and think, not sure what to do or how to understand the situation. Elsewhere (Jarvis, 1987), I have called this 'disjuncture'. Disjuncture occurs where there is not taken-for-grantedness between people's past learning experiences and their present situation. In other words, they have to stop and think. Time appears to stop, indeed time appears to be frozen at this point. We are no longer really conscious of time. Herein lies experience with a heightened consciousness. No longer can previous learning cope with the present situation, people are consciously aware that they do not know how to act. We have to think, to plan or to learn something new. Learning then always begins with experiencing, but this points to a major conceptual difference between experience and experiencing and their relationship with time. But our subjective experience of time is not of an unchanging phenomenon, for how often do we hear people saying 'How time flies' or 'Isn't time dragging?' When time flies we are hardly conscious of its passing usually because we are doing other things (Quadrant D in Figure 3.2), but when we are both aware of time and of the world around us (see Quadrant C) we are usually bored with what we are doing but may be powerless to change it. These are alienating experiences. Paradoxically then, when we are active in the world, effecting change on externality or when the external world is affecting us, we are not conscious of the flow of time, but when we are less active we are conscious of it. Nevertheless, when we are effecting change on external reality we are very conscious of that world in which we are functioning and, likewise, when the world is affecting us we are also conscious of the world, but in both instances we are less conscious of the passing of time. However, our consciousness of the world is not of the entire world, nor even of the entire situation in which we find ourselves, since we actually focus on a single part of our externality.

In Figure 3.2, we can see four ideal types of situation with which we are probably all very familiar:

- Quadrant A depicts taken-for-granted situations when we take for granted our actions and presume on our environment. This is duration.
- Quadrant B appears to be one which we might call *time-watching*, and they are similar to those situations in Quadrant C, neither of which we can change.
- Quadrant C depicts those *alienating* situations when we are aware both of the world and of the passing of time.
- Quadrant D depicts situations of *awareness*, when we are concentrating on either our activity in the world or our thoughts, almost to the exclusion of everything else. It is here that a great deal of learning takes place – but not all!

We often move between these quadrants rapidly since at one moment we can be concentrating on what we are doing, a moment later we can be time watching, and so on. Moreover if we are not concentrating fully on what we are doing, we may also become half aware of other things within the parameters of our attention. Therefore, we can see that in Quadrant D we can say that we are having an experience, time has, as it were, stood still and it is at this point we reflect, we plan and we learn. There can be

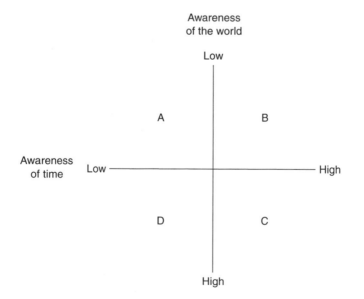

Figure 3.2 Awareness of the world and of time.

no learning without experiencing but a great deal of it actually begins with an experience – what I want to call episodic experience – although the level of consciousness of the learner plays a significant part in both the experience and the ensuing learning.

However, time is not an episode and once we consider the idea of endless time, we are forced to recognize that experience itself is in some way more than a sequence of episodes but seamless and we as people are never fully developed – always becoming. Consequently, we now conclude that experience is a continuous lifelong phenomenon rather than an episode, although there are episodic events within it, and these relate in some way to our levels of consciousness. Oakeshott (1933:10) was also quite clear about this:

> And the view that I propose to maintain is that experience is a single whole, within which modifications may be distinguished, but which admits to no final or absolute division; and that experience everywhere, not merely is inseparable from thought, but is itself a form of thought.

This is a view that is shared by other thinkers (Dewey, 1938:37; Schutz, 1972:45–53, *inter alia*) who also regarded experience as a continuous phenomenon. For Oakeshott, then, experience is subjective and always a form of thought, but those thoughts are constructed and influenced both by our biography and by the social and cultural conditions within which they occur. He argued that experiencing is always a 'world of ideas' which are within the individual, although he (1933:12) maintained that there are two phases in the process of experiencing: the first is the direct encounter with the situation and the second is a form of qualification and modification of the initial encounter by the previous knowledge that the person having the experience possesses. This observation has also been confirmed empirically by neurological research into brain activity (Greenfield, 1999). These two phases may occur simultaneously, or almost simultaneously, although in some situations we might recall specific sensations and reflect upon them at a later date.

Oakeshott, however, assumed that consciousness is much more of a constant unity than it actually is. For instance, we may be concentrating on one object or action in a situation and have only a fleeting awareness of others, but at a later time we may be able to recall some of those things that we were hardly consciously aware of at the time (Quadrant D in Figure 3.2). In addition, we might recognize a face in a crowd, although had we been asked to describe that person without seeing the faces in the crowd we would not have been able to do so. The same argument could apply both to taste and smell, and so on. This type of knowledge Polanyi (1967) called 'tacit knowledge'.

However, he assumed that experience is entirely cognitive whereas the person is at least mind, body and emotions. When I act upon the external world, for instance, I am also thinking and feeling about it – I both know how to do a thing and I have the ability to do it – which we might call practical knowledge, but also I usually have feelings about it, which may actually provide significant motivation to act. We also are aware that sports people train their bodies and musicians their arms and fingers to act in an almost instinctive manner. Consequently, the body acts, sometimes almost without the mind, or in response to an external stimulus, which might be a smell, a taste, an emotion, and so on. Experience is more than just the ideas, so Oakeshott placed too much emphasis on the mind and we see that the internal is cognitive, emotive and physical.

Experiencing, then, may be conceptualized, on one level, as the subjective awareness of a present situation – in this sense we are talking about an experience, or what I want to call an episode, or episodic experience. It is this episodic experience that lies at the heart of a great deal of thinking about experiential learning. However, this awareness occurs only in the light of previous experiences, and consequently the subjectivity is determined by individuals' past biographies and the socio-cultural milieu in which they experience situations. People bring to every new situation their own past, although the extent to which they are themselves aware of this is a point that Freud's researches have illustrated.

In experiencing, there is a combination of the biographical past with a sensation, or perception, of the present 'external' situation although, on occasions, that 'external' situation can actually be a memory of a previous experience, which occurs during contemplation. Adults bring to potential learning situations their memories of the interpretations and their emotions, which they gained from past experiences, which has both advantages and disadvantages for learning. Memory certainly affects the experience in a variety of different ways.

'I can't remember like I used to' is a common expression among adults and one that many educators of adults hear frequently from their students in the teaching and learning situation. The expression tends to give credence to the front-end model of education, but is it correct? Obviously it reflects an experience or else the person would not utter the exclamation, and yet Rogers (1977:59) pointed out that

> a young man and a man in his late fifties would both be able to remember and repeat an average of eight random numbers recited to him. But what does change is that if the older man is asked to remember something else between the time he was first given the numbers and the time he was asked to repeat them, he is less likely to remember the original numbers than the young man.

96

Yet older people may have many more commitments than younger people and often study part-time, and so additional information, etc. might be gained by them from a variety of sources, some of which will make it harder to recall specific facts. Hence, teachers of adults should provide opportunities during their teaching and learning sessions so that adults have time to begin the process of storing the information that they have gained. Additionally, it might not be wise to discourage last minute revision when adult learners are required to sit a traditional examination. Knox (1977:435) also pointed out that adults are more likely to retain information that they receive if it is meaningful to them and they are able to integrate it into the store of knowledge that they already have. All of these findings refer to what is now called the short-term memory, but once the material is stored in the long-term memory it can be recalled, and most people are familiar with the very elderly being able to recall, from their long-term memory, information that they learned decades before.

The discussion thus far has focused on the idea of sensing or perceiving a situation, and this is 'primary experience', but Husserl made the point that experience is frequently not direct in this sense, but indirect. He pointed out that once a person describes an object or an event, the description becomes an indirect experience for anyone listening to it. Indirect experience occurs through linguistic communication and this is 'secondary experience'. Secondary experience usually occurs in combination with primary experience because what is experienced directly, through the senses, is both the situation/interaction and the words or meanings that are communicated are only indirectly experienced through the language, picture, music, and so on. Husserl's insight into the two aspects of experience – primary and secondary – is very important when we consider education.

Primary experience

Most of the literature on experiential learning is actually about learning from primary experience, that is learning through sense experiences, and experience has been treated as having a sequence of episodic experiences. We can see this in Weil's and McGill's (1989:3) four villages discussed above, where they are all subsections of learning from primary experience. Learning from primary experience then is learning in a practical situation where individuals are learning through their sense experiences, as well as through their minds. They are learning to experience an actual situation and to learn from it. They may also be learning a skill where the objective might be to get individuals to perform a skill unthinkingly but which then becomes a taken-for-granted situation, from which no further learning may occur – this is the movement from Quadrant D to Quadrant A in Figure 3.2.

Obviously when learners enter the practical situation there are many primary experiences that they have for the very first time; some of these are ones where action is possible and may be of a repetitive nature because they have learned what to do previously. At the same time, other experiences are potentially non-action situations, because the learners have not learned about them in the classroom or they have no biographical knowledge to bring to the situation, which might make them feel impotent in the situation. Not knowing how to act is a potential learning situation and in order to act they might learn from trial-and-error, observation of others' performances, or from questioning other skilled performers (or mentors), and so on. This action is always experimental/creative in the first instance.

In none of these latter situations do the learners have the knowledge or the skill to cope with the situation so that there is disjuncture between their biography and the experience that they are having and, consequently, a potential learning experience has occurred. If the students have already had some instruction in the classroom about this type of situation, then they bring an informed biography to the situation and this affects their experience. At the same time they still have to stop, plan their actions and so on because the classroom knowledge cannot be applied directly to practice. Theory can never be applied directly to practice since the practice experience is primary whereas the classroom one is secondary. Any experience in which they have to stop, think, plan, and so on, is a potential learning experience. At the same time, if they have had no previous instruction in the classroom then they may not be in a position of being able to act at all, and so non-action occurs.

In primary experience, people enter a situation, experience it subjectively and they can either act or else they can reflect upon the situation. If they act, it is usually with a high level of consciousness, monitoring all aspects of the action, thinking about it and evaluating its relevance, etc. They do this as a result of recalling to mind their previous learning experiences and then they have weighed up the possible alternatives and acted on the best possible evidence. Now this is using previous learning in new situations and testing it to see if it works. If it does, then it was valid knowledge, but if it does not then it may be regarded as invalid and can be rejected.

It is in practice that skills are actually learned from practical experience. Individuals use their classroom learning, but they still have to plan their actions, monitor them, and maybe reflect upon them, and then learn from their new experiences. The point here is that in planning the action, skill, etc. the students have used their biographical knowledge and act upon that knowledge. They have not acted mindlessly or thoughtlessly: they act in the probability that their intended outcomes will be achieved, and they learn from the outcome. Herein lies the relationship between theory and practice – it is a pragmatic relationship in which the two coincide only if the theory works out precisely in practice. However, there are always many contingencies in practice that prevent intended outcomes from occurring. No generalized theory can take into account all the possible contingencies that might prevent the outcome occurring – the relationship between theory and practice must always be one of probability. Indeed, the primary experience is a completely different experience from the theory, which is a secondary one, taught in the classroom. Elsewhere I (Jarvis, 1999a) have argued that we actually develop our own theory from practice, rather than apply it to practice.

Secondary experience

This form of experience might also be called mediated experience. We have the experience mediated to us through a variety of means – the media themselves, the teacher or instructor, people with whom we talk, and so on. Secondary experience is often linguistic: it occurs through normal conversation, listening to lectures and debates, and any form of monologue, dialogue, and so on, including listening to the media. In a sense, it is not always interactive. In addition, reading books and other forms of linguistic and pictorial communication may be classified under this head. Simply, it is a matter of meaning being communicated through words and pictures but, simultaneously, there is direct sense experience with the other persons in the interaction, with the book or with the media, etc. rather than with the phenomenon, event or meaning being discussed, described, etc. in the communication. However, the meaning being communicated is always someone else's interpretation and never that of the learners, so that there is always need for critical, reflective learning.

This form of communication occurs extremely frequently in education, since it has traditionally taught the theory that was to be applied to the practice. Perhaps the most common image of education is that of the teacher lecturing to a class of students, an image that many educators of adults have wanted to play down. Yet to do this is to deny the significance of speech and conversation to the learning process. A great deal of everyday life consists of interaction and dialogue. Provided teaching is dialogue and not prolonged monologue, then it remains a valid exercise and relates to everyday experiences. In everyday life people converse about a variety of things, such as an overseas vacation, and so on. Often only the speaker has a direct experience of the situation being discussed and the other participants in the conversation have an indirect experience through the speech. In other situations, none of the participants may actually have had a direct experience of the subject contained in the communication, and yet it can still be meaningful. Consequently secondary experience is a common everyday occurrence through which we actually construct our understanding of the world, and of reality itself.

Learning occurs in secondary experience through the communication of meaning: words are given meanings, pictures are interpreted in meaningful ways, and so on. Communication is meaningful. The process of communication of meaning is threefold: the speaker encodes the meaning in words, the words are spoken, or transmitted through some other medium, and the receivers decode the meaning, or they interpret the communication for themselves. The fact that they decode the experience, or interpret the communication for themselves, is important to understanding the process of having a meaningful experience; it is not an experience of an objective phenomenon by the listeners or the readers – the experience of meaning is one in which the listeners have played their part by giving meaning to the words and by bringing their own biographical past to the surface. The experience is a total whole in which the words are heard and interpreted, and the experience they have is made subjectively their own. In this sense of interpretation, all secondary experience is hermeneutical.

Precise communication can only occur if these three stages are carried out exactly and the speaker's objective in communicating specific meaning is fully achieved. If what the speaker is saying is already known, or assumed, by the hearers then they simply take for granted what they hear. If the meaning being communicated is new but unproblematic, then they may merely seek to memorize it provided that the disjuncture between what they already know and what they received is not too great. However, if the hearers doubt the validity of what they hear, or even if they merely wish to test it out, then they stop and reflect upon the meaning of the communication. Suddenly the communication is bounded by time and the hearers turn time back upon itself, as it were, as they seek to analyse the truth, or validity, or even the practicality of the communication. At this point there may be a considerable awareness of disjuncture as the meaning being communicated is questioned. One aspect of testing out the validity of the communication may be the extent to which it works in practice.

Here, then, is the process of learning from secondary experience. Meaning, validity, truth, but also description and so on, are communicated by the originator of the communication and that communication may itself produce different reactions in the learners, and different forms of learning may occur. This depends on what the learners bring to the meaning experience, it depends upon their biography and their interpretation of the words and phrases employed in the transmission. Descriptive communication and telling people something may merely produce non-reflective learning, but questions about validity or truth may produce both non-reflective or reflective forms of learning. A number of factors will determine what type of response the learners make, among them the reputation of the speaker, the topic under discussion and the extent to which the hearers think that meaning and truth are objective and unchanging. If people are aware that any encoding of meaning or truth is a subjective and social process, then they might adopt something of a healthy scepticism to what they hear or read; but, unfortunately, this is not always the case.

Experiential learning, then, is usually regarded as learning from primary experience and educators have seen themselves as facilitating that learning, often by providing situations – some artificial and the others actual – in which learners can learn. Perhaps the most influential work on this has been by Kolb (1984).

Kolb's learning cycle

In a sense, Kolb's (1984) learning cycle incorporates the possibility of two modes of experience, because it allows for the learning process to start either with the concrete experience, or anywhere else on the cycle, including that of generalizing and conceptualizing, although the cycle is often assumed to begin with the concrete experience.

Experience is a subjective awareness of a present situation, the meaning of which is partially determined by past individual learning. Consequently, the experience is not merely of something external, but one of fusing of the external with the individual biography. There are two modes of experience – either directly through the senses, or indirectly through linguistic communication – and individuals can and do learn through both modes of experience.

Kolb and Fry claim that the learning cycle may begin at any stage and that it should be a continuous circle (see Figure 3.3). It will be noted that there are elements of previous theories in this cycle, which is quite understandable since no one theory of learning is able to explain the complexity of the many forms of learning that occur. Additionally, it may be questioned as to whether there is an implicit behavioural definition of learning contained in this cycle. Nevertheless, it raises significant issues about learning from experience. In addition, Kolb and Fry suggest that the movement in the vertical axis represents a process of conceptualization while that on the horizontal axis represents the variation between active and passive manipulation. They claim also that each quadrant represents a learning style, but we shall return to the idea of learning styles at the end of this chapter.

This cycle, which has become tremendously popular probably because of its simplicity, does not do justice to the complexity of human learning. Indeed, we have already shown that it does not do a great deal of justice to the concept of experience itself. Jarvis (1987) has tested the cycle many

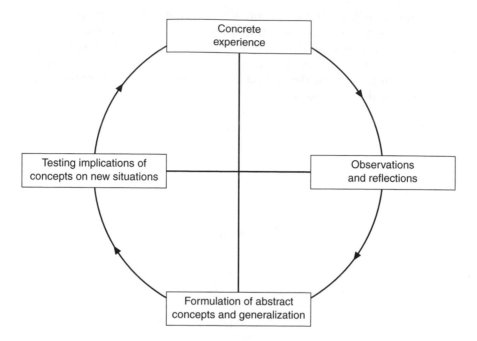

Figure 3.3 Kolb's experiential learning cycle.

Source: Kolb and Fry, 1975:33–37. From *Theories of Group Processes*, Cooper (ed). 1975 © John Wiley & Sons Limited. Reproduced with permission.

times with a variety of groups of adult learners and on each occasion the participants have demonstrated that it is an over-simple description of the learning processes, and we shall return to this shortly.

Even a cursory examination of books on experiential learning shows that the concept of experience is treated in a variety of ways by different authors. Sometimes, for instance, it is taken for granted (Boud *et al.*, 1983; Fraser, 1995; Marton *et al.*, 1984; Smith and Spurling, 1999; Tuijnman and van der Kamp, 1993; Vaill, 1996; Winch, 1998). Many writers imply that experiential learning is participatory. Elsewhere, Henry (1989, 1992) treats experience as having two modes: all learning is experiential and that experiential learning is about reflecting upon the experience (see also Eraut, 1994; Peterson, 1989). Others tend to use the term with reference to the sum of all past learning (Knowles, 1980a), which echoes Oakeshott's analysis.

Weil and McGill (1989:p.248) also make this distinction between the two phases of experience:

> Experiential learning is the process whereby people, individually and in association with others, engage in direct encounter and then *purposely* reflect upon, validate and transform, give personal

and social meaning to and seek to integrate the outcomes of these processes into new ways of knowing, being, acting and interacting in relation to their world.

(italics in original)

Here, they emphasize the idea that experience is having a direct encounter with the world and do not give due recognition to both perception and construction, but it does allow for the experience to be more than just a cognitive phenomenon. At the same time, we can understand why the idea of a direct encounter arises since we are rarely consciously aware of the processes by which we construct our reality, and even less aware, as Freud taught us, of the effects of sublimation and repression (Hall, 1954). Indeed, it might well be that it was previous unpleasant experiences that were repressed, or that the experiences might have been traumatic and, as Dewey (1938) pointed out, they can result in mis-education. This process, or these processes, of construction occur unconsciously and are influenced by both our biography and the situation within which the experience occurs. In other words, our biography – that is, the whole person – is involved both consciously and unconsciously in constructing the experience from which we learn, but it is also being changed throughout the lifespan by the experiences that it helps to construct. But as our life histories also include both our past constructed perceptions and our sublimations and repressions, it is difficult to regard all the thought processes as being entirely rational.

Carl Rogers (Rogers and Freiberg, 1994:36) captures something of the complexity of experience in experiential learning in a rather descriptive manner when he writes:

> Let me explain more precisely the elements involved in significant or experiential learning. One element is the quality of personal involvement: the whole person, both in feeling and in cognitive aspects. Self-initiated involvement is another element. Even when the impetus or stimulus comes from the outside, the sense of discovery, of reaching out, of grasping and comprehending comes from within. Another element is pervasiveness. It makes a difference in the behavior, the attitudes, even perhaps the personality of the learner. Yet another element relates to the learners' self-evaluation of the event. She knows whether it is meeting her need, whether it leads towards what she wants to know, whether it illuminates her dark area of ignorance. The onus of the evaluation, we might say, resides definitely in the learner. Its essence is meaning.

The idea that 'significant learning' is experiential and that it occurs at the intersection of arrested experience and frozen time is one that we discussed above. Rogers' emphasis on the whole person is important since, at this point of intersection, individuals are aware of more than just cognitive phenomena. It is the whole person who is consciously aware of the situation, i.e. it is the individual's skills, attitudes, values, feelings, emotions, beliefs, as well as cognitions. It is all of these that help construct the experience itself. However, there is a problem with this wholeness since we may be consciously aware of an odour, for instance, which points us beyond the cognitive when we experience. Smell is a sense experience, but we must hold the sense in our mind – this is what Polanyi (1967) called tacit knowledge – we could not accurately describe it but we would recognize it on another occasion. The wholeness of the person demands a tacit dimension to our knowledge.

The wholeness of the person is also reflected in the definition of experience given by Miller and Boud (1996:8): 'experience is the totality of ways in which humans sense the world and make sense of what they perceive'. Their definition echoes much of the discussion of Oakeshott. We are now at a point where we might draw together some of the previous discussions and develop definitions both of experience and experiential learning. Using Miller's and Boud's definitions as a basis, we can suggest that experience is the totality of ways in which human beings either make, or try to make, sense of what they consciously perceive. Once we have defined experience, we are in a position where we can offer a definition of experiential learning. Experiential learning is the process by which individuals, as whole persons, are consciously aware of a situation and make sense, or try to make sense of what they perceive, and then seek to reproduce or transform it and integrate the outcomes into their own biography.

From this discussion we can see that both experience and biography are lifelong, and so is our learning. Consequently, we now need to reach beyond the experiential and see learning as existential, and so it is not surprising that the wider benefits of learning should be being researched. But there is a sense in which this is what my own research into learning has been telling me as I have adapted my original model as new insights have emerged and new understandings have developed. Consequently, I now want to discuss this within the framework of existential learning.

Existential learning

Over the years since I first undertook my own research into learning, I regarded it as an experiential theory but which I frequently argued was the driving force of human growth. I (Jarvis, 1992) categorized it within an existentialist framework but did not extend my analysis for the better part of a decade. However, as I continued to work on my understanding of human learning during this period, I became increasingly aware that experientialism in itself was not sufficient to explain the complexity of the process and the more I saw learning as having broader benefits, as I argued in *Learning in Later Life* (Jarvis, 2001a). However, it was really in *Paradoxes of Learning* (Jarvis, 1992) that I argued that learning is actually existential, since it is through learning that the mind, the self and identity emerge from the body through the early experiences of life. Hence, learning is experiential but within an existential framework. In this brief section I want to recall the actual research process that I conducted and then to note that I have continued to work on the outcomes of that research so that my understanding is much more complex than it was when I (Jarvis, 1987) published my first book on adult learning.

Over a period of about fifteen months in 1985 and 1986 groups of adults participated in a project that did not actually begin as a research project, but as a series of workshops about learning – but which, as they proceeded, I recognized were generating research data and that I was actually a practitioner researcher. In each of the workshops, all the participants were first invited to write down a learning incident in their lives. They were asked to state what started the incident, how it progressed and, finally, when and why they concluded that it was completed. Having undertaken this exercise they were then paired in order to discuss their different learning experiences and it was suggested to them that they might like to examine the similarities and the differences in their experiences. Thereafter, two pairs were put together and they then discussed their four different learning experiences and soon the groups were actually discussing learning rather than just their own experiences. At this stage they were introduced to Kolb's learning cycle (Figure 3.3), which I told them was probably not sufficiently sophisticated to do justice to their four experiences and so they were asked to redraw it to fit their own experiences. We had all types of diagrams, many of them spirals, all more complex than Kolb's diagram, but all were modifications of it.

This exercise was conducted on nine separate occasions both in the UK and in the USA, with teachers of adults and teachers of children, with university lecturers and adult university students who were teachers of adults in their full-time occupation, with younger people and with some not so young participants, with men and women. In all about 200 people participated in the exercise, although the sample was middle class and not tightly controlled. A complex model of learning was constructed, by combining the many modifications of Kolb's diagram that the different groups of four produced. This model was subsequently tested in seminars, etc., over another nine-month period, again both in the UK and the USA, with some 200 or 300 people participating in these. The final model appeared, with a full description of this methodology in a book (Jarvis, 1987). However, since that date I have continued to use this model and to adapt it as I realized how it was still not accurate. Even now I realise that the model in Figure 3.4 is still only an over-simplification of the complexity of human

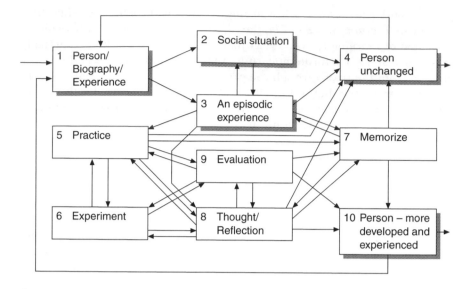

Figure 3.4 A model of the learning processes.

learning, that I will no doubt change it again and that we may probably never know sufficient to embrace all the processes in a single model.

There are a wide variety of routes through this diagram that will be discussed thoroughly below, but before we do this we must acknowledge that there are also many difficulties with such a complex model – one of which is to display the continuous nature of time: this is done here through the arrow entering box 1 and leaving at box 4 and box 10, whereas the continuous nature of learning is displayed in the arrows that leave boxes 4 and 10 and go back to box 1. This seeks to capture the nature of a spiral or the continuous nature of human learning. The fact that it is the person who learns is emphasized by the shadow behind boxes 1–4 and box 10, while box 1 demonstrates that it is the whole person – knowledge, skills, attitudes, values, beliefs, emotions and the senses – having a lifetime of experience – biography – who enters the situations and constructs the experience. Box 3 represents an episodic experience, which is constructed through the person (box 1) interacting with the social milieu (box 2) and producing an experience from which learning might occur. Box 10 illustrates the fact that the person grows and develops as a result of the learning. But it is impossible to depict the ageing process of the body in a diagram such as this, suffice to note that it is still the person, with a lifetime's experience, that constructs an experience. The construction of this experience is also related to the individual's awareness of the world and the passing of time – depicted in Figure 3.2 – with those four quadrants relating to taken-for grantedness (A), time watching (B), alienation (C) and awareness (D). Different forms of learning will occur relative to the person's state at the time of the experience, and this will be discussed in the next section on types of learning.

However, there is another issue that needs to be clarified at this point – what is it that makes an individual deflect from the path boxes 1→2→4 and go from box 2→3? This is a crucial question and has often been discussed in terms of motivation to learn – which has usually meant motivation to enrol on a course of study. The pathways mentioned here do not relate to enrolment at all, but neither is motivation included in this figure. The issue lies in the idea of duration – when we can take for granted our world we can act and speak and so on, without having to think about it. However, we often encounter situations in which we do not know the answer and are forced to ask why? how? and so on, and then we are forced to think, or reflect on what we have experienced. It is this moment in time when the recognition occurs that the situation has become problematic that I have called *disjuncture* – it is the crucial time at which learning can commence, and the more complex and rapidly changing our global society, the more frequently will we experience disjuncture and, therefore, lifelong learning. Each reaction to disjuncture might result in our memorizing new knowledge, or it might result in problem solving or even in planning future action. Hence the construction of the episodic experience always follows entering the situation, even if only momentarily and then we relate our inner selves to the wider world – reflection follows the construction of an experience whereas planning looks forward from the reflection. Once more we see the complex relationship between learning and time.

Since the person is so complex, having knowledge, skills, emotions and so on, and because social milieu are not totally controllable, the learning that might occur can either be intended or not intended, as Figure 3.5 shows. We can now illustrate the type of learning that might occur in each of these six different learning situations.

- Box A is *formal education and training* that occurs in an educational institution and any other bureaucratic organization.
- Box B can refer to the ongoing nature of learning that occurs in places such as the work place, community, and so on. Sometimes the learner is actually mentored in these situations.
- Box C is both *learning in everyday life* and *self-directed learning*. It is the type of learning that we undertake when we decide to teach ourselves a computer program, and so on. It can be individual learning or part of a group project.
- Box D refers to that *incidental learning* that occurs in formal situations, not always educational, but which the planners of the learning experience did not intend. For example, the realization that the

Type of learning

Type of situation	Intended	Incidental
Formal	A	D
Non-formal	B	E
Informal	C	F

Figure 3.5 Possible learning situations.

instructor is not really as knowledgeable as we thought, or that the
room is badly designed, or that the carer does not really treat me as
an autonomous individual, and so on.

- Box E also refers to *incidental learning* situations in non-formal learning episodes.
- Box F refers to *everyday learning*, which is probably the most common
situation of all, especially in rapidly changing societies. In these we
find ourselves in new situations and we have to learn how to cope – by
thinking on our feet about our next action, and so on (Heller, 1984).
If we fail to respond to this situation quickly, we usually have to plan
our learning and then the situation moves to Box C.

However, the degree of formality is not the only variable in the subcultures of social situations that might affect either the type of learning or
the behavioural outcomes of such learning: the politics and culture of the
social context, the social position of both learners and teachers (leaders,
managers and so on) and even the status given to the knowledge being
acquired will be amongst the factors that affect the type of experience
from which the learners learn (box 3).

Types of learning

It is clear from Figure 3.4 that there are many different forms of response
to possible learning experiences, and we are claiming that there are at
least three forms of non-learning and eight types of learning:

- Non-learning:

  i taken for granted/presumption
  ii non-consideration

iii rejection

- Incidental learning about self – through non-consideration and rejection
- Preconscious knowledge learning (incidental learning)
- Preconscious skills learning (incidental learning)
- Basic skills learning (non-reflective)
- Memorization (non-reflective)
- Reflective cognitive learning
- Practice learning (reflective)
- Contemplation (reflective)

We will now illustrate the way that these different forms of learning occur in respect to the four quadrants of Figure 3.2.

Quadrant A: In situations where we presume on the world, we take it for granted and there are no experiences of disjuncture nor is there motivation to change the world; as Schutz (1972:47) put it: 'when I immerse myself in my stream of consciousness, in my duration, I do not find any differentiated experiences' (see boxes 1→2→4) in Figure 3.4. Consequently, there is no learning – we call this non-learning. Nevertheless, we are often aware of other things in the situation and we may unconsciously sense the world and memorize the sensation, like the face in the crowd or the smell that we associate with certain places, and so on almost unknowingly. In these situations we acquire tacit knowledge. This is *preconscious learning of knowledge* and it follows the route – boxes (1→2→3→7→4). Preconscious learning can occur at any time and in any situation. In order to learn from it in a conscious manner we need to recreate an experience and then learn from it, so that we can see a move from Box 7 to Box 3 – and then the normal learning processes can occur. In a similar manner experts can adjust their skilful actions without necessarily being conscious of it and have a *preconscious skills learning*, then the route would be boxes (1→2→3→5→4). In this case there is little or no reference to memory since we usually assume that memory is cognitive. It is often very hard for experts to explain how they have adjusted their actions, as Nyiri (1988:20–21) explains: experts 'rarely have the self-awareness to recognize what it (practical knowledge) is. So that it must to be mined out of their heads painstakingly, one jewel at a time'. This is the same type of process we all experience in everyday life (Heller, 1984) where so much of our behaviour is based on presumption that the world has not changed and so we act on our tacit knowledge.

Non-learning may also occur when we are in either alienating or time watching (Quadrants B and C) situations, although it is always possible that *preconscious learning* might also occur. These situations are ones in which we might experience a variety of emotions, boredom, frustration, and so on. Nevertheless in alienating situations, when our awareness of the world is high, but when we might be unable to change it, then we may actually learn more about ourselves incidentally. These *incidental self-learning* (boxes 1→2→3→8→10) experiences, which are often accompanied by strong emotions, might actually become powerful motivating factors for action at a later date.

When the whole person is enabled to focus on the world and lose awareness of time (Quadrant D), learning is more likely to occur but, as we have seen already, learning is not a simple, nor a single process. We focus on the world because we have episodic experiences, which are either triggered by disjuncture or by a motivation to act on the external world. When we experience disjuncture, a sense of being, we are aware that there is a gap between our biography (total experience) and our perception of the situation in which we are: we can then choose to learn or not to learn. If we deal with the latter first, we might choose not to learn because we are too busy to think about it (*non-consideration*) or because we do not wish to learn something new for a variety of reasons, some of which are emotional (rejection). Nevertheless we might well learn something more about ourselves, incidental self-learning. But we may not even give it a second thought and in this case it is non-learning. In these incidents, the processes are boxes (1→2→3→8→10) and boxes (1→2→3→8→4), respectively.

However, we can also learn just to repeat something, either a skill or knowledge. In a sense we hardly think about either, but just repeat that with which we have been presented. In both of these incidents we do not reflect although we may still have an emotional orientation to the situation, but there is little change in the external world although there is some change in the learners. This is *non-reflective* learning and they might be called *basic skills* learning (boxes 1→2→3→5→7→10) and *memorization* (boxes 1→2→3→7→10). Rarely, if ever, will we not be changed in some way by the learning that ensues from the experience, even if it is only emotionally, and hence the route is from box 10 rather than box 4.

Finally, there are three types of reflective learning. The first is *contemplation*, when individuals are totally lost in their own thoughts, and this can either occur as a result of a social experience (boxes 1→2→3→8→9→7→10) or individually and alone (boxes 1→3→8→9→7→10). Then, we can learn new knowledge as a result of reflecting on our actions and experiences (boxes 1→2→3→5→6→8→9→7→10), which is *reflective cognitive learning*, or *new skills learning* which is always accompanied by thought (boxes 1→2→3→8→6→5→9→7→10), which is *practice learning*. (This might also be called *action learning*.) These latter two types should be differentiated from contemplation, since they occur as a result of thinking on our feet, something discussed by Schon (1983). Moreover, in all three reflective forms of learning, we can see that there is a continuous loop

110

(5→6→8→9, or 9→8→6→5) and this can continue for as many times as is necessary in the learning process.

We have traced eight different learning routes through Figure 3.4. and we have also highlighted non-learning situations. In all of these learning processes the emotional element plays a major part being part of nearly all experience; there are also both learned and motivating factors in future action, so that no definition of learning can be complete without emotion being recognized. Naturally, it is possible to find many other routes through this model and the different learning processes can occur simultaneously so that there are many combinations of routes. However, those outlined here illustrate something of the complexity of the processes of learning.

We are now in a position to offer a definition of human learning: *Human learning is a combination of processes whereby whole persons construct experiences of situations and transform them into knowledge, skills, attitudes, beliefs, values, emotions and the senses, and integrate the outcomes into their own biographies.*

Not everyone processes their experiences in the same way and this relates to their biographies, perceptions of the situation, personalities, ways of thinking, and so on. The most common term for all of these aspects of learning is learning styles, and this constitutes the final section of this chapter.

Learning styles

There has been considerable research over the years into what came to be known as learning styles, and in Table 3.2, I have summarized some of the main ones; there has always been a question as to whether these are different ways of learning or different personality characteristics. It has been widely recognized that we have different strategies for learning, but few educators have tried to match their teaching to these different approaches to learning with the exception of the work undertaken at Lancaster (Entwistle, 1981). Some of the impetus for the work at Lancaster was that of Marton and Säljö (Marton *et al.*, 1984:39–40) who examined the way that students learned from reading and discovered that those who focused on the text and tried to remember it never really learned what it was trying to convey, which they called a surface approach to learning, but those students who adopted a deep approach to learning tried to understand its meaning.

Table 3.2 summarizes some of the different approaches to learning styles that have been adopted by different writers on the subject.

However, there have also been other pieces of work which have avoided the terms 'learning' and 'style' and in drawing this chapter to a close we will look at two of these: Belenky *et al.*, (1986) used the phrase 'ways of knowing' and Sternberg (1997) wrote about 'thinking styles'.

Table 3.2 Learning styles

Learning style	Comment
Active versus passive	It will be seen from the learning cycle that some learners may actively initiate their experience and seek out information and these are self-directed learners, while others may be more passive in the receipt of information provided for them.
Assimilator versus accommodator	Kolb (1984:78) described the assimilator as one whose dominant learning abilities are abstract conceptualization and reflective observation, and the accommodator as one whose strength lies in active experimentation and learning from concrete experience.
Concrete versus abstract	Some learners like to start with the concrete situation, such as the experience, while others prefer to start from the abstract, theoretical idea. This is similar to the preceding type.
Converger versus diverger	The converger is best at abstract conceptualization and active experimentation while the diverger's strengths lie in reflective observation and concrete experience (Kolb, 1984:77).
Field dependence versus field independence	Wilkin describes these as in the former mode 'perception is strongly dominated by the overall organization of the field, as fused"' (1971:24). In the latter mode 'parts of the field are experienced as discrete from organised background' (ibid).
Focusing versus scanning	If learners have a problem to solve, focusers will examine it as a totality and generate hypotheses that will be modified in the light of new information, while scanners will select one aspect of the problem and assume it to be the solution, until subsequent information disproves it, when they have to recommence the task.
Holistic versus serialistic	This approach reflects Gestalt psychology: some learners see phenomena as a whole while others string together the parts.
Reflection versus impulsivity	This is similar to focusing and scanning and Kagan, who undertook his studies with children, wrote that 'a child who does not reflect upon the probable validity of alternative solution sequences is likely to follow through the first idea that occurs to him. This strategy is more likely to end up in failure than one that involves reflection' (1971:54–57).
Rigidity versus flexibility	Some people are rigid in their approach to learning since once they have discovered a successful method they always seek to apply it. This creates its own difficulties, since problems emerge that cannot be solved by the normal approach.

Belenky et al.

The work of Belenky *et al.* has a number of major strengths, one being that their research was an intensive study of the lives of women and so their discussion about 'ways of knowing' is quite existentialistic. While their work was with women, they did not view this as an exclusively feminist study and recognized that these ways of knowing might be as relevant to men as to the women they studied, and this I believe to be true. They traced the life history of 135 women through in-depth interviews and as a result of their analysis they suggested that there are five different ways of knowing – the fourth, however, is subdivided into two: silence; received knowledge; subjective knowledge, procedural knowledge (separate and connected), constructed knowledge.

SILENCE

This is described as being 'deaf and dumb' since they could not learn from the voices of others and they felt voiceless. They felt passive, reactive and dependent, unable to speak out or protest. They did not feel that they could learn from their own experience and they depended on authority – the higher the authority the more they accept. Consequently, secondary experience is by far the more important to their learning. They could only describe themselves by how others described them; in a sense they were alienated persons.

RECEIVED KNOWLEDGE

They learned to listen to the voices of others but they had no confidence in their own ability to think. Once again, authorities (experts, teachers, professors, and so on) have the right answers – they know the 'truth'. The idea that there is no truth but probably the idea of conflicting perspectives rarely crosses their minds. They believed what they were told. Knowledge always lies outside of them and so they always seek to learn from the expert – in a non-reflective manner. Belenky *et al.* describe these as 'selfless selves'.

SUBJECTIVE KNOWLEDGE

To reach the state of subjective knowing, individuals have to wrest control of their lives from others. This period of transition, which is not age-related but about half of their interviewees were subjectivist, rarely had anything to do with learning in an educational setting, although it could be described as a transformative learning experience. However, it is described as a realization of failed authority (Belenky *et al.* specify failed male authority) – now the authoritarian position is no longer valid. For some, however, a return to education follows from reaching this stage of subjective knowing, but since they had considerable doubts about the authoritarian atmosphere of educational institutions, they found it hard to conform without retreating into a position of silent conformity while they privately disputed much of what they hear and see.

> Subjectivist women distrust logic, analysis, abstraction and even language itself. They see these methods as alien territory belonging to men. As we listened to subjectivist women describe their attitudes about truth and knowing, we heard them argue against and stereotype those experts and remote authorities whom social institutions often promote as holding the keys to the truth – teachers, doctors, scientists, men in general. It was as if, by turning inwards for answers, they had to deny strategies for knowing that they perceived as belonging to the masculine world.
>
> (Belenky *et al.*, 1986:71)

Now the primary experience is more important since they have the confidence to know how to handle it – for these women truth is experienced. They tended to be intuitive in the existential sense of just knowing what to do. Feelings play an important part – knowing what to do comes from within but ideas come from outside, for these women.

PROCEDURAL KNOWLEDGE

This approach sees the subjectivist approach as being in conflict with a recognition that there is external validity. This creates a major dilemma in education when teachers and professors tell students how to handle/ describe data, since procedural knowing is the conflict between external authority and the subjectivist position.

Knowledge is acquired by systematic analysis and the content becomes less important than the method by which the knowledge is acquired. It is now something that is gained objectively and dispassionately. Learners have to be critical thinkers, and there are two forms.

Separate Knowledge becomes something that is objective and information has to be treated with a degree of scepticism. Experts are now only as good as their arguments, but the doubting information is still regarded as doubting the informer/teacher – it is personal rather than impersonal. Being critical in this way is not a congenial form of conversation, even between friends. There is still an underlying 'will to truth' as Foucault describes it (Sheridan, 1980). Since the knowledge is now important the self has to be played down – for example, write in the third person, and so on.

Connected In this form of procedural knowing, there is an attempt to understand the other's perspectives and points of view. Now empathy enters into the equation: 'If one can discover the experiential logic behind these ideas, the ideas become less strange and the owners of the ideas cease to be strangers' (Belenky *et al.*, 1986:115). No longer is the approach judgmental.

But

> in the institutions of higher learning most of these women attended, the subjective voice was largely ignored; feelings and intuitions were banished to the realm of the personal and private. It was the public, rational, analytical voice that received the institutions' tutelage, respect and rewards.
>
> (Belenky *et al.*, 1986:124)

There is a developing feeling at this stage that we are all connected in a common quest to gain knowledge. At the same time, academics who appear to let personal feeling enter into their judgement are a little bewildering to procedural knowers, because they have lost the sense of seeing knowledge as subjective.

CONSTRUCTED KNOWLEDGE

Now there is a realization that all knowledge is subjective and that the knowers construct their own knowledge – it is integrated and personal between those who can both listen and share in a collaborative manner. Knowledge about reality is complex and experts are aware of the complexities of their subject. Now all knowledge is challenged but the process is intimately connected with caring. Constructivists become passionate knowers and emphasize the never-ending search for truth.

What we have seen in this typology is a developmental sequence, one that is not connected with age. It reflects different approaches to learning and illustrates something of the complexity of the person in box 1 and the interaction between the person, the situation and the experiences (boxes 1, 2 and 3 of my diagram). We can also see, however, that it is the growing and developing experience of the women that takes them through these different ways of knowing.

Robert Sternberg

Sternberg also demonstrates something about the complexity of the person who enters situations, has experiences and learns and acts. For him a thinking style is a 'preferred way of thinking ... but (w)e do not have *a* style but a *profile* of styles (Sternberg, 1997:19 – *italics* in original).

He stresses that the style is a preference and not an ability and that people have different styles which they use in relation to the situation in which they find themselves. His work is concerned with mental self-government (Sternberg, 1997:20–26) in which he argues there are three *functions*:

- Legislative – people who like to decide for themselves, and are usually creative.
- Executive – people who like to follow rules and procedures and prefer pre-structured problems; they do what they are told.
- Judicial – people who like to evaluate rules, they also like problems.

However, there are four *forms* of mental self-government:

- Monarchic – people who are single-minded and driven.
- Hierarchic – people who have a hierarchy of goals and recognize the need to set priorities.
- Oligarchic – people who are motivated by several competing goals of perceived importance.
- Anarchic – people motivated by a potpourri of needs who have trouble adapting to formal organizations.

But there are also *levels, scope* and *leanings*. There are two levels – global and local: global thinkers like large abstract problems, while local ones prefer concrete problems and working with detail. There are two scopes – internal and external: the internals tend to be introverted, task-orientated, aloof and not socially aware, while external individuals tend to be extroverted, out-going and people-orientated. There are also two leanings – liberal and conservative: the liberal likes to go beyond existing rules, maximize change and seek ambiguous solutions, whereas the conservative individual likes to stick to existing rules, minimize change, avoid ambiguous situations and stay with familiar situations.

The strengths of Sternberg's approach are that his research is based on empirical research, he tries to capture the person – both as a learner and as a doer – and he recognizes that within the profile he goes beyond the normal dichotomy of learning styles. He also recognizes that styles vary across the lifespan. Thinking styles are related to culture, gender, age, parenting and schooling and occupation. While I think that his work could easily be extended to take in some of the dimensions of the whole person that he does not explicitly refer to, it offers a realistic understanding of the person.

Earlier in this chapter, we made reference to self-directed learning (Houle, 1961; Tough, 1979; Long and assoc, 1988, 1993, 1997, 1998, *inter alia*), and we can now see from Sternberg's studies the type of person who is likely to be self-directed. Additionally, we can see another framework by which we can analyse self-directed learning.

Summary

This chapter has endeavoured to cover a lot of ground about learning, looking at the characteristics of adult learners, basic theories of learning – especially the experiential – it has introduced readers to an existentialist approach to learning in which the complexity of learning processes themselves are recognized and, finally, the complexity of the person's approach to learning has been discussed. Ultimately, it is argued that learning is the driving force of the individual, and that through learning people grow and develop. Philosophically, learning is both about 'being' and 'becoming'.

This chapter has concentrated on the learning processes through life, rather than lifelong learning in the way that it has more recently been treated in policy statements about lifelong learning since, it is argued, this more ambiguous use of the concept of learning not only confuses the issue, it detracts from the richness and complexity of learning itself and has a tendency to dehumanize learning. Despite recognizing this complexity, it has to be maintained that what is written here is but a brief introduction to learning and it might be too complex a phenomenon ever to understand entirely.

Having examined adult learners and adult learning, it is recognized that few of the learning theorists have been examined in detail and, consequently, the next chapter is devoted to elaborating upon the work of a number of the main ones.

4

ADULTS LEARNING – SOME THEORISTS' PERSPECTIVES

Having developed an approach to adult learning in the previous chapter it is now necessary to examine the fields of adult education and lifelong learning more broadly and to investigate some of the writings about adult learning that have been produced in recent years. This chapter, which is closely linked to the previous one, highlights the work of five major writers, each of whom, in their various ways, has examined different aspects of adult learning. Four of the writers concentrate on adult education and the fifth is an educational psychologist; three assume a psychological and the remaining two a sociological perspective. They are: Paulo Freire, Robert Gagné, Malcolm Knowles, Jack Mezirow and Carl Rogers; the main works of each referred to here are listed in the bibliography. These five have been selected because, in their differing ways, they have contributed to the theoretical knowledge of adult learning and their writings are examined here, comparing and contrasting their ideas to those presented in the previous chapters.

Paulo Freire

The writings of Freire are very well known among adult educators, even though some have confessed to finding him difficult to comprehend. Freire's ideas emerged against the background of the oppression of the masses in Brazil by an elite, who reflected the dominant values of a non-Brazilian culture. His writings epitomized an intellectual movement that developed in Latin America after the Second World War, which was a synthesis of Christianity and Marxism and which found its theological fulfilment in liberation theology: its educational philosophy was Freire's own work. From this background, it may be seen that at the heart of his educational ideas lay a humanistic conception of people as learners, but also an expectation that once they had actually learned they should not remain passive but become active participants in the wider world. Hence, for Freire, education could never be a neutral process; it is either designed to facilitate freedom or it is 'education for domestication' (Freire, 1973c:79), which is basically conservative.

In a sense Freire never really distinguished learning from teaching and so we will briefly return to him two chapters from now when teaching theorists are discussed, but he is included here because of his emphasis on the learners and the ways that they can be emancipated from their socio-cultural milieu. This is only an implicit theory of learning throughout his work and it is this that we will try to focus on here.

In order to understand Freire's thinking it is helpful to recall Figure 1.1 in which it was suggested that objectified culture is transmitted to the individual through the lifelong process of socialization. Since the culture that was transmitted is foreign to the values of the Brazilian people, who were its recipients, Freire claimed that this was the culture of the colonizers and implicit in the process of the subordination of the culture of the indigenous people. He illustrated this in the following manner:

> It is not a coincidence that the colonizers refer to their own cultural practices as an art, but refer to the cultural production of the colonized as folklore. Similarly, the colonizers speak of their language, but speak of the language of the colonized as dialect.
>
> (Freire, 1973c:50–51)

Since a construction of reality is contained within language, the common people have a construction of reality imposed upon them that is false to their own heritage. Thus the idea of a false self-identify emerges, one that perpetually undervalues the indigenous culture and, therefore, native people come to see themselves as subordinate. Hence, the oppressed are imprisoned in a cultural construction of reality that is false to them but one from which it is difficult to escape, since even their language transmits the values that imprison them.

Through the process of literacy education Freire and his colleagues were able to design experiential situations in which the learners were enabled to reflect upon their own understanding of themselves in their socio-cultural milieu. It was this combination of action and reflection that he called praxis (Freire, 1972b:96). Herein lies the difference between human beings and the other animals, argued Freire: people are able to process their experiences and reflect upon them. Through the process of reflection individuals may become conscious of realities other than the one into which they have been socialized. Freire wrote that conscientization 'is a permanent critical approach to reality in order to discover it and discover the myths that deceive us and help to maintain the oppressing dehumanizing structures' (1971, cited in 1976:225). He then expressed it slightly differently: conscientization 'implies that in discovering myself oppressed I know that I will be liberated only if I try to transform the oppressing structure in which I find myself' (ibid.). Later, he claimed that he no longer used this term 'conscientization' and this may be because it had become too closely related to the Marxist idea of 'false class con-sciousness', which is much more restrictive than his understanding of the process. Nevertheless, Freire still regarded education as 'the practice of freedom' through which process learners discover themselves and achieve something more of the fullness of their humanity by acting upon the world to transform it.

In his later books, he continually returned to the themes of his earlier ones – in *Pedagogy of Hope* (Freire, 1996) he continued to insist that edu-cators understand the language of the oppressed, that they denounce the dominant elite practices and they understand the immense resilience of the poor who need their voices to be heard in this capitalist world that continues to oppress them. Throughout his work, it is possible to detect ideas contained in Figure 1.2, where having received and processed inputs from the objectified culture that engulfs them, learners can externalize and act back upon their socio-cultural milieu. Implicit, therefore, in Freire's formulation is a social theory of learning, although he never described it in this manner.

How do Freire's ideas differ from those suggested in earlier chapters? Fundamentally, there is one major difference and some minor ones. In the first instance, the socio-cultural background from which his theory emerged has resulted in him depicting the objectified culture as being false and hostile to that of the indigenous learner, so that his approach was often viewed as being political rather than literacy education. However, this interpretation of culture is not something that was unique to Freire: many Marxist writers would concur that the dominant cultural knowledge and values, etc. acquired by most members of a society are the cultural perspectives allowed by an elite, so that some form of cultural hegemony exists. (See Westwood, 1980 for a discussion in which this approach is applied to adult education and Bowles and Gintis, 1976 for their analysis of American schooling from a similar perspective.) Thus, Figure 1.2 actually allows for such an interpretation to be assumed and, indeed, teaching might even be viewed as an activity that encourages it. Nevertheless, there is a significant difference between the model pre-sented here and Freire's thought: he incorporated two opposing cultures into his understanding of the process – that of the ruling elite and that of the oppressed. This is the crux of Freire's argument that no education can be neutral since the culture of the oppressed is in opposition to that of the elite. Hence literacy education can only assume a political perspective. The model produced earlier has not sought to analyse the culture of the United Kingdom in this way, although some sociologists and community educators might consider that such an analysis is necessary, and this will be discussed below in relation to the relevance of Freire's work for Western Europe and the United States.

Freire placed considerable emphasis on the teacher being a learner of

the culture of the learners so that he stressed the teacher–learner/
learner–teacher dialogue. Thus, teaching and learning consists of a two-
way model of human interaction. He recognized that the teacher may
facilitate the experience on which reflection occurs, which thus becomes a
learning process. Thus Freire regarded the role of the teacher as a facilitator who is able to stimulate the learning process rather than as one who
teaches the 'correct' knowledge and values that have to be acquired. For
him this was a fundamentally democratic and humanistic process – a
theme he was to return to at the end of his life (Freire, 1998). However,
this does not differ significantly from the model produced here since the
teacher is regarded as either one who transmits cultural knowledge or one
who facilitates learning. This distinction will be discussed further in the
following chapter.

Freire's approach is a model for teaching adults but it is also useful for
teaching children. It concentrates upon the humanity of the learners and
understanding their language so that they are able to learn from what is
being communicated to them. It places great value upon the human
being, the consequences of which are more structural and political in
their emphasis. While he maintained that education could never be
neutral, with which we agree, learning need not be understood in political
terms even though we both locate learners in their socio-cultural milieu
and regard them as recipients of cultural information and experiences
transmitted through personal or impersonal means. Learners are also
agents who are able to act back upon their environment in order to try to
change it.

Having pointed to some of the apparent differences between Freire's
approach and that discussed in this book, it must also be recognized that
there are many similarities, including: his emphasis on the humanity of
the learners; his concern that learners should be free to reflect upon their
own experiences and to harmonize their reflections and actions (he called
this 'praxis') and to act upon their socio-cultural milieu in order to
humanize and transform it; his connection between the socio-cultural
environment and individual learners; his recognition that learners are
able to create their own roles rather than become role players performing
roles prescribed by others. As a result of all these aspects, Freire maintained that education is always a political process since it is a social institution controlled by the social and political processes, which almost
automatically ensure that social pressures are brought to bear on learners
in order to make them conform to what is socially prescribed in both cognitive and behavioural terms.

Out of the political condition of Latin America emerged a
Christian–Marxist approach to education that is both humanistic and
radical. Yet the term 'radical' is often the 'kiss of death' to innovative
approaches, as was seen with the concept of recurrent education.

However, if there is not something radical about the educational process, the question needs to be posed as to how it differs from socialization. If education actually provides people with an opportunity to process and to reflect upon their experiences, it must allow them to reach different conclusions about them and to choose whether, or not, they will behave in a conformist manner.

From his earliest writings, Freire continued to produce radical analyses of education, often writing with another author, in the form of dialogues, which he called 'talking a book'. These books are of interest because they help introduce readers to Freire's ideas and the way in which he developed them in discussion. There have been a number of books like this, one of the last being with Myles Horton from Highlander, a Folk High School in Tennessee (Horton and Freire, 1990). While they can be inspiring they also tend to confuse Freire's reflections about his own previous writings and actions with the discussion ongoing in the dialogue. This is natural in discussion but it is difficult to trace the developments in his thought from his earlier writings. Perhaps these dialogues serve as a full introduction to Freire, his world and his thoughts.

Since Freire's ideas emerged in Latin America, do they have any relevance for contemporary Western society? This is a most important question to pose, since he could be dismissed as someone whose views are of significance only within the context in which they emerged. Yet this approach would be quite wrong, since many dominant ideas and values in contemporary society owe their origins to historical cultural milieux completely different from this one. London reflected upon Freire's work in the context of North America and he claimed that in that society adult education has adopted a 'bland approach . . . (a) non-controversial stance, and (b) safe and respectable perspective' (London, 1973:59). But he maintained that a:

> central problem for adult education is to undertake programming
> that will raise the level of consciousness of the American people
> so that they can become aware of the variety of forces – economic,
> political, social and psychological – that are afflicting their lives.
> (London, 1973:54)

Hence, it may be seen that from the earliest time when Freire's work became known in the USA, commentators were sympathetic to the adoption of his approach. At the same time there were some who felt that his work was insurrectionary and that he should be opposed (Berger, 1974). Perhaps his argument might have been even more compelling had he focused on the different cultures and subcultures in America as well, but his views emerged from the situation in Brazil, where the cultural and political power differences between rich and poor were much more pronounced and which illustrated his understanding of teaching and learning extremely clearly. The conditions of the poor there are caused by global capitalism, just as they are elsewhere in the world. Clearly Freire's work is relevant throughout the world and even more so as globalization is widening the gap between the rich and powerful and the remainder of the world's population.

Not all educators recognize the political significance of their role, although in the United Kingdom, for instance, community educators, such as Lovett (1975) and Newman (1973, 1979), adopted similar perspectives, and Kirkwood and Kirkwood (1989) reported on a community education project carried out in Edinburgh using Freire's methods. However, a great deal of community education and literacy work has been much more instrumentalist and narrow, but it is still humanistic and valuable, although it has not assumed Freire's more radical approach. Indeed, it is possible to argue that many people in Western Europe and elsewhere are no more aware of the variety of forces that afflict them than are their counterparts in the United States. Consequently, it is important that the radical Christian perspective adopted by Freire is not lost from the world of lifelong learning as education and learning are being more closely related to employment.

Robert M. Gagné

Gagné (1977:284–286) developed a model for understanding a relationship between learning and instruction. He suggested that learning progresses through the following phases as the instructional process was undertaken. These stages are: expectancy; attentive; selective perception; coding; storage entry; memory storage retrieval; transfer; responding; reinforcement. In a later publication it was suggested that there are nine phases in instruction:

- gaining attention
- informing the learner of the objectives
- stimulating recall of prerequisite learnings
- presenting the stimulus material
- providing learning guidance
- eliciting the performance
- providing feedback about performance correctness
- assessing the performance
- enhancing retention and transfer

(Gagné et al., 1992:203)

Like with Freire, an emphasis on teaching as well as learning may be found here. Nevertheless, there is another element of his work that is also significant to adult education and this is his types of learning. He proposed eight types, seven of which he regards as a hierarchy and the eighth may occur at any level. These are: signal learning; stimulus–response learning; motor and verbal chaining; multiple discrimination; concept learning; rule learning; problem solving.

He claimed that signal learning may occur at any level of the hierarchy and it may be understood as a form of classical conditioning, which was discussed in the previous chapter. Clearly this happens with both children and adults and it is one of the ways in which everyone acquires many attitudes and prejudices throughout the whole of their lives. The remaining seven types of learning are, according to Gagné, seven stages of a hierarchy and they are now discussed.

Stimulus–response learning is the same as operant conditioning in which the response is shaped by the reward. The following two types of learning, motor and verbal chaining, Gagné placed at the same level in the hierarchy: the former refers to skills learning while the latter is rote learning – both of which can be found in the model of learning discussed in the previous chapter. With both, practice is necessary to achieve correctness whilst reinforcement is necessary to ensure that the acceptable sequence is maintained. In multiple discrimination learning, Gagné moved into the area of intellectual skills; this, he suggested, is the ability to distinguish between similar types of phenomena, so that the learners themselves are able to decide which of similar types is correct for any specific situation. In contrast to discrimination is the ability to classify. Concepts are abstract notions which link together similar phenomena so that, for instance, friendship is a concept but individual friendships are actual occurrences, education is a concept but in actuality there are educational processes. Gagné suggested that the ability to learn concepts is the next order of the hierarchy and it may be recalled that developmental psychologists, such as Piaget (1929), would claim that the ability to think in the abstract commences mostly during adolescence, so that it is necessary to recognize that the education of adults may be different from the education of children, since the levels of conceptual thought in the various learning processes are different. This is implicit in Gagné's hierarchy of types of learning but one that is important in relation to any consideration of adult learning. One particular type of classification is that of rules and he maintained that the ability to respond to signals by a whole number of responses is successful rule learning. At this level of thought it is clear that Gagné perceived the individual to be a little more free than some of the behaviourists and this is quite fundamental to seeing his work in the context of the education of adults.

Problem solving is the highest order of learning in Gagnés hierarchy and this occurs when the learner draws upon his previously learned rules in order to discover an answer to a problematic situation. It will be recalled that among the different styles of learning discussed in the previous chapter was the dichotomy between the flexible and the rigid learner, in which the former clearly has the mastery of more sets of rules than the latter. Problem solving is an approach to learning and teaching used frequently in the education of adults, so the problem solving sequence that Gagné proposed is quite significant for adult educators. He suggested that the following sequence occurs, in which the flexibility is apparent. Initially a learner proposes one or more hypotheses concerning the problem and these are based upon the rules that have already been learned. These hypotheses are then tested against the actual situation and once an answer has been discovered to the problem the solution will be assimilated into the learner's repertoire of rules, so that the next time a similar situation arises the learner will not experience it as a problem. There are similarities at this point between Gagné's approach and that of Schutz and Luckmann (1974) mentioned earlier. Another psychologist whose analysis is similar to Gagné's in this context is George Kelly (1955), who claimed that all behaviour may be regarded as a form of hypothesis testing to enquire whether the actual world is really like the perception of it constructed by the individual. If it is, then the experience merely reinforces the construct, but if it is not, then the construct (hypothesis) has to be modified in the light of experience. (See Candy, 1981 for a direct application of some of Kelly's ideas to adult education).

The problem solving sequence has formed a basis of many learning exercises in adult education and in recent years a number of problem solving cycles have been devised which are similar to the learning cycles that were discussed in the previous chapter. Figure 4.1 depicts a problem solving cycle that combines the sequence proposed by Gagné with some of the ideas mentioned by Kolb and Fry (1975). Thus it may be seen that this type of problem solving cycle actually relates back to the learning cycle, but it also highlights some of the most important aspects of Gagné's hierarchy of learning. Since Gagné started from a psychological perspective some of the wider cultural implications of learning, discussed in the previous chapters and in the work of Freire, are not so apparent. Indeed, Freire was more concerned about problem posing than problem solving, since more innovative and radical ideas were likely to emerge from it. Yet the learning process that Gagné has highlighted is significant for adult educators, so that educators of adults need to be aware of the wider literature on learning.

Malcolm S. Knowles

Knowles may almost be regarded as the father of andragogy because, while he did not actually invent the term, he was mainly responsible for its popularization in the USA and Western Europe. Indeed, the term derives from the Greek *aner*, meaning man, and it was first used in an educational

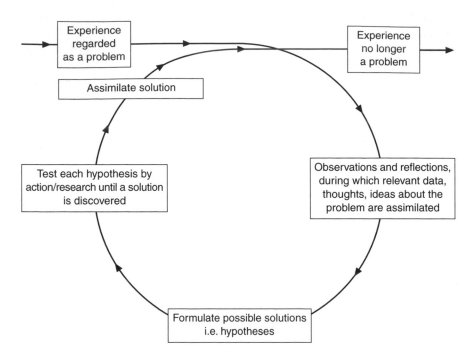

Figure 4.1 A problem solving cycle.

context in nineteenth-century Europe. Nevertheless, Knowles is most fre-quently associated with the concept, which he originally defined as 'the art and science of helping adults learn' (1980a:43).

Knowles (1978:53–57) initially distinguished sharply between the way in which adults and children learn and claimed that there are four main assumptions that differentiate andragogy from pedagogy. These are:

- a change in self-concept, since adults need to be more self-directive;
- experience, since mature individuals accumulate an expanding reservoir of experience which becomes an exceedingly rich resource in learning;
- readiness to learn, since adults want to learn in the problem areas with which they are confronted and which they regard as relevant;
- orientation towards learning, since adults have a problem centred ori-entation they are less likely to be subject centred.

However, in 1984 he added a fifth assumption about the motivation to learn (Knowles and assoc, 1984:12) and in his autobiographical book he added another one about the need to know (Knowles, 1989:83–85). Knowles had clearly given the idea a great deal of thought and has frequently reconceptualized it, demonstrating his own willingness to

126

rethink his position – a characteristic which is to be admired. However, the fact that he has reformulated the idea on a number of occasions illustrates the fact that each of the assumptions is open to considerable discussion. It might be asked, for instance, whether children are any less motivated than adults to learn about those phenomena that they regard as relevant and problematic to them, or whether Knowles had actually specified all the relevant points in any discussion about the differences in adults and children learning. The fact that Knowles had, to some extent, rethought his ideas is significant since the concept of andragogy has been, and is still being, accepted uncritically by many adult educators. Indeed, when Knowles' work was first published in America it stimulated considerable debate in the American journals about its validity. Initially, McKenzie (1977) sought to provide Knowles' pragmatic formulation with a more substantial philosophical foundation and he argued that adults and children are existentially different – a point with which Elias agreed, although he suggested that this was not necessarily significant since men and women are existentially different but no one has yet suggested that 'the art and science of teaching women differs from the art and science of teaching men' (Elias, 1979:254). To this point, McKenzie (1979) replied, without having undertaken the necessary research, that the differences between men and women, while pronounced, are not significant when related to their readiness to learn nor are they important in relation to their perspective of time. He also argued that andragogy is similar to but not precisely the same as progressivism. Yet McKenzie did not really focus upon the point that children might actually have the same readiness to learn as adults, and indeed probably do, when they are confronted with a problem the solution to which they wish to know.

Another set of issues arose in the debate about andragogy: Label (1978) suggested that the education of the elderly should be known as gerogogy, since education should recognize the phases of adult development; but are there only two phases in adult development? Knox (1977:342–350) suggested otherwise, so that to include gerogogy as a separate element in the art and science of teaching would be the 'thin end of the wedge' in a multiplication of terms, which prompted Knudson to suggest that all of these should be replaced by a single concept of 'humanagogy' which is:

> a theory of learning that takes into account the differences between people of various ages as well as their similarities. It is a *human* theory of learning not a theory of 'child learning', 'adult learning' or 'elderly learning'. It is a theory of learning that combines pedagogy, andragogy and gerogogy and takes into account every aspect of presently accepted psychological theory.
>
> (Knudson, 1979:261; emphasis in original)

127

Perhaps Knudson's position is a logical outcome of the debate, but the term 'humanagogy' has not gained any acceptance and, in any case, what makes humanagogy any different from the process of teaching and learning? It appears that Knudson has merely invented a new term for an old process, even though he has emphasized one aspect of the process that is regarded as significant to our understanding of the educational process: the humanity of the participant.

In 1979, Knowles chose to re-enter the debate, while he recognized that andragogy and pedagogy are not discrete processes he claimed that 'some pedagogical assumptions are realistic for adults in some situations and some andragogical assumptions are realistic for children in some situations' (1979:53), and that the two are not mutually exclusive. However, since the debate was prolonged in America and as a number of questions were raised throughout this discussion, it is worth enquiring whether Knowles' formulation is actually correct.

Knowles placed a tremendous emphasis on the self, something with which many adult educators would agree. Knox (1977) pointed out that the self undergoes development throughout the lifespan and that some aspects of that development may be related to physical age. However, it will be seen from the discussion on learning as an existentialist phenomenon in the previous chapter, that to focus only on the self is too narrow; we would suggest here that the emphasis should have been on the whole person.

But other scholars, such as Riesman (1950), have pointed out that some adults are 'other-directed', so that when they come to the learning situation they may seek to become dependent upon a teacher. While it may be one of the functions of an adult educator to try to help dependent adults to discover some independence, it must be recognized that this may be a very difficult step for some learners. But the fact that there are other-directed people suggests that Knowles' formulation was a little sweeping in this respect.

Knowles also claimed that adults have an expanded reservoir of experience that may be emphasized as a rich resource for future learning; but do not children and adolescents also have some experience that may be used as a resource in their learning? Do only adults learn from their relevant problems? What of those adults who study with the Open University or attend university extension classes? Once again, we see that because he differentiated between andragogy and pedagogy, he was forced into making rather difficult claims. Moreover, his treatment of the concept of experience is rather sketchy and yet it was a focal point for his theory of experiential learning.

It appeared that while Knowles focused upon something quite significant to adult learning, i.e. experience, his formulation was rather weak, not based upon extensive research findings, nor was it the total picture of adult learning. Indeed, it was not a psychological analysis of the learning process, it did not describe why specific aspects of experience are relevant, nor did it generate a learning sequence for an adult, so some of the claims that Knowles made for andragogy now appear to be rather suspect. It is not surprising, therefore, that in his later work he made less all-embracing claims for this concept, nor is it surprising that many scholars have been rather critical of it. Day and Baskett, for instance, concluded that:

> Andragogy is not a theory of adult learning, but is an educational ideology rooted in an inquiry-based learning and teaching paradigm – and should be recognized as such. ... It is not always the most appropriate or the most effective means of educating. This distinction between andragogy and pedagogy is based on an inaccurately conceived notion of pedagogy.
>
> (Day and Baskett, 1982:150)

There have subsequently been many other criticisms of the concept of andragogy: Hartree (1984:209) concluded that while Knowles

> has done an important service in popularizing the idea ... it is unfortunate that he has done so in a form which, because it is intellectually dubious, is likely to lead to rejection by the very people it is important to convince.

Tennant (1986:113–122), writing from a psychological position, also rejected many of Knowles' arguments although he did not reject the ideas of individual autonomy, which underlie much of Knowles' work.

Yet despite its apparent conceptual weaknesses and the many criticisms being levelled at the concept, it has became a popular term in adult education; so what are the strengths of the formulation that have resulted in its gaining support? Day and Baskett (1982) have perhaps located one of these when they suggested that it is an educational ideology, for clearly it is humanistic and liberal, which captured the frequently expressed beliefs among adult educators. It also focused upon the self-directed learner and emphasized the place of the self in the learning process, both of which are very significant to learning theory. One of the worrying features about this term was that, because of its huge popularity in the USA and Western Europe in the 1980s, it is still being accepted uncritically by others – especially in the emerging countries of Eastern Europe at the start of the twenty-first century, without reference to the wider debate, and often without reference to the long history of the concept in the former Yugoslavia, amongst other places.

Additionally, it arose in a period of history in the twentieth century, which L.C. Martin (1981) characterized as romantic, in which the value of the individual was emphasized and the boundaries of the institutions of society were weak. These boundaries resulted in an increased emphasis on integrated approaches to academic study and a wider acceptance of the ideological perception of progressive education. Indeed, the popularity of the concept in the 1980s reflects the fact that the education of adults needed a symbol as it became differentiated from school education and so perhaps it is serving the same function at the present time elsewhere in the world.

Knowles' emphasis on self-direction resulted in his (Knowles, 1986) book on learning contracts assuming considerable importance in many circles. The learning contract is one made between teacher and learner, for the learner to undertake specific work by a given date. In a tutorial that preceded it, there might also be discussion about how the work is to be undertaken, which experts should be consulted, how the work should be presented and also the standard that should be achieved. This teaching and learning method has assumed a great deal of popularity among some sectors of adult education, possibly because it encourages individual autonomy and, maybe, because it appears less time-consuming for the teacher. But this latter assumption probably belies the reality of the situation! Another reason why learning contracts are popular at present is because of the current emphasis upon correct performance rather than correct academic knowledge, and the learning contract can be utilized in very practical ways.

Andragogy, then, was a theory that grew out of a specific period (Jarvis, 1984) although Knowles emphasized certain values, such as individual autonomy, which were to transcend the 1960s when Knowles first formulated the idea. By 1986, however, the andragogical teacher had become the manager and designer of the learning process and the learning contract the agreement between the manager and the managed as to how the learning was to be undertaken. Knowles' work remains popular despite all its failings and one of the main reasons for this is probably because it reflects popular ideological currents.

It may be concluded from this brief discussion that, despite the claims sometimes made on its behalf, andragogy is not a distinct approach to adult learning, but it does contain some elements of experiential learning theory. Neither is it a theory of adult teaching even though its humanistic perspective might provide some guidelines for an approach to teaching adults. Is it a philosophy? Certainly, it includes within it an ideological perspective that is both idealistic and humanistic, so that it is not surprising that it has been found by many to be acceptable. However, andragogy might also be employed as a term to denote the body of knowledge that is emerging about the education of adults, in the same manner as pedagogy might be used to describe the body of knowledge about the education of children.

Knowles was, therefore, an important practitioner in the education of adults and some of the points that he raised are based upon the humanistic ideals of education itself. It is significant that these points are discussed within this theoretical context since, while andragogy is not a theory of adult learning, its implications are quite profound for the practice of teaching adults.

Jack Mezirow

The work of Mezirow on transformative learning has been well known in the USA for over twenty years now, although it is not as widely used elsewhere. Mezirow (1977, 1981) draws upon the insights of a number of established disciplines and synthesizes them in an original manner. This section summarizes some of the ideas that he presents, although the emphasis of his work has changed in more recent years as he has endeavoured to produce a more complete theory of learning. His early work will be discussed first and, thereafter, reference is made to his more recent publications.

Mezirow starts from the assumption that everyone has constructions of reality which are dependent on reinforcement from various sources in the socio-cultural world. He calls these constructions of reality 'perspectives' and notes that they are transformed when individuals' perspectives are not in harmony with their experience. In this situation of disjunction, the individual's construction of reality is transformed as a result of reflecting upon the experience and plotting new strategies of living as a result of their assessment of the situation. Mezirow notes that life crises are times when this occurs and his conclusion is both in accord with his own observations and those of Aslanian and Brickell (1980), who discovered that people tended to return to studying at times like this. Hence, the crux of Mezirow's analysis is that when a 'meaning perspective can no longer comfortably deal with anomalies in the next situation, a transformation can occur' (1977:157). He goes on to suggest that a learning sequence is established as a result of a discordant experience, which may be depicted in the form of a learning cycle (Figure 4.2).

In a later work, Mezirow (1981:7) extends this cycle to include the following ten stages:

1 A disorientating dilemma
2 Self-examination
3 Critical assessment and a sense of alienation
4 Relating discontent to the experiences of others
5 Exploring options for new ways of acting
6 Building confidence in new ways of behaving
7 Planning a course of action

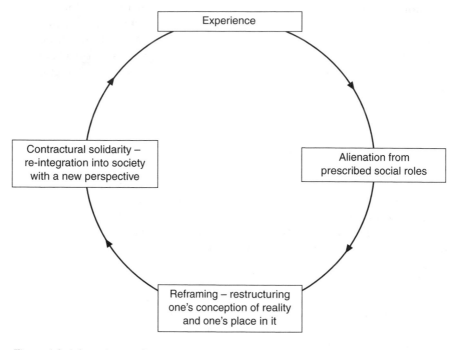

Figure 4.2 A learning cycle.

Source: Mezirow (1977:158).

   8 Acquiring knowledge in order to implement plans
   9 Experimenting with new roles
 10 Reintegration into society

The extent to which this is actually a sequence is not clear since Mezirow suggests that there are two paths to perspective transformation – one sudden and the other gradual. However, he regards these transformations as 'a development process of movement through the adult years towards meaning perspectives that are progressively more inclusive, discriminating, and more integrative of experience' (1977:159). However, there are a number of points now that perhaps require additional evidence since not all people may develop as a result of their experience, nor may they necessarily learn from it. Additionally, should individuals' universes of meaning necessarily change in the same direction as each others' as they age? and do these processes not also happen with children?

It is this movement along a maturity gradient that Mezirow regards as a form of emancipatory learning and here he draws heavily upon the work of Habermas (Mexzirow and assoc, 1990). In his latest work (Mezirow, 2000:8) he also stresses the difference between instrumental and communicative learning. Even so he had already used Habermas' third domain – emancipation – which is, according to Mezirow, 'from libidinal, institutional or environmental forces which limit our options and rational control over our lives but have been taken for granted as beyond human control' (1981:5). Hence, perspective transformation is an emancipatory process

> of becoming critically aware of how and why the structure of psycho-cultural assumptions has come to constrain the way we see ourselves and our relationships, reconstituting the structure to permit a more inclusive and discriminating integration of experience and acting upon these new understandings.
>
> (Mezirow, 1981:5)

By the year 2000, Mezirow claimed that this related to both instrumental and communicative action. In this latest book, there is considerably more reference to the emotional aspects of living than in his previous work, although his (Mezirow, 2000:5) definition of learning as 'the process of using a prior interpretation to construe a new or revised interpretation of the meaning of one's experience as a guide to future action' focuses on the cognitive domain and is rather narrow. He (2000:19) claims that learning occurs in four ways:

- elaborating existing frames of reference;
- learning new frames of reference;
- transforming points of view;
- transforming habits of mind.

At the heart of Mezirow's work is meaning, which despite his references to emotional intelligence, and even to the spiritual, his is a rather restricted approach to learning. In addition, not all learning need result in 'future action', as he claims. Nevertheless, this is an important attempt to understand the cognitive domain of learning, and it is clear that there are certain similarities and some differences between Mezirow's work and that of other theorists who consider the wider socio-cultural milieu. Both he and Freire regard education as a liberating force: Freire views it as releasing the individual from the false consciousness in which he has been imprisoned as a result of the dominance of the culture of the colonizers, but Mezirow regards the freedom from a more psychological perspective; both Freire and Mezirow focus on the social construction of reality and regard learning as a method by which this may be changed. Like a number of theorists of adult learning, Mezirow focuses on the idea that learning occurs as a result of reflecting upon experience, so that much of his work is relevant to understanding the learning process in socialization and in non-formal learning situations. However, he also suggests that there are different levels of reflection and he (1981:12–13) specifies seven of these, some of which he claims are more likely to occur in adulthood:

1   Reflectivity: awareness of specific perception, meaning, behaviour
2   Affective reflectivity: awareness of how the individual feels about what is being perceived, thought or acted upon
3   Discriminant reflectivity: assessing the efficacy of perception, etc.
4   Judgemental reflectivity: making and becoming aware of the value of judgements made
5   Conceptual reflectivity: assessing the extent to which the concepts employed are adequate for the judgement
6   Psychic reflectivity: recognition of the habit of making percipient judgements on the basis of limited information
7   Theoretical reflectivity: awareness of why one set of perspectives is more or less adequate to explain personal experience

The last three of these, Mezirow maintains, are more likely to occur in adulthood, but this claim might run into the same difficulties that Knowles ran into with his distinction between andragogy and pedagogy. Even so, the final one he regards as quite crucial to perspective transformation.

It was only in 1991 that Mezirow brought together thoughts that he had expressed in numerous articles and papers in *Transformative Dimensions of Adult Learning*, and he extended these in his more recent work *Learning as Transformation* (Mezirow, 2000). In both of these he sought to synthesize perspectives and research from different academic disciplines to demonstrate how adults learn. In the former, he suggested that learning is the process of making meaning from experiences as a result of the learner's previous knowledge, so that learning is a new interpretation of an experience, which has not changed greatly in the ensuing years. He went on to show how people make meaning in a variety of different ways and he also analysed the distorted assumptions that stem from prior experiences. Making meaning is an important element in learning although, as we have pointed out, he restricts it to the cognitive domain, which is a pity since skills, emotions and even the senses are also learned from experience. This is an important study although it is not as unique as the publishers claim on the dust jacket (see, for instance, Marton *et al.*, 1984 whose work Mezirow does not appear to know).

Indeed, there is a sense in which his approach is very similar to the phenomenological approach suggested in the previous chapters. He also focuses on disjuncture – that is if a person's stock of knowledge is inadequate to explain the experience, then the questioning process is reactivated. Additionally, his emphasis upon reflection is important since he has extended the analysis quite considerably by suggesting different forms. Here his approach is actually similar to that of Gagné but he concentrates upon meaning and reflection as learning. However, his idea of progress and development during the ageing process requires some further evidence, but it leads logically to the idea of the 'wisdom of the elders' and to the notion that the self-knowledge of the elders is always more mature than that of younger people (Jarvis, 2001a). Furthermore, the influence of social change plays little part in Mezirow's analysis although sociologists of late modernity (Giddens, 1990, 1991) have written a great deal which would have enriched his analysis. Mezirow has, however, accepted some of the central tenets of Habermas' theory of communicative action without fully analysing the academic debate that the work has generated. Nevertheless, his approach is a significant contribution to recent literature on adult learning.

Carl Rogers

Carl Rogers is the final theorist to be discussed in this chapter: he was a humanistic psychologist who expounded this psychological approach in the fields of education and learning. Having this theoretical perspective, it is not surprising that he emphasizes the self-actualization of the learner and he (1969:279–297) argues that the goal of education is a fully functioning person. However, this orientation reflects the therapist in Rogers and the distinction between education and therapy is occasionally blurred in his writings. Indeed he uses therapeutic techniques for educational ends. His fusion of these two distinct activities is highlighted by Srinivasan's (1977:72–74) discussion of the curriculum distinctions between self-actualizing and problem-centred education, which are:

- emotional versus intellectual;
- involving the learning group in developing its own curriculum versus identification of appropriate subject matter;
- planning learning experiences so that learners can reassess their feelings versus building learning around a problem;
- support in active learning versus using prepared learning units;
- using a variety of audio-visual approaches versus standardized printed materials and group discussion;
- using the group's spontaneity versus a programmed learning text;
- decentralized educational opportunities versus formal educational provision;
- participatory techniques versus teaching; assessing personal growth versus assessing learning gains.

Clearly, Srinivasan has polarized the distinction since a number of the theorists mentioned in this chapter would focus upon the significance of some of the former elements in the dichotomies as significant aspects of their understanding of education. Certainly Rogers would not draw the distinction in quite the way that Srinivasan has done but she has attempted to clarify an important conceptual issue. However, Rogers and Knowles are close in their emphasis on the self and the need for self-development and self-direction: indeed, Knowles acknowledged his debt to Rogers. Knowles (1980a:29–33) specifies fifteen different dimensions of maturation and he certainly regards maturity as one of the goals of education. Like Rogers and Knowles, it will be recalled that Mezirow was concerned about the maturation process of the learner, so for a number of theorists this plays a significant part in the education of adults.

Unlike some of the other writers discussed here, Rogers records the results of his approach to experiential learning in the context of graduate teaching in a university and he also records incidents of others in a formal setting who have attempted similar techniques. He suggests that experiential learning has a quality of personal involvement, but he recognizes that the teacher has a facilitating role; is pervasive in as much as it makes a difference to the learners; is evaluated by learners in terms of whether it is actually meeting their needs rather than in terms of its academic quality; has an essence of meaning. It is perhaps significant to note that while Rogers regards experiential learning as self-initiated, he does not actually dispense with the teacher although does claim that teaching 'is a vastly over-rated function' (1969:103), so that he is describing a different form of self-directed learning to that discussed by Tough. In the third edition of his book (Rogers and Freiberg, 1994), there is both a greater emphasis on schooling and also on teaching – yet the emphasis on whole person learning still remains and the goal of learning is still a fully functioning person.

Like Srinivasan, Rogers (1969:157–164) regards experiential learning at one end of a spectrum but at the other he places memory learning. He claims that experiential learning is typified by the following principles:

1 human beings have a natural potentiality to learn;
2 significant learning occurs when the learner perceives the relevance of the subject matter;
3 learning involves a change in self-organization and self-perception;
4 learning that threatens self-perception is more easily perceived and assimilated when external threats are at a minimum;
5 learning occurs when the self is not threatened;
6 much significant learning is acquired by doing;
7 learning is facilitated when the learner participates responsibly in the learning process;
8 self-initiated learning involves the whole person;
9 independence, creativity and self-reliance are all facilitated when self-criticism and self-evaluation are basic;

10 much socially useful learning is learning the process of learning and retaining an openness to experience, so that the process of change may be incorporated into the self.

His approach is clearly based upon the idea that the learner is the agent and that the social structure is not too oppressive to the learner. However, omission of any discussion about the wider socio-cultural milieu appears to be a weakness in this approach, so that while the above ten principles provide considerable insight into the learning process and offer some guidelines for the teacher, they do not present a comprehensive theory of individual learning in the wider socio-cultural environment.

Overall, Rogers' approach to experiential learning has much to offer and may provide inspiration for the teacher, as it did for Knowles, but it does not provide a comprehensive theory of adult learning. At its heart it reflects a humanistic belief system that has been quite fundamental to many individuals who work in adult education, but it also reflects the age in which he was writing when there were also a number of quite radical studies about schooling published as well.

Summary

The work of five major theorists has been briefly examined in this chapter and the intention has been to highlight some of the similarities and some of the differences between them. Both Freire and Mezirow consider the socio-cultural milieu as a significant factor in the learning process in common with the model presented earlier, although they treat culture in rather different ways: Freire has a two-cultures model of society whereas Mezirow is content to regard it as rather static and homogeneous. The process of reflection plays a significant part in the work of a number of these theorists, since they recognize that human beings are able to sift and evaluate the external stimuli received from their experiences. Experiential learning is quite central to all of the writers' considerations, since they recognize that the adult learns most effectively when the learning process is in response to a problem or a need. All of the writers, with the exception of Gagné, have placed considerable emphasis on the self and, although it is most exemplified in the works of Knowles and Rogers, it reflects the humanistic concerns of adult education. Even so, it is a much more debatable point as to whether the aims of education should be specified in terms of the development of the learner because the success of the educational process is then being evaluated by non-educational criteria. The cognitive dimension of the learning process is insufficiently emphasized in some instances while in others the practical and the emotional are under-played. The emphases that different writers put upon different elements of learning points to the need for a more comprehensive and integrated theory of learning rather more like that offered earlier in this book.

Most of the theorists focus upon the human need to learn, Rogers being the most explicit about it being basic to humanity, but none of them sought to incorporate it into such a comprehensive theory of learning. Mezirow and Freire have both developed comprehensive theoretical perspectives but Knowles' andragogical approach appears to have achieved the status of a theory, without having been systematically worked out. In all cases there are similarities with the model produced earlier in this study but in each instance the theorists have emphasized those elements that are most central to their own concerns, so that there are naturally also a number of points of divergence.

Learning might have been more clearly separated from teaching in this chapter, but it is much more difficult to draw this distinction when examining the work of practitioners since while conceptually learning can be separated from teaching and teaching from learning it is much more difficult to do so in practice. Nevertheless, the following two chapters examine the teaching of adults.

5

TEACHING ADULTS

Teaching may be an overrated activity, as Rogers (1969:103) maintains, but it remains at the heart of the educational process, so that consideration needs now to be given to it. Hirst and Peters (1970:78) defined it as the intention to bring about learning, and if this broad definition is adopted it may be seen that any activity that is performed in order to produce learning, however it is conducted, may be considered to be teaching. Hence, it is clear that Rogers and Hirst and Peters used the term in slightly different ways and it is, therefore, essential to clarify its use at the outset. Teachers can adopt a variety of approaches to the performance of their role: didactic, Socratic, facilitative or experiential. It might be argued that critical and feminist pedagogies constitute another approach to teaching, but it is suggested here that these should be included in all forms of teaching rather than being seen as a separate genre. If teachers play their role in a didactic fashion, they expound the knowledge to be learned by the students; if they are Socratic, they lead students towards a conclusion to their enquiry by shrewd questioning; if they are facilitative, they create conditions under which learning can occur but they do not seek to control its outcome; if they are experiential, they will seek to provide learners with experiences which involve the whole person. In a globalized world, where divisions between the 'haves' and the 'have-nots' gets wider, all teachers should be aware of critical and radical positions and should, at the very least, give their students opportunities to consider them.

Both the didactic and the Socratic approaches are teacher-centred and may lead to the teacher's perception of reality being accepted by the students, although the Socratic is more likely to result in conclusions other than those held by the teacher – whereas the facilitator and the experientialist have little control over the outcome of the learning. Rogers was clearly condemning the didactic approach and, maybe, the Socratic one. By contrast, the definition proposed by Hirst and Peters is sufficiently broad to include all four. Their definition is broad enough to include informal teaching but not broad enough to incorporate unintended teaching experiences that may occur in the process of human interaction. This, therefore, raises two major questions: to what extent is unintended teaching actually teaching and to what extent is the failure to produce learning, even though it was intended, actually teaching? If unintended teaching in informal situations is to be regarded as teaching, then the intention to bring about learning outcomes is too narrow and it should be seen as the provision of any situation in which learning might occur. If this is the case then unintended teaching is still teaching. Hence, teachers may be anyone who provides an opportunity for another person to learn, irrespective of whether they are part of the educational institution or whether or not they intended the learning to occur. But, clearly, this is too wide a definition within the context of the occupation of teacher. In this instance, a teacher may be defined as one who is employed to provide an environment in which learning may occur. In this instance the 'intention' is what distinguishes the process of teaching from the occupation.

Hirst and Peters acknowledge that teaching is not essential to education but claim that serious mis-education may occur if too much emphasis is given to this. However, it may be that this is a point at which Rogers, and other adult educators, would diverge from Hirst and Peters. They certainly do appear to place much more emphasis on the role of the teacher than many of the learning theorists discussed earlier might wish to. Learning can and does occur without a teacher but teaching is one way in which learning is facilitated, and many adult educators would claim that one of the teacher's fundamental aims should be to help the learner to become independent. Hence, it might be claimed that teaching is one of the occupations whose aim should be to make the client independent of the practitioner, a slightly different approach to that of first school-teachers who try to dissuade parents from teaching their children until they are sent to school!

Learning, then, is considered to be the most significant element in education and it will be recalled that the definition of education adopted in this study broadened it to an intended process of learning rather than restricting it to the transmission of culture. Hence the position adopted here is quite different from that proposed by Peters (1966:25) who argued that one of the criteria for education is that knowledge of a worthwhile nature is transmitted to the learner. Learning is a much broader phenomenon than teaching, and the humanistic basis of education adopted here places the learner at its focal point. It is, therefore, the relationship between conditions of learning and approaches to teaching that occupies the first section of this chapter. Thereafter, the processes of teaching and teaching techniques are examined in some detail.

But before this is done, it is necessary to recognize that the world in which teachers perform their roles today is different from that in which they performed a generation or two ago. In that world, the teachers' role was primarily about enabling the learners to learn, as we defined it above, and this was normally undertaken by didactic methods. In today's global society, there has been a division of labour within teaching itself. The following list indicates some of the different roles that teachers now perform:

Group 1
- Teacher/Facilitator
- Teaching assistant
- Supervisor
- Trainer/Coach
- Mentor
- Counsellor/advisor
- Administrator
- Assessor

Group 2
- Researcher
- Trainer of teachers/trainers
- Author of learning materials
- Programme/curriculum planners
- Educational policy makers
- Programme administrators
- Programme technical staff
- Consultants and evaluators
- Retailer/marketer

The first group of teaching roles are in direct contact with the learners whereas the second set are one stage removed, with the very last one recognizing that the knowledge-based economy has also produced a knowledge market. It might be claimed now that with the continuing development of e-learning, teaching through video-conferencing, through the World Wide Web, and so on this list could be extended considerably. Indeed, in higher education in Singapore, it is expected that every new course produced will be put 'on-line', and government has given money to ensure that this happens. We shall discuss this in chapter 7. Education has become a very complex and multiskilled business, and these are some of the skills that teachers and trainers need – both in their initial professional preparation and also in their continuing professional development, or in-service training – if they are to be regarded as professionals.

This now has serious implications for teaching itself and since not all these roles can be performed by a single teacher it is not unusual to see team teaching occurring. Team teaching can take a number of different forms: it can be two or more teachers teaching the same class at the same time, at different times on the same course, or that a team of staff produce the learning material and use their different skills in order to transmit that material successfully. We shall return to this latter approach in the chapter on distance learning. However, all forms of team teaching need careful planning in order to be successful, which is also a time-consuming process, especially when courses or modules span more than one academic specialism. In times of financial constraint it is easy to overlook the amount of 'new' time spent in the preparation of teaching and learning.

Not only is collaboration between teachers occurring in the teaching and learning process, but new courses in adult education are being undertaken when the collaboration is between the academic staff and the students. In the University of Tennessee, for instance, a Masters degree in Adult Education is being undertaken entirely in this collaborative manner, in which part of the students' learning process is being undertaken in the collaborative process. Thus it may be seen that teaching and learning actually overlap in the contemporary world rather than being two separate processes.

Conditions of learning and approaches to teaching

In the previous two chapters a number of points have been raised about how adults learn effectively and it is now necessary to draw many of them together and to relate them to various approaches to teaching. Table 5.1 summarizes many of these conclusions.

Whatever links are drawn between the conditions of learning and the approach to teaching it is clear that teachers of adults do not always stand in front of the class and expound the wisdom that they consider the students need to know (see the exercise in Rogers, 1973:82–84). This is not to claim that there is no place for didactic teaching but it does suggest an approach to teaching in which exposition is less significant than it often appeared to be in the education of older children and young adults; the fact that it occurs with children does not necessarily mean that it is either the most efficient or human way of facilitating their learning either! However, it is clear that the teachers of adults, besides having either the relevant knowledge or experience, require certain other characteristics in order to help adults learn, including: knowledge of the educational process, appropriate philosophy and attitudes and teaching and personal skills. Hence, it is rather surprising that the preparation of educators of adults has occupied such an insignificant place in teacher education; but, since this is the topic of a subsequent chapter, no further reference will be made to it here.

Teaching styles and teaching methods

Table 5.1 has not stipulated how teachers should perform their teaching role with adults but it does imply that certain styles of teaching may be more appropriate than others. In most courses preparing individuals to become teachers of adults, considerable emphasis has been placed upon the variety of methods with which teachers should be familiar but much less has been placed on teaching styles. This is a major omission from teacher training since the style that the teacher adopts may play a considerable part in the outcome of the learning. Indeed, it may be even more important than the teaching method adopted. For instance, teachers may say that they are facilitative but their style might actually communicate that they expect learners to reach the outcome that they would have been taught had the session been didactic! There is an old maxim that teaching is about 'truth through personality' and while I do not now subscribe to it entirely, it does communicate the importance of teaching style.

Perhaps the most significant early piece of research that has affected thought about teaching styles has been that developed by Lippett and White (1958) in a project directed by Kurt Lewin in the 1930s. They examined leadership styles of youth leaders in youth clubs with 10-year-old boys in the United States. Basically they noticed three styles of leadership: authoritarian, democratic and *laissez-faire* and discovered that group behaviour tended to be consistent with leadership style. They found that: the authoritarian leaders create a sense of group dependence on the leader, that their presence held the group together and that in their absence there was no work undertaken and the group disintegrates; the *laissez-faire* leadership results in little being done irrespective of whether the leader was present or absent; the democratic leaders achieve group cohesion and harmonious working relationships whether or not they are actually present. However, there are a number of problems in applying these findings to adult groups, or indeed to any other teaching and learning interactions: the subjects were children; the location was a youth club; the task undertaken by the groups was a specific type of craft work. Even so, it may not be without significance that the democratic style of leadership achieved the types of results that it did.

In more recent years, and perhaps more significantly for educators of adults, McGregor's (1960) work has assumed greater importance. This stems from the field of management studies. According to McGregor, there are basically two approaches to managing people which he terms Theory X and Theory Y: the former assumes that average human beings dislike work, needs to be controlled, directed or coerced in order to do what is required and prefer to be directed; the latter commences with the conception of self-motivated adults who seek to fulfil their own human potential. Hence, if teachers start with the perspective of Theory X they

143

Table 5.1 The conditions of adult learning and approaches to teaching

Conditions of adult learning	Approaches to teaching
Learning is a basic human need	Teaching is not essential to learning but may facilitate it
Learning is especially motivated when there is disharmony between an individual's experience and his perception of the world	Teachers and learners need to structure the process of learning together so that it may be relevant to the experience/problem that created the felt need to learn
Adult learners like to participate in the learning process	Teaching methods should be Socratic or facilitative rather than didactic in many learning situations
Adult learners bring their own: • experiences to the learning situations • meaning systems to the learning situation	Teachers should use these experiences as a learning resource Teachers should try to build on the meaning system, rather than seek to be contrary to it, so that students may integrate their new knowledge with their old: methods should be used that enable students to use their previous knowledge as a resource
• needs to the learning situation	Teachers should help students to be aware of the relevance of what they are learning; subject matter will be 'applied' rather than pure: learning will be individualized where possible
Adult learners bring to the learning situation their own: • self-confidence • self-esteem	Teachers need to be empathetic and sensitive to the humanity of the learner at all times and, when appropriate, always anticipate a successful learning outcome Teachers should 'reinforce' all 'correct' knowledge and understanding in order that students are enabled to maintain a high level of self-confidence and self-esteem. Teachers should provide opportunities for adult students to reflect upon 'incorrect' knowledge, so that they can 'correct' it for themselves, where this is possible. Teachers should encourage self-assessment rather than teacher-assessment

• self-perception	Teachers should encourage self-assessment rather than teacher-assessment
Adults learn best when the self is not under threat	Teachers need to create an ethos in which no adult feels threatened or inhibited – this is especially true at the outset of any new course of learning. Cooperation rather than competition should be encouraged
Adult learners need to feel that they are treated as adults	Teachers should not regard themselves as 'the fount of all knowledge' but they should attempt to create and facilitate a teaching and learning engagement between all the participants
Adult learners have developed their own learning styles	Teachers should recognize that different learning styles exist and encourage learners to develop effective and efficient learning. Hence, teachers also need to be flexible and adopt teaching styles relevant to the teaching and learning transaction.
Adult learners have had different educational biographies so they may learn at different speeds	Teachers should encourage adults to learn at their own pace
Adults have developed a crystallized intelligence	Teachers should not be influenced by previous academic record, especially that from initial education
Adults bring different physiological conditions to the learning situation, e.g. declining visual and/or audio accuity, less energy, failing health.	Teachers should ensure that the physical environment in which the teaching and learning occurs is conducive to adult learning

will seek to manipulate the students either by a hard approach of threats or a soft approach of rewards and permissiveness; but teachers who adopt a perspective that derives from Theory Y will be more concerned about the potentiality and growth of the students even though they may vary their approach and teaching method to suit the situation.

Hence, it is evident that the democratic approach in the research of Lippett and White and the Theory Y perspective in McGregor's work are most consistent with the philosophy of this study and with the picture of the educator of adults as seeking to aid adult learning and to develop the full potential of the learner. However, it must be borne in mind that neither of these approaches actually prescribe the manner in which teachers should perform their role, although it does circumscribe the number of methods that might be used. More recently there has been work on teaching styles (see Entwistle, 1981 *inter alia*), although in some of it, especially in relation to schooling, there is a tendency to confuse teaching style and teaching method. Perhaps Kidd summarized the humanistic perspective on teaching adopted in this book, recognizing that there are differences between learners, he pronounced his own decalogue for teachers of adults:

1 Thou shalt never try to make another human being exactly like thyself; one is enough.
2 Thou shalt never judge a person's need, or refuse your consideration, solely because of the trouble he causes.
3 Thou shalt not blame heredity nor the environment in general; people can surmount their environment (or perhaps some of their heredity) [author's addition].
4 Thou shalt never give a person up as hopeless or cast him out.
5 Thou shalt try to help everyone become, on the one hand, sensitive and compassionate and also tough minded.
6 Thou shalt not steal from any person his rightful responsibilities for determining his own conduct and the consequences thereof.
7 Thou shalt honour anyone engaged in the pursuit of learning and serve well and extend the discipline of knowledge and skill about learning which is our common heritage.
8 Thou shalt have no universal remedies nor expect miracles.
9 Thou shalt cherish a sense of humour which may save you from becoming shocked, depressed or complacent.
10 Thou shalt remember the sacredness and dignity of thy calling and, at the same time, 'thou shalt not take thyself too damned seriously'.

(Kidd, 1973:306–307)

Roby Kidd's creed summarizes much of the humanistic philosophy explicit in this discussion. Having examined some of the approaches to teaching, it is now necessary to explore the teaching processes.

It may be seen from Kidd's *Ten Commandments* for an adult educator that they reflect the value of personal relationships in the teaching and learning process. Naturally all relationships are moral ones and we will discuss the morality of teaching a little later in this book, but teaching style is also important to what Goleman (1998) sees as working with emotional intelligence. Emotions are one of our most powerful components and yet it has been a neglected factor in teaching, although we have argued that we learn our emotions and through them as well, often incidentally and pre-consciously, but if we do this, then it is incumbent on teachers that they should be providing the right situations for positive emotions to be learned.

This is most certainly to do with our teaching style – it is about our people skills. We have to provide situations in which learners feel cared for because their being matters, as much as their progress, to the teacher. This sense of care needs to be purveyed to the learners, not only through verbal communication but also through the non-verbal – as Goleman reminds us this is an empathic relationship. But, at the same time, learners still have to own their own learning, so that teachers should never 'take over' the learning task – in modern parlance, learners are stakeholders in the teaching and learning process. Nevertheless, teachers are still concerned about correctness, so that we have to learn the art of being the friendly critic, and so on. Additionally, students must feel that they are being successful, or are going to be successful, in order for them to succeed. Teachers who convey to their students a sense of failure create a self-fulfilling prophecy and so does communicating a sense of success. Belbin and Belbin (1972:167–168) record a discussion with the most successful London trainer of older men to become bus drivers: 'I never mention the word "fail". I always act as though I know they're going to pass'.

Learning is also a risk-taking business since as we learn we question our past knowledge and even our previous attitudes, beliefs, values and emotions so that teachers need to provide a safe environment for risks to be taken. It is crucial to all adult learners that they feel safe and supported as they launch out into the deep and learn new things. There is a growing body of evidence, including a doctoral study by one of my own students (Hesketh, 2003) that shows how students who feel safe and supported get far higher grades than their contemporaries; this study was conducted with black under-privileged students in a Management Studies programme in a South African university. The fact that they are more successful underlines the significance of the human side of teaching.

Consequently, it can be seen that building a relationship with the students is a key to the success in teaching but, more is the pity, in this instrumental age little time is allowed for teachers to do this part of their job properly because it is not seen to have immediate effects. Perhaps it is time for all the people-based professions (nursing is another) to emphasize the human side of what we do and try to show, as Hesketh has done, that the longer term outcomes are actually better if teachers are allowed to work with the emotions of their students.

Teaching style, therefore, is vitally important because it is through our styles, through the way that we manage the teaching and learning process that we can enable more successful learning to take place. Having argued for the importance of teaching style, we will now look at the wide variety of teaching methods that there are and while the following list is not exhaustive, it would be expected that professional teachers would be competent in very many of them.

The processes of teaching

In contrast to initial education, adult education has tended to emphasize the learner and learning more than the teacher and teaching. Traditionally, in initial education teachers and their skills have constituted a subject for discussion but rarely has that discussion sought to be related to the process of learning. Adult education has tended to regard the teacher as an adjunct to learning, often necessary and frequently important, but never as essential to it. Consequently, the process of adult learning has been explored but rarely in relation to adult teaching. Hence the focus of this section is upon the teaching process in adult and continuing education. Four types of teaching were mentioned earlier – didactic, Socratic, facilitative and experiential – and it is necessary to recognize that they are not totally different approaches. Initially, therefore, an oversimplified model of didactic teaching is discussed. Thereafter, the Socratic approach. Finally, the facilitative and emotive approaches to teaching are discussed, and it is recognized that the experiential is most often facilitative. However, it must also be recognized that one of the domains of human being that is learned in every teaching situation is emotion. Emotions are learned in an unintended manner and may be learned consciously or pre-consciously, and it is for this reason, amongst others that the style of teaching is at least as important as the methods chosen.

Didactic teaching

Teaching has traditionally been regarded as the process of making a selection of knowledge, skills, etc. from the cultural milieu, those aspects which 'it is intended that pupils should learn' (Hirst and Peters, 1970:80), and transmitting it to them by the use of some skilled technique. It has been assumed that such rewards as the teacher's approval, good grades in assignments and successful examinations (all forms of conditioning) would ensure that the pupil learned and was, therefore, able to reproduce that selection of culture thereafter.

Figure 5.1, which is very similar to Figure 3.1, locates the teaching process in the wider socio-cultural milieu and it may be seen that the teacher is the agency of transmission of a selection of culture (a curriculum); that selection may have been made by an examination board, an education committee of a profession, or an acknowledged expert in the field, and so on. Students ares expected to learn that which is transmitted to them and to be able to reproduce it, which may equate with the lower order of Gagné's (1977) hierarchy of learning but it is certainly no higher than the middle. In terms of Bloom's (1956) taxonomy of educational objectives – the students may be expected to have understood what was transmitted and, perhaps, be able to apply it but not necessarily to be able to analyse, synthesize or evaluate it. In university education, however, it might be argued that expectations are higher than this, but Hegarty has suggested that legal education may 'easily degenerate into mindless book learning ... any student of university calibre could obtain a comfortable honours degree by doing little more than memorising the set text book in each subject and doing the occasional problem' (1976:81). The extent to which Hegarty's assessment is applicable to all undergraduate courses is another matter, but it is doubtful if that assessment of legal education is unique in this respect.

Not only does the level of learning not necessarily scale the heights of the learning hierarchies but the selection of what is to be learned is made by agencies other than the learner, so that the relevance to the learner of

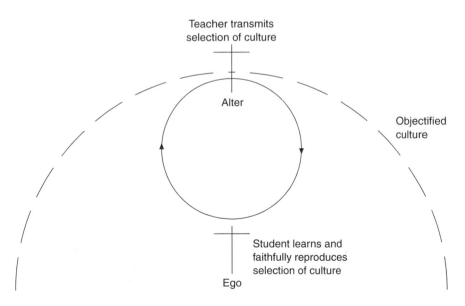

Figure 5.1 A stereotypical picture of teaching.

what is learned may often be reduced to the rather instrumental end of being successful in the assessment procedures, rather than being able to learn and understand something relevant. This approach frequently results in the reproduction of the status quo and while it might be argued that this is no bad thing in initial education, it is much less convincing in the education of adults. Even so, following the philosophy of Freire, even this assertion might be considered dubious!

Is there, then, no place for didactic teaching in the education of adults? Such a claim would be too sweeping, but perhaps its place is less significant than it is generally accorded to be. An exposition can actually transmit knowledge and the students may:

- be encouraged to consider the validity of what has been presented to them;
- be provoked to think;
- have their learning facilitated;
- be motivated to continue their learning, especially if it is superbly presented.

Hence a didactic approach may prove very useful, especially if the students are encouraged to analyse what is transmitted to them, rather than merely reproduce it.

In the past decades, as the theory of the education of adults has developed, vocational education has assumed a greater relevance and it would be fair to say that training might be regarded by some as a form of didactic teaching although many industrial trainers would claim, quite correctly, that they employ a variety of teaching and learning methods. However, didacticism is also the traditional image of training since in many instances employers are only interested in their employees acquiring specific knowledge and skills, which has often resulted in this image. Studies, such as Marsick (1987) and Casner-Lotto and Associates (1988), demonstrate the variety of approaches used in workplace learning, which would certainly deny this traditional image.

A variation on this theme is for teachers to encourage the learners to ask questions, so that they actually initiate the learning process but the teachers still provide the answers. By adopting this approach teachers overcome one of the initial problems of didactic teaching – that it may not start from a diagnostic basis. Yet it is the teachers who still transmit knowledge and expect it to be received and learned by the students who are still the receptacles of knowledge, rather than the 'creators' of it. Frequently during the education of adults, students ask questions that teachers are unable to answer, so that they discover that they can confess their ignorance without losing credibility. Indeed, it is possible to argue that a display of fallibility may help to establish the teacher's position in the group, both as a teacher and as a human being. After all, why should the teacher know everything? No other profession expects its members to be omniscient! Many conscientious teachers, having admitted that they are unable to respond to the question, ask the class if anybody is able to answer. Here the experience and expertise of the group can be put to good use and teachers can learn from the class as well as contribute to the class learning. However, many very conscientious teachers, when confronted with a question that they cannot answer, tell the group that they will go and find out the answer. This they do, and they inform the students on a future occasion. A certain irony emerges in this situation: the student's question has revealed a teacher's ignorance. The teacher is made aware of a learning need and goes and learns in order to provide the students with an answer. Examine closely what has occurred. The students' question facilitated the teacher's learning! But what did the teacher do for the student's learning? The teacher merely made the students more dependent, but the teacher actually became a more independent learner. Two points emerge from this: first, perhaps the teacher should encourage the students to seek an answer as well; second, it is the questioning process that facilitates independent learning and so, perhaps, a good teacher leads students from question to question rather than from answer to answer. After all, that is how the learning need becomes apparent in children, as it has been argued in earlier chapters, and it is also a way that effective learning may be facilitated with adults.

Socratic teaching

This method introduces questioning into the teaching and learning process; it consists of the teacher directing a logical sequence of questions at the learners, so that they are enabled to respond and to express the knowledge that they have, but which they might never have crystallized in their own mind. However, unless teachers are actually skilful in the use of questions and also perceptive in responding to the students, this approach is still likely to result in an expression of knowledge reflecting the accepted body of cultural knowledge and, therefore, a type of conformity. This method assumes that the learners have internalized a great deal of cultural knowledge incidentally and this approach brings the answers to conscious awareness. This is part of the process of externalizing depicted in Figure 1.2. However, conformity to and expression of the established body of knowledge is by no means wrong, and thus it is a useful method to employ, especially in teaching adults since it utilizes both their store of knowledge and their experience of life, which are essential learning resources in the education of adults. However, it must also be noted that if this method is used with great skill it can and does help the learners 'create' rather than reproduce knowledge. Another advantage to its use is that the learners are always actively involved in the learning process.

A learning and teaching cycle

The above discussion indicates that the teacher often plays the role of an agent in the transmission of the culture of a society in the formal educational process, even in the education of adults. However, it is clear that Figure 5.1 does not really discuss the actual process of teaching and learning, so that it is now important to draw together some of the conclusions about adult learning and these observations on teacher-centred teaching. Figure 5.2 suggests a learning and teaching cycle in which these are combined.

It may be seen in Figure 5.2 that teachers are agents transmitting a selection of culture to the learner(s) and, at the same time, they may have devised methods whereby the students have the opportunity to reflect on it through a discussion group, tutorial or written assignment, etc. Thus the process of reflection may be regarded as an integral part of the learning and teaching cycle. However, it must be borne in mind that unless the opportunity for reflection on the knowledge and ideas that are presented by the teacher occurs individually, the decision that a person reaches may

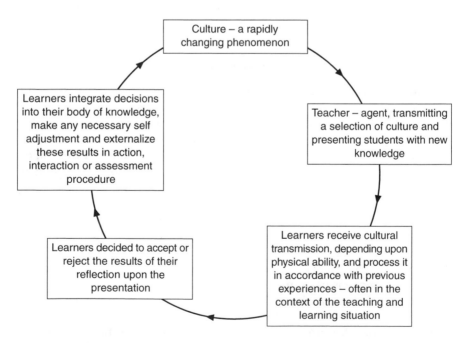

Figure 5.2 A learning and teaching cycle.

be influenced by the dynamics of the learning group, and considerable research exists to show that group pressure results in conformity in many situations (e.g. Krech *et al.*, 1962:507–515).

However, the process of selecting that aspect of culture to be transmitted is itself an important one, but it is sometimes omitted as a phase in these considerations. Some teachers merely take for granted, without recognizing their power in the process, that they will seek to transmit all the knowledge, etc. that the examination board of syllabus specifies. Yet if teachers see themselves as agents for the transmission of cultural knowledge, it may be that they should become more active agents in discussing with the learners what they should transmit. This should also be determined by the amount of knowledge and understanding that the students bring to the teaching and learning situation. It is, therefore, incumbent upon teachers to diagnose the students' level of knowledge and, thereby, their learning needs, before actually endeavouring to teach anything at all. Diagnosis is, consequently, an intrinsic element in the selection of knowledge to be transmitted and this is especially significant with adults since they bring to their learning a considerable amount of previous knowledge and skill, etc. That adults do bring such resources to their learning has led some adult educators to regard themselves as facilitators of learning rather than teachers in the traditional sense discussed here.

Facilitative teaching

Teachers of adults may not always want to employ teacher-centred techniques in the performance of their role. They may seek to create an awareness of a specific learning need in the student; to confront students with a problem requiring a solution; to provide the students with an experience and encourage reflection on it. In all of these instances the outcome of the activity should be that learning has occurred, but teachers have performed their role differently: they have facilitated learning. Hence, it is possible to reconstruct the experiential learning cycle discussed in chapter 3 in order to incorporate the teacher's role in the process.

It may be seen from Figure 5.3 that teachers can create the situation in which the learning cycle is activated and, additionally, they may help in the process of observing or reflecting. But should they actually influence the process in this way? Dewey has suggested that, with children, the teacher should be involved:

> Sometimes teachers seem to be afraid even to make suggestions to members of the group as to what they should do. I have heard of cases in which children are surrounded with objects and materials and then left entirely to themselves, teachers being loathe to

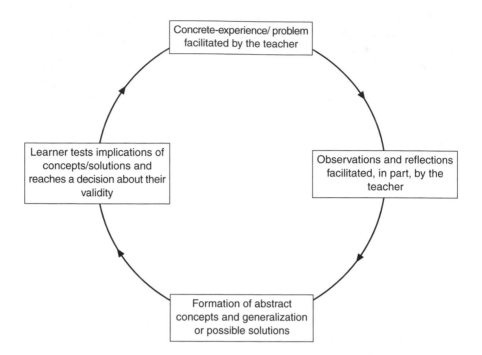

Figure 5.3 A facilitative learning and teaching cycle.

suggest even what might be done with the materials lest freedom
be impinged upon.

(Dewey, 1938:71)

Dewey went on to warn of the opposite extreme: of teachers who abuse
their office and who channel children's work along the paths that suit the
teachers' purposes rather than those of the children themselves. He maintained that teachers should be intelligently aware of the capacities, needs
and past experiences of those under instruction, so that they may assist
them in creating a cooperative learning exercise. Obviously Dewey was
writing about children learning in a progressive educational environment
but the same observations are relevant to the education of adults. Indeed,
it might be recalled that McKenzie (1979) recognized the similarities
between progressive education and andragogy.

Thus it may be seen that the teacher's role may be that of facilitator
and/or guide, but not in this instance that of the director of the learning
process, since that would detract from the adult's own autonomy and
independence. (See Williams, 1980 for a practical outworking of some of
the ideas presented here, but see Jarvis, 1992 for a discussion about the
concepts of self-direction and autonomy.) Thus the facilitator is one who

assists in the students' learning, even to the extent of providing or creating the environment in which that learning may occur, but is never one who dictates the outcome of the experience. Consequently, it would be impossible for a facilitator to set behavioural objectives for any learning experience that may be created, but they should be expressive ones. Because the learning experience is open-ended, facilitation is often a difficult role to play since the learners may reach conclusions other than those held by facilitators but the latter should not seek to impose their opinions on the learners.

It should be noted in Figures 5.2 and 5.3 that teachers have a role in the early stages of the teaching and learning cycle but that, since they cannot make any individual learn and since one of the aims of adult education is the creation of the autonomous learner, teachers play little part in the final stages. Even in distance learning, where adults meet with tutors for an occasional tutorial after having learned from the teaching material, the teaching and learning cycle is only recreated with the students bringing more of their own learning from the initial stages. However, it might be objected that even in these two diagrams the teachers' involvement in the learning process, even as facilitator, inhibits the students' freedom to learn. But, it may be asked, what is freedom in this context? Boud and Bridge (1974:6), for instance, distinguish four types of freedom: pace, choice, method and content. By this they mean that students should be free to work at their own speed, choose to study particular aspects of a course, adopt whatever learning style suits them best and be free to choose what to learn. Boud *et al.* (1975:18) modified this slightly and suggested that the four types of freedom are: pace, method, content and assessment. The extent to which any of these is achievable in any institutionalized course of study is open to question; the expectations of the educational organization and the influence of the teachers are never completely overcome. It is doubtful whether there can be complete freedom in any type of institutionalized learning – see Candy (1991) and Jarvis (1992) for a full discussion.

Clearly the traditional teaching role does not seem to fit easily into the teaching and learning process for adults if these freedoms are considered to be an important element in it since class teaching seems to recede into the background. Indeed, one of the outcomes appears to be an individualized or small group approach in which the participants are engaged in the pursuit of knowledge that is relevant to their own problems or experiences. Certainly, the class as a whole is perhaps a little less significant; small group learning is frequently undertaken in adult education and individualized learning has been developed in both adult basic education and in higher education. Considerable research has been conducted into individualized learning and although it appears to have an idealistic perspective, Crane noted that:

Unexpectedly perhaps, in view of the persuasive role played by committed Romantics in decrying the old and urging a renewed concern for the individual and individual differences, it was largely men with behaviourist training and outlook who actually produced innovations of value.

(Crane, 1982:33)

Certainly the group/class versus the individual is one of the problems that emerges logically from any analysis of this type of teaching and learning. Students' learning should be regarded as their own, so the teaching and learning cycle must ultimately relate to individuals, although this does not preclude teachers interacting with the learners during the learning.

Finally, it has to be recognized that a great deal of teaching is providing a secondary experience through which learners acquire cognitive knowledge consciously and, perhaps, emotions pre-consciously. The situation of learning is the classroom, something far removed from the reality of practice and daily living. Consequently, there has been an increasing emphasis on having a primary experience – entering a practice-situation – and so experiential teaching is becoming more popular. In professional preparation we are finding more work-based experiences provided, so that learners might actually learn in the workplace. In addition, role play and simulations are being devised so that learners can, at least, experience something of what it is actually like to be in a 'real' situation. It is not surprising, therefore, that we are gradually beginning to see such approaches as problem-based learning and, even, work-based learning being introduced.

The focus of this section has been upon the teaching process and four types of teaching have been discussed: didactic, Socratic, facilitative and experiential. These may be seen as being either teacher-centred or student-centred, and it has been suggested that those approaches that are extremely teacher-centred may be inappropriate for some education of adults. Having looked at the broad approaches to teaching, it is now necessary to look at specific methods.

Teaching methods

It is impossible in the space available in this section to elaborate adequately upon every aspect of each teaching method that can be employed in the education of adults. Indeed, since the first edition of this book there are been many books on teaching in all types of education, e.g Hargreaves, (2003) in school education; Light and Cox (2001) in higher education; Jarvis (2002) as a more general book. Consequently, it is intended only to highlight the variety of methods that can be used. Since there is such a wide range it is initially necessary to classify them for the purposes of discussion. Chadwick (personal communication) has suggested that one approach would be to consider the three modes of search, interactive and presentational. While this is a very attractive form of classification, it might be more consistent here if the division between tutor-centred and student-centred approaches is maintained. However, it must be borne in mind that a variety of methods might be employed in any single teaching and learning process and that it might be more stimulating to the learner if such an approach were to be adopted.

Teacher-centred methods

Before individual methods are itemized, it is necessary to recognize that tutors may lead a session and still adopt two basically different approaches: be didactic and teach the subject in the traditional method of providing the information, or be Socratic and seek to elicit the information from the students by careful questioning. The art of questioning is a technique that teachers should acquire, so that they are aware of how to gain the most effective response from the learners; but, frequently, it appears to be assumed that this is a skill that teachers have either naturally or as a result of their socialization process. However, this assumption may be false.

Seven frequently employed teacher-centred methods are discussed in this subsection: demonstration, guided discussion, controlled discussion, lecture-discussion, lecture/talk/speech, mentoring and the tutorial.

The demonstration

This is one of the most frequent approaches to skills teaching. The teacher shows the student(s) how a specific procedure is undertaken whom they are expected to emulate. However, the demonstrator is usually very skilled so that the performance appears easy and effortless. But if the students are unable to repeat the same skill with the same fluency they may become discouraged. Perhaps this is because teachers may not have analysed their own techniques sufficiently in order to be aware of all the minutiae of correct procedures that combine to produce effortless action, or because they wish to be role models for students and then to coach them.

In addition, teachers may have acquired tacit knowledge (Polanyi, 1967) which they cannot articulate. Practical knowledge is extremely complex and Nyiri, for instance, suggests that it has to be 'mined out of their heads painstakingly, one jewel at a time' (1988:21). (See also Baskett and Marsick, 1992 for an edited volume which endeavours to outline a number of these significant issues.) Belbin and Belbin (1972:44–45) suggest that if a skill is broken down into a number of discrete stages and that in both the demonstration and in the subsequent practice sessions each sequence is initially performed slowly, it is possible for learners to acquire new skills fairly rapidly. They recognize that 'it takes time for someone who hitherto has been pressed toward greater speed, to accept that a really slow performance is ... required' (ibid.).

Additionally, there is a possible danger in teachers being seen as role models transmitting their own imperfect skills to their students, which could prevent them learning even better ways because they may not have the opportunity to be exposed to an even more accurate performance of the skill that they are endeavouring to acquire.

Guided discussion

This approach has been separated from the more general discussion techniques because it is one of the approaches that epitomizes the Socratic method: it is sometimes called step-by-step discussion. In this approach the teacher has a carefully prepared sequence of questions that are directed towards the end of drawing from the learners the knowledge that they have implicitly but which they may not have articulated, crystallized or related to a wider theoretical perspective. It is a method that can be employed to elicit from students their own understanding of experiences that they have undergone. For instance, a teacher of theory may endeavour to draw from the students their understanding of some elements of a practical work experience in which they have already participated as part of their vocational education. However, the teacher should be careful not to artificialize the approach by being inflexible, since the students' responses may actually direct the discussion along paths other than those planned. If this is so, it might be wise for the teacher to follow the students' lead and redirect the questions, although there are times when the teacher has to ensure that the steps prepared should be followed. While this method sometimes appears simple and easy to prepare, it is one that requires confidence in the teacher as well as a great deal of knowledge and preparation.

Controlled discussion

By contrast to guided discussion, controlled discussion is quite didactic and much closer to the next method to be examined. In this approach the teacher sets the theme for the class and begins to talk about it, but the students are encouraged to contribute to the learning process or to elicit information. However, the teacher is still at the centre of the scene to whom most of the questions or comments are directed. One of the problems in this approach is that there is a tendency for only the dominant or the confident to interject so that the learning needs of the silent members of the group may not be met. If teachers want the learners to address each other they must ensure that the environment is arranged so that there is no dominant seat, etc. and that the learners have eye contact with each other. Seating must be arranged in a circular formation (with or without desks). It is difficult sometimes for teachers to change the seating arrangements of a room, especially if they arrive after many of the students, and so it is often wise to ask a caretaker to have the room arranged in the required manner in advance. If this is impossible, it is useful to explain to adult students why the room should be rearranged and, in the majority of instances, they will undertake the task themselves.

Lecture-discussion

The lecture-discussion is very similar to the previous method mentioned but it may assume a different form: a short lecture/address followed by discussion. Once again, however, it is self-evident that the teacher controls both the learning process and its content. By contrast to the previous method, the teacher has a larger initial input rather than merely focusing on the topic to be discussed, so the discussion may tend to develop or to demonstrate the weaknesses in the position taken in the lecture. It is worth remembering that unless the content of the lecture is controversial or provocative then the discussion may not be particularly valuable since it may merely rehearse the arguments previously presented.

All forms of discussion require careful preparation on the part of the teacher and a willingness to endure silence by the class especially during the early part of the discussion. It is a common failing to try to prompt the class to talk by too much early tutor intervention. Confident and talkative adults are, consequently, useful allies during early phases of a discussion session, but then it may be necessary for the teacher to draw other people into the debate and help the talkative members of the group to contribute a little less. It is, however, part of the human process that the teacher should facilitate both of these aspects without injuring the self-esteem of any of the class members, so that it is often unwise to ask individuals directly either to participate or to contribute a little less to the discussion. Hence, the social skills of the teacher are as important to the teaching and learning process as are knowledge and teaching techniques (Legge, 1971a).

Lecture

Lecturing is perhaps the most frequently employed teaching technique despite all the criticisms that have been levelled against it at various times. Bergevin et al. define the speech, or lecture, as 'a carefully prepared oral presentation of a subject by a qualified person' (1963:157). However, many students know to their cost that lectures are not necessarily carefully

prepared on all occasions, nor is the presentation always given by a qualified person. Hence, this is more of a description of an ideal type and it
may be more accurately defined as 'an oral presentation of a subject',
although this still leaves the definition of 'subject' open to question. Thus
far the distinction between lecture, speech and talk has not been raised,
but it is significant to note that Beard (1976) discusses the lecture in her
work on higher education but neither Bergevin et al. (1963) nor Legge
(1971a) concentrate upon it a great deal, preferring to use the other
terms, but they are teachers of adults. This reflects a little of the conceptual problems of chapter 2, but higher education has traditionally been
discussed separately to the education of adults, despite the fact that students in higher education are adults. This separation has been to the
detriment of higher education. Bergevin et al. clearly regard the speech as
a rather formal presentation while Legge's orientation towards non-
examinable liberal adult education enabled him to focus upon the less
formal concept of the 'talk'.

Many criticisms have been levelled at this particular approach to teaching but, despite these, nearly all teachers continue to use the lecture
method. Perhaps it is important to put the lecture in perspective and
Bligh summarized the research on this topic when he argued that:

> (1) with the exception of programmed learning, the lecture is as
> effective as any other method of transmitting information, but not
> more effective; (2) most lectures are not as effective as more
> active methods for the promotion of thought; and (3) changing
> student attitudes should not normally be the major objective of
> the lecture.
>
> (Bligh, 1971:4)

Thus it may be seen that only in the transmission of information is the
lecture as effective as other methods of teaching and then it must be
borne in mind that most of this research was not conducted with adult students. However, Davies (1971:163) claimed that the lecture is a useful
teaching method with less able adult students. Yet adult basic education
has tended not to employ this method, so that this raises questions about
his claim. The lecture is no more effective than a variety of other teaching
techniques, why is it so frequently employed? This question certainly
requires consideration.

It might be argued that since many educators of adults are not actually
trained to perform the teaching role they do not have evidence of the
effectiveness of other approaches, or that they do not know how to teach
apart from the lecture, or that they do not have the confidence to attempt
other approaches. This may be an argument for introducing more teacher
training into the education of adults, a point that will be developed in a

subsequent chapter. Additionally, it is clear that because students are familiar with this approach to teaching, or because it means that some of them may be passive learners, they prefer this approach. But these may be quite superficial and even wrong reasons: students may put pressure on a teacher to give a lecture because they may not want to reveal their level of knowledge or understanding of a topic and they may feel threatened if they think that their lack of comprehension will become apparent for others to see. Teachers, or at least some tutors, may also obtain satisfaction from having given a 'good' performance, or they may simply like it because it enables them to control the content of the session in such a way as to ensure that any gaps in their own knowledge may not become apparent – which might occur if the students directed the session. The maxim 'if you don't know a subject well lecture it' is perhaps a reflection of a teacher's sense of insecurity, especially before a class of adults, and the lecture is perhaps a novice's approach to teaching, despite the fact that many lecturers are not novice lecturers. Programme planners also like the lecture method because of the ease of timetabling and room planning.

In addition, it might be argued that the lecture can be an instrument of motivation and it may be true that the superb lecture may actually produce this result; but, perhaps, few teachers actually possess such oratorial skills, and so Legge's ironic comment that 'the really hopeless teacher, i.e. the one who fails to communicate at all, drives the good student to the library to do the work for himself' (1971a:57) may be closer to the real situation! Lectures, it has been claimed (e.g. Beard, 1976:101; Legge, 1971a), may be economical in teaching many students at the same time and ensuring that the whole syllabus is covered. While there may be some truth in these claims, it must be recognized that covering the syllabus without ensuring that the students learn it is far from efficient (Bligh, 1971:3) and, since there is evidence to show that the level of concentration varies at different phases of the lecture (Legge, 1971a), it is difficult to ensure that learning actually occurs during the presentation. Additionally, individual learning needs may not be catered for and unless the learners have an opportunity to question the lecturer they may never actually interact with the speaker. Even if they are provided with the time to raise queries, individual students may not do so because they may not wish to reveal their ignorance or to hinder the remainder of the group. If a student does interrupt the speaker with questions, the rest of the class may become frustrated while they are answered. This is a dilemma that is intrinsic to the lecture method and it appears to have no resolution that would result in effective learning from every participant. The lecturer may seek to resolve the problems by not taking any questions but this may result in reduced learning efficiency. But even if questions occur they may interrupt the thought processes of other learners, who may then lose the flow of ideas with which they were grappling. Thus it may be seen that many unresolved problems surround this approach.

Where the lecture method is employed there are a number of errors in techniques that should be avoided: conscientious lecturers may prepare too much material for the time available but still endeavour to complete the self-appointed task by speeding up the presentation, so that they actually deliver all the content but to the detriment of the learner. Hence, out of the best intentions the lecturer may hinder rather than help learning. Additionally, lecturers may be bound to notes, even to reading them, so that little eye contact is achieved with the class which results in teachers being unable to detect and respond to any of the students' manifest learning needs. Hence, it may be wise for teachers to reduce the volume of notes, even to headings, sub-headings and references, in order to ensure that they have both contact and fluency of delivery. This is one of the reasons why PowerPoint presentations might be useful, although we will return to these later in the chapter. In a similar manner teachers may wish to illustrate a point by writing on the blackboard, but if they continue to speak whilst they have their back to the class some adult learners, especially those with deficient hearing, may be unable to follow every word. This is also true when a lecturer, who is not bound to notes, wanders around the room while speaking. Since the lecture has to be prepared before its presentation, it may not always be sufficiently appropriate or relevant to the learning needs of all the students and it may prove difficult for the lecturer to adjust the content of the presentation to the needs of the learners during the actual lecture.

Finally, the lecture may not provide sufficient opportunity for the adult students to remember and internalize all the ideas presented, neither may they always have the opportunity to reflect upon the knowledge transmitted after the presentation. Hence, it is useful to provide the opportunity for group discussion or question and answer during the session, or for a handout to be distributed at the end of the session, in order to help adult students memorize ideas, etc. Other forms of audio-visual stimuli may also be useful in helping students to recall the information and ideas with which they have been presented.

Having raised a number of critical points about the lecture, it is a useful teaching tool, especially when it is well used, but only for the transmission of knowledge. It should perhaps be employed a little less frequently than it is at present and used only by those trained in its use rather than it being the basic technique used by those who are employed to transmit ideas to others.

Mentoring

There are different interpretations of mentoring although it is clearly a significant teaching method in contemporary education and training.

In his excellent book on mentoring Daloz (1986:215–235) suggests some of the major things that good mentors do in the situations of mentoring adult students: support, challenge and provide a vision. Each of these is subdivided into a number of different functions:

- Support – listening, providing structure, expressing positive expectations, sharing ourselves, making it special.
- Challenge – setting tasks, engaging in discussion, heating up dichotomies, constructing hypotheses, setting high standards.
- Vision – modelling, keeping tradition, offering a map, suggesting new language, providing a mirror.

In a sense, in these instances, the role of the mentor is to help the protégés to reflect on their practice, to learn from their experiences and to improve so that they might gain more expertise. In mentoring, this is done through an in-depth relationship, i.e. a primary experience. Indeed, it is the relationship that makes mentorship so important – not just to professional practice but to life itself. It is here that the mentor gains from the relationship – but the mentee should gain as much.

Murray (1991:5), however, points out that there are two schools of thought about mentoring: one suggests that it can be structured or facilitated, while the other maintains that it can only happen when the 'chemistry' between the two people is right. However, these are not automatically exclusive, since a facilitated relationship might actually develop into one where the chemistry appears to be right for the relationship to continue and to deepen. Clearly, in education and training, structured or facilitated mentoring is called for; but this is not something that can just be turned on and off with the passing of every two-month module, etc. This has already been discovered in nursing when, as Barlow (1991) reported, short-term mentorship did not seem appropriate for clinical practice with students. Indeed, these mentors were often new staff nurses who would no doubt have benefited from being mentored themselves.

During studentship and early years of practice, however, beginners might benefit from having a mentor, which might be performed by the personal tutor or a senior colleague – especially if the individual is acknowledged to be concerned about excellence in practice. Mentorship might also be facilitated for junior qualified staff, in the way that Murray indicates. She records a top level executive as saying:

> I'm always mentoring, both formally and informally. My role is to help my subordinates make decisions. I let them bounce ideas off me and I give my input. But ultimately, I want them to make decisions. If I were making all the decisions for them, I wouldn't need them, would I? So taking on what you call an 'additional

protégé' is no great hardship for me in terms of time. It's what I do anyway.

(Murray, 1991:58)

Elsewhere, she cites a mentor from AT&T Laboratories who claims that 'having a protégé from a different department helps her to bring an objectivity to the relationship that a supervisor might not have' (ibid:61).

If the chemistry is right, however, it is the relationship which is important in mentoring – in Buber's (1959) words, it is an I–Thou relationship. But he takes it even further in his characterization of the educative relationship:

> I have characterized the relationship of the genuine educator to his pupil as being a relationship of this kind. In order to help the realisation of the best potentialities in the pupil's life, the teacher must really *mean* him as the definite person he is in his potentiality and his actuality; more precisely, he must not know him as the mere sum of qualities, strivings and inhibitions, he must be aware of him as a whole being and affirm him in his wholeness. But he can only do this if he meets him again and again as his partner in a bipolar situation.
>
> (Buber, 1959:131–132; emphasis in original)

Mentoring, then, may be seen in a variety of different ways and in all of them it is in a one-to-one situation, where the mentor seeks to assist the learners to reflect upon their practice and improve it.

The tutorial

This teaching method is more likely to occur in the formal system of education rather than in liberal adult education. However, it might be possible to classify some small classes in the latter as group tutorials. In addition, it must be remembered that in the university extension tradition a three-year course was referred to as a tutorial. But the normal use of the word refers to a teaching and learning method and, according to Davies (1971:167–168), there are three basic types: supervision, group and practical. The first type involves a student and a tutor and the former is often expected to read a prepared piece of work to the latter and then to defend the argument in the ensuing discussion. This is quite normal practice at Oxford and Cambridge universities, but since it is labour-intensive it is not so widely practised elsewhere. Another similar use of this type of tutorial is for the student and tutor to meet after the latter has marked an assignment by the student and then the student may seek to clarify an argument or challenge the tutor's assessment grade, while the tutor may

164

seek to explain comments, point out ways in which the work might have been improved and, even, to defend the grade that has been awarded. By contrast, group tutorials employ one tutor to a number of students. Davies (1971:134–135) argues that the optimum number in the group depends on the ability of the tutor rather than a figure beyond which the group cannot function. Nevertheless, he suggests that six or seven is probably sufficient because of the number of possible relationships that can exist between the students. Practical tutorials may be either individual or group and are often based in a laboratory, gymnasium, workplace, etc. In all of these tutorials, the tutor's role may be either didactic or Socratic, although it may result in a more effective tutorial if the latter approach is adopted. Apart from teaching style, it must also be stressed that the tutorial requires a tutor who is trained and sensitive in human relationships, and in the group tutorial the tutor should have some understanding of the group dynamics, or else the tutorial may fail as a teaching method.

Thus far all the teaching methods examined have been tutor-centred, but in the education of adults the tutor should play a less dominant role than that generally assumed by the teacher, so that it is now necessary to discuss these teaching methods in which the tutor also acts as facilitator.

Student-centred group methods

In this section student-centred teaching methods are considered, demonstrating throughout the discussion that since the students referred to here are adults each brings to the teaching and learning situation a vast and unique experience of life. This is a major resource since they have knowledge, reflections on their experiences and an interpretation of meaning and purpose of life for them. Peer teaching is not, therefore, necessarily 'the blind leading the blind' as some people have claimed, since it can be an approach that capitalizes on the resources of the learners themselves, although it has to be borne in mind that there may be technical knowledge, etc. that none of the members of a group possesses and then the teacher may have a more didactic role. Generally, however, in student-centred teaching the teacher is a facilitator of the learning rather than a source of knowledge, and whilst responsible for creating the learning situation, teachers do not control the learning outcomes. Indeed, if they ever do this, they may actually be involved in indoctrination rather than education.

There are many different methods of teaching that might have been incorporated in this section, but to discuss them all in detail would require a whole book, so seventeen different approaches have been selected here because they are frequently used, or have the potential for future use. Even so, the list does not purport to be exhaustive, but it is: brainstorming; buzz-groups; debate; fishbowl; group discussion; interview;

listening and observing; panel; problem-based learning; projects and case studies; role play, simulation and gaming; seminar; snowballing; therapy groups; visits and study tours; workshops; work-based learning.

Brainstorming

Bergevin *et al.* call this an 'idea inventory' (1963:195–196). It is an intensive discussion situation in which the quantity of ideas produced, or potential solutions offered to a problem, is more important than the quality. All the points made by the participants are recorded over the period of time mutually agreed by the group for the brainstorming to operate. No group member may criticize any idea or suggested solution during this initial period, irrespective of how strange or ludicrous it might appear, since this might create inhibitions in the learners contributing to the inventory. At the close of the agreed period, the group is free to analyse the points raised and to arrive at a consensus, if possible, about potential courses of action or solutions to the problem under scrutiny. Clearly this approach is an aid to creative thinking in decision making or problem solving but Davies reported one study that raises questions about the effectiveness of this method since, it is claimed, the notion of expressing 'all ideas may have a deleterious effect on the group members' (1971:170). By contrast, he reports another in which many good quality ideas were produced, suggesting that some of the claims made for it are valid. The construction of a list of ideas, or possible solutions, may be seen as the initial stage in the facilitative learning and teaching cycle (Figure 5.3), and the next phase in the process is that of observing and reflecting upon the outcome of the first one. Since this is true of many of the methods discussed in this section no further reference is made to the theoretical perspectives outlined initially.

Buzz-groups

In many ways these are similar to the previous method, but in this approach smaller groups, usually between two and six members, are used for a short period of time during the process of a lesson in order to discuss a particular item or topic. Small groups encourage participation by all members of the class, and may help in the process of reflection. It is often a useful technique to use in conjunction with a lecture, especially to help divide the session and retain student concentration.

Debate

This is a more formal approach to teaching and learning and one that is not used so frequently in adult education although it is often regarded by students in higher education as an enjoyable leisure time pursuit. Nevertheless, Legge (1971b:87) claimed that the debate is a useful method of presenting students with sharply contrasting viewpoints and demonstrating how these different opinions can be analysed and assessed. In addition, he pointed out that because the debate is a staged performance it provides certain protection for the point of view expressed by the participants, even though there may be quite fierce denunciation of it. Even so, Legge suggested that opinions may be modified as a result of reflecting upon the arguments presented during the performance.

Fishbowl

The object of this method is to get as many people in the group as possible to participate and discuss their views on a given subject. It can be used in a variety of settings, although it is best used when the room is large enough to have a circle of chairs sufficiently large to get all the members of the group in one compact circle. At the same time, if there are too many in the group it is not a very useful method, and so it should be restricted to classes under about twenty students, who can sit in the circle. There is then a small inner circle of chairs in which the individuals involved in the discussion sit. Those who sit in the outer circle must remain silent.

The idea of this approach is to get two or three members of a class discussing a proposition and they sit in the inner circle, with the remainder in the large outer circle. Once the discussion is underway, any member of the outer circle who wishes to participate in the discussion can do so by replacing a member of the inner circle. This is usually done by touching the shoulder of one of the inner group when that person is not speaking (!), replacing that person and participating in the discussion. There can be any number of moves between the inner and outer circle with individuals coming into the inner circle as many times as they wish – but inner circle participants must concede their place if they are not speaking when a member of the outer group wishes to replace them.

It is possible for the teachers to join in this discussion if necessary, although it may be that teachers do so early on to encourage others to participate, although they can do so later if they wish to redirect the discussion in specific directions. It is a useful discussion tool that allows as many people to participate as wish to while everybody is sufficiently close to the process to follow the debate.

It is often useful to put a time limit on the fishbowl – say about half of the session – so that it gives time afterwards for the class to consider and write up some of the points that they have gained from the discussion. It may be useful for the group to list the main points of the discussion in some form of feedback before they write it up.

Group discussion

Discussion reoccurs on the list because it is one of the most frequently employed teaching methods in the education of adults. Many aspects of group discussion exist, all of which could have been covered separately. Bligh mentions *free-group discussion*, which he defines as 'a learning situation in which the topic and direction are controlled by the student-group' (1971:126) and which the teacher may, or may not, observe. He suggests that this is a useful method in which attitude change may be produced in the participants. It may also enhance human relations, self-awareness and create a willingness to consider new ideas. But if the group fails to function smoothly these positive gains may not be achieved and problems of human relations, etc. may arise, which the teacher should not ignore. In contrast to this, there is *problem-centred discussion*, in which the group has a task to perform, which may have been set by the tutor. The outcome of this approach may be enhanced analytical thinking, ability to make decisions and to evaluate them.

Bergevin *et al.* (1963:95) claim that a good discussion topic should meet four criteria, it must: interest all group members; be possible for participants to acquire sufficient information to discuss it meaningfully; be clearly worded and understood; suggest alternative points of view. These criteria are a useful guide since adult students may opt out of the discussion if it is not of interest or relevance to them, or if they do not think that they have anything to contribute to or learn from the discussion. Hence, it is important for the teacher to pick discussion topics with care and maybe to do so in conjunction with the students. Although discussion groups are frequently organized in adult teaching there are a number of weaknesses in the approach: the topic may not be suitable or relevant; the end-product may not be regarded as useful; the technique relies heavily on the ability of the participants to articulate and to listen to each other; dominant personalities tend to come to the fore and quiet people remain passive. By contrast, there are a number of strengths in this method: it encourages learners to accept responsibility for their own learning; it facilitates group sharing; it assists individuals to develop a sense of teamwork; it helps people develop a sense of self-confidence. Legge claims that many 'of the weaknesses of discussion as an aid to learning . . . result from the failure of the teacher to use the method with skill and the failure of the students to take the role of good discussion group members' (1971a:78). Hence, it is incumbent upon teachers to insure that they understand the technique and are aware of group dynamics, so that they are able to help students prepare for the role that they play and to understand the reasons why this method is used in adult teaching. Perhaps teachers are less prone to inform students about why specific teaching methods are being used than they ought to be, especially since the students are adults.

In recent years the discussion group has become a favourite teaching method for a number of reasons, including the fact that teachers realize the expertise of the adult learners with whom they are working, but this brings a danger; if the discussion group is used too often or unimaginably then students can be heard to mutter: 'Not groups again!' Overuse of this, as of any method, is detrimental to the teaching and learning process.

Interview

The interview, sometimes called a witness session, is not employed quite so frequently within the education of adults as it might be, but it is a technique with considerable potentiality. In this instance, the resource person is the subject to be interviewed, so both the topic and often some of the questions are prepared in advance. However, it is not a scripted exercise since this would result in an artificial situation. The aim of the technique is for the interviewer to elicit information from the resource person by means of the questions that the learners want answered. Hence, the students often prepare the questions for, and submit them to, the interviewer in advance, so that the session is relevant to their interests and learning needs. This approach may help clarify issues, provide information, explore and analyse problems and even to stimulate an interest in a topic.

Advantages of the use of this method include: it helps the resource person to communicate knowledge without having to present a lecture; it helps to articulate an idea in response to direct and relevant questions; it is relatively easy to employ; it helps the less dominant members of the group because they are enabled to submit their questions before the session. It is a technique that might be used more often when visiting specialists are not trained educators, but it must be borne in mind that the resource person need not be a visitor and it might even be one of the members of the class who has specific specialist knowledge that the remainder of the group consider relevant or interesting to them. However, the interview does not allow for detailed presentation of an argument and much of the success of the session depends upon the skill of the interviewer. If the latter talks too much, is unable to modify his approach or cannot stimulate the learners, then the interview may fail through no fault of the resource person.

Listening and observing

This is a group technique that is designed to promote active listening and observing during a lecture, speech or film, etc. Each group, or each person in a group, is given a specific task to undertake, e.g. one group may be given the job of listening for bias during a lecture while another is expected to assess the relevance of the presentation for a specific category of learners. Once the presentation is complete the group members confer amongst themselves and reach decisions that are then reported back to a plenary session. Plenary sessions are themselves teaching and learning periods and, in some instances, they are similar to what Bergevin *et al.* (1963:83) call a forum. Listening and observing has the advantages of encouraging active listening or active observation and then of helping students crystallize their ideas about the presentation, but it may have the disadvantage of the students missing other elements of the presentation because they have concentrated upon the task that they undertook to the exclusion of all else.

Panel

Like the interview the panel can utilize both the experience and expertise of visitors to the group or it may use the class members themselves. The panel may be established with a number of slightly different approaches: each member can deliver a short address to the whole group and at the end of three or four talks there can be a period of questions and answers; the panel members can discuss aloud a specific topic for a specified length of time while the class listens to their deliberations and then the class may be invited to raise questions; the discussion between panel members might occupy the whole time; a panel might be set up merely to respond to the questions of the class, without an initial input or stimulus, but, in this instance, a considerable amount of preparation is necessary beforehand in order to ensure that the questions are forthcoming. The panel technique may be used in order to present opposing views on a topic and to create a wider understanding of the subject. As a method, it is useful in stimulating interest and demonstrating to a class the validity of opposing perspectives. By contrast, it has a number of difficulties: the chairperson needs to be proficient in the arts of chairing; the class might have to undertake considerable preparation beforehand in order to familiarize themselves with the complexities of some of the arguments; class members should have sufficient confidence to pose questions, since there is a tendency to consider that students' queries are not worthy of an expert's consideration. However, if these problems can be surmounted successfully the panel session can be both a stimulating and relevant teaching and learning method.

Problem-Based Learning (PBL)

Problem-based learning has grown in popularity over recent years with the gradual realization that the knowledge used in professional practice and, for that matter, in everyday life is not academic discipline-based and neither is it theoretical. Indeed, the difficulties in relating theory to practice have become very great and some (Jarvis, 1999a) believe that this is no longer really possible in the areas of social living and working, or in the social sciences in general. Theory is more likely to be constructed after the practice and it is integrated knowledge rather than single discipline-based. As we pointed out earlier, Lyotard (1984) argued that a great deal of legitimated knowledge in the current age is performative. As learning occurs in practical situations, so the idea of setting learners practical and problem-orientated activities has grown in popularity. The method was pioneered in the Faculty of Health Sciences at McMaster University in Canada, but it is now popular in progressive educational establishments throughout the world.

Kwan (2000:137) summarizes problem-based learning in medical education thus:

> In the traditional curriculum, preclinical disciplines, such as anatomy ... are a prerequisite for proceeding to paraclinical subjects and clinic specialities. ... In contrast, in PBL curriculum, health care problems are used to guide the direct learning from an integrative perspective ... Knowledge ... (from the disciplines) ... will come into place as long as they are of sufficient relevance to achieving the learning objectives.

In this method the learners work in syndicate groups on a problem that has been suggested – maybe by the tutor – and they define their problem and then seek to solve it. Groups are given a set period of time and then they can submit their report – even teach the other groups as a result of their own activities.

Some 'watered-down' approaches have also been used, when the tutors teach the disciplines in the first part of the course and then introduce learners to problem-based approaches, but this does not occur when PBL is fully implemented. At the same time, not every academic finds this method acceptable.

Projects and case studies

These methods are frequently employed in the education of adults, but it is widely recognized that they are difficult techniques to use in courses that are assessed, since grades are generally awarded to individuals rather than groups. Yet they do incorporate the highest level in Gagné's hierarchy of learning, so they are techniques that should be encouraged. There are some notable examples in liberal adult education of group projects. Coates and Silburn (1967) conducted, with their class, a sociological study of a deprived area of Nottingham and after three years of research they had gathered enough data to write a book that was published. During the course of the project the students gained considerable knowledge of the discipline, of the area of Nottingham in which the research was conducted, of the social and political processes of society and of research methods. Such approaches do not have to be restricted to the social sciences for it would be just as possible to undertake such work with the environmental, health and natural sciences. Fletcher (1980a) regarded community studies, such as that conducted by Coates and Silburn, as a form of practical adult education – almost the practice-based education discussed in the previous section, but if a class makes discoveries about a community it might want to use the results in an active manner thereafter. Tutors mounting such project type courses should be aware before they commence that this is a possible outcome of studies of this nature. Case studies are very similar to group projects but the group may seek to focus upon a specific phenomenon and in this instance it may incorporate a multidiscipline perspective. Group projects and case studies can, therefore, assume an exciting and innovative ethos, in which the class learn by doing and then use the results in a practical manner. However, the attrition rate from such classes may be greater than average, especially if the activity becomes politically orientated in the community; but more research into this is necessary.

Role play, simulation and gaming

These are other approaches to teaching in which the student group actively participates and they are included together in this section because of their similarities, but discussed separately for the sake of convenience.

Role play is similar to psychodrama and socio-drama but it has educational rather than therapeutic aims. It can be employed when tutors wish students to experience something about which they are cognitively aware. However, it must be recognized at the outset that it is an approach that has difficulties, so it should not be used carelessly or thoughtlessly. It should be used naturally and students should feel that what they are doing fits logically into a planned learning sequence. Rogers and Lovell state that it 'often makes for a smooth, easy introduction to the techniques if at first role playing is done by the teacher' (Rogers, 1973:78), so the students see the significance of what they are undertaking. Usually role playing is a brief episode acted from someone else's life or from the role for which an individual is being prepared. Hence, in vocational education it is possible to devise many learning situations in which role play would be a most natural method to employ, and when this has been done with adult students they are often most positive about the use of the techniques. Stock (1971:93) suggested that role play encourages active participation, enables problems of human behaviour and relationships to be presented and extends the cognitive into the emotional. Rogers and Lovell (Rogers,

1973:77–78) also indicate that students of any ability can be involved, that this approach helps to break down social barriers in the class, motivates students to learn more, telescopes time so that a longer procedure may be enacted in a brief period, and that it may be therapeutic. Hence, this method has much to commend it, especially in the education of people who are socially mature enough to participate seriously and then willing to reflect and to learn from their experiences.

However, some students may feel reluctant to participate and it is wise for the teacher to leave them to respond to the situation in whatever way they wish, so that they will not feel over-embarrassed by it. Additionally, the technique has other disadvantages: there are difficulties relating role play to reality in some instances; role play cannot be predicted precisely, so the learning outcomes will vary with the role players; it may be time-consuming in preparation; it is hard to evaluate its effectiveness; it may create emotional crises in individuals to which teachers, if not trained as counsellors, may be unable to respond competently. However, in order to help overcome this last potential problem there should always be a period of debriefing afterwards, during which students can readjust to their normal situation; and, obviously, the more the emotional involvement demanded by the role play the greater the need for a debriefing period. Indeed, if teachers do not provide it they may discover that adult students request it. Such a period also provides an opportunity to reflect upon the experience, a stage in the facilitative teaching and learning cycle. Stock (1971:93) also claimed that role playing should not be used when the educational objectives are complex, where there is any danger that they may be obscured by the involvement and he notes that bad casting may destroy the learning situation.

Role play is often a constituent element of simulation, when the teacher may involve the students in a much more complex problem and even relate it to a future occupational role in vocational education. For instance, it is possible for trainee lecturers to simulate a complete board of examiners' meeting, so that each member of the group learns something about the process before actually having to attend a meeting in a professional capacity. However, the preparation of a simulation is extremely time-consuming and unless the simulated situation relates closely to reality the point of the exercise might be lost. Since role playing is also expected in these types of learning exercises most of the problems noted above are significant here also. In addition, since simulations involve a specific number of actors it may be difficult to involve all the students in any one exercise, so the learning experiences of participant and observer will vary. Simulation should also be followed by a period of debriefing, during which time the learning experience may be reflected upon and ideas be allowed to crystallize in the minds of the participants.

Unlike the previous two techniques, gaming may not involve role play in quite the same way, and so there might be a greater cognitive element to the initial learning experience. Since there are patterns of behaviour in human interaction and regulation in social living it is possible to design games which highlight these patterns and regulations. Because the same is true of the physical universe it is possible to learn about aspects of that through gaming techniques. Rogers and Lovell (Rogers, 1973:78) note that they are aware of a Marxist economics lecturer who gets his students to play 'Monopoly' in order to demonstrate the working of the capitalist system. Other games are appearing on the market in a variety of topics, but one of the problems with educational games is that their potential sale may not be large enough to attract the volume games producers and thereby keep the price low, so that, while lecturers should be aware of the games that have been commercially produced in their own area of expertise, they might also consider producing their own. Davies (1971:169) also points out that some business games have been produced that involve role play as well. He also notes an important fact that evaluation on the use of gaming is scarce and such a conclusion is also more true in the education of adults than it is in the education of children.

Seminar

This is in complete contrast to the methods discussed above since there is usually an introductory statement or paper by one, or more, students or a visiting specialist and this forms the basis for a group discussion. The thesis of the paper should be sufficient to insure, or provoke, discussion so that it may be controversial, provocative, topical and relevant. The method has all the advantages and disadvantages of lecture-discussion but it also results in active learning by the presenter(s) of the topic as well as passive learning by the remainder of the group who are recipients of the presentation. However, the seminar may prove to be a daunting method to students if they are to teach their peers and this may prove too off-putting to insure success. This highlights the significant fact that this method is dependent upon the ability of the presenter to provoke discussion or else the tutor may have to intervene to insure that the session is a useful learning experience.

Snowballing

This is an approach that starts with each individual learner but then becomes a group process. Initially, individuals are asked to reflect upon a task, proposition, etc. and to reach some conclusions about it. Thereafter, they are asked to work in pairs and to reflect upon their original conclusions and reach a joint conclusion. Thus each individual has the opportunity to share their own thoughts and ideas with another member

174

of the class. When this process is complete, the pairs are asked to form groups of four and to repeat the process. There is a likelihood that all will join in the discussion, knowing that they have the support of their partner from the previous stage. Each group should then elect a rapporteur to report upon the group's collective findings in a plenary session.

Gibbs (1981) advocated this approach since, initially, the individual's own experiences are utilized and all members of the class actually participate in the process. Since this method actually assists in demolishing the barriers of interaction it is a useful technique early in a course, as an ice-breaking exercise. However, there is an important point to note in this method: the timing is very significant and it is very easy to overrun, so that the plenary session is cut short. Tutors have also to beware in this type of teaching and learning session, especially when the time is restricted, that they do not seek to provide a summary of the group's reports in which they superimpose their own ideas upon them. Even so, this is a useful method which can be employed with large numbers of students and which encourages full participation by all of them.

Therapy (T) groups

This is 'a method of teaching self-awareness and interpersonal relations based upon therapeutic group techniques in which individual group members discuss their relationship with each other' (Bligh, 1971:128) – it is a form of experiential learning. This approach may be employed in sensitivity training and in developing individual self-awareness, so it can be useful in certain forms of professional education where the trainees have to learn to work closely with other people in order to practise their profession effectively. However, this approach can result in situations in which the outcome is social disharmony within the learning group that may continue for long after the learning session has been completed. Indeed it is an approach that can, unless used with professional care, be damaging to an individual's self-esteem, and so it is unwise to use it unless all the participants have consented to participate and unless there is easy access to a trained counsellor.

Visits, tours and field trips

Adult education has a long history of arranging study tours both at home and abroad and also of arranging field trips. The purpose of these has always been to provide personal experience for the learner; but it should be noted that it can also provide a common learning experience for a group and that this may become a resource for further learning activities. Not only does a visit provide a learning experience, it may also help integrate a group, so that it may be a useful technique to use early in a course – although it might also constitute the whole of the course. It is significant that this approach is being used by the European Union to help create a common European awareness, through such programmes as Erasmas and Socrates.

It is often necessary to have some form of debriefing session, or group discussion, in order to insure that the learning experiences are reflected on and shared. However, there are limitations to this approach: trips take a lot of time to organize and may be relatively expensive; they may preclude some people from participating in them, especially the handicapped or those who are extremely busy with many different activities; they may have to be organized in conjunction with another party, and thus the tutor may not be totally responsible for the arrangements of the learning activity. More recently, study tours have been organized in continuing professional education but the problems of organization are exacerbated when the applicants for the course have to gain study leave, paid or unpaid, in order to participate.

Workshops

The penultimate method to be examined in this section is the workshop, which has similarities to the project and case study method. Here a group of students are encouraged to relate theory to practice in some area of their interest or occupation. Students may actually design their own working programme or participate in one devised by a tutor. In the workshop situation, students are enabled to undertake a piece of work, either individually or in groups, and the product of the exercise may be subjected to the critical scrutiny of the class for discussion and appraisal. The end-product of such a workshop may be improved skills, a product useful to professional practice, or, merely, additional learning. This approach can be employed in liberal adult education and one branch of the Workers Educational Association, for instance, offered a public workshop on Robert Tressell. No tutor was present, although the local tutor-organizer acted as convenor. The group which was formed not only studied his work *The Ragged Trousered Philanthropists* but went on to write about it and then proceeded to publish a book on the subject entitled *The Robert Tressell Papers* (WEA, 1982). The group actually undertook all the production of the book, so the end-result of the workshop was a total learning experience. Hence, the workshop may be seen to provide a wide range of learning experiences and is a method that is attractive to adults, especially those who have some previous experience of a topic.

Work-based learning

Following the discussion that has occurred throughout this book about the rapidity of change of artificial knowledge, the fact that learning comes from human experience and that legitimate knowledge is practical knowledge, it is perhaps not surprising that some institutions have recognized the fact that individuals in certain workplaces are in continuous learning situations. In a real sense, their workplace is their classroom. This is a stage beyond problem-based learning because now the problems are being examined in the workplace itself by the workers. Consequently some educational institutions have devised ways of helping work-based learners reflect on their learning and demonstrate the depth of their understanding. They are sending academic staff into the workplace in order to help them understand the situations in which the learners are working and then they are arranging evenings and weekends when the workers can come together to share their learning and also have some of the more theoretical elements explained to them to help extend their understanding. Now some institutions are awarding qualifications for work-based learning. Later in this book we shall also examine the idea of the practitioner researcher (Jarvis, 1999a), which might also have been called work-based research.

Whilst a considerable number of student-centred group methods have been examined in this section, no attempt has been made to insure that the list is exhaustive. The main purpose has been to demonstrate that a variety of approaches exist, so that adult teaching should not always follow the same format. Additionally, a number of different methods may be employed in a single teaching session. Hence it is necessary for the teacher to be proficient in the use of a variety of methods in order to provide stimuli to the students and to enable them to learn in ways to which they are best suited. Yet, thus far, the discussion has focused only upon student-centred group methods, and so it is now necessary to examine some individual student-centred methods.

Individual student-centred methods

In contrast to the previous section, the focus in this one is on individual students and the methods that might be employed to facilitate their learning. There are a variety of approaches that can be employed ranging from self-selected learning to tutor-set projects. It will be noted that the traditional adult education approach of self-directed learning occurs in one form or another in many of these. Significantly, self-directed learning in the way that Tough (1979) envisaged stands outside of the educational system, although educational programmes might be incorporated into the self-directed learning project. It is proposed, therefore, to discuss only eight methods in this section, chosen because of their significance to the education of adults: the assignment, computer assisted learning, contract learning, experiential, personalized systems of instruction, the practical, the personal tutorial and self-directed learning. Each is elaborated upon briefly, in the order listed above.

Assignments

Assignments are a common feature of most courses of teaching and learning and may involve, for instance, writing an essay, a case study, or a research project. In addition, assignments may have a more practical application, and students may be asked to produce a teaching aid, or some other piece of equipment relevant to their course or occupation. If more practical assignments are produced it is necessary to insure that expert assistance is available for consultation. An advantage of encouraging students to work in media other than the written word is that adults bring to their learning their own interests and skills, which may stretch beyond the written word, and these may be used to the benefit of the learning process. The written word is only one method of communicating knowledge and it may be one which some adults have not used extensively since their initial education. At the same time, writing an assignment is perhaps the most common method by which results of research undertakings are communicated, and so adult students should seek to be proficient in the use of this medium. But the proficient use of the written word may be a skill that adults have never been taught, and so it may be necessary to diagnose adults' learning needs in the art of writing prior to setting such assignments; and if there is a learning need, tutors should help students acquire the necessary skills to undertake the task (see Sommer, 1989). Recently, many books have appeared offering guidance to students on the art of writing, preparing a thesis, and so on (see, for instance, Murray, 2002).

Once the tutor is sure that students are able to use the written form, assignments of this nature may be set. The title of any assignment may be tutor-set, student-set, or a choice of either may be given to the group. Advantages of tutor-set assignments include: ensuring that the whole syllabus is covered and producing a standardization of grading at the end of the process. Yet grading is a subjective process, affected by many variables, including handwriting, length and style, and so it is dubious whether the latter advantage could actually be substantiated. Encouraging students to select their own topic may mean that they are more likely to choose an area relevant to either their learning needs, or interests, or both. However, there is also a tendency to choose subjects that are already known, especially if the assignment is to be graded, and this may partially defeat the object of allowing students to select their own assignment topic. Even if this disadvantage can be overcome, it is not always easy for students to select a subject which they can handle in the time or space available, so that the tutor may have to offer help to the students to get sufficient precision into their titles to enable them to do justice to their topic, within the limitations imposed upon them. Essays are perhaps the most frequently employed method, which may be because the tutors themselves were expected to write them, although projects and case studies are assuming a more important place in adult learning and teaching. The use of these methods is significant because they enable students to follow the sequence of the learning cycle: engaging them in an analytical approach to the problem; discussing the title and its implications; collecting data to construct an argument in response to the analysis; planning a structure in which they can reveal the results of their reflections and evaluations of the data collected; showing something of the process of reflection during the sequence of the argument; reaching conclusions and testing them against the wider reality. Hence, the preparation of the written assignment is a method of learning, and setting assignments is a technique of facilitating that learning.

Usually written assignments are submitted to the tutor who marks and returns them to the student. Little training is given to tutors in marking written assignments since it is generally assumed that the tutor, as an expert in a subject, is able to assess and grade a piece of work. There are a number of problems about this assumption: that the tutor is competent to assess both the structure and content; that the completed assignment is the end-product of the learning process; that there is some objective standard against which the work is judged. Clearly some tutors do not assess the structure, only the content of the argument, even though the structure may constitute as important an element in the learning process and reveal the way in which the learners have been able to organize their thoughts and manage data. This suggests that tutors might need to be trained in the art of marking assignments, which may be even more true when the students are adults and we will return to this in a later chapter. However, it is perhaps a totally false assumption that the completed assignment is the end-product of the learning process which reflects the behaviourist psychology that has dominated education for so long. Many adult students continue to reflect upon what they have written and tutors are often asked for feedback about work that they have marked. The written assignment, therefore, actually constitutes another medium through which teachers and learners engage in dialogue. Since marking may be regarded as part of that dialogue, and it is a delicate part, tutors may be required to correct misunderstandings that the adult students have acquired, and it is often useful to adopt a Socratic technique. Hence tutors highlight strengths and weaknesses by means of questions, so that students are enabled to reflect upon what they have written and reach conclusions of their own, which may be more beneficial to their self-image and self-esteem than being corrected. In addition, the questions facilitate a continuing process of learning, whereas didactic comments might inhibit the learners from continuing to pursue ideas in the assignments that they have written. This is not to deny that there is a place for didactic comment, but only to claim that too much information may not be helpful, so that didacticism should play a less significant role in marking than it frequently does (Jarvis, 1978a). However, if grading is to be regarded as part of the teaching and learning process, perhaps the tick or the cross is the least helpful of all comments since it merely provides reinforcement, positive or negative, for what is written and, unless it is used in response to empirical fact, it suggests nothing necessarily about correctness, or otherwise – only agreement or disagreement on the part of the tutor.

Computer assisted learning

With the growth in popularity of the personal computer, the majority of the population are familiar with its use, so that more learning packages are becoming available and it will be easier for educators of adults to use these. Even so, the popularity of the computer might well result in more privatized learning projects, such as those discussed by Tough (1979), being undertaken; no doubt there are already a multitude of such learning activities being undertaken in Western Europe and America. Most educational institutions now have the facilities for adult teaching to be assisted by computer programmes. Its potentiality for responding to the learning needs of students is great. Nevertheless, the lack of personalized contact with tutors may not always prove satisfying to learners, so that it does not necessarily mean that there will come a time when human teaching is redundant.

Contract learning

Knowles (1986) helped to make this method of teaching and learning well known. Adults bring a great deal of experience to learning situations, are highly motivated to learn and are capable of being self-directed in their learning, so that the idea of adult learners entering a contract to learn with their teachers is a logical step forward. Clearly this approach recognizes that learning is an individual process, learners have different experiences and different motivations so that classroom teaching and learning might not always be as effective and individualizing a process. Contracts are, therefore, developed between teachers and learners spanning a variety of aspects of what is to be learned, e.g. teachers and learners may agree individually upon the aims and objectives of the learning, the resources and resource persons to be used, the date by which the learning is to be achieved and the mode by which the learners demonstrate that they have achieved the desired ends. The contract may be a written one or an informal agreement and this may depend upon whether the contract is made during a normal face-to-face course where there is frequent contact between teachers and learners, when it can be informal, or where there is less frequent contact, when it may be more advisable to write the contract. If it cannot be kept, it becomes the responsibility of the one who cannot keep it to renegotiate the terms with the other party so that, for instance, if students cannot achieve the desired end by the agreed date, then they take the initiative and renegotiate the contract.

It is also possible to enter a contract about the grade to be awarded for a piece of work, so that the criteria for each level are agreed upon in the contract and then students demonstrate that they have met those criteria when they present their work. If the tutors do not agree then they have to demonstrate to the students why they wish either to lower or to increase the contracted grade.

In many ways this is an extremely attractive approach to teaching and learning but it is extremely time-consuming for teachers if they have big classes, more so than teaching by more traditional methods, and so they should understand the commitment that they make at the outset as well as expecting this to be understood by the students.

Experiential learning

Experiential learning is included here as something entirely different from the previous discussions about experiential learning in the learning theory section. Here it is a teaching technique, in which tutors provide students with an episodic experience of what they have been learning in the classroom or what they are about to experience when they enter the world of work. These experiences may be 'artificial' in as much as they are provided for the purpose of teaching only and the learners are not exposed to the actual social forces of the situation in everyday life. In a sense, it is an attempt to provide primary experiences, a sense of reality, to counterbalance the secondary experiences of the lecture theatre. In this sense, we see experiential learning as a teaching method.

Personalized systems of instruction

The personalized system of instruction refers to the Keller Plan (Boud and Bridge, 1974; Keller, 1968), which is perhaps the most well known of the early programmed learning systems to emerge, and it is included here as an example of the way that these developed. Crane (1982), for instance, refers to: Postlethwait's audio-tutorial system; individually prescribed instruction; programme for learning in accordance with needs; the personalized system of instruction. The Keller Plan consisted of units of work, or modules, which students studied at their own pace and in their own time without a teacher. Each unit had to be passed successfully before they proceeded to the next one, which is referred to as mastery learning. Lectures and other learning activities are provided but attendance is not compulsory since they are regarded as an additional and occasional stimulus. Keller summarizes his plan in the following five points:

- the go-at-your-own-pace feature, which permits the student to move through the course at a speed commensurate with his ability and other demands upon his time;
- the unit-perfection requirement for advance, which lets the student go ahead to new material only after demonstrating mastery of that which preceded;
- the use of lectures and demonstrations as vehicles of motivation rather than sources of critical information;
- the related stress upon the written word in teacher–student communication; and, finally:
- the use of proctors, which permits respected testing, immediate scoring, almost unavailable tutoring, and a marked enhancement of the personal–social aspect of the educational process.

(Keller, 1968:83)

This method was acclaimed by Taveggia as 'proven superior to conventional teaching methods with which it has been compared' (cited by Holmberg, 1981:127). Rogers (1977) discusses British counterparts to this approach in her chapter on discovery learning but it was Leytham who elaborated a set of principles for programmed learning, when he suggested that:

- aims and objectives should be clearly specified
- materials selected for learning should relate to aims and objectives
- each new stage should only introduce sufficient new material to ensure that it is not too difficult so that students make few, or no, mistakes
- the level of difficulty of new material should be commensurate with the students' previous experience
- students should work at their own pace
- students should be active learners
- students should receive feedback
- no new stage should be inserted before the previous one is mastered

(Leytham, 1971:140)

Clearly Leytham's principles are in accord with the points stressed by Keller, with the exception of the latter's use of proctors who undertake the administration of the tests and provide the feedback. While this approach to teaching can be instituted within the educational organization, it is also clear that many of the principles of modular and distance learning are encapsulated within these formulations. However, one of its drawbacks is that all the material that is taught and learned is selected by the teacher, and while the learner is left to learn it, it remains the teacher's choice and the learner's need is not necessarily a determining factor in the selection of content. Perhaps this is one reason why it has found a niche in adult basic education (see Crane, 1982 for an example) and in higher education but, as yet, it has only established a place in liberal adult education through distance learning. Yet this approach appears to offer considerable potential as disciplines become even more specialized and interests even more diverse.

Practicals

In many professions the teaching of practical skills had, until recently, been left to the learner to copy the demonstrator, and stress had been laid on learning through experience. We have already pointed out that there has been a renewed emphasis upon the value of practice and the place of practical knowledge in recent times. New forms of apprenticeship are appearing, but one of the main problems with the government's policy of trying to get more school leavers into universities is that some of the highly skilled manual occupations are not getting sufficient recruits. These occupations demand prolonged periods of practical placements so that the practical skills can be learned under the guidance of a mentor, or an expert teacher of practice. Theory had assumed too great a significance to the detriment of practical skills in some cases, although it is possible that the pendulum might be swinging too far in the other direction, with certain government policies assuming that all relevant theoretical knowledge can be learned in the practical situation. At the same time Beard has pointed out that 'there is some evidence that this method is unnecessarily slow since students have insufficient practice and feedback' (1976:147). Hence, there has been a gradual movement in some areas of education to teach practical skills in a simulated situation, so that students can practise the skills until they are mastered. Belbin and Belbin (1972) emphasize that most adult students, left to learn at their own pace, can master skills especially if each skill is subdivided into separate elements and each element mastered separately. It is immediately noticeable that there are considerable similarities between skill teaching and the programmed learning discussed above: much of the learning is tutorless, students are left to work at their own pace and in their own time, and each phase is mastered before progression to the following one.

However, in some other forms of education for adults there is another aspect of the practical and that is the work undertaken in the laboratory. In this instance, it is necessary for the tutor to decide whether the purpose of the exercise is merely to learn the use of experimentation by repeating other people's experiments. Naturally, these are not mutually exclusive but if one of the aims is to help students understand the process of experimentation it is necessary to combine the practical with some other learning technique, such as a discussion or a tutorial, so that reflection upon the process can be stimulated and additional learning occur.

Personal tutorial

The tutorial has already been discussed from the perspective of the tutor but it can be used in order to respond entirely to the student's learning needs. In this instance, the tutor plays the role of respondent to the questions and problems raised by the adult student about the content and method of what the latter is studying. Hence the tutor is merely answering questions and the student is effectively guiding the progress of the tutorial, but when this occurs it is perhaps wise to agree beforehand upon the length of time to be allocated to the session.

Self-directed learning

In the same way as experiential learning has assumed significance in the education of adults in the United Kingdom, the idea of self-directed learning has become an important element of American thought. There is an annual conference each year on the topic. Many of the methods discussed in this chapter employ self-directed learning strategies so we can see that it is a significant teaching method in its own right.

It may well have become clear from the discussion on contract learning that self-directed learning might be regarded as a teaching technique and a development from andragogy (see Brockett and Hiemstra, 1991). Certainly, Knowles regarded self-directed learning as one of the manifestations of andragogy and a vital element in his understanding of contract learning. Underlying the whole idea is the idea that the individual is an autonomous learner. While there are degrees of autonomy, Jarvis (1992) endeavoured to demonstrate the paradox of this position.

However, Candy (1991) also showed that however free the learner appeared to be within the framework of an educational institution, there is still a residue of teacher influence and so he distinguished between autodidaxy and self-directed learning. He (1991:15) regarded autodidaxy as self-directed learning outside the educational institution in which the learners' autonomy is retained, which he (1991:108–109) claims has a number of characteristics of autonomy:

- conceives goals and policies independently of pressure from others;
- exercises freedom of choice and action;
- reflects rationally;
- is prepared to act fearlessly in accord with the foregoing;

- has self-mastery;
- individuals perceive of themselves as autonomous.

Candy recognized that there were threats to the idea of individual autonomy, which he then discussed. However, for the purposes of this study,
the distinction between self-directed learning within an educational institution and that outside is of major significance since the influence of the
teacher is never far removed from any form of student-led learning within
the institution, and it is only with distance education that learners are
apparently free from the immediate presence of teachers. But, and
necessarily, distance education institutions are very centralized in many
ways so there is no genuine learner autonomy in this form of education
either.

Thus far in this chapter there has been a division between tutor-centred
and learner-centred methods and this has been done for ease of discussion. Clearly, however, in any teaching and learning session it is possible
to combine a number of approaches, and it is often a useful technique in
teaching adults to negotiate with them about aspects of both content and
method. This is not relinquishing professional responsibility but rather
exercising it in a mature manner with adult learners who may contribute
greatly to the teaching and learning process. Finally, in this chapter, it is
now necessary to move from methods of teaching to aids for teaching and
this constitutes the next section of this chapter.

Teaching aids

In the same way that teachers of adults should be aware of and able to
employ a variety of teaching methods, they should also be aware of and
able to use a variety of teaching aids. A multitude of different ones exist
and, with the continuing growth of technology, there is an increasing
sophistication of equipment. Table 5.2 lists many of the teaching aids and
much of the equipment about which teachers of adults should be aware,
some of which they should also be competent to use in the classroom.

Many of the aids listed in Table 5.2 are in daily use so that they require
little comment here, although there are many publications that deal with
the technological aspects of teaching which may be referred to as appropriate. Therefore, it is intended to raise only a few points here.

Initially, it is important for teachers of adults to know that such a variety
of audio-visual aids exist and that it is useful to have some expertise in
their use. Many teaching and learning aids are produced commercially
and can be purchased either by individual teachers or by the educational
institution in which they are employed. At the same time, most educational institutions have audio-visual aids departments and it is always
worthwhile discovering precisely what services they offer, so that lessons

Table 5.2 Teaching and learning aids and equipment

Aids: Audio	Audio-visual	Visual	Learning aids
Audio cassettes	Films	Artefacts/models	Articles/journals
Audio recordings	Tapes	Charts	Books
Radio	Slides	Diagrams	Computer
Records	Television	Drawings	programmes
	programmes	Graphs	Handouts
	Video recordings	Illustrations	Home experiment kits
		Photographs	Games
		Slides	Media programmes
			Role play
			Simulation exercises
			Study visits
			Work books/sheets

Equipment: Basic	Technical
Chalkboard	Camera/cine camera
Flannelgraph/	Cassette recorder
Feltboard	
Flipchart	Closed circuit television
Magnetic board	Computer
Plasticgraph	Epidiascope
Whiteboard	Episcope
	Projectors: cine
	overhead
	slide
	Radio
	Record player
	Television
	Video recorder

may be enhanced by the technical help that such a department can render. Additionally, if the library facilities in the college/institution are limited, many of the public libraries are prepared to cooperate with teachers of adults in order to ensure that they have sufficient stocks of books on a specific subject to enable class members to borrow them. Local museums also are often prepared to loan boxes of teaching materials, e.g. relevant artefacts, on specific topics if they are approached. They are, of course, also pleased to receive class visits when it is appropriate.

In more recent years probably the most frequently used audio-visual aid is PowerPoint. It has assumed a central place in many presentations and yet it is nearly always used in the same rather traditional manner – that is having bullet points for the points to be raised and occasionally variations on the theme. Yet PowerPoint can be used much more adventurously if the presenters are experts in its use. In addition, when PowerPoint is used with a class or a group of learners not all of whom have the same first language, I have found that summarizing the whole of a presentation, including the full quotations etc., helps them follow the presentation more easily because they can both hear and see the text.

When teachers of adults either prepare their own aids, or use the services of the audio-visual aids department, it is wise to be aware of the laws of copyright, since infringement of these may occur out of ignorance. It is also worthwhile checking to see if their employing educational institution has signed the copyright agreement because this allows them to photocopy specific materials for use as handouts, under certain conditions to which they must adhere, without reference to the publishers themselves. Even so, many companies and organizations are prepared to grant permission for the reproduction of their materials, given acknowledgement, and so it is often advisable to seek permission from them if they themselves are not included within the agreement. Moreover, some companies and organizations will also provide teaching resources to teachers who approach them.

Such a variety of teaching aids and equipment ensures that students may be able to learn in accordance with their preferred learning style. Indeed, the greater the variety of appropriate aids employed the more likely it is that students' learning will be helped; but teachers should not employ too many aids in a single session for the sake of their performance because this artificializes the learning environment and interferes with the learning process. Considerable research has already been conducted into the relationship between learning and audio-visual communications and it is necessary for the teacher to be aware of some of this. For instance, Sless (1981) examined the relationship between learning and visual communications and, while he admitted that his own coverage was incomplete, he maintained that students were not trained in the use of visual stimuli, so that if teachers use them they must 'also show how people can learn from these forms' (1981:77). Nevertheless, the technologies have now been in common use for a number of years and many adults are adept in this use.

Thus it may be seen that a wide variety of aids and equipment are available and teachers will enrich the learning experience if some of the techniques are employed in their work. It is, therefore, the responsibility of teachers of adults to be aware of what provision is made by their own educational institution and by other institutions in the locality, so that they are able to perform their role effectively.

Summary

This chapter has reviewed a great deal of material about teaching adults. It began by seeking to draw relationships between learning and different approaches to teaching, in which it was recognized that the humanity of the adult students and the teachers are paramount in the process. It was clearly seen that there are a wide variety of styles, methods and audio-visual aids available to teachers, who should be competent in all the domains, even if not with every method and aid, etc. Now it is necessary to examine the ideas about teaching that occur in some of the well-known writers on the education of adults.

6

SOME THEORETICAL PERSPECTIVES ON TEACHING ADULTS

In the previous chapters the processes of learning and teaching were discussed and it will have become apparent from the numerous methods mentioned that there are a diversity of approaches to teaching and many theoretical perspectives about it, so that it is now necessary to examine some of the latter. Before undertaking this, however, there are two other aspects that we need to explore: in this light of the discussion on teaching styles it is essential to ask whether teaching is an art or a science and, second, since teaching and learning is a process of human interaction in which both sets of participants should be affected, it cannot be a neutral process. It is a moral one!

In the first section, we will argue that teaching is both an art and a science; it is about teaching styles as well as teaching methods (technologies). Indeed, in this study it has been consistently maintained that education itself is humanistic although teaching and learning processes may fall short of these ideals. Hence, it is necessary to consider not only the aims, methods and content of a particular teaching session, but also the teaching style and the morality of the approach in relation to the participants in the process.

This chapter will, therefore, have two sections; the focus of the first is on the art and science of teaching and then on some of its moral aspects. The second will examine the work of five theorists: Bruner, Dewey, Freire, Illich and Knowles.

The human process of teaching

In this section we will first examine the art and science of teaching and then we will look at the idea of teaching as a moral process.

The art and science of teaching

Bourdieu and Passeron perhaps capture the traditional model of teaching in a very illuminating manner:

189

The ideal lecture theatre is vast, truly vast. It is a very sombre, very old amphitheatre, and very uncomfortable. The professor is lodged in his chair, which is raised high enough for everyone to see him; there is no question that he might get down and pester you. You can hear him quite well, because he doesn't move. Only his mouth moves. Preferably he has white hair, a stiff neck and a Protestant air about him. There are a great many students, and each is perfectly anonymous. To reach the amphitheatre, you have to climb some stairs, and then, with the leather-lined doors closed behind, the silence is absolute, every sound stifled; the walls rise very high, daubed with rough paintings in half tones in which silhouettes of various monsters can be detected. Everything adds to the impression of being in another world. So one works religiously.

(History student, female, aged 25 – cited by Bourdieu and Passeron, 1994:1)

Academic discourse, as Bourdieu and Passeron make clear, uses a vocabulary far removed from the students' everyday experience and not well understood by them. When they try to use it, usually incorrectly, it merely reinforces the professors' perception of them as unintelligent, since they try to repeat the professors' ideas in a language that they have not mastered. But even if they do master it, it contains only limited forms of knowledge that might, or might not, be useful to the students in their own everyday life, or even their own professional life. It is about certain forms of cognitive knowledge, omitting the other dimensions of human living and human practice that we have already discussed. But the question that we might want to ask is – is what we have described here actually teaching? It has certainly passed for teaching in universities for a long while. But how do we evaluate it – is it because 'correct' knowledge is being transmitted or is it because the process facilitates the learning. Universities have traditionally been concerned about the former and only recently have they become concerned about the latter. Therefore, before we can seek to answer the question posed, we need to explore what we mean by teaching. This remainder of this subsection has three brief parts: the concept of teaching; teaching as a technology; teaching as an art.

The concept of teaching

In this subsection, we will review and expand some of our earlier discussion about the nature of teaching. As we have already seen, a great deal of emphasis in contemporary education has been placed on learning and the learner, although concerns about teaching have continued to surface – as the Quality Assurance exercise in universities and the emphasis in the

Dearing Committee's (1997) report make clear about it. In the latter, we read:

> We recommend that, with immediate effect, all institutions of higher education give high priority to developing and implementing learning and teaching strategies which focus on the promotion of students' learning.
>
> (Recommendation 8)

> We recommend that institutions of higher education begin immediately to develop or seek access to programmes for teacher training of their staff, if they do not have them, and that all institutions seek national accreditation of such programmes from the Institute for Learning and Teaching in Higher Education.
>
> (Recommendation 13)

While the Dearing Committee was concerned that the image of the professor sitting high above his students had to be eradicated, the committee did not really consider the aim of teaching itself, although it did include distance education within its deliberations. Pratt (1998) offers five different approaches to it: transmission (effective delivery), apprenticeship (modelling ways of doing), developmental (cultivating ways of thinking), nurturing (facilitating self-sufficiency), and social reform (seeking a better society). His five different aims of teaching, like all the discussions that we had in the previous chapters, show that there are many approaches and that it might be considered to be a technology.

Teaching as a technology

Since education has been an Enlightenment product, it is no surprise to find that the traditional concept of teaching has embraced many of its philosophies, such as the emphasis on an end-product, rationality, efficiency, scientific ideals of measurement and evidence, and both an empirical and pragmatic approach to knowledge. Significantly, learners were treated almost as if they were passive recipients of the information that they were receiving; they could be treated almost as inanimate objects so that the process could be likened in some way to natural science. Teaching could, therefore, be examined in the same way as material objects, so that the techniques by which knowledge was transmitted were regarded as crucial to the process. Therefore, teaching as we have traditionally known it, might be regarded as the product of the era of Modernity. It is an activity that had to fit this paradigm, so that this calls for a discussion of at least three aspects of teaching: the end-product of teaching, the means to the end and an assessment of the process.

191

The outcome of any teaching process had to be measurable so that the emphasis on behaviourism is instrumental rationality. If teachers could understand how the learning process occurred they could endeavour to ensure that their activity is efficient and achieved the predetermined outcomes. Hence scientific experiments were needed to demonstrate how individuals learned and Skinner, amongst others, was able to demonstrate this case in laboratory experiments with animals. This satisfied the scientificism of Modernity. Consequently, the more teachers understand processes of reinforcement in learning, the more effective their teaching might become and they achieve their specified objectives – usually behavioural in nature. Skinner (1968:59) actually believed that teaching is a technology in which we can 'deduce programs and schemes and methods of instruction'. Therefore, lessons and teaching materials could be designed that provided the type of reinforcement necessary to achieve the predetermined outcomes, that could then be measured either by behavioural change or by examination and assessment of the knowledge taught. In precisely the same way he (1968:65) believed that teaching machines are devices that 'arrange the contingencies of reinforcement' and, therefore, effective distance education could use the same psychological processes as face-to-face teaching and their effectiveness could be assessed in precisely the same manner.

While there is considerable evidence that conditioning is effective, fundamental questions have to be asked about the extent to which the laboratory experiments with rats and mice can be transferred to human beings. Nevertheless, behaviourism is a product of that period, and this approach to teaching seemed self-evident and was widely accepted.

Teaching techniques are means to an end. In basic curriculum theory we see the logical pattern of aims of the lesson, content to be taught and, therefore, the methods to be used. Finally, in this model, evaluation occurs – of the content and of the methods selected. The choice of method bears little or no relationship to moral or philosophical principles but only to an understanding of human behaviour and teaching's effectiveness in producing the desired outcomes. This 'scientific approach' is even more pronounced in the various approaches to instructional design, which are more common in the USA than in the UK (Gagné et al., 1992; West et al., 1991). Here the models for designing instruction are extremely sophisticated; they provide rational processes and programmes that instructors should implement in order to make their instruction more effective. Once more, it is the technique and not the teacher, which is important, so that individual instructors or the teachers are almost dispensable to the process.

Perhaps we see this even more with the use of Powerpoint presentations – I have attended conferences where there has almost been a competition for the most sophisticated power point expertise, almost irrespective of the conceptual level of its content. It is almost as if the technology has assumed a greater importance than the content or the teachers and learners.

This argument has been pursued even further when it comes to distance education, since it is possible to design the types of materials that Skinner (1968:65) advocated when he suggested that 'the teaching machine is simply a device to arrange for the contingencies of reinforcement'. In another way we see teaching as no more than a transmission of knowledge to more students than a single lecture theatre could hold. Otto Peters (1984) equated the production of distance education materials to a process of manufacture. Now teaching was becoming efficient since it was enabling one set of teaching materials to be mass produced and used with a far greater number of learners. However, in later work, Peters (1998) has also noted that other distance education material does take philosophical and humanistic concerns into consideration, as we shall see in the next chapter.

Nevertheless it is quite significant that in teacher training there has been a considerable emphasis placed on teaching methods, as we argued in the previous chapter. It is the method that is important rather than the personality of the teachers or of their behavioural and ideological dispositions. Teaching techniques are important, and few people would deny this, but the emphasis placed upon them reflects the era of Modernity. Skinner (1968:91), however, actually recognized that if these techniques are used unwisely they might inhibit learners' creativity, so that he indicated that teaching might be more than technique, as do other theorists of education. Not all objectives, for instance, are behavioural – some are expressive (Eisner, 1969), and more recently we have focused on other elements of teaching such as teaching style.

With the emphasis placed on instrumental rationality, it is little wonder that one of the ways of measuring teaching success has been on the outcomes of the process. Teachers must be effective if they produce students who gain good grades – this is a measurable outcome. This might actually be the case, but we do not necessarily know whether it is the teaching process, or the teachers themselves or the learners, who help achieve the success. But there is at least one other problem: students can learn from many other sources and it might even be that poor teachers drive good students to the libraries. But so does the fear of failure! Our professor sitting on high might actually be communicating relevant knowledge but fear of failing his course might mean that students spend hours in the libraries and then it is their study skills that are as, or more, important than the lecture.

The other way of assessing the teaching process is to observe it and in some way record it. In this numerical world, we have seen teachers graded, and in some places the grade is used in helping to determine

193

whether, or not, teachers should be promoted. But as we know from all the research on marking essays that there is a tremendous difference between different markers and how much more is this likely to be when each teaching event is unique and when it is not really possible to revisit the event and reconsider it? We are all aware that students' evaluations of the same lesson do not all agree, and a similar disagreement might well be found if experienced lecturers all assessed a teaching process. Indeed, many years ago we tried an experiment in a workshop when we asked thirty teachers to assess a video of someone cleaning a pair of shoes – there was considerable variation in their assessments! This is not to claim that bad teaching cannot be identified, only that it is more difficult to do than many of the over-simplistic methods that are often employed in many situations.

With distance education materials, we can only evaluate the content and the way that it is produced and presented, but the writer of the material may not actually be the person who designs the format or produces the final structure. In this sense, the writer as academic can be evaluated but the presentation of that material is a skill that other professionals might possess, so that teaching itself becomes a team activity with at least one partner not necessarily being an academic. However, it is also clear from this discussion that distance education has changed the nature of teaching; it is about content, process and design that captures the spirit of the technological age. It is an ultimate form of manufacture; it comes much closer to being a technology and a science of production than does classroom teaching. Like other occupations, the uniqueness of the person is removed. The human relationship of the classroom is displaced by impersonal transmission of knowledge and individual learning and achieving. However, in certain forms of on-line learning we are beginning to see the possibilities of relationship and individuality emerge in distance education – it is a more human and a neo-Fordist approach to education.

What we have shown in each of these points is that there is validity in the idea that teaching is about technique. It is a technology and this is all it need be to provide learning opportunities intentionally. Teachers might merely be the instruments choosing the right methods, communicating the 'correct' knowledge and getting the desired results. In the process the students are treated as passive and are moulded like materials in other production processes – but this does not exhaust the process of teaching since students need individual help, need to be motivated, and so on. Learning and teaching needs a personal relationship in order to achieve the best outcomes and this is also recognized by the fact that many distance education institutions also provide opportunities for face-to-face contact.

The art of teaching

The concentration on content and method has led many of us to say that 'I teach sociology' or 'I teach mathematics' – but this is incorrect. Actually, 'I teach people sociology' or 'mathematics', and so on. Sentences of the former type betray the values of a technological age, but they are incorrect – we do teach individuals.

Brookfield (1990:2) has denied that importance of the technology of teaching by suggesting that it is rather like 'white-water rafting'. In a sense the conditions in which it occurs are not controllable. In a similar manner Eble (1988:11–12) seeks to dispel at least twelve myths of teaching, although he concentrates rather more on the teaching process than on the conditions; three of his twelve myths are that:

- teaching is not a performing art;
- teaching should exclude personality;
- popular teachers are bad teachers.

Basically he is saying precisely the same thing as Freire (1998) when he calls teaching a human act, but he goes a little further than Freire by implying that there is something of a performance in teaching, as we suggested in the previous chapter. I do not think that Freire would disagree with this.

Kidd (1973:295) suggests that teaching styles are often presented as dichotomies:

- Permissiveness versus control;
- Aggressiveness versus protectiveness;
- Emphasis on content versus emphasis on participation.

We have already discussed teaching styles but we can begin to see their significance when we think about teaching as an art. However, there is more to humanistic teaching than just style. This form of teaching involves a relationship, one that is necessarily moral, for all human interaction has a moral component (Jarvis, 1997). Once these moral elements enter teaching and the focus is on the humanity of the learners much of the instrumentality of teaching disappears. It is about enabling human beings to achieve their own potential, without imposing on them predetermined outcomes, although we recognize the importance of what is learned in the process. Fundamentally, teaching is a human process, in which the teachers themselves may well be the best instruments that they have in helping learners to both learn their subject and achieve their potential. We are now beginning to see recognition of this when campaigns to attract teachers have celebrities saying which teachers most influenced

195

them, and so forth. But the emphasis on the values of the Enlightenment era in which modern conceptions of teaching emerged have always underplayed the human part of the process – the art of teaching.

Teaching, then, is both a technology and an art – but I would argue that it is more of an art than a science or a technology. It is through interaction that the art is realized.

Teaching and learning: transaction or moral interaction?

Roby Kidd (1973), following Dewey, described teaching and learning as a transaction – and to an extent this is true. There is a sense in which both the teacher and the taught bring something to the classroom and it is there that a transaction occurs. This appears to be a valid metaphor in contemporary society where education is viewed as a commodity to be marketed to potential learners, although it is intended to demonstrate here that such a metaphor is most problematic when applied to the educational process. Additionally, the idea of the transaction hides something of even greater profundity, and yet much more basic. What occurs between teachers and the taught is a human interaction – a relationship is formed between teacher and the learners. Of course this is obvious, but the fact that the potentiality of human relationship occurs in this situation means that it is necessarily a moral interaction, for there can be no relationship between people that is not essentially moral.

One way of analysing this interaction, which has been undertaken by some scholars such as Caffarella (1988) and Clark (1990), is to look at a number of case studies and seek to draw conclusions from the ensuing analysis. This is an excellent starting point but has certain limitations since it does not ask the fundamental questions about human interaction and human values. Indeed, there is a sense in which these have to be assumed in this form of analysis and there is a possibility that every case chosen for examination might reflect the contemporary immoralities of society, so that it is considered more appropriate to begin with an exploration of human values and then to assess the relevance of this investigation for education. Many philosophers have embarked upon the quest to understand values in human relationships, but such a study would constitute the basis of the study of moral philosophy as a whole – and so it must be recognized that the approach adopted here has it own presuppositions, the fundamental one being that human value can only be realized in relationship. This assumption itself seems to be flying in the face of the individualism of contemporary Western society, and so it is, but this is because it is suggested here that Western society has placed too much emphasis on the individual and self-interest and lost its moral direction in the process.

We first examine a few possible outcomes for a world in which self-interest underlies the teacher–learner transaction, then we explore the moral philosophical foundations of interaction, and, finally we look at some of the implications of the discussion.

A self-interested teacher–learner transaction

Underlying the morality of the modern world are the twin ideas of individualism and self-interest. These stem from the Enlightenment and from the morality implicit in the division of labour and, consequently, in the market place. Fundamental to the division of labour is the idea that human beings produce different commodities, which they then seek to offer in the market place in exchange for others that they also need. Clearly this is an efficient method of production and one that has been generally accepted in modern society. In 1759, Adam Smith, in *The Theory of Moral Sentiments* developed the idea of self-interest which was applied in a more narrow economic fashion in *The Wealth of Nations* in 1776 (Brown, 1992), where he recognized the moral significance of the division of labour and suggested that the exchange in the market is based upon the philosophy of self-interest, i.e. 'give me what I want and I will give you what you want'. In other words, it is a transaction – but certainly not the type implied by Kidd. This outworking of self-interest, it was claimed, functions for the social good, and society seems to function efficiently as a result – as if an 'invisible hand' has guided its transactions.

As a consequence of this approach to social life, instrumental rationality has become widely equated with rationality itself, and it is regarded as quite natural for people to act in such a manner in order to further their own self-interest in a market situation. Imagine a transaction where two people are bartering over the sale and purchase of a commodity; it is regarded as quite natural that both should be concentrating on getting the best deal for themselves. The outcome of this might well be amicable agreement in which the social good results. But this market approach also means if the actors are unable to reach agreement then the more powerful usually get their way and the less powerful become even more dominated, so that while there is social cohesion as a result of the power relationship it does not mean that the good of all the actors in the transaction has been achieved. (See Poole, 1990 for a full discussion of relationship between modernity and morality.) This power relation might also have immoral implications. Taylor (1991:17) states quite specifically that 'some forms of life are indeed higher than others, and the culture of tolerance for individual self-fulfilment shies away from these claims'.

If these approaches are applied to the teaching and learning transaction, the following two scenarios may be drawn. In the first, both students and teachers act in self-interest. Students might approach the transaction with their needs and with the intention of satisfying these but by doing as little work as possible in order to gain the best qualification

197

for themselves. The qualification is the sign of ownership of the commodity that has been provided by the teacher. Teachers are aware of, and have often experienced, this instrumental approach to education by some students. Teachers, on the other hand, bring their own knowledge and skills to the transaction, but what if they were also to approach it in such a manner as to see how they can satisfy their other needs and get the best out of the transaction for themselves, while still trying to get the greater majority of students through their examinations? They might seek to do as little preparation as possible, provide as little of the necessary knowledge as possible, see the students as infrequently as possible, expect more self-directed learning and projects, etc. – not that these are bad in themselves. It might be argued that if the learners actually gain their qualifications then the conservation of energy and time to use on other activities is perfectly acceptable, both sets of actions are perfectly rational and that the actions of the role players are right. But what if, in the long term, the teachers have not really kept abreast with developments in their discipline and their students begin to fail examinations and courses because they have also done little work? Then the students will not achieve their qualifications and they will become dissatisfied with the provision and might well look elsewhere for their education. The logic of this position, therefore, is false. It is not really possible for both teachers and learners to try to get the best deal for themselves all the time and still to maintain a high quality of education.

It will be noted that in this instance the language of needs has been used and this is because some of the philosophy underlying ideas commonly used in the education of adults is problematic. Maslow's (1968) hierarchy of needs, for instance, placed self-actualization at the apex of human development, as we discussed in the first chapter, but this is an individualistic perspective which can easily be used to justify individuals striving to self-fulfil or to actualize their own self-interest at the expense of others. It can easily become a legitimating ideology for this bartering transaction, so that Maslow's position apparently reflects something of the same set of values as the market discourse.

In the second scenario, teachers might use their position to dominate the learners and get the best out of the situation for themselves. One way in which this occurs is when teachers impose their will on the class and use the teaching and learning situation as an opportunity for self-aggrandisement, while their students are forced to be the recipients of the tutors' performance, eloquence, wit, etc. When education is so teacher-centred that the teaching and learning transaction is a process which the teachers control for their own personal or psychological benefit, then the students are given no encouragement to grow or develop. Teaching, or the teachers' performance, is the end-product of the process and the students' learning is almost incidental. The teachers might come away from such a class claiming that it has been a 'good session' and untrained observers might also regard it as an excellent lesson. The students, also, might have enjoyed the performance, but the outcome of the session might be that they might have learned very little. Indeed, this approach to education is in accord with the thesis of Bourdieu and Passeron (1977:5) that all 'pedagogic action ... is objectively, symbolic violence insofar as it is the imposition of a cultural arbitrary by an arbitrary power'. In this instance, teachers use their dominant position for their own self-interest; a form of teaching has occurred but educators might question whether good education has actually happened. Indeed, Buber (1961:120) suggested that the educator is not '"the man (sic) with the will to power," but he was the bearer of assured values'.

Neither of these approaches incorporate the values that most people would associate with teaching and learning in adult education or, in other words, the morality underlying much of contemporary society is flawed, since teaching and learning is more than a transaction. It might well be argued that this morality is also suspect for many other aspects of daily life, since being flawed for education demonstrates quite clearly that it is not applicable to all aspects of contemporary society either. It is necessary, therefore, to examine a philosophy of human interaction, as an ethical basis of teaching and learning.

Teachers and learners in relationship

Perhaps the crucial idea in teaching and learning lies in the word 'relationship'. Teaching and learning in the classroom situation, although not in all forms of distance education, involves a relationship between the teacher and the learner, and, consequently, it is with the work of some philosophers who have concentrated their analyses on 'relationship' that this part of the discussion begins. Of these, perhaps the most well known is Martin Buber, after whom the adult education institute of the Hebrew University in Jerusalem is named, although there are many other eminent philosophers whose work is important to this discussion.

Buber, in a number of major works, explored the idea of relationship, especially in *I and Thou* and *Between Man and Man*. In the former he (1959) explored the idea of personal relationship, as opposed to I–It relationships. He might also have, but did not, postulate a third form of relationship, I–Group relationship, since there are many occasions, especially in education, where individuals are confronted with a group, or an agglomeration of individuals. While such interaction might be regarded as impersonal, it is not the same as trying to interact with a tree, so that it must be seen as a form of personal relationship.

For Buber, the personal relationship is conducted at three levels – with living beings, with individual persons and with spiritual beings; each of which could be expanded upon here but only the second of these is relevant to the present discussion. People enter personal relationships through direct experience, usually because they share the same space at the same time, and through so doing they have opportunity to interact with each other during which time they share a mutual bond. Before a relationship is formed, I exist in my world and the Other is a stranger, a significant idea since the stranger is free (Levinas, 1991:39) over whom I have no power. When I enter relationship with the Other it is usually through the medium of language in the first instance, although relationship is more than an exchange of words. When I and the Other are face to face, the distance between the Stranger and me recedes and some form of bond begins to be created, but the very formation of that bond impinges upon the freedom which is the prerogative of the Other. At the same time, my own freedom in respect to the Other is curtailed. The bond's existence, however weak, signifies that I am prepared to forego some of my freedom in order to enter a relationship. This relationship may be only for a brief period of time, although there is potentiality for it to continue beyond the first interaction.

I am able to enter such a relationship with the Other for whatever period of time it exists because of our common humanity. Where there is no humanity, the relationship is of necessity an I–It one. Relationships with a group, because all its members are human beings, share many of the same characteristics as with the Other, but they tend to develop the bonds of community rather than those of the more exclusive personal relationship. (The exclusive personal relationship always puts at risk the community since it has the power to fragment the group.) The potentiality of individual personal relationships always exists in the educational situation. Herein lies a fundamental truth, when the I–Thou relationship is formed the Stranger, or the group member, becomes a person with whom I, as a person, can share a human bond. My personhood can only be realized in relationship with another person – or as Buber (1959:18) put it, 'In the beginning is relationship', and MacMurray (1961:17) suggested 'the Self is constituted by its relation to the Other'. Elsewhere, MacMurray (1961:24) claimed that 'the idea of an isolated Agent is self-contradictory. Any Agent is necessarily in relation to Other. Apart from this essential relationship he [sic] does not exist'.

As the relationship becomes established, certain patterns of interaction begin to appear and it is these which curtail freedom. Sociologists call these norms and mores and some scholars, such as Heller (1988), wrongly I believe, regard these as the foundation of ethics, although it must be recognized that values, both moral and immoral, are manifest within norms and mores. Like the case studies, norms may not reflect the morality of the interaction for a number of reasons, including the fact that the norms of modernity were shown earlier in this section to be morally flawed in certain situations. Additionally, if there is an unequal power between the actors the patterns of interaction may reflect the selfish desires of the more powerful actor even though they may not be presented to the less powerful or even to the general public, in this manner. Hence, it appears that the actual location of morality lies with the intention of the actors rather than with the behaviour itself. One of the problems with this is that individuals can claim that they had good intentions, even though their actions had unfortunate outcomes and, in other situations, bad intentions can produce a good outcome – but in these latter situations the morality underlying the action has to be questioned. Consequently, ethics is not an empirical science! It is grounded in human intention, wherein the morality of action lies.

It is in a common humanity that the arguments for ethics lies and in the formation of the relationship in which personhood may be realized rests the practicalities of ethics. Indeed, Levinas (1991:43) argues that ethics arise when an individual's spontaneity is inhibited by the presence of Other, and if this position is accepted then teaching must always be seen to be an occupation grounded in the moral debate. (He actually regards the bond that is established between the Self and the Other, the I–Thou relationship, as religion and MacMurray develops his discussion in a similar manner with a discussion of the celebration of communion, although this point will not be developed further here.) However, it is clear that in the potentiality of personal relationship itself lies the basis of any discussion of the nature of ethical value. MacMurray (1961:116) would agree with this analysis and claimed that the 'moral rightness of an action . . . has its grounds in the relation of persons'.

It is significant that whatever the relationship, whoever the people and whatever the historical time, this argument still applies. It is for these reasons that it can be claimed that the basis of moral value is that it is universalizable. It may thus be seen why Kant claimed that values had to be generalizable in this manner, which is implicit in MacMurray's (1961:122) claim that:

> To act rightly is . . . to act for the sake of the Other and not of oneself. The Other . . . always remains fully personal; consequently its objectives must be the maintaining of positive personal relations between all agents as the bond of community.

The underlying point here is that the intention behind the action is some form of care, or concern, for the Other. It is maintained that such an intention is never wrong in itself, except when the desire to care for one Other may put many others at risk, and this illustrates the distinction between the I–Thou and the I–Group relationship. Clearly in this instance, there is a major ethical debate about putting one's loved ones before unknown Others, or the teacher devoting more effort to favoured learners than to the class as a whole. Teachers must be concerned for all those with whom they work and act for their own sake rather than the teachers' own self-interest. At the same time teachers interact with all the class individually, so that there is both an I–Group interaction and a potential I–Thou relationship with each individual member of the class. Since these are both personal in nature, the I–Thou relationship will constitute the basis of the following analysis and its significance for the I–Group relationship will be discussed in the conclusion.

There are many studies that have sought to demonstrate the significance of the moral relationship in teaching (Daloz, 1986; Freire, 1998; Palmer, 1998, *inter alia*) and they recount the lengths to which teachers should go to help students achieve their own fulfilment through the processes of teaching and learning. This is the vocation of teaching. Included in the three books mentioned above are: caring, commitment, humility and self-confidence, integrity, joy and pain in relating to learners and to their successes and failures, respect for the learners' autonomy and freedom, and tolerance. These show how committed teachers 'go the extra mile' for their students; they exemplify the morality of the teaching vocation. There is nothing more honourable nor sometimes more demanding than seeking always to help other human beings achieve their own potential.

Ethical implications of teachers and learners in relationship

It is clear from the above discussion that underlying the teaching and learning relationship should be an intention to care for the Other. In the first instance in this analysis, the I will be the teacher in relationship with both the Thou and the Group, but this does not exclude the individuals in the Group each seeking to play the same role in relationship with the teacher and, indeed, with each other since the group itself constitutes a moral community. Part of the intention of the teacher should be in trying to establish the climate where such relationships are encouraged. However, for the purpose of this analysis the I is the teacher and the Thou, or Other, a student.

The potentiality of the teacher–learners relationship is created by the fact that the interaction occurs at the same time and in the same space – the classroom/lecture theatre, etc. There is a sense with a new class that a lot of strangers come together in a common space, so that there are potentially many I–Thou relationships, but they must be made freely. It may be seen, therefore, that the class is not only potentially a group, by virtue of its becoming a moral community.

Three issues constitute the focus for this enquiry hereafter, since they are constituent issues in any understanding of the teaching and learning relationship – the students' autonomy, authenticity and personhood, and each is now discussed.

It was pointed out that the essence of the process of forming relationships means that I am prepared to curtail my freedom and the Other is prepared to do likewise – but neither should inhibit the autonomy of the other, the I has to reach out to the Thou – with concern for the Other being the only intention underlying the action. Paradoxically, it is the teachers who control the space of the classroom but they do not and cannot control the learners, and if they try to do the latter they are likely to fall into the trap of seeking to exercise power for their own self-interest rather than out of concern for them. If the relationship is to be created, it must be a free process and it is only through the exercise of that freedom that the autonomy of the participants can be retained. I and Thou have both freely to be prepared to forego a degree of freedom so that care can be exercised.

Language lies at the heart of relationship for being open to the Other is to be open to conversation with the Other (Levinas, 1991:51) or as Buber writes it is about a dialogical relationship. Such a conversation is itself the sign of an ethical interaction and Levinas (1991:51) regards the conversation as itself a process of teaching:

> Teaching is not reducible to maieutics (maieutics is the Socratic mode of teaching by drawing out knowledge from within an individual – author); it comes from the exterior and brings me more than I contain. In its non-violent transivity the very epiphany of the face is produced.

Teaching, then, occurs through any open conversation in a relationship of caring during which ideas are shared freely and it is in a similar context that the teaching and learning relationship in education should be created. Teachers should share their knowledge, skills and ideas through conversation, or in a style that enables conversation to begin in the process of sharing, but in the conversation learners also share their knowledge, skills and ideas with the teachers and with each other. To stifle the learners, through a teacher monologue, is to prevent the I from gaining what the Other can bring to the relationship, and this can destroy the educative relationship in which care and concern for persons is manifest face to face.

Only through recognizing that the actors in the I–Thou relationship have freely chosen to forego some of their autonomy for the period of the relationship can such a conversation occur and, paradoxically, it is then that both I and Thou retain freedom. I's control of the space of the classroom is such that I do not seek to control the Other, only to reach out to the Other in the space that I control out of concern for the Other.

There is no agreement among philosophers as to what is an authentic person: three different approaches can be be detected (see Jarvis, 1992): the Polonian, the Dadist and the interactionist. Polonius said to his son 'To thine own self true' whilst the Dadist claims that the only requirement for authenticity is that an individual's action and commitments should 'issue from spontaneous choices, unconstrained by convention, opinion or his own past' (Cooper, 1983:10). Before discussing the third position, it must be noted that both of these positions revolve around self-concern. They are both individualistic and take individual freedom to its limits, so that they provide no opportunity for the Other to enter into relationship with the I and there can be no manifestation of concern for the Other. They are, therefore, immoral positions reflecting the morality of the age but should not be adopted in the teaching and learning relationship.

It is important for educators of adults to recognize this since both 'strong' persons who know their own minds and those 'whose behavior is not easily predictable' (Rogers, 1969:225) fall into this category. For Carl Rogers, the end of life is to be the self that one truly is, and as such his position is a statement of self-interest and in respect to teaching and learning it is fatally flawed. Both of these arguments for authenticity reflect a position that does not enable the highest moral values to be manifest.

Contained within the above critiques lie some of the problems in defining authenticity: individuals have to be true to themselves and free to act or else they become subservient to others, but this freedom and emphasis on the self excludes the Other from I's immediate ambit of significance. Too much emphasis on the Other and I's justifiable concern for selfhood disappears under the demands of the Other. There is an ambivalence about authenticity that is captured in Taylor's (1991:66–67) endeavours to define it: on the one hand it is about being free to be creative, constructive, original and free to question the power that others impose upon the self but, on the other hand, being open to others and dialogical. The authentic person must both be free to enter relationships and to terminate them if it is necessary, but the decision to do the latter must also be made in the light of concern for the Other and it is here that some of the ambiguity of authenticity lies. That I should act out of concern for the Other is not doubted but at what point does I act out of concern for self and to the detriment of the Other is the question? Perhaps the concern for the Other should never die and so the I should always be concerned for the Thou. For so long as the relationship is vibrant it will be a teaching and learning relationship and both I and Thou will find satisfaction in it. In these cases I should not wish to terminate such a relationship but when that dynamism disappears then individuals might wish to dissociate themselves from each other, although in such sad situations the concern for the Other should never die.

Following Taylor, the teacher should encourage learners to be authentic – that is to encourage creative, constructive and original thought, and to question the established rules and principles, but the teacher has also to encourage learners to be open and dialogical. In a sense, the teacher should endeavour to provide a situation in which learners can realize themselves as different and as individuals in relationship, rather than to mould learners to be either like themselves or like some other idealized picture of the learners that they wish to produce. To do less than encouraging the learners to establish their own authenticity is to fall short of the high ideals of teaching, but the danger lies in adopting an understanding of authenticity that enables the self to grow and develop at the expense of the Other.

Teaching and learning is a dialogue between persons in which the teacher is concerned for the learner – the I is concerned for the Thou. But as Buber (1959:34) makes clear 'he who lives with It alone is not a man'. It is only in relationship that the Thou becomes a person – an I, and then the possibility of inter-subjective dialogue becomes possible. It is the person with whom the teachers interact and the purpose for their interaction lies in the dialogue – the teaching and learning. Clearly in that dialogue teachers have a duty to ensure that in as much as they are able that which is considered to be correct knowledge, skills, attitudes, etc. constitute the subject of the dialogue. But the person is also being developed through this interaction – a development that continues until the end of life – for persons are centres of consciousness. Persons develop by having a greater variety of experiences and richer interaction with others, and this must be one of the fundamental aims of education. Indeed, Paterson (1979:17) claimed that 'education is the development of persons as independent centres of value whose development is seen to be an intrinsically worthwhile undertaking'. While it would not be claimed here that the undertaking is intrinsically worthwhile, it is maintained here that it is worthwhile because it emerges from a concern for the Other that can only be realized through relationship. The person is, therefore, more important than the content of the dialogue and personhood more important than correct knowledge, although this rather stark dichotomy does not do justice to a reality where both are possible!

It may be seen from this discussion that the manner through which teachers interact with learners (teaching style) is probably more important than the actual teaching methods employed. This does not relegate method to the sidelines but it does point to the fact that underlying technique is something even more significant. However, concern with issues of human relationships in teaching and learning has not constituted a major factor in the preparation of educators of adults.

From this analysis it may be seen that the teaching and learning relationship should also embrace moral values which are contrary to those that are dominant in contemporary Western society. But it is significant at this time that there are considerable pressures being exerted by governments to make education conform to market values – the values of transaction – while the values underlying education are those of interaction. Education must endeavour to resist the pressure being exerted upon it at the present time in Western society, since its interactive processes are more profound than those of a transaction in a market place.

I and Thou interact out of concern for each other and through which both are developed as human persons. Such an interaction can only occur if teachers use the space that they control to facilitate the human interaction. Teaching adults is, therefore, an invitation to explore human relationships and education is itself a humanistic process. Above all, being a teacher provides an opportunity to facilitate human becoming, and so teaching and teachers must be prepared to respond to the current social pressures and retain the ethic of concern for persons that forms the very essence of education itself.

It will be recognized from this discussion that the moral dimension of teaching is a significant but often neglected aspect of the role (see also Jarvis, 1997). Many of these points will become apparent in examining the following five theorists: Bruner, Dewey, Freire, Illich and Knowles.

Some major writers about teaching

None of the following writers has actually developed a theory of teaching adults. Bruner's *Towards a Theory of Instruction* is a systematic theory of teaching but not directly orientated towards adults, while the other four are all concerned with adults but none has an explicit theory. Knowles' theory of andragogy clearly relates learning and teaching in a much more integrated approach than most, and this is to its credit, although there are other problems with it. In the remainder of this section each of these five are now discussed.

Jerome S. Bruner

Bruner, in his classic study *Towards a Theory of Instruction* (1968), recognizes that the human being is a natural learner and he claims that schools often fail to 'enlist the natural energies that sustain spontaneous learning' (1968:127). This might appear to be an indictment upon modern schools but it is also a recognition that they perform a socializing and moulding function to equip children to take their place in society as much as an educational one, or one that creates individuals who can perform an innovative role in contemporary knowledge society (Hargreaves, 2003). Bruner (1968:53), therefore, recognizes that any instruction that is given in school should be regarded as having an intermediate as well as a long-term aim, the latter being that the learner should become a self-sufficient problem solver. However, it might be claimed that any didactic process, such as formalized instruction, is actually helping to create a sense of dependency in the learner rather than one of independency, especially if the school teachers are unable to detach themselves from the process and encourage independent learning in children. Consequently, by the time children grow into adults they will have learned to expect that teachers will instruct them. Indeed adult students do exert considerable pressure upon educators of adults to conform to their expectations of teachers playing a didactic and, often, an authoritative role.

It is against this discussion that Bruner's theory of instruction may be viewed. He (1968:40–41) claims that a theory of instruction should have four main features, and these are that it:

- should specify the experiences which most effectively implant in an individual a predisposition towards learning;
- must specify the ways in which the body of knowledge should be structured so that it can be readily grasped by the learner;
- should specify the most effective sequences in which to present the materials to be learned;
- should specify the nature and pacing of rewards and punishments in the process of learning and teaching.

Clearly Bruner has positioned his theory against the background of initial education, so that some of the above points appear to be diametrically opposed to some of those already mentioned in the education of adults. Yet the first of these four points is quite significant since Bruner maintains that instruction should facilitate and regulate the exploration of alternatives and a major condition for undertaking this is curiosity. Curiosity, in Bruner's work, is an outcome of disjunction which was discussed earlier. It will be recalled that curiosity is aroused in adults, as well as in children, when their interpretation of their socio-cultural environment no longer provides them with relevant knowledge to cope with their present experiences. Hence, in teaching adults it is possible for the teacher to provide experiences that arouse this questioning process, so that the adult students' questioning is orientated in a specific direction. Clearly the structure and form of knowledge are significant in teaching adults and Bruner recognizes that the mode of representation, the economy of presentation and the effective power of the representation varies, 'in relation to different ages, to different "styles" among learners, and to different subject matters' (1968:44). Hence, this second point may be seen as relevant to adult teaching. The relevance of his third point is also clear since he claims that instruction 'consists of leading the learner through a sequence of statements and are statements of a problem or body of knowledge that increase the learner's ability to grasp, transform, and transfer what he is learning' (1968:49). Finally, all learners need some reinforcement, so the relevance of this is very evident in the education of adults. However, it must be recognized that Bruner is discussing only one type of educational method, instruction, or a didactic presentation of knowledge, and the relevance of his theory must be seen in relation to this.

There are also considerable similarities in Bruner's formulation and those in the personalized system of instruction discussed in the previous chapter, and it may be seen that Bruner has highlighted many of the points that underlay a theory of instruction. Instruction is obviously didactic and there is a sense in which, as a teaching method, it controls the amount of knowledge to be learned by the students, so that it is open to the accusations that some of the analysts discussed later in this chapter would make about it. Nevertheless, many of the more informal methods of teaching also include some teacher direction and guidance, so that they may not be quite so free of control as might appear on the surface. However, it might be true to claim that all teaching methods may be located on a continuum between student-centred and teacher-centred, and perhaps more are located towards the latter end of the continuum than adult educators might like.

While Bruner is clearly concerned about the humanity of the participants in the teaching and learning process, there is no explicit place within his principles for a humanistic perspective, although he does recognize the importance of the relationship between teacher and learner. Nevertheless, Bruner has outlined a set of principles that educators of adults should be aware of because they form part of the theoretical perspectives of teaching.

John Dewey

Perhaps Dewey is the most significant of all educationalists for the development of adult education, and so it is hardly surprising that he should be considered here. Many of his ideas have already been discussed in earlier chapters, so it is not intended to repeat them at length here. However, Dewey was one of the major exponents of progressive education, and his earlier books were clear expositions of this position, and among his basic principles were that the concept of education had to be reconceived, so that it related to the whole of life rather than just of its early years. For Dewey, the human being is born with unlimited potential for growth and development, and education is one of the agencies that facilitates it. Another tenet of progressivism significant to understanding Dewey's thought is the recognition that prominence is given to the scientific method; so the individual needs to start with a problem, develop hypotheses about it and test them out by examination of the empirical evidence. Hence, the problem solving method, discussed in relation to Gagné's hierarchy of learning, is significant in the work of Dewey. He also recognized that this resulted in a changed relationship between teacher and taught, so that teachers might facilitate and guide the learning but they should not interfere with nor control the process in the way that a didactic teacher would.

Some of the above ideas appear in *Education and Democracy* (1916) but in many ways the book that Dewey wrote on *Experience and Education* (1938) reflects some of his more developed thinking on teaching. He was concerned to contrast his approach to that of the more traditional schools of thought and he considered freedom and experience to be significant. Additionally, he maintained that continuity of experience and interaction between young and old are both important to learning. While he was actually writing about initial education some significant ideas for the education of adults evolved, so it is important for the educators of adults to be aware of theoretical approaches to children's education.

Dewey considered that since experience is at the heart of human living and because continuity of experience leads to growth and maturity, then genuine education must come through experience. Hence, the teachers' role is to provide the right type of experience through which the learner may acquire knowledge and understanding and this facilitates the process of growth and development. Learners mature without having a structure of knowledge and the body of social rules imposed upon them. However, it might be argued that if the teachers' main task is to provide the conditions in which the students learn, and if teachers are actually directing the process when the students require help (Dewey, 1938:71), then they are involved in a much more subtle process of control than that which occurs in traditional, didactic teaching. However, Dewey recognizes that this possibility exists and he condemns those who 'abuse the office, and ... force the activity of the young into channels which express the teachers' purpose rather than that of the pupils' (ibid). According to Dewey, the teachers' leadership responsibilities include:

- being intelligently aware of the capacity, needs and past experiences of those under instruction;
- making suggestions for learning but being prepared for the class to make further suggestions so that learning is seen to be a cooperative rather than a dictatorial enterprise;
- using the environment and experiences and extracting from them all the lessons that may be learned;
- selecting activities that encourage the learners to organize the knowledge that they gain from their experiences in subject matter;
- looking ahead to see the direction in which the learning experiences are leading to ensure that they are conducive to continued growth.

These points are collected from different pages of Dewey's work but they reflect some of his major points about teaching. It is clear from the above that Dewey's work on teaching may be related to the facilitative learning and teaching cycle (Figure 5.3) in the previous chapter and that many of his ideas are similar to those expounded in earlier chapters of this work. It was Lindeman (1961 [1926]) who, influenced by Dewey, incorporated many of these ideas into adult education, so that theories of teaching in adult education reflect a progressive educational perspective which can be traced directly back to Dewey.

Paulo Freire

Freire's work was discussed in a previous chapter in terms of the theory of learning implicit in his writing, but the theory of teaching is much more explicit. Three elements are discussed here and these are summarized by Goulet (Freire, 1973a:viii), who suggests that the basic components of Freire's literacy method are:

- participant observation of educators 'tuning in' to the vernacular universe of the people;
- an arduous search for generative words;
- an initial codification of these words into visual images which stimulate people 'submerged' in the culture of silence to 'emerge' as conscious makers of their own 'culture';
- the decodification by a 'culture circle' under the self-effacing stimulus of a coordinator who is no 'teacher' in the conventional sense, but who has become an educator-educatee in dialogue with educatee-educators too often treated by formal educators as passive recipients of knowledge;
- a creative new codification, this one explicitly critical and aimed at action, wherein those who were formally illiterate now begin to reject their role as mere 'objects' in nature and social history and undertake to become 'subjects' of their own destiny.

Without raising issues of literacy education, the first significant point that emerges from this summary is that Freire advocates, and practises, going to those who have a learning need and listening to them, so that the educator can become the learner. While this serves a diagnostic function, it has more purposes than this because it enables the educator to learn the language of the potential learners and to identify with them. At the outset of the teaching and learning the teacher bridges the gulf between him and the learners in order to create a genuine relationship and dialogue, without which humanistic education cannot occur.

The second significant point about this process is that the learners are encouraged to participate in dialogue and to problematize the reality in which they are immersed. This is a deliberate attempt to make the learners question what they had previously taken for granted, so that they can become aware that they have been socialized into the culture of the colonizers and that their construction of reality may be false within the context of their indigenous heritage. This occurs through the analysis and use of language, since language is a significant carrier of the universe of meaning, and through becoming aware of what has happened to them the learners are enabled to reconstruct their universe of meaning. In this process the learners are not objects of a social process but they are creative subjects within it.

Finally, Freire does not regard the educator and the learner has having mutually distinct roles but thinks that in a genuine dialogue the teacher teaches the learners who learn and teach the teacher as well. Hence, in the dialogue there is also a mutual planning of the teaching and learning, so that it is relevant to the needs of the participants. It is in this dialogue that the humanistic nature of Freire's teaching method is apparent since he (1972b:61–65) claims that it is essential to the educational process and that it requires an intense love for and faith in humankind. Perhaps Freire's philosophy of teaching is summed up by a Chinese poem:

> Go to people, live among them,
> Learn from them, love them,
> Serve them, plan with them,
> Start with what they have,
> Build on what they have.

> (Author unknown)

Perhaps more than in most theories of teaching, Freire emphasizes that the teacher has to reach out to the learners and learn from them in order to be able to contribute effectively to the teaching and learning process. Like other theories of teaching adults the humanity of the learners is respected and emphasized.

Two significant points need to be made here. Clearly Freire presents a radical approach to teaching and he regards it as a method by which learners can act upon their socio-political environment in order to change it. Hence, the educator is the facilitator of learning and education is a process of change. The educator is not the 'fount of all wisdom' trying to fill the empty buckets: education is not a process of banking received knowledge. Rather education is an active process in which the teacher controls neither the knowledge learned nor the learning outcomes. Because of the politically radical elements in Freire, there is a danger that other aspects of his philosophy of teaching may be lost.

Freire offers a humanistic teaching method that may actually be divorced from the political radicalism, although to do so would fail to do justice to Freire' s philosophy. However, he highlights the fact that teachers: have to break down the barriers between teacher and taught; should speak the same language as the learners; should be aware of how they construct their universe of meaning and what they see as their learning needs; should start where the learners are and encourage them to explore and learn from their experiences.

From Freire's unique synthesis of Christianity, Marxism and existentialism he has produced a theoretical approach to teaching that is both inspiring and challenging. That he is regarded as a political radical should not detract educators of adults from seeking to emulate elements of his method, since it epitomizes the high ideals of humanistic education. Many of his early ideas about teaching have been reinforced by later writing (Freire, 1998).

Ivan Illich

Like Freire, Illich is a radical Christian who presents an alternative approach to education. He is included here, however, not because of his radicalism but because one of his major ideas is already finding expression in adult education in America and, to some extent, it is being incorporated into the University of the Third Age in the United Kingdom. His approach also presents a warning to those adult educators who seek to professionalize their occupation.

In order to understand Illich thoroughly it must be understood that he offers a radical critique of some of the established institutions in Western society, including medicine, the Church and teaching, and so it is necessary to summarize his concerns before they are applied to education. Illich (1977) claims that the professions dominate ordinary people, that they prescribe what the people need and institutionalize it within the professional's own territory, Hence, doctors determine when a person is ill, prescribe an acceptable remedy to the need and ensure that health cure takes place in 'hygienic appartments where one cannot be born, cannot be sick and cannot die decently' (Illich, 1977a:27). Similarly, teachers determine what children need to learn, and prescribe the educational remedy in a building which artificializes the real experiences of living. Professionals dominate people's lives, prescribing what they regard as right and proper, and the general populace are no more than the recipients of the process. This is the crux of Illich's position.

Since education has fallen into the trap of institutionalization, Illich (1973a) proposed that it was necessary to deschool society. He considered this essential because not only education but social reality itself has become schooled. Accepted knowledge and credentials for occupational advancement have become incarcerated within the institution of the school, but there is no equality of access to it, so that expenditure on education is unequally distributed in favour of the wealthy. Every time some other area of social living is incorporated into a school curriculum a new class of poor is generated; so that, for instance, with the introduction of new training initiatives for young adults in the United Kingdom a new class of poor who are unable to attend the courses and gain the advantages is generated.

In precisely the same way, Illich and Verne (1976) offer a critique of lifelong education. Continuing education specialists will generate the need for more learning, prescribe how and where it should be learned and perpetuate the school system throughout the whole of the lifespan. They claim that in 'permanent education we are no doubt witnessing a further reduction of the idea of education, this time for the exclusive benefit of the capitalists of knowledge and the professionals licensed to distribute' (1976:13). Clearly, Illich is offering a valid criticism of the process of institutionalization in Western society, and indeed in other societies as well, even though he has overstated his argument to make his point. What then does he propose as a remedy for the malady that he has diagnosed?

Illich (1973a) proposes that learning networks should be established and that resources are required to establish a web-like structure throughout a society. In short, long before the learning society he was advocating learning zones, cities, and so on. He (1973a:81) proposes four different approaches which enable students to gain access to any educational resource which may help them to define and achieve their own goals: reference services to educational objects; skill exchanges; peer matching; reference services to educators at large. This clearly requires organization and some of the resources spent on the school system could be used for this purpose, and the professional teacher, liberated from the bureaucratic control of the school, would be free to provide a service to these learners who require it. Such a scheme is idealistic and revolutionary, so there is no likelihood of a society reforming its educational institution in this manner since it is investing even more capital in the school system than ever before. But the free university system in America appears to be fulfilling these criteria. A free university, according to Draves is 'an organization which offers non-credit classes to the general public in which "anyone can teach and anyone can learn"' (1979:5). Some of the free universities are sponsored by traditional colleges, while others are sponsored by libraries and some others are independent. They exist to coordinate learning and teaching opportunities, to introduce potential students to potential teachers. There is a national conference of free universities each year and in 1979 there were over 180 free universities established in America, with over 300,000 participants. A similar approach is appearing in the University of the Third Age in the United Kingdom at present.

Illich, then, offers a radical critique of contemporary society and of the dominant position occupied by the professionals. While his radical alternative to schooling does not appear to have gained a great deal of support in initial education, there is evidence that some adult educators are seeking to respond to the learning need in people and to create networks where teaching and learning can occur outside the institutional framework. Nevertheless, such free institutions must run the danger of ossifying and becoming established, and so it remains to be seen whether learning networks will survive and multiply in the coming decades.

Malcolm Knowles

Like Freire, Knowles was discussed in the chapter on learning theorists but, unlike Freire, he is included again because he has actually produced a textbook in which he specifically discussed the two processes. It was pointed out in the previous chapter that he produced a table similar to Table 5.1, in which he specifies sixteen principles of teaching in response to conditions of learning. He demonstrates that he regards teaching as the process of designing and managing learning activities. His (1980a:57–58) principles indicate the process of teaching, and they are summarized below – teachers

- expose learners to new possibilities for self-fulfilment;
- help learners clarify their own aspirations;
- help learners diagnose;
- help learners identify life-problems resulting from their learning needs;
- provide physical conditions conducive to adult learning;
- accept and treats learners as persons;
- seek to build relationships of trust and cooperation between learners;
- become a co-learner in the spirit of mutual enquiry;
- involve learners in a mutual process of formulating learning objectives;
- share with learners potential methods to achieve these objectives;
- help learners to organize themselves to undertake their tasks;
- help learners exploit their own experiences on learning resources;
- gear presentation of their own resources to the levels of learners experiences;
- help learners integrate new learning to their own experience;
- involve learners in devising criteria and methods to measure progress;
- help learners develop and apply self-evaluation procedures.

This list of principles clearly demonstrates the facilitative teaching style of a humanistic educator of adults. Knowles saw andragogy as embracing the process of teaching, and learning rather than merely learning or teaching and, within this context, it is perhaps important to understand that these principles embrace progressive education for adults, so that they are rather different in perspective from the other approaches that have been examined in this chapter.

Elsewhere in the same work, Knowles (1980a:222–247) applies these principles to the process of teaching, which he regards as having seven stages: setting a climate for learning; establishing a structure for mutual planning; diagnosing learning needs; formulating directions for learning; designing a pattern of learning experiences; managing the execution of the learning experiences; and evaluating results and rediagnosing learning needs. Each of these phases is discussed briefly.

The climate of learning is perhaps more significant than many educators actually assume and this reflects an emphasis on teaching style. Knowles includes both the physical setting of learning and the psychological ethos. He recognizes that the learning climate is also affected by the way in which teachers and the adult students interact. This is especially true in the early sessions, a point that many adult educators focus upon, so that it is significant that teachers endeavour to establish good relationships between themselves and the class and between the learners themselves, from the outset of a course. Only within this climate can diagnosis occur within which Knowles claims that there are three stages: developing a model of the desired end-state of the teaching and learning; assessing the present level of knowledge; and assessing the gap between the two. Thereafter, learning objectives can be formulated by teachers and the learners together. Having reached this stage, Knowles advocated that the adult learners design the pattern of learning experiences, which should contain continuity, sequence and integration between different learning episodes. It is the teachers' role to manage the learning experience and Knowles maintained that teachers should serve both as strong procedural technicians – suggesting the most effective ways that the students can help in executing the decisions – and as resource persons, or coaches, who provide substantive information regarding the subject matter of the unit, possible techniques, and available materials, where needed (Knowles, 1980a:239). Finally, teachers should join with the students in both an evaluation of the process and a re-diagnosis of future learning needs.

Thus it may be seen from the above sequence that Knowles clearly regards the learners as active explorers in the learning process, participating in every stage, and the teachers as resource persons for both content and process. He is obviously in accord with many of the ideas that Dewey expounded, and so unlike McKenzie (1979), it is maintained here that Knowles has applied progressive education to the education of adults. Therefore, it may be seen that the ideology of andragogy is humanistic.

Summary

This chapter commenced with an introductory analysis of some of the moral issues involved in teaching, issues that need more exploration. At the same time it is possible to detect that each of the five theorists discussed in the second part point to some of these issues, without raising them explicitly. It may be seen, however, that Dewey and Knowles clearly have similar humanistic, idealistic approaches to education, seeing learners as individuals who are motivated to learn, so that the tutor's role is mostly facilitative; Illich and Freire both place their analyses in a wider context, Illich as a critique of professional institutions and Freire of the power of the elite; Bruner's analysis is much more specifically in relation to instruction. No doubt Freire and Illich would not want to dispute the humanistic perspective of Dewey and Knowles although the former may consider the latter as having a restricted analysis; but, indeed, all four might well agree with Bourdieu and Passeron when they assert that all pedagogic action 'is objectively, symbolic violence insofar as it is the imposition of a cultural arbitrary by an arbitrary power' (1977:5ff). Bruner may not wish to disagree too violently with this claim either, since he focuses upon humankind's curiosity as an activator in the process of learning.

If education is regarded as the process of learning that knowledge which society considers worthwhile, then it might be argued that skilled techniques that transmit that knowledge is 'good' education. But if education is regarded as the process of learning and understanding, then the content is less significant, and the ways in which the students are encouraged, or enabled, to learn become more significant. In this instance, it might be maintained that 'good' education is concerned with the process of learning, irrespective of what is learned, and that adult learners should become sufficiently critically aware to reject that which is incorrect or irrelevant to them. Hence, to transmit to learners accepted or received knowledge and expect them to learn it uncritically may be regarded as 'bad' education and, therefore, 'bad' teaching. If techniques are used to ensure that the students are persuaded to accept such knowledge, then it may be symbolic violence, in the way that Bourdieu and Passeron claim. However, it would not be maintained here that all pedagogic action is symbolic violence, although some of it most certainly is. Clearly there is a place for pedagogy in the education of adults, but it has been argued that it is not such a significant one as it is generally assumed to be and that the teaching method employed has to relate both to the learners and also to the nature of the topic and the knowledge being learned.

Hence, the issues raised by the more radical theorists do relate to the perspectives adopted by those educators assuming a more humanistic perspective. It is clear that there are moral and social policy issues involved in the process of teaching and while it has been one of the purposes to highlight them, it is not the intention of this chapter to resolve them. Yet the manner by which teachers resolve these issues for themselves may well affect the way in which they perform their own role, and, indeed, it is an issue with which they should be confronted during their own training.

7

DISTANCE EDUCATION

This book started with a discussion of globalization, during which it was pointed out that one of the two main driving forces of this process is information technology; it is not surprising, therefore, that educational systems have been affected by the changes in the substructure of the globe. It is unnecessary to rehearse all of these arguments again here, but to recognize that nearly all forms of education are changing in response to the wider social pressures. Even so, distance education has grown in popularity in recent years, popularized by the British Open University, although its history is far older, and even university distance education occurred long before the Open University was ever dreamed about (Rumble and Harry, 1982). Consequently, this chapter first examines the nature of distance education/learning and, thereafter, it looks at the way that it has developed, and continues to develop, and, finally, it examines some of its practices in contemporary society.

The nature of distance education and distance learning

In one sense, perhaps distance education actually began when James Stuart, the founder of university extra-mural adult education, experimented with correspondence education for women in the 1870s. There were societies for home study at about this time in both England and the United States. (See Garrison and Shale, 1990 for a historical overview in the United States.) Correspondence education became a relatively popular form of education for adults in the early part of the twentieth century, although it was always regarded as second best. With the development of the wireless, there were many experiments with educational radio and, naturally, now there are more high technology means of transmitting knowledge. However, it is only in more recent years that theories about distance education have begun to emerge. We can see, therefore, how distance education has moved from correspondence education, to hard-copy teaching and learning materials, to electronic communications techniques in the period of a half a century as a result of these forces for change.

218

Perhaps the most complete discussion of the meaning of the term is to be found in Keegan (1990:28–47). He (1990:44) characterizes distance education in the following manner: it has a semi-permanent separation of teacher and learner; is influenced by the educational organization in both the preparation of the teaching materials and the support of the students; uses technical media; is a two-way process; has a semi-permanent absence of a learning group. Naturally these characteristics are open to certain criticisms: for instance, it may well be true that in certain forms of distance education there is a two-way relationship between teachers and taught so that the learners may also initiate teaching and learning situations, but this is by no means universal. Consequently, this characteristic appears superfluous to any definition of the concept. Distance education is, there-fore, defined here as those forms of education in which organized learn-ing opportunities are usually provided through a technical media to learners who normally study individually, and removed from the teacher in both time and space. As each educational institution has its own proce-dures and provides its own facilities this definition endeavours to be narrow enough to be meaningful but not so wide as to include almost any form of learning. Even so, with the development of the World Wide Web, the idea of the teacher begins to be unnecessary to the education we pointed out before; education and learning are now distinct phenomena. At this juncture, we can see the appearance of distance learning, as opposed to distance education. The former is usually provided by educa-tional institutions and is accredited by them, but now learning opportun-ities like those provided by the Web can gain educational accreditation through the Accreditation of Prior Experiential Learning.

Just prior to the foundation of the Open University in the United Kingdom, Otto Peters (1967 – see Stewart *et al.*, 1984:68–94 for his analy-sis), who was a member of an important group of adult educators at the University of Tübingen in Germany, began to develop an influential theory about distance education being a typical form of education for the age; he regarded it as: a rationalized form of industrial production; a divi-sion of labour with each individual in the course team having a different role in the production and dissemination of knowledge; mechanization, as the dissemination of knowledge was achieved through assembly line pro-duction; mass production, since there was theoretically no limit as to the number of copies of the same course that could be produced or students who could study the course once it was produced. He regarded this as a process of standardization and the beginnings of a monopoly of the edu-cational market (see Keegan, 1990 for a clear summary of Peters' posi-tion); this is a position consistent with the one being argued here for social change in general and education in particular. Perhaps the idea of the monopoly was premature, but it was at least being realistic.

Another significant theorist of distance education is Holmberg (1989), who regarded it as a form of guided didactic conversation and who considered that there are seven postulates to distance education:

- there should be the creation of a personal relationship between the teaching and learning parties;
- there needs to be well-developed self-instructional material;
- there should be intellectual pleasure in the exercise;
- the atmosphere, language and conventions should foster friendly conversation;
- the message received by the learner should be conversational in tone, easily understood and remembered;
- a conversational approach should always be used in distance education;
- planning and guiding are necessary for organized study.

It will be clearly seen that Holmberg's approach is more humanistic than Peters' analysis, although Peters never claimed to approve of all that is occurring. Holmberg's approach is naturally open to question, especially the third of these points since intellectual pleasure may not always be on the learners' minds! Nevertheless, in order for it to work it is necessary to change the whole style of academic discourse, and a considerable degree of academic training in order to ensure that course writers are empathetic to their readers. Indeed, it might well be argued that a Socratic approach to writing distance education material is much more useful since the learners are challenged to think for themselves rather than just being presented with teaching material that must be learned.

Naturally, Holmberg's work is attractive to educators who have a humanistic approach to education, but there is a danger in making everything appear too friendly since the written word often assumes an aura of sanctity! The text appears to some readers as 'sacred knowledge', which cannot be criticized, and anything that is not included is regarded as less significant, or not important at all. Indeed, it is not uncommon to hear students studying distance education courses asking whether they should include material in their assignments that is not in the text – and occasionally poor tutors telling them that they should not do so! However learner-friendly the distance education, teachers and writers have to be aware that the curriculum of the distance education course is centralized and controlled, so that in this sense distance education has a tendency to be closed.

A theorist who was influential during the early years of the Open University was Charles Wedemeyer (1981); like many American writers, his concerns were self-study, independent learning and, even, individualism and in this he comes closer to the point made above about distance learning. He regarded distance education as an optimistic enterprise in the provision of lifelong learning – in which learners are independent of teachers. Wedemeyer's approach is optimistic but uncritical.

However, there have been dramatic changes in the world in recent years and it is now possible to extend Peters' analysis, since it is being claimed that contemporary Western Europe is entering a period of late, or post-, modernity. Basically, this means that the consequences of the Enlightenment are being recognized and questioned, with some scholars asking whether it was actually a success. This is not the place to pursue this discussion, but distance education can clearly be seen as a sign of late modernity. Giddens (1990) suggests a number of features which typify contemporary society as being late modernity, such as: industrial-capitalistic; space–time distanciation; disembedded mechanisms and expert systems; reflexivity; individual responsibility. However, industrial-capitalism is of a different order than the other four, being one of the driving forces of global change, and it should be regarded as different from the others. In this sense, the shift towards distance learning is a response to the driving forces of global capitalism and information technology and the other four are super-structural aspects that have been incorporated into the educational system as a result.

Distance education is, therefore, a form of education utilizing all forms of information technology to assist learners to learn and it has differing characteristics, depending upon the way that different educational institutions utilize it. But space–time distanciation, disembedded mechanisms and expert systems, reflective learning and individual responsibility are central to them. It is important to note that Giddens' 'reflexivity' is changed here into reflective learning to indicate that the educational system here is dealing with human learning processes as well as social and system changes. It is clearly a contemporary phenomenon that epitomizes each of these four features of late-modern society, and so they are now discussed in the order in which they appear here.

Space–time distanciation

Giddens indicates that in 'pre-modern societies, space and place largely coincide, since the spatial dimensions of social life are, for most of the population, and in most respects, dominated by "presence" – by localised activities' (1990:18). In other words, students had to be in the presence of the teachers to hear their profound words. The history of the university is of students travelling to places where teachers expounded; in order to gain a degree from certain universities, residence qualifications were imposed, and so on. Now it is possible to study for, and be awarded, even higher degrees from some universities without ever being physically present, neither at the university itself nor even in the country in which the university is located. Now the teachers record their lessons and they can be studied in the students' own time and place. The learning experience is no longer immediate and face-to-face, but mediated and secondary. Indeed, knowledge – like most other forms of capital – is now without boundaries (Walshok, 1995) and whilst Walshok's book is primarily about the USA, knowledge is not bounded in contemporary society. Consequently, distance education, by definition, symbolizes the process of space–time distanciation; we will return to this discussion in the next section when we examine space–time compression.

Disembedded mechanisms and expert systems

Disembedding implies a process of extracting the specific localized social relations and reimplanting them within a global context of space and time. Consequently, the distance teaching institutions can be experienced, not as places to which learners travel for study with a teacher, but as the mechanisms through which the pursuit of their studies is facilitated wherever they study – new learning sites – and at whatever time they choose to undertake their work. The distance teaching institution is disembedded and needs no campus and no geographical location. In other words, the academy is now no longer a place, it is a process and a system – its educational offering is now a product guaranteed to provide specific learning for the purchasers; now it is not only the teachers who are important, it is the whole system – producing, packaging, marketing, processing, support services for clients, and so on. It is removed from its localized context and the clients and learners have to be persuaded to trust in the efficiency and expertise of the whole system. This has progressed to such an extent that there are already virtual universities, to which we will return in the next section.

The idea of expert systems is also something with which we have become familiar over recent years; we do not need to know how the system functions in order to be serviced by it. The system processes its products – in this case both teaching and learning materials – and once students are registered they receive the products, i.e. the teaching and learning materials, without being aware of all the processes of production. But there is another sense in which the distance education institution is an expert system since once students are registered as students they are also processed. Open University students in the UK, for instance, are given a number on registration and everything to do with that student is processed by the system number.

Reflective learning

The reflexivity of modernity, according to Giddens, involves a constant examination and re-examination of social practices which are 'reformed in the light of incoming information about those very practices' (1990:38). Consequently, the traditional mode of doing things is no longer sufficient justification for continuing a practice. Indeed, change in the mode of production and distribution of distance education materials will alter as new technologies initiate different ways of doing things. For instance, the interactive compact video disk, and the interactive computer program, will begin to replace some of the traditional correspondence material as the market makes it a worthwhile financial investment. However, in seeking a worldwide sale such hi-tech productions will limit the size of the market able to purchase costly commodities and so many educational materials will remain in traditional, and cheaper, written form for a few more years to come.

However, the concern here is much more with reflective learning – there are more opportunities when students operate at their own time and pace and in their own space for them to reflect upon the learning material with which they are presented. While there is a tendency to treat written material as 'sacred text', there is also a tendency to treat what teachers say as true, and in the teachers' presence that tendency is enhanced. Exercises can and should be provided in distance teaching in order to encourage reflective learning.

Individuation

As the functioning of many elements of society has become organized and distanced from everyday life, there has been a new emphasis upon the individual rather than the group; on individual rights rather then human rights, as so on. Emphasis is also placed upon the existential questions of humankind – upon the self and upon self-identity. People do not always feel so constrained by the demands of organizations, because they do not always have to attend them to be part of them, although they are actually controlled by their procedures in precisely the same way! Consequently, individuals feel able to follow their own pursuits, at their own time and in their own way and, to some extent, be self-determining individuals. Distance education, therefore, provides the opportunity for people to continue their education individually in their own space, at their own time and pace and have that learning serviced by a disembedded educational institution – an expert system.

Distance education may, therefore, be seen to fit many of the characteristics of late modernity and it may be regarded as being a symbol of this form of society. This analysis highlights some of the contemporary issues that this form of education for adults raises. It is not considered important to pursue the consequences of these any further here, although it is necessary to recognize that some practitioners of distance education attempt to overcome some of the problems implicit in the previous discussion.

The continued development of distance education

As we have already argued, distance education is the product of industrial capitalism and information technology; there is a sense in which we have begun to look at the way that changes in information technology have already affected the education system, and we will suggest that more changes are occurring later in this section, but before this we do need to return to the topic of global capitalism and to some of the points made in the opening chapters of this book. This section, therefore, will have two parts: advanced capitalism and information technology.

Advanced capitalism

Peters has shown how thoroughly the production of distance education materials epitomizes industrial production, although he does not demonstrate its relation to the capitalist market in quite the same manner. However, inherent in capitalism are three features that can also now be discovered in distance education, namely privatization, commoditization, and competition.

In recent times, education has been provided by the State in most societies of the world although religious bodies have also been major providers. Private provision has been a small factor in what has generally been regarded as a welfare state responsibility. However, from the earliest of days of distance education, private organizations, such as Pitmans, have provided a small amount of education. When distance education really developed – especially in its university form, with the British Open University – it was still State provided. However, in more recent times there has been a proliferation of distance education 'universities' (Jarvis, 2001b), which have been totally private and some have successfully sought to gain accreditation for their courses. At the same time, the State system has not been inactive and we have seen the emergence of the University for Industry, with LearnDirect. As these processes develop we will no doubt see an enlarged learning market, provided by distance learning institutions in competition with the State sponsored organizations.

Once any commodity is technologically produced it becomes an object, and within a capitalist economy a commodity can be sold. A distance education package, or a course, or an interactive video compact disk is a marketable commodity and one which educational institutions have been encouraged to sell. Now they have marketing managers committed to selling educational courses and, of course, the market is limited if the commodity is a course offered only at a local college or university. However, if the programme is contained within an object that can be carried away from the vendor, or even mailed or transmitted electronically to the purchaser, then it becomes a more attractive marketable commodity. This is even more so if the language used is international, such as English or Spanish – and no doubt in the future, Chinese.

Even so, the capitalistic market is one of competition. The rhetoric of the market is that only the best quality commodities will survive, but its reality is that only the strongest and largest organizations survive irrespective of the quality of the product they sell. Distance education now advertises its wares and buyers wish to know not only about the nature of the course being studied, but also the length of time that it will take, the qualification that will be awarded on successful completion, the number of assignments that have to be submitted and the fee that they will have to pay. Purchasers can then decide for themselves what is their 'best buy' according to their own instrumental concerns. One of the obvious outcomes of this process is that those unsuccessful institutions, irrespective of the quality of their product or of their potentiality, will lose out and may be forced to close. Hence, the large get larger at the expense of the small, unless the small discover a gap in the market, etc., but the consequences of this are self-evident.

But the market cannot be limited to the local area of the producing institution. The market is bounded only by the size of the globe! Hence, globalization has entered into distance education, and many universities are running their courses internationally: for example, the British Open University is opening offices throughout the world and from the 1980s has now become a mega-university (Daniel, 1996), the University of Surrey organized a Masters Degree programme in post-compulsory education in the 1980s which could be studied anywhere in the world and now there are many universities offering similar programmes. Now it is possible to study for a British university degree from many UK universities whilst still living in the farthest reaches of the world. Naturally, there are tremendous advantages to this – but it might also be wondered about the effect that this will have upon small indigenous universities of poor Third World countries, and once again it might lead to accusations of cultural imperialism. However, it might be much more a matter for some of trade or, as others would argue, of aid rather than anything else. Indeed, it could be argued that once education has embraced the market, then the logical outcome is that the large will get larger and with it there will almost certainly be forms of cultural imperialism, hegemony of discourse and the impoverishment of many forms of local education. This can already be seen in many of the smaller countries of the world, where their students feel forced to abandon their own language in order to be able to gain recognition in the wider world. There is then a danger that local, cultural knowledge will be side-lined as the knowledge concerns of the dominant cultures become the focus of global distance education.

Information technology

We have already traced the development of distance education in conjunction with the developments in information technology. But the digital age has generated a new and major development in distance education, which can be associated with another aspect of space–time re-alignment – space–time compression (Harvey, 1990:240–259). Harvey associates space–time compression with the Enlightenment and whilst this is perfectly true, there is another sense in which the virtual age has exacerbated this process. It is now possible through electronic means to communicate with people throughout the world interactively. This development has given rise to the virtual classroom and the virtual university (Teare *et al.*, 1998). New private universities are beginning to emerge that are almost totally electronic and virtual and there are tremendous advantages to such systems since there are no boundaries and it is still possible to communicate with tutors and peers around the world in a more personal manner than the one-way communication of more traditional distance education teaching.

With these developments there has been some questioning about the place of more traditional education. Katz and his associates (1999) have called this 'Dancing with the Devil' – but they are serious when they ask whether the more traditional forms of education can compete in the learning market with these new developments. Clearly traditional education is having to adapt to these social pressures, or else – following the inevitable law of the market – it will not survive. Aronowitz (2000), however, sees these new institutions as 'knowledge factories', which he condemns as he argues for a more humanistic approach to education. Irrespective of the fears of Aronowitz and his plea for a more humanistic approach to education, it has to be acknowledged that education is moving in the direction of a greater degree of virtuality. Nevertheless, it is increasingly being recognized that there is still a need for the traditional face-to-face interaction so that many institutions are developing mixed-mode delivery systems. Indeed, it could be argued that it is only in face-to-face interaction that creativity can flourish in education, so that there is some justification for Aronowitz's position. Yet, Peters (2002:133) would argue that we are now presented with real opportunities for the development of autonomous learners but that we are faced with major challenges in developing new pedagogical models to utilize this new learning space effectively to empower autonomous learners.

Like most innovations, there are clearly advantages to distance education but, because it has been developed by market-driven forces, it is often associated with the good and the bad of the market, rather than the good and the bad of the delivery system *per se*. Obviously, there are many advantages in the system – people not having to travel to schools and colleges because of disadvantage or commitments, being able to study in their own time and at their own pace, and so on. But it can easily become an impersonal system that is open to all the criticisms that can be levelled at it, although it will no doubt continue to become an even more significant sector within the field of education and, like the capitalist market itself, it will continue to impose forms of cultural and linguistic imperialism on disadvantaged peoples and undermine local cultures and practices. Consequently, we have to see both the advantages and disadvantages of distance education at the present time – but above all, the system does have many advantages in contemporary society although, unfortunately, it can hardly ever be neutral or even democratic.

Contemporary practices

As the times have changed, distance education has not just dropped one approach and adopted a new one; rather new approaches have been added to what is already a very complex field, just leading to a greater degree of complexity. Peters (2002:40–45) has suggested that there are at least seven different approaches to distance education today:

- the 'examination preparation' model;
- the correspondence education model;
- the multiple (mass) media model;
- the group distance education model;
- the autonomous learner model;
- the network-based distance education model;
- the technology-extended classroom model.

In addition, he recognizes that there are hybrids of these taking a variety of forms. For instance, we still find educational institutions offering to prepare students for examination, offering 'model answers' to questions, and so on. There are still correspondence schools and some universities, as they move into this new world, are adopting correspondence-type approaches but often combining them with more technological extensions of the classroom. In addition, there are other universities that combine the second and the third approaches. In the fourth approach, there are universities, such as the Chinese Open University, where the more formal third approach is used, not with individual learners but with groups who have been released from work, etc. in order to follow the prescribed lecture, and so on. Institutions that seek to facilitate autonomous learners are sometimes criticized because they do not provide sufficient content and distance education students (perhaps all students) do prefer to be given information, or at least led to it through careful Socratic approaches which are not necessarily conducive to creating autonomous learners. Increasingly, as knowledge expands and academic departments are not expanding at the same speed, students are enabled to network across the Web and with each other and also use all forms of teaching and learning material through which they can create their own network of learning resources. This is being encouraged as different universities are putting whole courses on line and allowing a wider public to access them. However, there are increasing dangers of plagiarism when this occurs since not all academic staff can be expected to know everything that now occurs on the Web in their subjects! Finally, there is the technologically extended classroom – this can be done in a variety of ways. For instance, when Adult Learners Week was launched in Lithuania, the opening lectures in one university setting were teleconferenced to seven different centres throughout the country and the recipients enabled to enter dialogue with the lecturers in precisely the same way as did those who were present. In Taiwan, there is at least one example of two universities sharing courses through teleconferencing, and this can certainly be expected to increase as educational institutions are forced to network in order to cover the wider practical knowledge bases of different subjects and practices. Additionally, higher education in Singapore has been given government money to ensure that all new courses produced can be put on line.

Naturally, as we continue to recognize the growing complexity of the learning process, there are many more possibilities to expand distance learning. At the same time, more mundane and everyday applications will continue to develop as corporations provide work-stations for their employees that enable them to check every aspect of their job and also learn about new applications and situations as they are introduced in the wider corporation.

Basically, the World Wide Web has produced the most extensive 'library' of learning materials and opportunities that the world has ever known – more knowledge that anyone can imagine – and this can all be accessed almost instantaneously at any individual's convenience in the home. Consequently, the opportunities that this offers are too many to number, but there is a fear that traditional institutions will find it hard to adapt to all these new approaches, as Katz and his associates warned. Then it has to be borne in mind that those who do not succeed in the market may perish, and this could be to the impoverishment of education generally and to some fields of study in particular.

However, producing all this material is also a very highly skilled and complex process. As we shall note later in this book, new roles for the educators are rapidly emerging and insufficient training exists that enables educators to become proficient at many of the skills required. For instance, it is widely recognized that the preparation of distance education materials places a greater emphasis on the creation of a course team of which the teacher is but one member, and so on. The style in which the material is written, if it is written, needs careful consideration and Holmberg (1960:14) suggested that the material had to be conversational and almost two-way, which he later came to regard as guided didactic conversation. This is true also in assessing course work that is to be returned to the distance education learners: comments might be regarded as an invitation to dialogue through the medium of the students' assignments and the tutors' comments.

The practice of distance education is now extremely common, especially with the development of desk top publishing, and this has resulted in many more people being involved in the preparation and assessment of distance education material. Naturally the quality should be high since most aspects of it can be controlled before dissemination, but the skills of becoming a distance educator are gradually being learned and taught and slowly we are seeing degree courses emerge in distance education, as a separate field of study. There are not yet many such certificated courses in the techniques of distance education. Indeed, some people are beginning to suggest that practitioners should be trained before they become distance educators, in the same way as the training of educators of adults has emerged, and it will probably not be too long before initial training courses, and concurrently certificates, in distance education develop and become part of the educational scene.

Conclusion

Distance education is growing in importance, it is being recognized by such organizations as the Commonwealth of Learning as a means by which the First World can assist the Third, but it is only recently that theories of distance education are beginning to emerge. The University for Industry, with its system of LearnDirect, is a private–public partnership designed to help individuals learn so that they can improve their career prospects and competitiveness in the labour market. Hence, even the boundaries between the public and the private are beginning to disappear as more people seek to learn. Otto Peters (2002) has called his latest book 'Distance Education in Transition', which is a good reflection of the current state of play in this field – but perhaps it is a transition that will not have an end-product in the near future.

8

ASSESSING AND EVALUATING

The language of the market place has been familiar to liberal adult education for many years, but it is only now becoming a part of the vocabulary of other educators. Even so, it is necessary to recognize that education has become a marketable commodity like other commodities, and that educational institutions are more like other commercial organizations, so that more commercial methods of assessment and evaluation are beginning to appear. Indeed, educational organizations have increasingly been forced to seek new markets, and this has caused them to become more competitive and flexible.

Continuing vocational education has become a rapidly expanding field, and with universities and colleges all seeking to offer additional education to those who are in work, functional degrees and diplomas, e.g. the MBA degree, have become commonplace. Colleges and universities are striving to attract more students to their taught higher degrees (both masters degrees and doctorates), and even engaging in competition to recruit more students by seeking to undercut their rivals in terms of the fees that they charge or even the amount of remission that they are prepared to award for prior educational experience. In addition, as potential students might not be able to gain educational release in working time, educational courses are now being offered during evenings and at weekends and distance education is becoming much more widely accepted. Courses are becoming modularized, irrespective of epistemological considerations, so that they can be more flexible and be marketed as independent units or as parts of a wider qualification. Flexibility and costs have become major concerns and academic qualifications have become symbols of the education that has been purchased. Indeed, it is now common to find educational institutions advertising the symbol of the education, that is the qualification to be gained, rather than the knowledge to be learned or the advantages of studying that specific field of knowledge. A National Vocational Qualification advertisement for training read: 'If you're buying training, make sure you get a receipt', and the receipt was the qualification! (*Guardian* 19 October 1993).

Other forms of general adult education, through adult education classes, have traditionally not been certificated. Liberal adult education, for instance, has been a part of the educational provision for many years. Indeed, the folk high schools in Denmark, university extra-mural classes in the United Kingdom and the 150-hour programme in Italy have all eschewed certification. However, the market ethos has now overtaken many of these systems and there is discussion about certificated courses in Danish folk high schools and liberal adult education is rapidly moving towards a fully certificated form in the United Kingdom. Now the educational qualification is a sign of the cultural capital possessed by individuals and through the purchase of additional educational commodities the sign can be changed to demonstrate the amount of knowledge consumed through the institutionalized learning process. With the introduction of accreditation of prior experiential learning (APEL), the commodity can be bought at discount prices in the educational market place and wise buyers seek the best purchases for their own purposes. It is significant that often the courses that are certificated are the same, or similar, to those which were previously not certificated – change but no change – or as Baudrillard suggests:

> Everything is in motion, everything is changing, everything is being transformed and yet nothing changes. Such a society, thrown into technological progress, accomplishes all possible revolutions but these are revolutions upon itself. Its growing productivity does not lead to structural change.
>
> (cited in Kellner, 1989:11)

Educational institutions advertise their courses, just like other market providers. Indeed, the Further Education Unit, among others, recognized this trend a while ago and produced pamphlets on marketing strategy for adult and continuing education (FEU, 1992). Indeed, the educational market is now international, with many institutions of higher education advertising their courses throughout the world, and many of them adopting a variety of modes of delivery, including distance education.

However, it is more often than not the sign that is advertised – Study for a University Degree – rather than the education itself. In order to attract the consumer the commodity must become a sign, according to Baudrillard, who defines consumption as 'a systematic act of the manipulation of signs' (cited in Poster, 1988:21). Individuals are, therefore, free to purchase their own education, if they can afford it, and develop in the direction that they wish, or at least in one of the directions that they are offered through the market. They can reinforce their own understanding of themselves through the educational signs, among other signs, that they display. Indeed, the more prestigious the commodities, the greater the sign value. It must be recalled, however, that APEL and APL have been major advances to the education system that adult educators have advocated for many years but, like most educational reforms, it took the social pressures generated by the globalization process and the market place to ensure that they were instigated and accepted.

Before the certificates are awarded learners' work has to be assessed and so the first part of this chapter looks at the processes and assessment and the second at certificates and credits.

Assessing learners' work

In this section we will examine the nature of assessment, the rationale for assessment and some types of assessment.

The nature of assessment

When we meet a person for the first time we may often comment afterwards: 'What a nice woman' or 'I didn't really think much of him', and so on. In a sense, as a result of our meeting we have assessed our own reactions to that person. What we are doing in this case is to assess how we have responded to the other person: we have assessed our reaction – others may have reached a different conclusion! This is important when we consider any form of assessment – it is our subjective reaction although, as we shall see below, there are bounds to the subjectivity of assessment. However, the most important first point to make is that assessment is natural and many, but not all forms, contain an element of subjectivity about them. Assessment, then, is placing a value on a phenomenon – and in this sense it has the same meaning as evaluation. However, there is something of a convention in education that assessment is restricted to the process of placing a value (grade) on learners' performances, whereas evaluation is used more commonly about either the teaching and learning process, e.g. curriculum evaluation. Even so, we now see one fundamental difference, the value is often placed on the education by the consumer rather than educationalists – customer satisfaction, irrespective of the standard of education, is a vital necessity, and there is a fundamental danger that this will lower the standard of the education itself. Indeed, the term 'dumbing down' is beginning to be heard more frequently – suggesting that this is actually occurring. Consequently, not only do we find evaluation and assessment being used even in the larger organizational evaluations, such as the research assessment exercise in higher education, but now we are faced with such terms as total quality management. The processes are the same – placing a value upon – but the use of language varies by convention and the evaluators are different, and we shall return to this point below.

232

However, there is a second point to be made about this: when we as educators make an assessment, we assess the learners' work – we do not assess them as people. Nevertheless, when the learners receive our assessment they frequently treat it as if it is an assessment of them as persons. Hence, we have to treat the assessment process in quite a delicate manner, recognizing the humanistic nature of education itself.

Not all assessment is subjective, however, and we know that when we take a ruler and measure the height of a room, or the length of a piece of wood, we can get an accurate measurement. This measurement can be replicated whenever we wish. The same would be true to a considerable extent when we check a mathematical calculation; we are able to award a mark which is more objective. We could say that it is a measurement of the learners' ability to solve the mathematical problems that have been set. However, it is rather different when we come to marking an essay: what will always remain the same is that we can measure how many paragraphs and words there are in the essay – that does not alter. But two markers may well disagree on the mark to be awarded for the content of the essay itself. This is not surprising because we are now no longer measuring but assessing.

Many educators are faced with a major problem in contemporary society – examination boards, governments and policy makers all want to treat assessment as if it is measurement. It is not! Assessment is a subjective process, rather like when we met that person – it is the same person but different people assess him/her differently. It also happens with assessing essays! During my career I have conducted many marking workshops, when groups of teachers/examiners have been asked to mark the same essay individually and simultaneously. Rarely has there been total agreement – rather there has often been a difference by as much as 40 per cent! What the assessors were doing when they were marking those essays was placing their own value upon the essay – it might be only on the content, but it might have been on the structure and level of analysis, as well as the content. But we all see something different in an essay and what is a good point to one reader might not be such a novel one to another, and so on. This, by no means, denies the fact that there may be correct and incorrect content in an essay, but it does emphasize the fact that it is not only the content that is assessed. And so we must see that assessment is not measurement – even though we might place a percentage grade on the piece of work. The idea of the percentage grade is only to give the appearance that the marking is objective and, therefore, learners should accept it without question.

At the same time, assessors should have a level of expertise that should enable them to make a more authoritative assessment of a piece of work than non-experts. However, the authority of the expert does not transform an assessment process to one of measurement. Our society is bedevilled with the idea of measurement because of the prevalence of the scientific measurement of inanimate and empirical phenomena. This is a problem for educators and it is one that we have to confront. We need to be as fair as we can to learners – hence, we often double mark to try to eradicate some of the subjectivity and this is to be commended, so long as both markers mark the same script blind – that is a clean script without any markings, or comments, from the other examiner appearing on the script. If the script is not blind, there is a tendency to agree with the first marker, and so on.

The fact that so much assessing is subjective, but that our society is often loathe to acknowledge it, is a real problem since we can see that a great deal of the educational examination system is seeking to provide an incorrect picture of the examining process – even though many techniques, like double blind marking, are put into place to try to reduce the level of subjectivity. However, reduction is not eradication! Therefore we might need to ask ourselves why we assess at all?

A rationale for assessment

There are several reasons why we assess – in the teaching and learning process it is a diagnostic tool, that is, it is a way whereby teachers can discover the strengths and weaknesses of the learners. Teaching should always be a response to the learners' needs and, therefore, it is necessary for teachers to try to diagnose what those needs are. Teachers, therefore, need to incorporate a variety of techniques in the teaching and learning process so that they are enabled to make their teaching even more relevant – such techniques can vary from question and answer sessions, to open discussion and feedback, to tests and examinations. At this level, therefore, assessing is very important for the learners as well as the teachers because the former also become aware of what they know and what they do not know, or what they can do acceptably and what they need to improve upon. It is also at this point when it is necessary to remind ourselves that we are assessing learners' knowledge, skill and so on rather than assessing the learners themselves. Learners must not feel threatened by the process and we, as educators, need to recognize the moral nature of the processes in which we are engaged.

Perhaps the most common reason given for assessment – especially in recent government policy – is the maintenance of standards. Schools, colleges and universities must be seen in this educational market to be maintaining standards so that potential clients know the standard of the institutions in which they might enrol. At first sight this seems to be a laudable enterprise in which an open market is reinforced by transparency. Once we accept the subjectivity of the assessing process, however, we can see that it is not entirely possible for comparisons to be made unless the tests being taken are public and are all graded in the same way – which is precisely what the government of the UK has endeavoured to do. But the approach still has flaws in it, since the learners in the schools and colleges start from different positions; they come into their educational institutions from different backgrounds, and so on. Therefore the comparative nature of the exercise is problematic although it is more possible to claim that standards in schools and colleges can be improved against the general picture using different teaching methods, different teachers, and so on – but we still do not do away with the subjective nature of assessment itself, only to see that in the larger, public examination, there are ways of making the process of assessing fairer.

A third reason for assessing is that it provides evidence of the learners' attainments and as such provides evidence that they may progress to either another stage in their educational career or that they may enter the career itself. However, it must again be emphasized that attainment does not necessarily equate with ability, and examination marks may not reflect intelligence. It was easier to make this claim when it was believed that there was only one form of intelligence, but with current research suggesting multiple intelligences it is harder to make the claim. Nevertheless, it is a convenient way for a college to judge entry and a profession to assess someone's ability to enter the profession. Yet there is little research to suggest that the entry grade necessarily relates to career competence or attainment.

Overall, perhaps the best we can claim for assessment is that it provides a guide, an indication, rather than that it is an exact science of measuring and we could wish that this were more publicly acknowledged.

Types of assessment

In a book of this nature it is not possible to examine in detail every type of assessment and so Table 8.1 outlines some of the major types of assessment and explains briefly what they are.

Total quality management

We mentioned above the fact that as education is now a commodity that has moved into the market place, quality might be regarded as having something to do with customer satisfaction. Naturally, this might logically have no intrinsic connection with the standard of education, but with whether the learners enjoyed their studies, and so on. Hence we find Parsons (1994:20) emphasizing the learners, or customers, as one of the four aspects of total quality management, the other three being the processes, the people and the culture. Not all writers on total quality management education emphasize the consumer quite so much and

Table 8.1 Types of assessment

Type of assessment	Description
Formative	This is the diagnostic form of assessment that occurs during the process of teaching and learning
Summative	The assessment that occurs at the end of the process – the final mark
Continuous	A process of assessment that involves an ongoing process throughout a course/module, etc. rather than relying entirely on a summative assessment
Analytical	This is also part of the diagnostic process since the marker carefully works through the piece of work, evaluating every aspect and, usually, commenting on it – as a form of teaching
Global	A technique of rapid marking many scripts through reading a whole script and rank-ordering it against other similar scripts and then later awarding a grade on each script in relation to all the others
Self	An approach to assessing where the learner/practitioners assess themselves or their own work
Peer	An approach in which peers assess each other's work
Collaborative	When a number of people collaborate to agree a grade, usually involving the learner and the teacher

Murgatroyd and Morgan (1993) have '3Cs' – culture, commitment and communication – as their baseline. Culture is about the ambiance of the process, commitment is to the shared goals of the institution and communication is about the ability to communicate effectively and efficiently. Clearly the major baseline with some writers about total quality management is with success in the market rather than those other aspects of the teaching and learning process and it is here where the lowering of standards might occur, since learners want a certificate and there is a chance that with lower standards more learners might enrol in a course knowing that they will almost certainly gain the award.

Certificates and credits

All forms of education for adults are now being certificated, and different approaches to qualifying certificates have emerged, two of which are discussed here – National Vocational Qualifications and credit accumulation and transfer.

National Vocational Qualifications (SVQ – Scottish Vocational Qualification in Scotland)

Not only has education become a commodity, it is one that has to be assessed in terms of its outputs. Considerable emphasis is now being placed upon the competencies that are gained as a result of the learning. Competence is 'the possession and development of sufficient life skills, knowledge, appropriate attitudes and experience for successful performance in life roles' (Hermann and Keynon, 1987:1). Whilst knowledge, skills and attitudes might also be included within the general framework of competence, it is extremely difficult to assess all of these from the perspective of performance because individuals do not always perform consistently in accord with their own theoretical position, as Argyris and Schon (1974) have demonstrated. They argued that people had 'espoused theories' and 'theories in use': the former are the perspectives which individuals will say guide their behaviour whilst the latter are those which may be detected from a close observation and analysis of behaviour. They are not necessarily consistent and while the performance may be regarded as more important than the espoused theory, the coupling of knowledge and skills in any definition of competence is oversimple.

In vocational terms, a competency may be defined as 'a performance capability needed by workers in a specified occupational area' (Hermann and Keynon, 1987:1). Different levels of competence have been designated in National Vocational Qualifications:

- Level 1 – performance of routine and predictable work activities.
- Level 2 – performance of work activities involving greater individual responsibility and autonomy than Level 1.
- Level 3 – skilled performance of activities, involving complex and non-routine work. Some supervisory activity may also be involved at this level.
- Level 4 – complex, technical, specialized and professional activities, including planning and problem solving. There is personal accountability at this level.
- Higher Level – competence in pursuit of a senior occupation, including the ability to apply fundamental principles and techniques. Extensive knowledge and understanding is necessary to underpin competence.

(Summarized from Oakeshott, 1991:52)

Performance must be tested using valid assessment methods and endorsed by the best current practice. The standards are set by the Lead Industrial Bodies – that is the organization, or occupational grouping, which has been given this responsibility. Since it is the performance being assessed, it is not necessary for individuals having their competencies assessed to have attended a training course beforehand – it is the ability to perform the job that is important. This is regarded as the most efficient, since it allows for the shortest routes to be taken to the point of assessment, although the value of experience is not ruled out by this approach.

While it is clearly necessary to assess performance in the work situation, trying to categorize all performances into a few levels is a problematic undertaking, especially those which are required infrequently by the demands of the job. However, this approach has moved assessment away from the theoretical and artificial to the actual place of performance; but the assumptions underlying this approach are probably as problematic as those underlying more traditional modes of assessment, since successful performance on one day is no guarantee of it on another. Much more problematic, however, is the process of trying to subdivide an occupation into its competencies and arriving at a complete list upon which there is general agreement – indeed, the whole is always more than the sum of its parts!

However, a complex process of designating competencies and testing them is being evolved at the present time, although the surrounding bureaucracy is clearly too great and some providers of courses seeking NVQ accreditation have expressed dissatisfaction with it.

Even so, it is becoming possible to gain NVQs for participation in voluntary activities as well as vocational ones. Tiernan (1992) records how the Royal Society of Arts recognized the skills involved in voluntary work and has introduced an Advanced Diploma in the Organization of Voluntary Groups, based on the NVQ model.

In addition, there is a movement towards introducing a more general set of qualifications that will relate to, but not replace, the current General Certificate qualifications; these are General National Vocational Qualifications (GNVQ). These qualifications are more work related than subject related, although it is anticipated that they will achieve compatibility with the normal General Certificate – it is claimed that level 3 GNVQ will be equivalent to an Advanced Level General Certificate of Education (Smith, 1993).

Credit accumulation and transfer

Once courses are modularized, it becomes possible to award some form of accreditation for each module. Standardized credits for educational achievement in continuing education were first discussed in America in the late 1960s. A National Task Force of the National University Continuing Education Conference in 1968 provided a definition of a continuing education credit as: 'Ten contact hours of participation in an organized continuing education experience under responsible sponsorship, capable direction and qualified instruction' (Long and Lord, 1978:2). Long records how this idea developed and how the idea of accrediting experience developed from this, so that accreditation of prior experiential learning (APEL) emerged from within the same framework. However, the movement towards standardized accreditation of modules developed much more slowly in the United Kingdom, although it was heavily influenced by the American experience. Eventually, it was accepted by the Council for National Academic Awards in 1986. Since the Council only accredited higher education courses, its credit scheme related to the different levels of the undergraduate degree and the taught Masters courses. It assumed that an undergraduate degree has three levels, relating to each of the three years and that each year was equivalent to 1,200 hours of study. Consequently, the first year of an undergraduate degree was seen as a Certificate and worth 120 credits at level 1; completion of two years was equivalent to the Diploma of Higher Education and was the equivalent of the Certificate plus a further 120 credits at level 2; a bachelor's degree was worth 360 credits, at least 60 of which had to be obtained at level 3 and not more than 120 at level 1. An honours degree had to include 120 credits at level 3 and no more than 120 at level 1. A taught Master's degree consisted of 120 credits at M level and herein lay one of the major mistakes that the Council made, since a taught Master's degree has always been the equivalent of one full year's study (i.e. 120 M level credits) followed by a dissertation. This mistake by the Council effectively devalued the taught Master's degree by at least one-third.

Having produced a system that gradually achieved widespread acceptance it became possible for students to study some modules in one educational institution and gain accreditation for that work and then to transfer to another institution to gain further credits. Many universities and colleges, while subscribing to the scheme, will only award their own degrees if at least a substantial proportion of the credits has been gained in their institution, and this proportion is often as high as two-thirds of the whole. This is understandable, since there is not yet a national undergraduate or taught Master's degree, although there might have been if the Conservative government had not abolished the Council for National Academic Awards. The Open University now administers the remnants of the Council's scheme, and many of the Council's former 'clients' (the polytechnics) now have university status and award their own qualifications.

This principle has been used at lower level courses and even in liberal adult education where there has not been any assessment of achievement. For instance, in one or two places 'passport' type schemes have been introduced, whereby a record of attendance at courses has been retained by students who could then produce their own record as part of their own learning portfolio in seeking credit for their previous learning experiences. Assessment of prior learning has become widely accepted in post-compulsory education in the United Kingdom, with two types appearing: a general and a specific credit. The former is often given as a general remission of part of a course for the overall learning experiences in which students have engaged, while the specific credit refers to remission of part of a course of study because of previous successful study in that specific area of knowledge. While assessment of prior learning in the general sense is a recognition of the broad learning of adults, there is a danger that it will be given to induce students to specific courses because it will enable them to complete it sooner and more cheaply, etc. This danger becomes greater as education is being underfunded and colleges and universities are having to attract as many students as possible in order to make their courses viable. Specific credits are content based and, consequently, there is a greater certainty that academic standards and subject coherence will be retained.

In almost precisely the same way the European Community has introduced a transferable credit scheme – European Credit Transfer System (ECTS) – which stemmed from its concern to introduce study abroad programmes throughout the Community, and it is regarded as a way by which the EC can facilitate educational institutions cooperating with each other. The programme began in 1988 in a selected number of universities, but by 1996 both universities and non-universities were involved in the project, and the number has been increasing each year – in 1997–8 there were 772 applications from new institutions to become involved, and this number continues to increase. The scheme is still largely based on the study abroad programme and, unlike the UK system, it awards 60 credits for an academic year, 30 for a semester and 20 for a term (trimester). Since this is a study abroad programme institutions are required to agree on the programme before a student studies abroad, but as a result there is full academic recognition by participating institutions of each other's awards.

Accreditation is becoming a normal part of the education of adults, even of liberal adult education as it becomes part of mainstream general education. The process of integration into mainstream education is something that adult educators would generally welcome, but the price for this is high. In many ways accreditation is contrary to the ethos of liberal adult education – an ethos which was being destroyed by the policies of the Conservative government of the early 1990s, although more recently its value has been recognized once again. At the same time, if education is to be regarded as a passport to occupation or further study it is necessary to have some form of recognition for the standards achieved in those courses, and accreditation is, therefore, a necessary part of this process.

As liberal adult education moved towards accreditation in order to continue to get some funding from the government, it was also being recognized that many people do not want to study for additional qualifications.

Consequently, some courses are being offered which seek to combine both those students seeking the award and others who are learning for learning's sake. Indeed, this was something Houle (1961) researched and the most recent further research undertaken, the *National Adult Learning Survey* (La Valle and Blake, 2001:14), notes that 20 per cent of all taught courses were non-vocational, although this does not mean that there was no award attached to them. However, we do know that the University of the Third Age retains the ethos of learning for learning's sake and that there are few awards given in the UK for completion of their courses. These are self-financing because of the voluntary nature of the U3A, but the provision of self-financing liberal adult education courses would result in decreasing provision as fewer individuals would be able to afford the fees and, therefore, adult education would probably become even more open to the accusations that it is a middle-class leisure time pursuit.

Naturally, there are a number of other reactions to this and one of these is the emphasis being placed on self-directed learning, the study of which is becoming very prevalent throughout the United States and elsewhere (Candy, 1991, *inter alia*). In addition, new forms of educational opportunities are emerging, such as free universities (Draves, 1980) and the University of the Third Age, where no credit is given since the learning is about human being and becoming rather than human having and consuming (Jarvis, 1992). Here people can learn, grow and develop, even within a market framework, but without reference to qualifications.

It is becoming difficult to imagine that academic standards are being maintained with all the changes that are occurring, despite the valiant efforts of nearly all major educational institutions to introduce systems of quality control.

Quality

Curriculum evaluation was the normal manner through which educators assessed their work, although much of this was conducted in initial education. It was often assumed in adult education, for instance, that if tutors retained their students throughout the allocated duration of their course then they must be acceptable. Another approach was that of elaborating upon the principles of good practice (see Council on the Continuing Education Unit, 1984). Periodic reviews by both local and governmental inspectors were another sufficient check of the overall standard. However, this is beginning to change under the influence of the market, and now the language of quality is appearing in adult and continuing education.

The definition of the concept, however, is much more problematic. Quality has been defined as effectiveness, efficiency and even student or client satisfaction. However, equating quality with any of these is to be guilty of the naturalistic fallacy, because quality simply cannot be equated to another value. Quality is quality and this differs considerably from efficiency, since it is possible to be adjudged efficient even though the outcome is poor, and so on. Additionally, quality has been used in relation to quality teaching, quality learning, etc., but in these instances there is a tendency towards tautology. Quality is also used in relation to the outcomes of the teaching–learning transaction (see Muller and Funnell, 1991). Thus it may be seen that this is by no means an obvious concept, although it does appear to be treated as rather self-evident at times. (See, for instance, FEU 1989, where the concept is assumed throughout rather than clarified.) The ideas of good practice and quality assurance were brought together in two research projects conducted by de Wit (1992, 1993) who wrote that:

> Although there is no agreed definition of quality, there are several key themes in the current debate, which focus attention on the whole network of resources and procedures in CE. These themes are
>
> - fitness for purpose
> - need for a strategic approach
> - meeting customers' expectations
> - a cycle of continuous improvement
> - a cohesive system of interconnected processes.
>
> (de Wit, 1993:7)

While any attempt to distil the main characteristics from such an abstract concept is fraught with danger, this approach is more correct than that of equating the concept with any specific characteristic, in the manner that some of the previous descriptions have done. De Wit's study endeavoured to draw together in a practical manner some of the main issues that are generally agreed to constitute quality in continuing education, and she produced a clear and practical checklist, under each of the following headings:

- Policy
- Staff
- Courses
- Marketing
- Teaching and learning
- Outcomes.

Under each of these headings there are a number of questions that course teams and evaluators might ask about continuing education provision to ensure that good practice is being carried out in all instances. Clearly it does not overcome the conceptual problem, but this it acknowledges. It does, however, seek to provide practical guidelines within the limits it sets itself.

Conclusion

The whole nature of assessment and credit has been transformed with the advent of lifelong learning in a global market but, as we shall see in the next chapter, the nature of the curriculum itself has been transformed as teaching and learning has become a marketable commodity.

9

CURRICULUM THEORY AND PROGRAMME PLANNING

'Curriculum' is a relatively common word in initial education but one used less frequently in the education of adults, while 'programme' is more common. British writers, however, do use both curriculum design and programme design reasonably interchangeably, while American writers also use the terms 'instructional design', 'design of learning' (Verner, 1964) or 'design of education' (Houle, 1972). In the United Kingdom, the term programme is beginning to assume greater significance since it has been recognized that in the learning market educational institutions offer a wide 'menu' of courses/modules and that it is now easier for learners to construct their own learning programme.

The concerns of adult education in the past have tended to be centred around the topics that have already been discussed, but without a great deal of explicit curriculum theory and this may have been because of its non-formal nature. Yet there has always been an implicit curriculum theory and also explicit statements of rationale for adult education. Some of these elements will be discussed in the first part of the chapter and, at the same time, the curriculum theory implicit in the ideas already raised will also become apparent. The second part will focus on the more explicit discussions about educational programmes that have emanated from the USA and will be constructed around the three types of programme described by Cervero and Wilson (1994).

Studies in curriculum theory

At the outset it is necessary to clarify the concept itself and, thereafter, the reasons why the term has not been employed in the education of adults will be examined. Various types of curriculum models will then be discussed including the introduction of modularization. This will be followed by an analysis of the elements of the curriculum, including a discussion of the way that the concept of 'need' actually pointed to a market model of education long before the market was so prevalent.

The concept of curriculum

The word derives from the Latin '*currere*', which means 'to run' and its associated noun, which has been translated as 'a course'. Hence, the word has been used to refer to following a course of study; but, like many other terms, its meaning has been subtly changed over the years and Lawton noted that 'in the past definitions ... tended to emphasize the content of the teaching programme, now writers on the curriculum are much more likely to define it in terms of the whole learning situation' (1973:11). Similarly Kelly suggested that it is necessary to 'distinguish the use of the word to denote the content of a particular subject or area of study from the use of it to refer to the total programme of an educational institution' (1977:3). From these two brief quotations it is possible to see that even these writers are referring to slightly different usages of the word. Perhaps Griffin's comment that curriculum refers to 'the entire range of educational practices or learning experiences' (1978:5) summarizes the problem. The word can mean anything from the content of what is taught to the total provision of an educational institution; it can also refer to the subject matter of a particular course of study or even to the learning that is intended. Hence, it relates to both the known and the intended, i.e. the formal educational organization and provision, or to the unknown and unquantifiable, i.e. the learning experiences. Traditionally it referred to the former and in this sense to formal educational provision.

The term has been employed in a variety of different ways, especially in initial education and we can look briefly at some of the terms that have been used synonymously with curriculum. 'Educational provision' is one: it refers either to what is organized and offered to students by the institutions or what is organized and offered to the students by the teachers within those institutions. This might also be referred to as 'the total learning situation', referring to all the learning experiences, intended or unintended, provided by the educational institution since, as we have seen, the term 'learning' is replacing 'education' in some significant ways. The 'programme' may be either the prospectus provided by an educational institution, or a section of it, or it may refer to the actual number of courses that are organized after enrolment. A course may be the course of study followed by an individual within the institution or it may refer to a single course offered to a specific group of students, e.g. the nursing course. As modularization has developed, so the term 'course' has tended to refer to students' individual programmes of study. Modules, however, are individual courses.

There has been a subtle, but nevertheless significant, change with the development of modularization. Previously, individual courses were usually built around the epistemological demands of an area of knowledge, e.g. a course on the sociology of the family, by the end of which students were expected to have grasped the rudiments of the subject irrespective of the number of hours that they studied beyond the hours that they were taught. This was something of an open-ended commitment on behalf of the student, but it was not really quantifiable. A module, however, is usually designated by the number of hours of learning that a student is expected to undertake, so that, for instance, a 50-hour module might involve 15 hours of teaching in the classroom, 15 hours of private study and a 20-hour assignment – although the exact constitution of the 50 hours is a matter of college policy. This 50 hours might be designated to occur over a short period of time, e.g. a few weeks (a 'short fat' module) or over a longer period. A 100-hour module, on the other hand, might involve 40 hours of classroom teaching, 30 hours of private study and a 30-hour assignment and this might occur over a period of 20 weeks (a 'long thin' module). Three important things to note about this change in curriculum design are: that more modules can be offered so that there is more student choice; that the length of the module has no relationship to the epistemological demands of the discipline; that there has been little or no research to examine the relative advantages of cramming a module into a short period of time, like a week, or holding it throughout a longer period, such as a semester, although it is probable that the longer period is more effective for learning but the shorter one for timetabling and marketing.

It is perhaps easy to recognize how the confusion in the use of the terms has arisen, since each of these has an affinity with the others. It is also important to note that the emphasis on learning is a comparatively recent addition and builds upon the ideas of the romantic curriculum and progressive education that were prevalent in the United Kingdom in the 1960s. At this stage it is clear that the term curriculum tends to reflect the totality of the learning as if it is a comprehensive and coherent whole, whereas programme implies that there are several parts to the whole, parts of which students might choose for themselves. This is an important distinction and one that becomes more significant in any examination of the current situation in the education of adults. Certainly the scene has changed a great deal and much of the discussion about curriculum theory that occurred in the 1970s and early 1980s now appears extremely dated. This chapter will look briefly at this earlier material now before moving on to analyse the contemporary situation.

An historical overview of curriculum theory

A great deal of curriculum theory that emerged was as a result of studies in initial education; indeed, in the United Kingdom there was an obvious reference to this with specific reference to romantic and classical curriculum models. The same was not so true in the United States where there has been

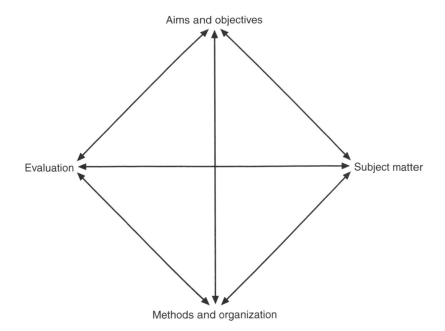

Aims and objectives

Evaluation ◄─────────────────────► Subject matter

Methods and organization

Figure 9.1 A learning and teaching process model for the education of adults.

a greater emphasis upon programme planning in adult education through-out the whole of this period, which we will discuss later in this chapter.

Many attempts have been made to produce a satisfactory model of the teaching and learning process in curriculum terms. Frequently, reference is made back to Tyler's (1949) classic study about school curricula, but Taba (1962:425), citing Giles *et al.* (1942), produced a model that, with slight adaptation, may be valid for the education of adults (see Figure 9.1). This model is a reasonably familiar one in curriculum theory since it contains the elements that occur in almost every learning and teaching process. Taba wrote:

> A curriculum usually contains a statement of aims and of specific objectives; it indicates some selection and organization of content; it either implies or manifests certain patterns of learning and teaching, whether because the objectives demand them or because the content organization requires them. Finally, it includes a programme of evaluation of the outcomes.
>
> (Taba, 1962:10)

The above model may be applied to every course offered in an educational institution rather than to the overall programme and thus there may be considerable variation with the elements of the curriculum between different courses. Hence, discussion about the aforementioned elements must necessarily still remain at the level of generality.

British educators, claimed Davies, 'have been more interested in defining aims than in studying objectives, while American teachers have been more willing to think in terms of concrete objectives' (1976:11). Certainly this claim would be true of the curriculum models of both Verner and Houle discussed later. By contrast, British theorists have focused upon the broader philosophical issues, as both Griffin (1978) and Mee and Wiltshire (1978) demonstrated, in their respective ways. Yet the broad philosophy of educators of adults may also affect their attitude towards the concept, and use of objectives in the design of a teaching and learning situation. Curriculum theorists have posited many types of objectives: instructional, teaching, learning, behavioural, expressive, etc. Davies (1976) discussed the whole area very thoroughly, so there is no need to expand it here. Even so, it is useful to examine the relationship between aims and objectives and to see whether the latter actually reflect the overall aims as even the general philosophy of adult education. For instance, considerable emphasis has been given to behavioural objectives, and while these might be quite valid on a skills-based course, their usefulness in cognitive learning courses is much more questionable and contrary to the overall philosophy of adult learning, but they do reflect this desire to measure rather than assess that we discussed in the previous chapter. Objectives specified in behavioural terms also tend to imply that the human learner will learn and behave in a manner designated by the teacher, like a pigeon or a rat! Another implication of this approach is that teachers will adopt a didactic and authoritarian approach to teaching and this is quite contrary to the philosophy of teaching adults. It is maintained here that any approach to teaching that designates how a learner will behave as a result of undergoing the teaching and learning process undermines the dignity of the learner and may be guilty of the charge of indoctrination; consequently, the process of teaching and learning then falls short of the high ideals of education elaborated in this study. By contrast, Eisner (1969) regarded expressive objectives as evocative rather than prescriptive, which is much closer to the general philosophy of the education of adults that is advocated here. Nevertheless, behavioural objectives have a valid place in some forms of education and also in therapy, but while therapy might involve learning it is not education.

The subject matter or content of some courses, especially those that are vocationally orientated or award bearing, is usually prescribed by the examining or the validating body. This reflects the point that the curriculum may be regarded as a selection of culture made by those who have status or power within the profession or within education. Elsewhere Jarvis (1983a:50–53) outlined other criteria for the selection of curriculum content in professional education including the demands of professional practice, the relevance of the topic, and its worthwhileness. However, there are courses in which the subject matter may actually be negotiated between tutor and students, but these courses tend to be exceptions rather than everyday occurrences since validating bodies tend to require the content of courses specified at validation. In liberal adult education these occurrences may have been much more frequent in the past since it was recognized that the subject matter depended on the interests of the students and might be negotiated between tutor and students.

Negotiated subject content may be much more common in continuing professional education since practitioners, being aware of their strengths and weaknesses in practice, will probably know what they need to learn during in-service education in order to improve the quality of their practice. Diagnosis of learning needs should occur either prior to a course or at the very least at its outset, so that it is essential for the teacher to join with the students in planning a teaching and learning programme. Often in continuing professional education it is useful to spend a planning day a few weeks prior to the commencement of the course, mapping out the areas of the subject matter that should be covered during it. Diagnosis should always precede learning and teaching, as we discussed in the previous chapter.

The location of the teaching, the organization of the room in which the teaching and learning is to occur, the content of the session and the methods to be employed are all part of the educational process. They should all relate to the learners, their learning needs or wants and to their learning styles, but they are also dependent upon the expertise of the tutorial staff. The organization of the environment relates to the adulthood of the learners and to the teaching methods employed. Similarly, the actual methods employed by the teacher are important considerations in the educational process. Bourdieu and Passeron claimed that all 'pedagogic action is, objectively, symbolic violence in so far as it is the imposition of a cultural arbitrary by an arbitrary power' (1977:5). It is important to recognize the symbolic significance of the teaching method. Moreover, the symbolism becomes an immoral reality if the teaching methods employed in any teaching and learning transaction inhibit the development, or undermine the dignity and humanity, of the learners; but it becomes moral, and good curriculum practice, when they encourage their growth and expression of humanity.

The philosophical issues involved in teaching are important considerations, especially in the education of adults, but the methods employed must also relate to the ethos of the group and the content of the session. Hence, the skill of the teacher is not only about techniques but also about human interaction, and it is a combination of these various factors that can lead to teaching and learning becoming an effective and stimulating process.

Clearly the aims and objectives that have been set for any single teaching and learning session or for a course as a whole provide one base for its evaluation. Yet these may prove to be too restrictive since the class may have deviated from the selected aims and even from the content decided upon in order to follow up ideas that arise during the process itself. This may have resulted in effective learning and class satisfaction and all the participants regarded it as successful. Hence, if learning and understanding has occurred, within a humanistic context, then the education may be assessed as successful.

Evaluation should not be undertaken by teachers by themselves since in the education of adults the students should be full participants in the process. In non-compulsory education this occurs in any case, since as Newman forcibly reminded his readers:

> Adult education is a cruel test of a tutor's skills. It is a sink or swim business. If the tutor does not have what it takes, people stop coming. His students vote with their feet, unobtrusively transferring to other classes or simply staying away. The class dwindles week by week, leaving him all too well aware that he has been found wanting.
>
> (Newman, 1979:66)

Perhaps this is a rather dramatic portrayal of the manner by which students are actually involved in the process of evaluation. Indeed, many students are very kind to their tutors and encourage inexperienced ones. Even so, students do evaluate their tutors and the process of teaching and learning that has occurred, and so it is beneficial to all concerned to involve them in the more formal process.

Classical and romantic models of the curriculum

The models discussed above owe their origin to theorists whose main concern was initial education, but many developments in school education curriculum theory were mirrored in the developments in adult education at this time. The classical curriculum reflected the teacher-centred approach while the 1960s emphasis on student-centred learning is reflected in the development of the romantic curriculum model.

The concepts of classical and romantic curriculum reflect contrasting educational ideologies, the latter coming to prominence in initial education in the 1960s, which has been regarded as a period of romanticism. These positions have been summarized by Lawton in two different tables and his argument is summarized here in Table 9.1.

Most models must necessarily overemphasize their salient points, so Table 9.1 presents a polarization of the two curricula models. Yet the fact *le 9.1* The classical and romantic curricula

Elements of the classical curriculum	Elements of the romantic curriculum
Subject-centred	Child-centred
Skills	Creativity
Instruction	Experience
Information	Discovery
Obedience	
Conformity	Originality
Discipline	Freedom
Objectives – acquiring knowledge	Processes – 'living' attitudes and values
Content – subjects	Experiences – real life topics and proposals
Method – didactic instruction – competition	Method – involvement – cooperation
Evaluation – by tasks (teacher set) – by examinations (public and competitive)	Evaluation – self-assessment (in terms of self-improvement)

Source: Lawton (1973:22–23).

that the major features are highlighted means that it is possible to see immediately the significance of these for a deeper understanding of the education of adults. Clearly the romantic curriculum, as formulated above, approximates to the more traditional forms of adult education and, indeed, to Knowles' interpretation of andragogy. It will be recalled that Knowles suggested that andragogy has four premises that are different from pedagogy: the learner is self-directed; the learner's experiences are a rich resource for learning; the learner's readiness to learn is increasingly orientated to the developmental tasks of social roles; the learner's time perspective assumes an immediacy, so that learning is problem- and performance- rather than subject-centred. Knowles (1989:83–84) later added two other premises to this list, and his new list is: adults need to know why they are learning; adults' self-concept is of being responsible for their own lives; adults bring greater quality and quantity of experience to their new learning; adults are ready to learn what they need to know; their learning is life-centred; adults have intrinsic motivations to learn. Clearly Knowles did not formulate andragogy in curricular terminology and perhaps his failure to do so has been a major reason why the debate about his work has been confused and so wide ranging. Can andragogy be equated with the romantic curriculum? In many ways the response to this must be in the affirmative.

Jarvis (1993b) also returned to the andragogy–pedagogy debate seeking to see why Knowles' work, which is so obviously wrong when applied to children and adults, has retained so much currency. It suggested that the major variable distinguishing andragogy from pedagogy is experience, not chronological age. If this argument is accepted it is now possible to formulate the andragogy–pedagogy debate within the framework of the education for adults, which is a rather different perspective from that initially presented by Knowles. Indeed, individuals having little experience in a subject might want a more pedagogic approach whilst those having a lot of experience in an area might prefer an andagogic approach. This leads on to the possibility of conceptualizing the initial vocational education curriculum in pedagogic terms and the continuing vocational education programme in andragogic terms. From this it can be seen that it is more possible to discuss initial vocational education in traditional curriculum terms but much clearer to discuss continuing vocational education in programme terms. In both cases it must be recognized that the process occurs within the humanistic perspective of the education for adults.

Without a humanistic student-centred approach it is maintained here that learning and human development may be impaired, and this is the crux of Macfarlane's analysis of literacy education in terms of these two types of curricula, as Table 9.2 demonstrates.

Once again, this type of approach overemphasized some of the differences, but he suggested that the student-centred approach aids the learner's development and growth. Macfarlane noted that for either approach to be successful in any way demands quite different methods and organization. He also maintained that these different approaches have ramifications for policy, staff recruitment, training and resource development. Yet it is clear from his own analysis that the student-centred approach is closer to the humanistic ideals mentioned earlier in this study, which are at the heart of adult education. Even so, this does not mean that all teaching need be of a facilitative style.

In the second chapter it was pointed out that continuing and recurrent education are two philosophies of lifelong education and that Griffin (1978) has examined these from the perspective of a curriculum theorist. Taking as his basis the teaching and learning process model, aims, content and method, he examined both continuing and recurrent education. His basic premise was that continuing education is related to the classical curriculum while recurrent education has a romantic curriculum basis. It will be recognized that this equation is not one that is maintained here, but Griffin's analysis is important because it is a genuine attempt to apply curriculum theory to the education of adults. Griffin himself recognizes that the task he undertook was 'a tentative curriculum analysis' and herein lies its value. His study may be summarized in tabular form and Table 9.3 contains many of his major points.

Griffin's work needs to be read in detail in order to follow his arguments, but it is clear from Table 9.3 that he saw a clear distinction in curricular terms between the two philosophies in the education of adults. That a practitioner may mix the two approaches is not denied, but it is

Table 9.2 Macfarlane's analysis of adult literacy education in terms of two curricula models

	Curricular attitudes among advocates of the traditional curriculum	Curricular attitudes among advocates of a student-centred curriculum
Role of the student	Passive recipient of externally formulated process	Active participant in defining own goals and needs
The literacy process	Hierarchies, centred upon skills and stages of progress	Holistic, task centred
Tutor's view of student	One who is deprived and handicapped (and hence inferior)	An equal who is not to blame for failure
Impact on student's self-image	Relatively unimportant, a by-product of progress in skills	Purposefully enhanced
Student's view of tutor	'The expert who will cure me'	'The friend who helps me sort things out'
Dangers	Maintains dependency and lack of confidence; transfer of skills to real world usage very doubtful	Threatens student and tutor with lack of structure and lack of perception of progress

Source: Macfarlane (1978:156).

Table 9.3 A curriculum analysis of continuing and recurrent education

	Continuing education	*Recurrent education*
Aims	Professional standards of provision	Autonomous learning
	Flexible and accessible structures of provision	Personal authenticity
	Unity of response to diversity of need	Diversity of learning experiences
	Institutionalized standards of achievement and excellence	De-institutionalized criteria of performance
	Means/ends rationality model of institutional response	Assimilation of education to life-experience of individual learners
	Access to common culture	Promotion of cultural diversity in the context of meaning and goals
Content	Public criteria of learning performances	Expressive criteria learning performances
	Subject structures reflecting forms of knowledge	Structures of knowledge contingent upon learning experience
	Mutual evaluation of subject demand	Problem solving response to conditions of alienation
	Mastery of, or initiation into, forms of knowledge and skill	Standards of learning performance relative to learning experience
	Knowledge for rational control and social mobility	Understanding for transformation through social solidarity
	Culturally appropriate institutional systems	Relevance for maintenance of subcultural identity
Methods	Effectiveness and evaluation	Methods stressing individual expression
	Professional criteria of relevance	Learners decide learning methods
	Professional standards based on adult learning theory	Methods reflecting diverse characteristics of learning situation
	Standards of teaching methods as a function of institutional provision	Standards as a function of a personal authenticity
	Methods reflecting the rationality of provision	Methods for transforming life-experience
	Teaching roles distinguish educational from social authority	Methods reflecting culturally significant aspects of learning

Source: Griffin (1978).

254

perhaps significant that as the 1960s were left behind, so the concept of romantic curriculum lost some of its appeal and thereafter the term recurrent education also lost favour. Even so, many of the curricular aspects that Griffin discusses within this context do find their place within the wider sphere of adult education because any form of education should have a humanistic basis if it is to achieve the high ideals of education itself.

In 1982, Griffin turned his attention to lifelong education and he noted that integration between initial education and education for the remainder of the lifespan is a significant issue that has resulted in an unbalanced policy debate, which has emphasized access above all other factors. Overall, he recognized that curriculum development in the context of lifelong education is 'by no means as straight-forward as the needs/objectives/evaluation model might suggest. The coexistence of various curriculum models makes it a much more complicated affair' (1982:119). This complexity was evident in Macfarlane's (1978) analysis and it is also clear in the distinctions drawn between initial and post-initial education curricula models. Griffin's later paper highlights that policy factors of social control are fundamental to education and most apparent in the provision of lifelong education.

Implicit in the debate about continuing and recurrent education and in the distinction between classical and romantic curricula is the matter of control: who should control the learning activities; who should control the learning outcomes? etc. Since the romantic education is student-centred there is a sense in which control moved in the students' direction. This is even more evident in programme models that appeared at about this time.

In more recent writings there has been a movement away from the terminology about curriculum produced by initial educational theorists. One example of this is Bines' (1992) threefold typology of professional education training models: apprenticeship, technocratic and post-technocratic models of initial professional education. She suggests that the apprenticeship model is one which involves on-the-job instruction with some day release in order to acquire some 'cookbook knowledge' which is basically practical knowledge. Technocratic curricula consist of a threefold approach to professional preparation: transmission of some systematic knowledge; the interpretation of that knowledge as it is applied to practice; practical placements. The third model, which is a response to the weakness of the positivist approaches contained in the second model, is built upon both the experience of practice and reflection on it, so that its focus is on professional competence, and the practical experience becomes the centre of the professional preparation. She recognizes, however, that as resources become scarce it becomes more difficult to staff practical training adequately. However, this model does not really develop a systematic epistemology, although it has a basis upon which this might be built, but it does reflect the concerns of writers like Schon (1987).

Competence, however, is a most difficult phenomenon to assess, as one experiment at the University of Surrey demonstrates. In general nurse training a few years ago it was expected that student nurses would successfully pass four practical assessments during their training. A student nurse was video-taped undertaking one of these assessment procedures and the ward sister in whose ward she was working adjudged that she had actually failed the practical assessment at the time when the video was made. It was then shown to a group of thirty experienced nurses who were on an assessment training course – about one-third of those watching would have passed the student on the performance that they witnessed, while two-thirds agreed with the ward sister and would have failed her. However, the student had already successfully passed that assessment a number of months previously! Professional competence is not necessarily an easy thing to assess. Another problem with the competence based approach to practice is that sometimes good practitioners are good because they know when not to act, as well as when to act, and it is difficult to assess the competence of active inactivity! Consequently, it appears that the post-technocratic approach which is currently in use is one which, while it seeks to overcome some of the problems of the previous curriculum approach, still requires a great deal more refinement.

Even so, the significant thing about Bines' approach is that it seeks to reconceptualize curriculum theory in terms of professional preparation and to produce models that are appropriate for education beyond school. In addition, she has endeavoured to make a distinction between curricula for initial professional education and programmes for professional continuing education. She does not develop this latter aspect, although there are instances of this in Bines and Watson (1992). However, this approach comes much closer to the American literature on programme development, which is explored in the second part of this chapter.

The hidden curriculum

Bourdieu's and Passeron's explicit discussion of the power involved in the process of teaching and learning may also be found in the hidden curriculum. Every institution evolves its own procedures, many of which contain values that are recognized and intended but some of which may be unrecognized and unintended by those who formulate them. Some of these values have been highlighted in this chapter and elsewhere in the book, such as those implicit in the teachers or students selecting the curriculum content, or in the use of various types of teaching. Yet there are others, and some of those that are unintended or unrecognized by the educators of adults may be apparent to the students who attend the institution, and it may be some of these that are learned and which affect their attitudes towards adult or continuing education. Hence, for instance, the differing status accorded to different types of programme may be very clear to students, and those whose class is given low status may feel deprived. Examination classes may be given precedence over non-examinable leisure time study, even though the latter may actually be more academic in some instances! Courses that bring in funds to the institution may be given preference to other forms of education. It may be called an adult education institution but the students may not be treated as adults either in the organization or in the teaching methods employed, or in the evaluation of the life and work of the institution. By contrast, other institutions may create such an ethos that the hidden curriculum purveys the humanistic ideals of education itself. The ethos of the institution is, therefore, the carrier of a message that may be received and learned by adult students who attend, and the carrier's subculture is contained within the hidden curriculum – it reflects its, and often wider society's, philosophy, social power and attitudes towards both individuals and people.

It will be recognized from the above that there are many different elements in the curriculum and the final section of this first part of the chapter briefly discusses some of these.

Elements in curriculum planning

The curriculum planning model is a development of some of the elements contained in Lawton's (1973:21) model of producing a school timetable and it is important to recognize that there is an affinity between the planning of the school timetable and the planning of the programme in the education of adults. However, Lawton's model required considerable adaptation in order to be relevant to the education of adults.

Figure 9.2 represents a complicated system that incorporates those aspects of the curriculum referred to above, and at the same time anticipates something of the programme planning models that are to be discussed in the second part of this chapter, since it seeks to demonstrate how the educational process is exposed to the influence of the wider society and its governing bodies, as well as being affected by the philosophy of the educator. In fact, an uneasy tension may exist as a result of the interplay of the forces stemming from factors mentioned in the first three boxes. Each of these elements will be elaborated upon in a subsequent section of this chapter, but it is clear from Figure 9.2 that the curriculum is always located in wider social systems. This is a systems model, similar to other systems models produced by organization theorists in order to assess the functioning of other types of organizations (e.g. Child, J. 1977:144–178), so it may be seen how the sociological study of the education of adults may benefit from similar sociological analyses conducted in other areas of social life.

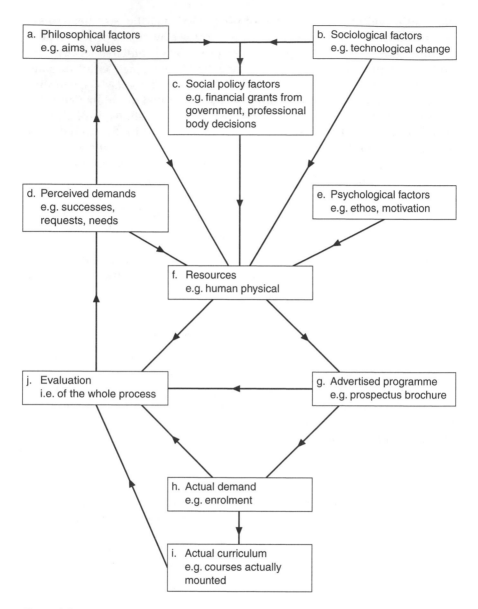

Figure 9.2 A curriculum planning model for the education of adults.

Philosophical factors

Underlying every programme of education there is a philosophy, whether it is explicit or implicit, considered or rarely thought about, consistent or inconsistent, and so on. It may be a philosophy constrained by other factors, such as social policy, but it remains a philosophy. At the outset of this study a rationale for the education of adults was produced which argues that every human being has a basic need to learn and that in a rapidly changing society each individual may need to make many adjustments in order to be in harmony with the socio-cultural milieu. Most individuals will develop as a result of their experiences, which should be provided in a humanistic manner, although it was recognized that growth is not inevitable, since there can be forms of mis-education. This approach, however, reflects Dewey's (1916) assertion that education is a means to human growth and that growth continues throughout the whole of life. Therefore, it is maintained here that underlying every curriculum should be a concern about the development of the learners as persons. This is a humanistic, progressive perspective and one that has traditionally been prevalent in adult education.

It was also recognized at the outset that society is changing rapidly and that some types of knowledge change so rapidly that they appear artificial. But it is essential that some people keep abreast with contemporary developments, so that it could be argued that society has the need to produce a specific type of person who will be a lifelong learner. Education is frequently accused of being a process that moulds and controls people so that they fit into a niche in society without disrupting it very greatly. The lifelong learner must be flexible, adaptable and totally commendable, and in the learning society it is to be hoped that education is becoming a more open and flexible process. If educators see their role only in terms of responding to the economic needs of the wider society primarily, they clearly have a different philosophical perspective upon education than the one being argued in this study. This does not mean that the humanistic, progressive approach to education has no concern about the economic needs of society, only that it sees the development of the learners as persons as they acquire a critical awareness, knowledge and understanding as more significant in educational terms.

Other philosophical perspectives may also underpin the whole of an educational programme. Elias and Merriam (1980) point out that both liberal and radical philosophies are also significant in curriculum design. Hence, it is possible to see that the literacy programme devised by Freire was considerably influenced by his own philosophy and that of his co-workers, and that this approach was totally different from literacy education in societies, such as the United Kingdom, in which this radical philosophical perspective has not been prevalent. Even so, Freire's own programme was not free to operate without influences upon it, such as the forces operating in the society that exiled him.

Sociological factors

It was recognized above and in the opening chapter that the curriculum itself may be regarded as a selection from culture, so that the social forces that operate upon the educational process are quite profound. Culture is changing rapidly and various aspects of knowledge are changing rapidly. Yet knowledge itself is not value-free: some has high status without being very practical whilst other knowledge has low status but is most useful (Young, 1971). The relevance of knowledge is also significant in its inclusion in any curriculum (Jarvis, 1978b). If curricula contain socially organized knowledge selected from culture, then it is significant to know where, why and by whom such a selection of knowledge is made. Clearly in self-directed learning and in some forms of adult education it is the learners who make the selection, but Griffin has suggested that this may not occur in continuing education. However, Westwood has indicated that perhaps the selection in adult education may not be from a wide range of knowledge and she claims that since adult education is a predominantly middle-class pursuit it 'has a reinforcing role maintaining the status quo, engendering a state of consensus and contributing positively to the mechanisms whereby hegemony is maintained' (1980:43). If her analysis is correct, then adult education curricula have reflected the middle-class attitudes and biases that maintain a 'bourgeois hegemony', so that it then needs to be asked whether this is a true reflection of its aims or whether it is a consequence of its existence. In precisely the same way we can argue that the culture of global capitalism is now finding its way into the curricula of lifelong learning and that this may be just as class orientated. Indeed, Sargant and Aldridge (2002) actually regard this social division as a prevailing pattern.

No curriculum in lifelong learning can escape the social pressures exerted upon it, and so it is necessary that more sociological analyses of the lifelong learning processes undertaken by adults should be conducted, as they were of adult education (see Elsey, 1986; Jarvis, 1985).

Social policy factors

Education is rarely free from the decisions of national and local government, and so policy factors also affect the curriculum in any educational establishment. Indeed, examining the development of educational policy decisions in the United Kingdom: continuing vocational education was distinguished from liberal adult education, and then continuing professional education became lifelong learning and endeavoured to incorporate liberal adult education within it. It then became a major focus of educational policy (see FEU, 1992; Fryer, 1997, 1998), but in more recent years there has been a division again and liberal adult education has become certificated as part of the mainstream provision and lifelong learning has been vocationalized, reflecting the European Commission policies which we will discuss in the final chapter of this book.

Not only have macro-curriculum decisions been affected by governmental policy, even the content of curriculum has been affected in this way. As long ago as 1859 John Stuart Mill (1962:239) deprecated the State being involved in the content of education since he regarded it as an infringement on human liberty, but when the Manpower Services Commission was established in the United Kingdom, it forbade the inclusion of any political material in the curricula, claiming that 'inclusion in the course of political or related activities "could be regarded as a breach of ... agreement with the MSC and could result in the immediate closure of the course"' (Harper, 1982). From this example it may be seen that even in a relatively democratic country, like the United Kingdom, government policy can and does exercise considerable control over the curriculum content.

Despite the government's claim that it wishes to leave a great deal to the market, it has constantly intervened in education in a way that many educationalists consider to be detrimental to education. Nevertheless, it should be recognized that even the policy decision to 'leave things to the market' has tremendous effects upon curriculum content since the market ensures the 'survival of the fittest', or in this case the more popular subjects, and enables the less popular ones to be offered at a higher fee in order to make them financially viable.

In 1987, Griffin examined adult education from this perspective, looking especially at three major models – the market model, the progressive-liberal-welfare and the social control. Indeed, it has been argued elsewhere (Finch, 1984; Jarvis, 1993a) that a great deal of government intervention is also a matter of social engineering. More recently, Griffin (1999a, 1999b) has concluded that:

> Lifelong learning and the learning society are simply ways of integrating education policy into wider policies for the reform of the welfare state. As has often been observed, it is possible to position lifelong learning at several points along a continuum running between utopian rhetoric to some fairly traditional arguments for the expansion of education and training provision.
>
> (Griffin, 1999b:451)

Perceived demands

In one sense, liberal adult education has always been a market model having also a welfare dimension, since it used the language of needs, but it also practised supply and demand. Newman wrote that:

261

> Adult education is designed in the simplest possible way to respond to demand. It is the other side of the numbers game. If classes can be closed on the basis of attendance, then they can also be set up. That is to say, if you have a group of people eager to pursue some activity, or if you have evidence of sufficient community interest you can approach your local adult education agency or centre and ask that a course be arranged, a room and basic facilities provided, and a tutor paid.
>
> (Newman, 1979:35)

The term 'need' should be distinguished from the idea of a basic need to learn, which was discussed in the opening chapters, since it has played such a significant part in adult education thinking it should be analysed and related to 'wants', 'interests' and 'demands'. In this sense the term captures some of the points made in Griffin's analysis of social policy – both progressive social, democratic and neo-liberal welfare reform models (Griffin, 1999b:438). It will have become clear from the previous discussion that education has become a commodity in the market, so that needs are changing from the needs for human being to needs of employability and becoming 'wants' and 'demands', and consequently the whole of this new discussion about curriculum in relation to both modularization and the market is referred to in a later section of this chapter.

Perception of demand is, therefore, one factor in the planning of a curriculum in adult and continuing education but one that is playing a larger part now than it appears to have done in the past. However, education has traditionally found it difficult to undertake market research, although a greater emphasis has been placed upon it in course validation exercises.

Psychological factors

One of the strengths of Knowles' formulation of andragogy is that it focused upon some of the psychological factors that need to be taken into consideration in planning adults' learning. If adults are, for instance, problem-centred rather than subject-based, then more courses should be planned that have relevance to the everyday life environment. If they are going to respond to the rapidly changing socio-cultural milieu with active questioning, then the programme should include courses/sessions that provide opportunities for them to seek answers. If some adults have developed an aversion to education as a result of their experiences in initial education or for any other reason, everything must be done to overcome the problem from the outset including the employment of tutors able to put adults at their ease, the way the accommodation is used and the programme advertised. However, it is appreciated that some of the psychological factors may not be fully responded to in planning because there may be limited resources available or because these dispositional factors continue to inhibit continued learning, so that the divide continues to persist (Sargant and Aldridge, 2002).

Resources

The above discussion has already indicated the interrelationship between the different elements of this curriculum planning model, since it would be impossible to consider resources without recognizing that these depend upon policy decisions, etc. Resources may be classified as financial, accommodation and staff. Little more needs to be written about the first of these since it plays a self-evidently important part in curriculum planning. Many education authorities, whatever they are called, make a financial grant to the educational institution and, thereafter, it has to be responsive to the market forces and fee income. Nevertheless, these grants have declined in real terms per student and so education has been forced to become a wealth producer. However, response to market forces means that the curriculum of an institution will depend upon the ability of the educational providers to perceive demands accurately or else it will result in a form of traditionalism in curriculum planning – the continuation of successful courses. Risk, therefore, has become an element in the educational institution's activities and many educators are not sufficiently entrepreneurial.

Accommodation for adult education was the subject of a report by ACACE (1982c) in which it was recognized that day schools should continue to form the main accommodation resource for adult education. Clearly it makes a good deal of sense to utilize premises for this purpose when they are not being used by children, but it is necessary to recognize that such usage may inhibit some adults from participating in post-initial education because of their experiences when they attended school. Research needs to be conducted to investigate the effect of this 'poor cousin' image of adult education and it may be that if this is to remain a pattern for the future, then new schools should be built having more facilities for wider community use. The Advisory Council Report also recommended that adults should have access to prime use accommodation, even though this may not be as close to their homes, but we are not actually seeing this form of expansion occurring.

Increasingly it is becoming recognized that a great deal of the education of adults is a service provision in the learning market and decent resources must be provided from which students can benefit. Consequently, educationalists are being required to work at 'unsocial hours', which is increasingly becoming evenings, weekends and holidays. This is also true for continuing professional education since employers, especially small ones, are loath to release staff for education and training purposes during their working hours. This does mean that teaching accommodation in colleges and universities might be easier to obtain, but we only have to look at many traditional university campuses to find that they are more than half empty at weekends and in the vacations.

The main resource in education of most kinds is the tutor and there has been considerable discussion in this study about the tutor's role, so that it is unnecessary to cover this ground again. There are, however, two issues that should be mentioned here: the use of staff untrained in teaching adults and the use of part-time staff to mount classes in minority subjects and interests. If there is a demand for a class in a specific topic and no tutor trained in the art of teaching adults, should the class be mounted? Since training is not mandatory then response to demand may necessitate use of untrained staff. By contrast, Hetherington (1980) suggested that part-time staff are asked by a principal of an adult education institute to mount a class in a minority interest topic. Having undertaken the commitment and a great deal of preparatory work, the part-time tutors discover that the class is closed after a few weeks because it has attracted so few enrolments and hence they lose their job. This might cause hardship and it certainly would cause loss of job satisfaction. In order to organize a wide and attractive programme it might be necessary to employ tutors in this manner, but the extent to which the part-time tutors should be regarded as a reserve army of labour is another matter. Unfortunately, the market mentality demands a flexible and, often, part-time work force that can be employed when there is work, and education tutors constitute part of this work force.

Advertised programmes

Two major issues here that need some discussion are the actual programme and the way that it is advertised, and both will be discussed in turn.

In the preparation of the programme at least three educational issues must be taken into consideration: scheduling, balance and level. The actual time when courses are programmed is a major curriculum issue since potential students may not be free to attend a class, even an in-service one, if it clashes with their work. Hence, it may be necessary for professional in-service education courses to be mounted on days when the pressure on that specific occupational group is least. In adult education classes it might be necessary to vary the time when they commence, since some topics may be attractive to those who commute to work and who might prefer a Saturday morning, or even a Sunday, class to an evening one. Clearly it is impossible to satisfy every demand since a mutually convenient time for all potential students may be impossible to discover and, even if it were, it may not be convenient for the caretaker! Hence, it may be necessary for different approaches to teaching and learning to be created if scheduling cannot be satisfactorily achieved, such as learning networks, individualized learning, etc.

Mee and Wiltshire (1978:41) rightly pointed out that in the 1980s adult education sought to respond to several publics, so that when adult educators referred to the idea of a balanced curriculum they may be suggesting that the balance should suit the demand. This is a different conception of balance to that in compulsory education when it might refer to the balance between different forms of knowledge or to that between the cognitive disciplines and physical skills, etc. Since that period, however, the education of adults has changed considerably: initially, educational institutions now function in a learning market, which means that instead of trying to balance a curriculum educators now offer a wide variety of short courses and modules that can be selected by the learners in order to fulfil their particular interest or to build up a certificated but individually selected educational programme. Once the learning market has assumed the prominence that it has it would be true to claim that educational philosophy has taken a back seat and now the profit, or at least the survival, motive reigns supreme and the fact that the course is award-bearing is said to be a guarantee of its quality. Consequently, a balanced curriculum may not be a major concern in the learning market.

There are different levels of awards from basic and introductory to bachelors degree. The National Council for Vocational Qualifications is trying to establish a national credit-based system at different levels, four of which are considered as being lower than higher education, and the university credit accumulation and transfer system also has three levels of first degree and also both honours level and masters level credits. (These developments have been discussed elsewhere in this book.)

Since lifelong learning seeks to offer individuals relevant opportunities to study according to their different educational interests and backgrounds, a very wide variety of courses have to be offered, or else there has to be a system of credit accumulation whereby credit can be gained from different educational providers. In addition, as higher education is gradually becoming more open and flexible it has to be more accessible to adults, so that it has become necessary to build progression routes, at different levels, to help adults gain access to advanced study. Further education colleges and adult education institutes are now offering a variety of lower level ACCESS-type courses that provide access to universities and institutes of higher education. However, this requires considerable planning and liaison between the various providers. Consequently, there are emerging systems of liaison, or compacts between providers at different levels, in which an agreement is reached to ensure that different access routes are open to adults: this has even led to discussions about universities and colleges of further education merging.

Courses and programmes must be advertised and two issues need to be considered here: to advertise successfully is a professional undertaking but to advertise too successfully might once have been contrary to the high ideals of education itself, although such a claim could no longer be made, for instance, Rogers and Groombridge (1976:76) argued that adult education is

> a service needing constant promotion and visibility [but] it remains largely unpromoted and directly invisible; where sympathetic understanding of all modern media is needed, it continues hopelessly to rely on methods which would have looked out of place in the late nineteenth century.

They suggested a variety of approaches that might be employed, including: focused distribution; a supplement in a local newspaper; direct mailing; skilful cultivation of the local press in order to ensure good coverage of newsworthy items; militant publicity. Obviously post-compulsory education must reach out to the wider populace and many of these suggestions are now included in the advertising programmes of many educational institutions. However, with the new market orientation of the education for adults, advertising has become a more prominent feature, with higher educational institutions competing against one another for students through mass advertising campaigns. As the education of adults has become a market orientated commodity, advertising has become more professional and commercial. Indeed, it is perhaps now necessary for education to take stock of what is occurring and ask itself if it is really happy with the route down which it has been forced to travel in recent years.

Advertising, as an occupation, is often accused of employing immoral, or at least questionable, methods. While the accusation is rarely substantiated it is important that education should not be seen to use methods to promote its courses that create a sense of need in, or manipulate, potential students. These techniques may be regarded as immoral and certainly fall short of the high ideals of education. Hence, it is important to prepare good publicity and to disseminate it widely, but the means used to persuade people to enrol on courses must always be in accord with the ideals of education; other means do not justify the ends.

Actual demand

At the commencement of the academic year, semester or term, the enrolment period brings the preparatory work into focus. The extent to which the advertised programme prepared by the educators actually responds to the demands of the potential students may now be revealed. In a recent study, Sargant (1990) discovered that 36 per cent of the adult population had been involved in some form of academic study over the previous three years, but by 1997 (Sargant *et al.*) discovered that the figure was closer to 40 per cent. They (1997:ix) also discovered that there was a considerable variation in the places where they studied: at a university (21 per cent); at a college (21 per cent); at the workplace (15 per cent); at home (11 per cent); at adult learning centres (9 per cent) being the most popular. Compared with the 1991 study, universities have assumed a much more prominent role, indicating how they have been forced to change to the demands of the global learning market, but studying at home has declined considerably. The subjects studied varied considerably but have also changed a great deal in a very few years. Sargant *et al.* (1997:37) wrote:

> Some jobs and functions have changed over the last 15 years, the most obvious changes being brought by the computer. The virtual demise of the shorthand and copy-typist, with the increasing multi-skilling in offices, has reduced the proportion learning secretarial/office skills from 8% ... in 1980 to 6% in 1990 and 2% in 1996. The same skill needs are now met by computer studies, which does not just achieve the same percentage as it did in 1990 (8%), but has doubled it to 17%. In 1980, computer systems were a male subject and presumably studied by people such as programmers and systems analysts. In 1990, men and women took computer studies in similar number, but shorthand/typing was also still important for women (12%). By 1996, shorthand/typing has virtually disappeared and computer-related studies has taken over, but more men (18%) than women are studying it!

> The decline in the study of all forms of engineering from 16% in 1980 to 7% in 1990 and 4% in 1996 is clearly a function of the decline of manufacturing industry. It is balanced by increases in the professional, managerial and administrative areas, where participating by women is now at a more encouraging level.

Similar changes have been recorded in a variety of other subjects and crafts, but Sargant *et al.* suggest that it is not that studying such crafts is declining so much as that people no longer consider them as learning. This may be because no credit may be gained from following them. But by 2002, Sargant and Aldridge (2002:17ff.) have shown that a persistent pattern of non-learning is occurring.

Clearly the programme may not respond to everybody's learning needs, and so there have arisen in recent years educational advisory services that can help potential students to find another course in the prospectus that responds to their interests or to discover another educational institution offering the course that the student requires. Adult education institutions have never been the sole providers of this service; public libraries, citizens advice bureaux and careers service offices have all contributed greatly to this, so liaison between providers and advisers is very necessary to ensure that an efficient advisory service exists. In the Advisory Council for Adult and Continuing Education's report on this topic, it notes that, for instance, the Guildford Adult Education Week held in the public library was a 'collective effort involving many agencies, including the University and the Women's Institute' (ACACE, 1979c:15).

But now there is a national service coordinated by the National Association of Educational Guidance for Adults (naega) sponsored by the Department for Education and Skills; it is an association which brings together organizations and individuals who provide work and lifelong learning guidance for adults. The association has its own publications and organizes its own conferences. The aims of naega are:

- To promote the formation and development of lifelong learning guidance for adults.
- To promote high standards of practice.
- To promote the understanding and acceptance of lifelong guidance for adults.
- To promote the training of all those involved in providing lifelong learning guidance for adults.
- To provide feedback at regional and national levels on issues affecting access to opportunities for adults.
- To assist in the exchange of information between services and practitioners.

While those special weeks, like the one organized at Guildford, provided guidance they also serviced a promotional function. Now, however, Adults Learners Week in May is both a publicity period and a celebration of the fact that lifelong learning is now accepted nationally – in a wide variety of countries – and that there are remarkable feats of learning undertaken by all types of people.

Actual curriculum

The actual content of the teaching and learning programme of any educational institution must, therefore, to some extent, rely on the response to the prospectus. Yet it will be recalled that demand itself is hardly sufficient reason for inclusion in the curriculum of any particular topic, so that there must be a place for some minority interests. Even so, the extent to which economically unviable courses may be continued does depend on the philosophy underpinning the educational institution's curriculum and on the social policy factors that affect the funding arrangements for specific courses.

The actual curriculum of an educational institution is more than its programme of courses, as will be recognized from the above discussion about the way in which the term is employed. Because it can refer to the total learning situation, the whole ethos of the institution, its hidden curriculum and the teaching and learning curriculum are all united at this point.

Evaluation

In Figure 9.2 it will be noted that the curriculum planning model demands that educators of adults should evaluate many of the elements of the process. Evaluation was discussed in the previous chapter and so it will not be repeated here. However, the basis of this evaluation must be educational philosophy, but even that may be called into question by the economic demands on the programme. In addition, there are certain factors that may be evaluated by other criteria, e.g. the use of physical resources by financial criteria, the whole of the operation by criteria of organizational efficiency, since the educator of adults clearly plays an administrative and managerial role. Hence, it is necessary to use the criteria of management in evaluating the planning and implementation of the curriculum, but because the end-product is an educational curriculum the major criterion by which the whole is evaluated must remain the educational philosophy of the educators of adults.

From needs to demands – the way that the language of curriculum changed

Traditionally, the language of adult education was the language of welfare provision, with the concept of 'need' being fundamental. Educators used to discuss the needs-led curriculum. However, responding to need was not far away from responding to demand and a great deal of the traditional liberal adult education offered in the United Kingdom was always market-led, consequently in this section we will analyse the way that change occurred during this period, starting from 'need'. Thereafter the idea of the market will be examined with reference to modularization, certification, advertising and quality. It will be seen that the traditional approach to curriculum theory is being replaced by one which has great similarities to the programme planning literature.

The concept of 'need' was regarded as one of the bases of the adult education curriculum and the moral overtones of the term have provided adult education with an apparently deep and unquestionable rationale for its existence. That the adult educator could provide an educational programme that responded to the welfare needs of individuals and communities has been an ideologically important factor to those whose occupation is at the margins of the educational service. The Russell Report (1973:5) was unable to provide a consistent analysis of the term but used it to provide legitimation to the activities undertaken by adult education. Mee and Wiltshire (1978) showed clearly how full-time adult education staff regarded their work as compensatory, while part-time staff viewed it as recreational – 'wants'. Hence, for the full-time staff 'needs' was the more significant term. The Advisory Council for Adult and Continuing Education has also adopted the term (ACACE, 1982b), but the term was clearly confused and, on occasions, 'wants' or 'interests' could be substituted for 'needs' without any change in meaning, although the moral overtones would be lost in the process.

That such a substitution was possible suggested that the term required considerably more analysis than it received before it could legitimately be regarded as a basis for a curriculum theory. Indeed, once such an analysis was undertaken, it was not difficult to concur with Hirst and Peters when they suggested that 'a major book could be written solely round the problems raised by the emphasis on needs and interests' (1970:33). They actually specified a number of different ways in which the term might have been used to illustrate their contention: diagnostic, e.g. a poor person needs more wealth; basic, e.g. the need for a bed; biological, e.g. the need for oxygen; psychological, e.g. the need for love and security; functional, e.g. the teacher needs his books. Clearly they did not exhaust the possibilities, and Bradshaw (1977) specified four more types of need of which social workers should be aware: normative, felt, expressed and comparative needs. Halmos (1978) drew attention to the distinction between primary and secondary needs: the former referring to bodily requirements while the latter are learned or acquired. Needs could also be classified as individual, community or societal. From the above discussion it can be appreciated that the concept of need was ill-defined and, therefore, an inadequate basis for curriculum development.

Educational analyses of the concept have revealed a number of other reasons why it may be a dubious concept to employ in this context. Dearden (1972) illustrated its weaknesses in a number of ways: those needs diagnosed as such against a norm may be rebutted by rejecting the validity of the norm, since it is not absolute (perhaps the exception to this is the basic learning need referred to in the opening chapter); those expressions of need that imply motivation may be rejected since learners may not want what they actually need, and needs and wants are not synonymous concepts; needs are not free from value judgements despite their apparent objectivity; needs are not empirically based. Dearden conceded that it 'might be said in connexion with needs and the curriculum. . . . that there are certain general injunctions about needs which do have a point in that they lay down something called "basic policy"' (1972:54–55). Dearden's criticisms might have been less familiar to adult educators, however, than that made by Wiltshire (1973) who rightly claimed that the use of the term begged a number of significant questions and he specifically noted that, by giving adult education an ethic of service to the needy, it drove a wedge between thinking and practice, which prevented practice from being fully analysed. Lawson (1975) also highlighted some of the weaknesses of the concept, concentrating upon the value judgement and the prescriptive issues. While he (1975:37) maintained that needs statements should not be abandoned he argued that they should be recognized for what they are. Paterson (1979:242) also criticized the use of the word because he claimed that the idea implies that people have the right to achieve a specific level of educational attainment, whatever that might be, and this is patently not the case. Armstrong (1982) also suggested that needs meeting was both an element in liberal ideology and also a justification of compensatory education. Yet do such needs exist?

Coates and Silburn (1967) claimed that no such needs exist. Illich noted the implicit ideological bias in the term and claimed that 'Need, used as a noun, becomes the fodder on which professions were fattened into dominance' (1977:22–23). This suggested that the term was used in order to achieve power and that need was a construction of the power seeker. Perhaps, therefore, the need to learn, as recognized by the potential learner, is a better basis for the education of adults and perhaps learning needs rather than educational needs are more significant.

Consequently, the concept was weak and ill-defined. For instance, once a learning need is recognized by a potential student it creates a want, an interest, or a desire in the potential student. Learners may, thereafter, exert pressure upon educational providers to respond to their demands and so the bases of demand are varied rather than just needs. But 'wants', 'interests' and 'demands' are not words that occurred frequently in the vocabulary of adult educators, nor did they carry the same moral overtones as does the term 'need'. However, they are terms that are analytically more convincing and demand may have been one of the foundations of adult education curricula and this does not detract from the value of the education (Jarvis, 1982a). Indeed as adult education became demand orientated, it might conceivably have broken away from the ethos of middle-class respectability that it carried but also demonstrated clearly that it was a middle-class leisure pursuit for many; however as we have seen, this has clearly not happened.

However, it might be asked whether this analysis is only theoretical or whether adult education did respond to people's demands. Mee and Wiltshire (1978:41) claimed that there seems to be some sort of national consensus that these are the things (their core curriculum) that institutions of adult education ought to be offering to the public and that there is something wrong if these subjects are not given something like their due place in the programme.

Commenting upon their work, Keddie (1980:54) suggested that their findings merely indicated that adult education had been operating a provider's model rather than a needs model of curriculum. For her, therefore, the needs meeting ideology merely provided legitimation for the retention of the status quo. Certainly it would be true to claim that there were no, or very few, genuine attempts to reach the people who needed adult education in the way that Freire (1973a, *inter alia*) practised it, in which he went to the people, learned their language and, simultaneously, their educational needs and then devised teaching and learning situations which responded to them. Even if there had been outreach to discover expressed learning needs, or demands, they were not in themselves sufficient reason for the inclusion of the appropriate learning activity in the curriculum unless there was already an implicit market model.

Needs, then, provided an unsatisfactory basis for a welfare model of educational provision, one with which theorists were most unhappy but which appeared to provide an important rationale for the provision of education for adults. Already it was being suggested that 'want' or 'demand' might be better bases for a great deal of the provision – although it might have been appropriate to have recognized that the provision of adult basic education might be justified in terms of citizens rights or even justice – and consequently need (Jarvis, 1993a).

Radicals, however, were also undermining the concept of need in a variety of ways during that period, and in the same way as Illich was arguing that needs might be created, Marcuse (1964:4–6) discussed the idea of true and false needs: the former being vital to human life and the latter superimposed upon individuals by societal interests and which may become repressive. Implicit in this analysis was the idea that the needs created in people are a 'product of a society whose dominant interest demands repression' (Marcuse, 1964:5). Indeed, these needs might have been created through advertising, etc., so that people feel that they need a certain commodity and feel the need to purchase it, and the dominant interests are those of the providers, or suppliers of the commodity, which in this instance is education.

As government funding to education declined in per capita terms, educational institutions were forced to find additional funding from student fees. This was especially true with the education of adults, where there had traditionally been even less government support and local government found it easier to cut back funding in the provision of education for adults than for the education of children. Consequently, education became a marketable commodity seeking to respond to the demands of potential students. Such language did not seem that strange for many adult educators because there is one sense in which it has always marketed education, albeit under the banner of a 'needs meeting' approach!

However, selling a whole course might be a different undertaking, but selling a course a piece at a time is much easier – and this was facilitated by modularization. Hence, most new courses have modular designs that allow for flexible study. This is even more appropriate where there are learning packages, which enable packages of learning material to be marketed like any other commodity as part of the wider provision of the institution or organization.

The above discussion has sought to highlight some of the major elements in the curriculum planning model and it is clear that the curriculum, when employed in the context of the total learning situation provided by the educational institution, has connotations for organization and management that demand that those full-time staff employed in this role should have additional training if they require it.

Programme planning

American adult education, by contrast, has rarely used the term curriculum – I well remember talking to Malcolm Knowles about this and he said – 'we don't have a curriculum, we have a programme', and so it is to the American literature that we turn our attention briefly. Cervero and Wilson (1994), who seek to provide a theoretical basis of curriculum planning, suggest that there are three broad programme planning models: the classical, the naturalistic and the critical. We shall examine each in turn.

The classical

As we pointed out in the earlier chapters on Knowles, perhaps andragogy is better understood as a curriculum/programme planning model than as a model for either teaching or learning. Indeed, he (1980a:26–27) suggested six stages in the process:

- Helping learners diagnose their learning needs;
- Planning with learners a sequence of learning experiences to answer them;
- Creating conditions conducive to learning;
- Using appropriate methods for learning;
- Providing the necessary resources;
- Helping learners measure the outcomes of the learning.

It is clear from the above sequence that there is little difference here from the traditional models of curriculum that relate it to the teaching and learning process, underlying it is a humanistic philosophy but lacking a theory of curriculum and a discussion of teaching style and also the sociological factors that also underlie the programme. For instance, there is no recognition of the critical debate that was discussed in the previous part of this chapter.

There have been many similar statements from a classical position, all of which are open to the same criticisms as are those made of Knowles. One of the earliest was that by Verner (1964) in which he located the teaching and learning processes in the educational institution (Figure 9.3).

It may be seen from this figure that Verner bases his planning on a needs meeting approach, a topic discussed in detail earlier in this chapter. He also distinguishes between planning, administration and the actual teaching, but it will be recalled from the discussion on the role of the educator of adults that the managerial and teaching roles were clearly highlighted, so that Verner's threefold distinction may be a little artificial in relation to role performance. Nevertheless, the distinction that he draws between planning and administration, on the one hand, and managing and learning experiences, on the other, does reflect the earlier discussion. Verner employs the

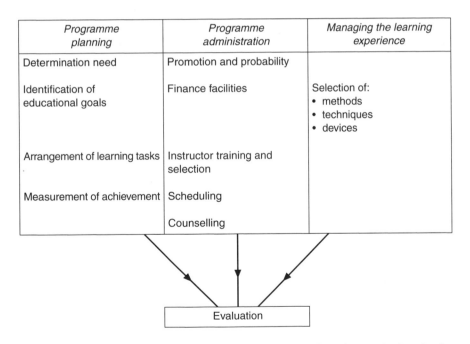

Programme planning	Programme administration	Managing the learning experience
Determination need	Promotion and probability	
Identification of educational goals	Finance facilities	Selection of: • methods • techniques • devices
Arrangement of learning tasks	Instructor training and selection	
Measurement of achievement	Scheduling	
	Counselling	

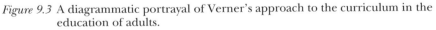

Figure 9.3 A diagrammatic portrayal of Verner's approach to the curriculum in the education of adults.

Source: Verner (1964).

term 'techniques' to refer to the ways in which the teacher establishes a rela-tionship between the learner and the learning tasks, while 'devices' are the audio-visual aids that the teacher uses to assist him in his task. Verner's model is a clear taxonomy of some of the elements of the curriculum but he did not seek to build it into a comprehensive curriculum theory.

In 1985, Boone produced a comprehensive overview of programme planning and in this case he used the term in rather the same way as British educators tend to use the term workshop or specially designed course. In his approach he examined many of the major American theo-ries and then proceeded to produce his own model in which he recog-nized two stages in programme planning: the organization and its renewal processes and linking the organization to its publics; two stages of design and implementation and a final stage of evaluation. This is a classical and practical approach since he proceeded to list in each of these five stages the essential elements to consider, as Table 9.4 indicates. Clearly this is a

Table 9.4 Summary of Boone's model of programme planning

Stage 1 – Understanding the organization and its renewal processes, including:
- Commitment to its function
- Commitment to its structures
- Its processes
- Its commitment to using a tested framework for programme planning
- Its commitment to renewal

Stage 2 – Linking the organization to its publics, including:
- Mapping its publics
- Identifying its target publics
- Interfacing with leaders of these publics
- Collaborative assessment of needs

Stage 3 – Designing the planned programme, including:
- Translating expressed needs to macro-needs
- Translating these into objectives
- Identifying educational strategies
- Specifying intended outcomes

Stage 4 – Implementing the programme, including:
- Developing action plans
- Developing and implementing strategies for marketing the plans
- Following through on plans
- Training leaders
- Monitoring and reinforcing the teacher–learner transaction

Stage 5 – Evaluation and accountability, including:
- Determining and measuring programme outcomes
- Assessing programme inputs
- Using results for programme revision and organizational renewal
- Using results as appropriate in accounting to sponsors etc.

Source: Boone (1985).

behaviourist and empirical model, but it is quite realistic about the way that educational activities have to offer themselves on the market and seek to demonstrate their usefulness. Boone's model comes close to what Cervero and Wilson call the naturalistic model, as we shall see when we look at the work of Houle.

At about the same time, Langenbach (1988) also wrote on the subject but he is one of the few American adult educators who used the term curriculum. He examined a variety of curricula prevalent in adult education and defined a curriculum model as 'a plan that creates access to education and training' (1988:2), which illustrates that his major concern is with elements of programme planning. Nevertheless he does examine a variety of the American approaches to adult education, plus the work of Freire, from a curriculum perspective.

The naturalistic approach

Cervero and Wilson (1994:17) distinguish this from the previous one by suggesting that that was based on idealized principles while this is based on an examination of the actual process. However, this is a very difficult distinction to sustain, since Boone's model could also have been located here. Indeed, many of the classical approaches have come from practical concerns, although it is true that the classical models do not indicate the influence of the educator on the planning and implementation process. They suggest that Houle's (1972) work does provide this perspective. He was one of the most well known of writers on this topic in America, who sought to illustrate the design of education.

Whilst recognizing the complexity of designing an educational programme, Houle produced two different types of models. He recognized that there are a variety of different educational situations in which a programme may be designed, and Table 9.5 illustrates the eleven different ones that he considered significant.

It will be seen that these various situations listed by Houle encapsulate a variety of adult learning situations, so that it is possible to fit within this framework self-directed learning, on the one hand, and planning an informative documentary television programme for a mass audience, on the other. Houle discussed each of these situations very fully, which is a most valuable exercise in the study of the design of education. Nevertheless, such a classification records nothing of the actual process that underlies the production of these educational situations, and so he also produced a second systems approach, which is summarized in Table 9.6.

Houle also recognized that in the design of the format it is necessary to consider the following points: resources; leaders; methods; schedule, sequence; social reinforcement; individualization; roles and relationships; criteria for evaluation; clarity of design. In addition, he suggested that in

Table 9.5 Houle's major categories of educational design situations

---

Individual

c1 An individual designs an activity for himself

c2 An individual or group design an activity for another individual

Group

c3 A group (with or without a continuing leader) designs an activity for itself

c4 A teacher, or a group of teachers, designs an activity for, and often with, a group of students

c5 A committee designs an activity for a larger group

c6 Two or more groups design an activity which will enhance their combined programmes of service

Institution

c7 A new institution is designed

c8 An institution designs an activity in a new format

c9 An institution designs a new activity in an established format

c10 Two or more institutions design an activity which will enhance their combined programmes of service

Mass

c11 An individual, group or institution designs an activity for a mass audience

---

Source: Houle (1972:44).

contextualizing the format, programme planners should also consider: guidance or counselling; lifestyle; finance; interpretation. This model has become quite widely cited as a clear approach to programme planning, as indeed it is, but it does omit a number of issues, some of which will be discussed later in this chapter.

Houle stated that in 'applying the model to a situation, one may begin with any component and proceed to others in any order' (1972:46–47). However, this is not really what the actual diagram in his study suggests since it is a sequential cycle which, while the process may begin at any point in the process, takes the programme designer through seven stages. The fourth and fifth stages have a number of individual facets. This model

Table 9.6 Summary of Houle's decision points in programme planning

---

1 Identification of possible educational programme
2 Decision taken to proceed
3 Identification of Objectives
4 Refining the Objectives
5 Designing the Format
6 Contextualizing the Format
7 Putting the Plan into operation
8 Measuring the results
9 Evaluating the results

Source: Houle (1972:47).

is meticulous in its production and Houle's discussion admirably thorough but it does adopt the perspective of the adult educator who is able to design an educational programme free from external constraint, which may not actually reflect the reality of what happens during the process. It is, therefore, necessary to include external factors as a variable in the process.

About the same time that Houle was producing his model, Verduin (1980) wrote a book in which he discussed curriculum building. The book claimed to produce the first curriculum model for adult education, although this is rather a problematic claim in the light of the programme planning books that were already published – and like many American writers he seemed totally unaware of the wider UK literature on the subject. While he used the term 'curriculum' he did not produce a theoretical discussion of the concept, although he outlined five elements in his model: aim (which he called direction), outside political forces, goals, instruction and evaluation. In addition, he was very concerned with practical processes of planning instruction, with a behaviourist orientation. For instance, in one place he (1980:102) produced a fivefold chart: assess entering behaviour; specific behavioural objectives; specify learning unit and procedures; present learning unit and tasks; student performs and learns. This was an early book in this field and one that at least recognizes the possibility that adult education might have a curriculum in the USA.

The critical perspective

Throughout this work it has been recognized that education cannot be removed from the social and political context within which it occurs and so Cervero and Wilson point in the direction of more critical thinkers, such as Freire, Habermas and Griffin, whose work has already been cited above. Once again this discussion reverts to the idealized and theoretical and does not look at either the constraints or the practicalities of programme planning in a market situation. Consequently, this discussion then takes us back to the earlier chapters of this book where we examined globalization and the market in a critical manner – but it does have to be recognized that there is frequently a conflict between what the educators might want to do and what the market will sustain – the reality being that educational programmes need learners who are also fee payers.

Conclusion

Perhaps, therefore, even the more practical approach of Houle is not really a practical one and more research needs to be undertaken in order to demonstrate this as the research of Martin (1999) illustrates. His study was of art teachers in the UK who wished to teach creative art but whose learners wanted to learn to copy pictures, and so on. The lecturers recognized that if they taught the type of creative art that they wished to teach, encouraging the learners to be original and creative, they were in danger of their learners leaving their class, whereas if they taught the learners what they wanted then they would keep them. The market was bound to prevail – they could not implement a providers' model of the curriculum but it did create the possibility of role stain and declining job satisfaction for the lecturers. Such studies as this take us beyond the critical theoretical perspective and back to the practicalities of the teaching and learning situation and also demonstrate that most curriculum theory and programme planning is in the realms of grand theory and are illustrations of the gap between theory and practice.

Another approach to programme planning is to study a case that has been successful and emulate it in some way. Recently, Beisgen and Kraitchman (2003:98) have offered a list of things that programme organizers might do to generate creativity amongst older learners, based on their study of a seniors' centre:

- Provide the right environment
- Provide opportunities to create
- Encourage ideas
- Provide challenges
- Help older adults not to be afraid to fail
- Provide time and resources
- Develop expertise
- Provide positive, constructive feedback
- Encourage a spirit of play and experimentation
- Provide opportunities for group interaction
- Provide a safe place for risk taking
- Offer rewards that recognize achievement
- Provide opportunities for brainstorming
- Help older adults develop thinking patterns to create new ideas
- Stimulate all the senses
- Provide opportunities to recognize and display creative work of older people.

Whilst their work points us forward to the need to prepare adult educators professionally, it also illustrates that practical programmes might point a way to theorizing about curriculum and programme planning, but that theorizing may have to be retrospective analyses.

10

PRACTICE, THEORY AND RESEARCH

The relationship between theory and practice and research is one that has been touched upon elsewhere in this book, without the word theory being defined. Theory is usually taken to be the body of knowledge that a professional occupation regards as essential to practise. However, we have already raised problems about this in at least two ways: the role of the educator has become much more complex, so that the knowledge necessary to practise may only relate to a specialized part of the whole professional role and, second, our understanding of knowledge itself has become so much more complex that we now question the extent to which theory can actually be applied to practice (Jarvis, 1999a). Indeed, I have argued that in many situations a personal theory is generated from practising rather than the other way around. This chapter, therefore, has two main parts: the relationship between practice and theory, and research into adult education and lifelong learning.

Practice and theory

In 1974, Argyris and Schon also raised one of the basic issues of this chapter when they distinguished between espoused theory and theory in use; the former being the theory to which practitioners give allegiance whilst the latter is that theory which can be constructed as a result of observing their performance. They recognized that there was not always congruency between the two; indeed, they (1974:7) actually claimed that there may, but need not, be compatibility between them at all. However, what the practitioners espouse may relate to what they learn during their professional preparation in the classroom whilst what they practise may relate to what they learn in practice, and further reference will be made to this later. At the same time Argyris' and Schon's concern was not really with the body of knowledge as theory, but only the manner by which practitioners made sense of the world and increased their effectiveness within it.

The relationship between the body of knowledge, as theory, and practice re-emerged in the United Kingdom (Bright, 1989; Usher and Bryant, 1989) and in the United States (Cervero, 1991) in the 1980s and 1990s, with many papers in professional journals questioning that theory could be applied to practice. If we recall Scheler's (1980) discussion about the speed of knowledge change, and we recognize how rapidly things are actually changing in practice, we can see that before research data can be gathered, interpreted and disseminated, the world of practice might have changed considerably and so the theory has already become history! Hence it is unwise to think that theory should be applied to practice in adult education and lifelong learning.

The other issue that we raised in our discussion about the nature of knowledge was that we are concerned with practical knowledge that is integrated rather than academic discipline-based. This raises a question: what is educational knowledge? This was a topic of concern in America in adult education as early as 1964 (Jensen et al., 1964), when Jensen thought that adult education borrowed from the foundation disciplines and was a combination of them, so that the foundation disciplines have long been regarded as one of the academic bases of educational knowledge, but this discussion gives rise to a subsequent one – what is the nature of the study of education? We need to answer this before we respond to the first question about the nature of educational knowledge.

Adult education and lifelong learning as fields of practice and study

Adult education is a field, or many fields, of practice and this appears to be a fairly unproblematic claim. But it is not quite so self-evident with life-long learning, since it can refer both to learning throughout the lifespan and the provision of learning opportunities throughout life. If we take the latter meaning then lifelong learning can also be treated as a field, or fields, of practice. However, both adult education and lifelong learning may also be fields of study, and when we examine them as fields of study it is quite easy to interpret the phenomenon that we investigate from the perspective of the disciplines – from a sociological, psychological, economic perspective, and so on. It is also possible that we undertake that interpretation from a more critical perspective (Carr and Kemmis, 1986), a feminist perspective, and so on. But then we are actually producing feminist, sociological, psychological or economic knowledge rather than educational knowledge. In other words, we are producing a philosophy of adult education, a sociology of lifelong learning, and so on. Educational knowledge, in contrast, is about the fields of practice and this is practical knowledge. But as we can see from this discussion of adult education and lifelong learning, the education of adults is not about one field of practice, but many. They can occur in educational institutions or outside of them; in professional or community settings; they can be vocational or leisure time occupations, etc. The only common phenomenon is the educational process so that the major conceptual problem that now arises is not 'what is education?' but 'what is educational?' No attempt will be made here to resolve this problem since this is also an ideological problem, as we have implied elsewhere in this book.

Nevertheless, it is clear that the common feature of all of these fields of practice is the practical activity. In order to practise it, some practical knowledge is necessary, which was one of the conclusions to Usher's (1989) study, where he called for more analysis of practical knowledge. This effectively meant that it was necessary to return to the writings of Ryle (1963) who, as early as 1949, differentiated between *knowledge how* and *knowledge that*. Discussion of practical knowledge has not constituted a significant aspect in adult education or lifelong learning literature in the English language and so one of the purposes of this chapter is to extend that discussion by considering it in relation to theoretical knowledge and to research in the field (see also Jarvis, 1994, 1999a).

Practical knowledge and information about practice

Teachers of adults, then, are practitioners and education is a practice. In order to be an expert teacher of adults it is necessary to know how to teach. As an educational practice, there are considerable similarities with school teaching, and we have highlighted this relationship elsewhere. However, Ryle (1963:40–41) made the point that knowing how to play chess means that the player does not have to be able to articulate the rules only observe them during the game. He suggested, in rather the same way as Argyris and Schon (1974) did about theory in use, that so long as the player observes the rules and so long as the chess player is seen to obey the rules, onlookers know that the chess player knows how to play the game. In a similar manner Nyiri (1988:19) discussed the knowledge necessary to know how to ride a bicycle. He pointed out that this ability is learned, not through knowing the theories of dynamics underlying riding the bicycle, but rather by trial and error.

Consequently, it is necessary at this point to ask what relationship exists between the actual performance of the action and the knowledge in the mind: that is, what makes practical knowledge? This is a much more difficult question to answer because the chess player might not always be able to articulate the rules of chess and the bicycle rider might not know the scientific rules that explain how balance might be maintained and the bicycle be ridden. Is it just the ability and the confidence to perform the correct actions, because they have been habitualized and memorized? Is *knowledge how* no different from *being able to*? In some ways it is because whilst an instructor might be able to tell student teachers how to teach until they have actually taught they do not know that they are able to do so. The instructor's information is information, some of which might then become part of the learners' practical knowledge at a later date. Knowing how to perform the action is not the same as having the skill to do it, and so learners can be taught the procedures about how to perform a skill but they still have to learn how to do it for themselves – this they cannot be taught in the classroom, although they can be coached, or mentored, by an expert in the practice situation. In addition, learners can be taught that if they perform a skill in a certain manner, there are most likely to be certain outcomes; in other words, they can learn *knowledge that* in the classroom but then they have to learn in practice how to practise – this is knowledge about practice.

However, the chess player knows when the rules are being broken and the cyclist is aware when someone else has not got the confidence to ride the bicycle. Naturally, this gives rise to the idea that some elements of practical knowledge are tacit (Polyani, 1967), or even that it is merely a matter of confidence that the skill performance is correct, and so no actual thought need go into why it is correct until such time as an action does not quite fit the situation. At this point of disjuncture actors have to think about it and perhaps devise some new ideas that need to be tried out in practice. If they work, then they can be internalized but their precise formulation may be forgotten, for expert practical knowledge is fundamentally subjective, pragmatic and presumptive upon the world, and the relationship between this form of personal theory and practice is pragmatic. In fact, practical knowledge is not only *knowing how*, in Ryle's terms, but it is also *knowing that* something will most likely occur given certain conditions and having the *tacit knowledge* that develops through experience. Practical knowledge consists of a personal combination of certain forms of knowledge.

How then is practical knowledge learned? Nyiri suggested that:

> One becomes an expert not simply by absorbing explicit knowledge of the type found in textbooks, but through experience, that is, through repeated trials, 'failing, succeeding, wasting time and effort ... getting a feel for a problem, learning when to go by the book and when to break the rules'. Human experts thereby gradually absorb 'a repertory of working rules of thumb, or "heuristics", that, combined with book knowledge, make them expert practitioners'. This practical heuristic knowledge, as attempts to simulate it on the machine (computer) have shown, is 'hardest to get at because experts – or anyone else – rarely have the self-awareness to recognize what it is. So it has to be mined out of their heads painstakingly one jewel at a time'.
>
> (Nyiri, 1988:20–21; all quotations from Feigenbaum and
> McCorduck, 1984)

Whether education is one or many fields of practice is irrelevant since this discussion is applicable to the practice of the education of adults, whether it is adult education or lifelong learning. Knowledge of the practice of education can be learned partly in the classroom and also in practice from experts; it is grounded in the field of practice. This is confirmed from students' reports on teaching practice – they say that they try things out to see if they work, they observe other teachers performing and they learn from experience. They learn the process by direct participation in it. They have developed their own practical knowledge of teaching as well as having been taught knowledge about practice. Clearly practice is an important area for learning, and Schon (1983) highlighted practitioners are not necessarily mindless in the performance of their occupation, although they can presume upon repetitive situations, but they are responsive to new situations and reflective in practice in order to improve their overall performance.

Such analyses have led to calls to reintroduce the apprenticeship model of training school teachers in the United Kingdom, and this could also be extended to the preparation of educators of adults as well. However, there are some fundamental questions to be raised about this claim, namely:

- that if there is no research into, or agreement about, what constitutes good practice then what every practitioner learns from any experienced practitioner must be acceptable if it works, even though not all experienced practitioners are experts. But we have also argued that education must be humanistic, which is a belief perspective, and its beliefs and values, as well as efficiency, underlie the idea of 'good' practice;
- that not all aspects of practice can be learned through observing the expert because unusual situations are likely to occur in most forms of professional practice, and so all practitioners are likely to experience something in the course of their practice that they have not been able to observe in their apprenticeship with the expert – but working with the expert does allow practitioners to learn practical knowledge itself;
- if there is only apprenticeship then every new practitioner needs to reinvent every aspect of the wheel, which might be an even greater waste of time than learning some aspects of practice in the classroom first!

However, the apprenticeship model does not rule out classroom learning, although it is only one form of learning and is not of superior status to learning in practice. Hence it is advantageous to have a body of knowledge about how the education of adults is undertaken, whether this be about teaching, curriculum design, management, etc. in the field, and this should be gathered from observation of practice rather than from theoretical explication of how a procedure should be performed, a teaching method practised or a lesson prepared.

Preparation for teaching adults should, therefore, include classroom instruction into the knowledge of practice, but this remains information for the practitioners, and it only becomes knowledge when it becomes embedded within their own understanding of their own practice – their own practical knowledge. Preparation for practice is providing information about practice both in the classroom situation and in practice, and the opportunity to learn practical knowledge in practice. Exposure to experts in practice is an essential part of learning practical knowledge. Nyiri (1988) claimed that a great deal of practical knowledge is learned through exposure to custom, convention and ritual. But it also has to be recognized that exposure to bad practice is also a way of learning because learners not only learn from experts, they learn from the mistakes of others. Naturally, this approach is traditional but the transmission of the ethos of practice is necessarily conventional and conservative. But social change is gradual, and a great deal of practice adapts to, rather than initiates, change.

Hence, it is possible to construct what we might call a body of practical knowledge to be included in a curriculum for the preparation of educators of adults, but which is actually only information about practice and this is its status when it is taught. Theory, in this sense, is information about practice rather than practical knowledge. It is about the practice of the education of adults, and it might be applicable to practice of both adult education and lifelong learning – but it is not necessarily always so. Once this body of information about education has been constructed, it might be called a body of educational knowledge or even a body of adult educational knowledge, etc. and this is confusing because what we call a body of knowledge is not knowledge in the sense of being known by the practitioners; it is actually potential information, that is theory, that might become an element in practitioners' practical knowledge.

Does having a body of knowledge (information about practice) mean that education is a discipline like other social sciences? Response to such a question must be negative. The body of educational knowledge is a body of information that is drawn from practice but once we interpret practice (knowledge why) then we will always be forced to use knowledge that is drawn from the other social sciences. The point about this is that in everyday life actions are performed that, if they are ever analysed, might be seen to be an integration of distinct but applied disciplines – such as psychology or sociology or philosophy, or even from beliefs and ideologies such as Marxism or feminism, etc. However, in everyday life people do not, when they think about how they are going to behave, always consciously decide that they are going to use a little bit of psychological, a lot more philosophical, some sociological knowledge, etc. and mix it together to constitute the practical knowledge underlying a specific behaviour. Nevertheless, there may be times when actors are aware that they have applied some philosophical ideals, etc. to their behaviour, so that it would be untrue to claim that the foundations of practical everyday knowledge are never recognized. (See Heller, 1984:185–215 for a discussion on everyday knowledge.) The same is true of educational knowledge – it is a unique constellation of applied knowledge that falls within the ambit of the other social science disciplines. It is only independent in as much as it relates to the fields of practice and this can be demonstrated in the following manner: it is possible to have a philosophy of adult education or a sociology of continuing medical education, but it is not possible to have an adult education of sociology or a lifelong learning of psychology, and so on. In this sense, education is not an academic discipline, but it is a field of practice that can be studied from a wide variety of perspectives.

There is necessarily a close link between the body of practical knowledge (information about practice) and practice. However, it is necessary to explore this relationship a little more specifically here. Traditionally, it has been argued that the body of knowledge (or theory) of practice should be taught before the new recruits enter the field, so that they can implement what they have learned in the classroom when they get into practice. This rather positivist approach, however, is flawed, as Schon (1983) showed when he pointed out that practitioners do learn in and from practice and when he argued for an end to technical rationality. Indeed, this body of practical knowledge does not determine practice. If it did, it would imply that practitioners mindlessly perform their professional duties in a totally unchanging world. Consequently, it is suggested here that this form of theory does not determine practice but neither does practice totally determine theory, but rather, as Lukes (1981:396ff.) suggested, it is a relationship of underdetermination. If it were not such a relationship, then actions would be predetermined and the social world would be regarded as unchanging and unchangeable. Such a view of both society and humankind is unacceptable, and so it is suggested here that there must always be incongruence between even the body of practical knowledge and practice itself. Indeed, it would constitute a much bigger problem if there were congruency between them.

Research into practice

Research is generally divided into two camps: quantitative and qualitative. There has been a tendency in the past, and it still exists in some uninformed circles, for some advocates and practitioners of quantitative research to dismiss a great deal of qualitative research as anecdotal. This is totally false, but qualitative research is a different form of research to quantitative.

286

Quantitative and qualitative research

Quantitative research, as its name suggests, is about measuring things. However, once we have measured something, it still tells us nothing – facts have no meaning. For instance, we can count the number of words, paragraphs and sections in this chapter and we will have measured it. But it tells us nothing about the meaning of what is written here. This can only be done by interpretation of facts – that is we give them meaning. Meaning is not self-evident and we are well aware of many instances where experts have disagreed about the meaning of facts and in some cases this has had disastrous consequences when an expert in a court of law, for instance, gives an interpretation of facts that is later shown to be wrong. Meaning is not quantitative!

Another aspect of quantitative facts about which we have to be sure before we undertake interpretation is that what we are saying we are measuring we are actually measuring. We have all seen this with intelligence testing. For instance, if Gardner's (1983) theory of multiple intelligences is correct then there is no way that an intelligence test can measure intelligence, it can only tell us how an individual performs in answering the questions in a specific test paper on a given day. Indeed, it cannot even be used for comparative purposes since individuals may have different strengths in different intelligences and will, therefore, perform differently in response to the same paper. However, there is a tendency to give a score to intelligence testing – an IQ – or to give a grade to an essay. This gives the interpretation an appearance of being objective and scientific and, therefore, indisputable and for as long as the policy makers accept it (as in examinations, for instance) then the appearance of being objective will be treated as if it is a fact rather than something not quite so empirically factual. It is something that we may see as part of the hegemony of the pure sciences.

However I am not claiming that quantitative research has no validity, only that its validity – like that of qualitative research, is limited. In the pure sciences it is necessary to measure and measurements, when interpreted by experts, enable us to know more about the nature of phenomena. In fields of practice, like adult education and lifelong learning, we can measure enrolments, participation in the some forms of formal and non-formal learning, and so on. We can also measure the number of people who are affected by certain barriers or opportunities to continue their learning, and so on. This does enable us to interpret facts and, perhaps, those interpretations may affect both policy and practice. But it must be emphasized at this point that since the meaning of facts is not self-evident, there is always an element of qualitative interpretation even in the most quantitative of research – data need interpretation to have meaning and become knowledge.

Qualitative research is a different form of research – it is about assessing and understanding rather than measuring – and in recent years it has assumed a greater significance as the social sciences are beginning to gain greater acceptability. Adult education and lifelong learning fall within the field of the social sciences but, as we pointed out above, there is still a place for quantitative research in education, although it is by no means as great as some of its proponents would claim.

There are many different methods of qualitative research, each with its strengths and weaknesses and, since this is not a research methods book, we shall not go into them here. Suffice to say, these approaches tend to be interactive, between the researcher and those individuals being researched, which has given rise for greater concern about the ethics of research than ever before, both in the protection of personal data but also in the way that the researchers conduct their research – ethical concerns are also very important when personal quantitative data are being collected. There is a real sense in which research is always an intrusion into people's privacy and the researcher has no rights to do this, but can only do so with the consent of those being researched.

One of the features about qualitative research, which may be one of the reasons why it is seen as anecdotal, is that it is nearly always local and small scale. To the quantitative researcher this is a fundamental weakness, but in the complexity of contemporary society there is a danger that large-scale research projects fail to uncover the diversity of the potential respondents. However, this does mean that results of small-scale qualitative research projects – which can and do probe more deeply into the beliefs, attitudes and lives of the respondents – cannot be conclusive about a wider population. Crudely, we can say that quantitative research starts with hypotheses that it tests and from which conclusions may be drawn whereas qualitative research starts with research questions or problems and ends with hypotheses that the findings might have some significance beyond what have been discovered.

Research has now become very complex indeed and so it is not surprising that more training is being offered in research methods than ever before. Most Masters degrees in adult education and lifelong learning contain at least one, and often two, modules in research methods that are often compulsory. The Economic and Social Research Council (ESRC) has recently introduced a new structure for many PhDs – what is commonly known as the 1+3 – that is a one year Masters of Research degree plus three years of research for the PhD. Some universities and departments are mistakenly claiming that all PhDs should be like this according to the ESRC. A Master of Research might be very important for someone entering the field of research, or for young academics who are going to enter teaching in higher education and who will be supervising PhD work in the future. However, it is more questionable whether more mature individuals who are seeking to undertake PhD research on a part-time basis need to undertake the whole of a Masters degree in research before undertaking the research that concerns them. Consequently, we may argue that once again adults are being marginalized from the mainstream but, let it be said that, all individuals undertaking research do need some training in research technique since poorly conducted research lowers the reliability of the findings and lowers the status of the field in the eyes of professional academic researchers.

Part-time researchers are often practitioner or action researchers, which points to the need for a properly developed and regulated practitioner doctorate, of equal but different status, to the PhD. Some practitioner doctorates are being developed, although the distinction between them is not always clearly enunciated. Such an approach should ensure that it is a field of practice that is being researched and practical knowledge and its relationship to the disciplines are well understood. An award of a Doctor of Adult Education (EdD) or even one in lifelong learning, or human resource development, would recognize the developments.

Practitioner and action research

Practitioner researchers (Jarvis, 1999a) are usually individuals involved in researching their own practice for no other reason than that they want to understand it better. In this sense, research is a focused and disciplined approach to learning under supervision – but it is still a form of learning and may be understood from within the model of learning discussed earlier in this book. In this sense, research has been democratized and is something in which practitioners can be involved whilst they are still carrying out their daily work. Research grants are not so necessary for this approach to research, so that it is little wonder that in this knowledge society there are an increasing number of such research projects, especially in adult education and continuing learning.

Action research is often like practitioner research (McNiff, 1988) in as much as it is the practitioner who undertakes the research, but this need not always be the case. The objective of action research is seeking to understand some field of practice so that it can be changed to improve it in some way.

Relationship between theory, practice and research

Having analysed theory, practice and research, we have begun to explore their interrelationship. Perhaps Usher's and Bryant's (1989) study has undertaken this most consistently thus far in the literature of adult education. Their contention that this is a triangular relationship in which each affects the other is recognized as having some validity, but as we have already pointed out the relationship is even more complex than this. Traditionally, the data discovered from research about practice was regarded as the new theory, or then the new theory was taught and put into practice and then researched, but this is now insufficient. The concepts are much more complex than this and we need to see that this inter-relationship has a number of possibilities:

- Research into practice becomes the personal practical knowledge of the practitioner researcher and, possibly, any publication from the research might become information (theory) that is taught to others who might in their turn, but need not, use it in practice;
- Personal knowledge (personal theory – practical knowledge) might be used, but not applied, in practice and the practice might be researched, and so on.
- Research data might be interpreted and incorporated into a curriculum that might be used in practice, but if the practice is undergoing rapid change then the research data will itself be out-of-date before it has been learned – in other words it is already history!

It is clear from this discussion that the relationship between these three is not automatic, nor predetermined in any way and, as we said earlier, it is one of underdetermination.

Relationship between research and policy

It has been traditionally believed over the years that policy is based on research findings but this is too strong a claim for this relationship. Rather research findings might be used if they fit into the already existing policies and ideological belief systems of government. For instance, if a government department will only accept quantitative research, then it will tend to ignore qualitative data however well researched it is. Neither is government likely to suddenly reverse its already existing policies, which may be based on their ideological systems, just because research findings contradict those belief systems or the policies. Research findings might be like water dripping on to a rock, which might have some effects in the long run, whereas if the research findings are popularized in some way so that they have some effect on public opinion government might actually respond more rapidly, which is an irony when we consider the fact that within the academic and research communities research gains status if it is published in peer reviewed journals which have very limited circulation amongst fellow academics!

Conclusion

The purpose of this chapter has been to open up some of the questions about research rather than to write a chapter about how research should be conducted. It points to the growing complexity of research itself and indicates that it is necessary for practitioners in adult education and life-long learning to be aware of the academic debates about research rather than necessarily being researchers – but in the contemporary climate there is every possibility that they are already practitioner researchers learning in their own practice. However, it does point to the need for practitioners to receive professional preparation for their role, which is the subject of the next chapter.

11

THE PROFESSIONAL
PREPARATION OF TEACHERS
OF ADULTS

When this book was first written there was considerable concern and inter-est in getting adult educators trained and I discussed this within the framework of the professionalization of an occupation. However, there has been a vast change in adult education in the UK since then, as has become apparent from the way that the second edition of this book has had to be radically revised, and it is quite significant to note that the last paper on the training of adult educators to appear in *Studies in the Educa-tion of Adults* was that by Harrop and Woodcock in 1992 – which is only one year after we (Jarvis and Chadwick, 1991) conducted our study of the training of adult educators in Western Europe. Currently, however, there is a pan-European Grundtvig project seeking to establish an andragogy curriculum for adult educators, with a UK partner, but in many ways events in the UK have moved beyond this with the introduction of lifelong learning and yet, as the Dearing Report (1997) and the White Paper *The Future of Higher Education* (DfES, 2003) demonstrate, the issue of the pro-fessionalization of educators has not disappeared, and we shall return to it in the third section of this chapter.

This lack of published research in the preparation of lifelong educators is significant in the light of current European Commission policies about the training of educators. Following a report from the Education Council to the European Council (Council of the European Union, E.C., 2001b), which the Swedish Presidency European Council in Stockholm adopted, three strategic goals were outlined for European education and training:

- improving the quality and effectiveness of education and training systems in the EU;
- facilitating the access of all to education and training systems;
- opening up education and training systems to the wider world.
                                                    (European Commission, 2002:8)

This was the first time that a document sketched out a comprehensive education and training system for the whole of Europe. These three aims were then subdivided into thirteen objectives – five for the first objective, three for the second and five for the last. Following the adoption of this project, the European Commission issued a work programme and this was followed by a further policy document on the need to invest efficiently in education and training in Europe (E.C., 2003) since it was claimed there has been a significant underinvestment in human resources within the European Union.

It is beyond the scope of this chapter to examine all of these objectives but it is significant that the first objective is: Improving Education and Training for Teachers – which is about both their initial and their continuing education. It is also necessary to recall that education and training in the European documents includes both higher education and lifelong learning and that both sectors are included in this discussion. Consequently, it is on this objective that we focus here since for educators in both lifelong learning and higher education, it is claimed that:

> Teachers and trainers are the most essential actors in the overall strategy towards a knowledge-based economy ... Europe needs to improve the ways in which teachers and trainers are prepared for, and supported in, their profoundly changing role in the know-ledge society.
>
> (European Commission, 2002a:14)

We can see, therefore, that training and continuing professional development are regarded as an essential stage in the development of the know-ledge society; it is also an indicator of being professional, or of professionalism. It is also significant that the document from the Euro-pean Commission specifies, amongst the key issues to be addressed:

- Identifying the skills that teachers and trainers should have, given their changing roles in a knowledge society;
- Providing the conditions which adequately support teachers and trainers as they respond to the challenges of the know-ledge society, including through initial and in-service training in the perspective of lifelong learning.

(European Commission, 2002:14)

The aims of this chapter, therefore, are not simply to update the informa-tion from the previous editions of this book but to contextualize the process of change by, initially, examining the process of professionalization and then providing an historical picture of what occurred in the UK in the 1970s and 1980s and finally, by examining recent developments in the UK which bring us back to the process of professionalization, albeit the profes-sionalization of lifelong learning educators. Clearly the professionalization process is quite central to understanding what has occurred but only when we recognize that the nature of the occupation has changed from adult education to lifelong learning in both further and higher education. Some of these changes were already being anticipated when the second report of the Advisory Committee on the Supply and Training of Teachers (Haycocks, 1978) treated adult education teachers as further education teachers.

The process of professionalization

The introduction of training schemes for adult and further education was a step in the process of professionalization, but it also reflected something of the changes that were beginning to occur in society, as more adults were returning to education. But, as I argued earlier (Jarvis, 1985) adult education at that time was a semi-profession, that is an occupation that has the following characteristics: no firm theoretical base; no monopoly of exclusive skills nor special area of competence; the existence of rules to guide practice; less specialization than occupations generally regarded as professions; control exercised by non-professionals; service ethic. Space forbids any full discussion of each of these points, although it is essential to note that the development of a theoretical curriculum about the education of adults received a stimulus from the introduction of training courses for adult educators. Whether adult education could have ever actually professionalized along the classic lines of professionalization is doubtful. It should, however, be noted that there never has been a complete and agreed typology of a profession, nor an agreed definition, so that it was easy in those early days of training for writers to treat adult education as a profession (see for example Mee, 1980:105). Yet Illich's (1977) analysis of disabling professions should also serve as a salutary warning to educators that while there may be advantages in pursuing this process, there are also dangers.

Even if it were to be possible to agree on a definition and characteristics of a profession, it might be argued that in a time of rapid change it is unrealistic to try to achieve a static and unchanging definition by which to decide what occupations are professions. Indeed, it might well be asked whether such an approach has a great deal of value. Using the term profession also gives the impression that an occupation to which it is applied is a homogeneous 'whole', but many years ago Bucher and Strauss (1966:186) developed the idea that professions are 'loose amalgamations of segments pursuing different objectives in different manners and more or less deliberately held together under a common name at a particular period in history'. The following different roles suggest that we are seeing this loose amalgamation of roles in teaching adults subdividing and, as we shall suggest in the final section of this chapter, new occupations forming. I want to suggest that there are at least eighteen such roles:

- Teacher/Facilitator
- Teaching assistant
- Supervisor
- Trainer/Coach
- Mentor
- Counsellor/Advisor
- Administrator
- Assessor

- Researcher
- Trainer of teachers/Trainers
- Author of learning materials
- Programme/Curriculum planners
- Educational policy makers
- Programme administrators
- Programme technical staff
- Consultants and evaluators
- Retailer/Marketer
- Manager.

The first group of roles are those that have direct contact with the learners while the second is at least one stage removed from them. Moreover, the education of adults has always demanded many different roles from its practitioners as early writers on the subject also suggested. For instance, Newman (1979) characterized the multifarious roles of adult educators as:

- entrepreneurs – they have to establish courses and then ensure that there are sufficient students to make them viable;
- wheeler-dealers – they have to overcome all the problems of entrepreneurs employed in a bureaucratic education service;
- administrators – they are responsible for planning programmes and employing staff;
- managers – their job is to manage the part-time staff and the educational premises;
- animators – they have to make things happen;
- trouble-shooters – they have to deal with the multitude of problems that complex organizations like adult education institutes create;
- experts on method – they might be called upon to provide guidance and assistance to part-time adult education staff;
- campaigners – since adult education, as a marginal branch of education, is always under threat.

It is quite significant that Newman did not include teaching amongst these roles. Hence, it may be concluded that for some full-time staff in

295

local education authority, adult education teaching played a fairly insignificant part of their work.

However, models about the process of professionalization might also be useful in order to guide our thinking about what is happening in education. A number of attempts to describe this process were published at about the same time, for example Caplow (1954), and Greenwood (1957), but one that was very widely accepted was Wilensky's (1964). He suggested that as occupations professionalize they undergo a sequence of structural changes that, while not invariant, form a progression.

- The occupation becomes full-time.
- It establishes a training school, which it later seeks to associate with universities.
- It forms its own professional association which seeks:

  i to define the core tasks of the occupation;
  ii to create a cosmopolitan perspective to the practice of the occupation;
  iii to compete with neighbouring occupations in order to establish an area of exclusive competence;
  iv to seek legal support for the protection of the job territory.

- It publishes its own code of ethics to assure the public that it will service its needs.

Using this approach it may be clearly seen that adult education and lifelong learning have not achieved the first stage of the process in the early developments referred to above. However, this model was formulated many years ago when it was assumed that most jobs would be full time, but now this is no longer the case and many practitioners, even in the higher status professions, no longer practise full time. Consequently, this first stage is not really relevant to education any longer, and may not even be relevant to the process of professionalization. Having its own training school in association with universities is certainly something that has occurred, and a great deal of professional preparation of educators is now undertaken within the university setting, a point to which we shall return later in this chapter. The next stages have not yet been achieved.

Yet it may be asked further whether it was important that adult education should have been regarded as a profession. Indeed, in this age of managerialism, perhaps even the question about professionalization is redundant; it is certainly not as relevant as it was in the past since performance is probably now more significant than status. Changes in society have resulted in managerial and organizational effectiveness and efficiency, so that the professions have in part been marginalized in as much as they have lost some of their autonomous power. All the welfare services have experienced these changes and the education of adults has not escaped them either.

However, a much more important question may be whether education practitioners were, and are, professional. The term 'professional' has at least three meanings: those who receive emoluments for the performance of their occupational tasks; those who practise an occupation generally regarded as a profession; those who are experts. It is this last meaning to which reference is being made here, since it is much more important that adult educators be professional than it is that the occupation should be regarded as a profession. Nevertheless, if its practitioners were generally regarded as experts then it would, perhaps, be easier for the occupation to progress along the pathway of professionalization, or at least be recognized as a legitimate field of practice, even if this is only to ensure that its practitioners are more professional in their performance.

There was considerable concern during the 1970s and 1980s about training and about professional status and so the second part of this chapter provides a brief historical overview about the developments that occurred during this time.

An historical overview of the development of the professional preparation of adult educators in the UK

Adult education, like most other branches of education in the United Kingdom, except initial education, was slow to produce a national pre-service teacher-training scheme. While it was hoped that this would arise from developments in the UK, which are discussed below, it now appears to have been rather idealistic even when in-service training was beginning to occur nationally. Campbell (1977) and Caldwell (1981) both indicate that a similar situation prevailed in North America. Indeed, many who entered adult education on a full-time basis, let alone those who are part-time teachers, had no qualification in the education of adults at all – their teaching qualifications often being in the education of children. Hence, it is possible to see that the discussions that emerged about the differences between andragogy and pedagogy had practical relevancy since, while there are common elements, there were enough significant differences to raise questions about the appropriateness of a pedagogic qualification for teaching adults.

Training for adult education teachers was raised as early as the 1919 Report (Smith, 1919), when it was suggested that more opportunities should be provided for training (para. 261) and that such teachers 'should have adequate remuneration and a reasonable degree of financial security' (para. 271). Thereafter, tutor training occupied the minds of adult educators on a number of occasions (see Legge, 1991:59–73 for a summary). Peers also noted that:

The matter was raised again by the Adult Education Committee of the Board of Education in a report published in 1922 (The Recruitment, Training and Remuneration of Teachers). In a report published by the Carnegie United Kingdom Trust in 1928, the result of an enquiry undertaken jointly by the British Institute of Adult Education and the Tutor's Association, the problem of training was discussed more fully and an account was given of existing experiments. Finally, after some years of discussion by a subcommittee of the Universities Council for Adult Education, the whole ground was surveyed again with some thoroughness in a report published in 1954 (Tutors and their Training).

(Peers, 1958:217)

Peers (1958:223) claimed that training for adult education should be a major activity for all university extramural departments, but this suggestion was slow to be adopted and, for a while after the 1954 Report, tutor training ceased to occupy a significant place in the concerns of adult education. Martin (1981), for instance, noted his disappointment that Mee and Wiltshire, whose work was published in 1978, 'dealt so little with training' (1981:124). Indeed, when Legge (1968) wrote about the topic in the late 1960s there were few other adult educators expressing the same interest. This was very evident from the relatively little space devoted to tutor training in the National Institute of Adult Education's national survey which stated that the 'proportion of Local Education Authority tutors claiming some kind of training was markedly higher than among their Responsible Body colleagues (34%:8%) and [that] a higher proportion was in favour of the provision of training facilities (74%:57%)' (Hutchinson, 1970:177). However, there were movements at that time to initiate training schemes and the East Midlands Regional Advisory Council for Further Education introduced the first in 1969 which had three stages (Elsdon, 1970): an introduction, a more advanced course and, finally, a certificate course which was to be validated by the University of Nottingham. This scheme was introduced, a description of which was provided by Bestwick and Chadwick (1977). It subsequently assumed greater significance since it was the model that the Advisory Council for the Supply and Training of Teachers used for its recommendation a decade later. However, before these recommendations are discussed it is necessary to review the research that puts these developments into perspective.

As Martin noted, little empirical research was actually published during this period to demonstrate either the expressed or felt needs of part-time or full-time staff for training or the extent to which provision was being made for their training, although the Russell Report (1973) suggested that part-time staff might be prepared to be trained and argued that appropriate training should be introduced. By the time that such research was published the Russell Report's recommendation had been acted upon and the Advisory Committee Report published. Even so, Martin (1981:122) noted that while 41 per cent of his sample of 3,313 part-time tutors in the East Anglian Regional Advisory Council area were qualified day school teachers, 37 per cent had no qualifications or had undertaken only an induction course mounted by the local adult education institute to familiarize new recruits with the institute, its procedures and adult education generally. The remainder of his sample had a variety of teaching qualifications ranging from the City and Guilds of London Institute, course 730, and teachers certificates of the Royal Society of Arts, to specialist sports coaching qualifications. In addition, a few actually held an ACSET Stage I award. Handley discovered a similar picture in her smaller sample and she records that from:

> the total sample 49% had attended training courses for primary education, 11.8% for secondary school teaching, 11.8% for further education and 24.5% for adult teaching. Another 7.8% had attended combined further education/adult education teacher training courses, 2% had attended both primary and adult training courses and 1% secondary and adult courses. Of significance is the 23.5% who had not attended any type of training course, and the further 12.7% who were non-respondents.
>
> (Handley, 1981:72)

Graham *et al.* (1982:54) also reported: 30 per cent (462) of their sample had some qualification in adult education, 34 per cent had school teaching qualifications, 12 per cent had subject qualifications only, but 23 per cent had received no training at all. They noted that women were more likely than men to have undertaken training in adult education, which may indicate that women who might otherwise have been restricted to the role of housewife regarded this training as important to their future careers. Of the 30 per cent who had received adult education training about half had a Stage I qualification from the East Midlands and a quarter had started the second level, or City and Guilds 730, course. Only 3 per cent, however, had acquired a Stage III qualification, from either the Universities of Leicester or Nottingham, which indicated that the length of time and amount of study required to complete this course might have deterred some part-time staff. Bestwick and Chadwick (1977) also record that out of the 28 part-timers who originally expressed interest in the East Midlands Stage III scheme, only eight actually completed it. Clearly if part-time staff were not going to spend longer than four or five years teaching in adult education, there was little incentive to study part-time for two of those years. However, possession of a Stage III certificate may, in itself, have been an incentive for part-time staff not to depart after a short time in the service.

The variety of courses attended by and qualifications held by part-time adult educators was considerable: Handley (1981) noted that the 68 tutors in her sample who had attended courses in adult and further education held 14 different qualifications between them. Graham *et al.* (1982:37–46) actually listed the variety of different teaching and coaching qualifications awarded by 19 organizations whose teachers were employed in part-time adult education and yet they did not exhaust the list by any means. In addition, some of the professions, such as nursing, awarded their own variety of teaching qualifications, so that before a national scheme for the training of educators of adults could be introduced it was necessary to work out equivalences in these qualifications, something that was occurring to some extent since nurse tutors were being allowed to enrol as registered nurse tutors if they held specific teaching qualifications, such as the Post Graduate Certificate in the Education of Adults from the University of Surrey and the Certificate of Education (Further Education) awarded by the Council of National Academic Awards in specified colleges.

In nursing, unqualified tutor status was regarded as temporary, so that all nurses appointed with this status were expected to seek a course of study as soon as they were able. This was not the case in some other professions and neither was it in adult education. Both Handley and Martin, however, recorded some statistics that indicate that a number of part-time adult education staff experienced the need to undertake training: Handley (1981:76) discovered that 50 per cent of her sample would be prepared to take advantage of any training provision whereas 38.2 per cent were unsure and 11.8 per cent were unwilling to do so; Martin (1981:12) recorded that 240 of his sample had actually attended the Regional Advisory Council's Stage I course during their first year of teaching adults.

It is apparent from these research findings that training educators of adults had become a significant issue by the late 1970s and that the East Midlands scheme was playing an important part in the process. Yet an adult education qualification was not mandatory for practice and no qualified teacher status actually existed for them. Indeed, qualified teacher status, i.e. having been trained to teach children, was still regarded as valid educational qualification for adult education, and Elsdon noted that while some school teachers undertook training in adult education they 'would have been theoretically exempted' (1975:29).

In precisely the same way as adult educators in the United Kingdom were advocating the need for training, there was a similar movement in the United States. Lindeman (1938), for instance, advocated that all students training to be school teachers should also study 'one unit of adult education covering one whole academic year' (cited in Brookfield, 1988:96). Overstreet and Overstreet (1941) noted that most adult educators had been trained by experience and by the end of the 1940s there was concern being expressed about the extent to which adult education was a profession and the type of training necessary for this (Hallenbeck, 1948). By 1964, Houle could write about the emergence of graduate study in American adult education in America, although it is still clear that the greater majority of this study was in-service rather than pre-service, and theoretical rather than practical.

However, the movement in the UK recognizing the need for training for adult education was to bear fruit with Elsdon's own publication on training part-time staff reflecting this development, since he was a Member of Her Majesty's Inspectorate. It appeared just about the time that the Advisory Committee on the Supply and Training of Teachers was established. This advisory committee, under the chairmanship of Professor N. Haycocks, published three reports on the training of teachers in further and adult education. The first, in late 1977, concerned itself with the training of full-time further education staff and recommended a two-year part-time Certificate of Education (Further Education) course, with a qualification to be awarded at the end of the first year for those who did not wish to progress to the second year. The first year, it was suggested, should be more practical but should be planned in conjunction with the second year centre in order to ensure continuity. This report was published at the time that school teacher education was just recovering from the reorganization forced upon it by the James Committee, during which a number of colleges of education were amalgamated with polytechnics (now the 'new' universities) and universities and had either become, or expanded, their departments of education. Hence, they, and some of the colleges of education that had retained their independence, were in a position to develop certificate courses in further education and, therefore, became centres for their training.

These colleges, once they had been approved by their Regional Advisory Council, were able to submit their courses to the Council for National Academic Awards (the Council was disbanded during the period in which the polytechnics were being granted university status) for validation. Initially, the Further Education Board received mainly submissions that led to a certificate of education but, during the first four or five years courses were developed and submitted leading to first degrees, postgraduate certificates and higher degrees. All of these courses concentrated on full-time staff, or at least upon those who were teaching at least ten hours per week, although a few demanded only five hours' class contact, but this tended to be the exception. Since the courses were devoted almost exclusively to further education, many adult educators were excluded by the teaching requirement.

In March 1978, the Haycocks Committee published its second report, the subject of which was the training of part-time staff in further and adult education and the training of full-time staff in adult education. This report commenced by reviewing the then current provision for training for adult educators and noted that the College of Perceptors and the City and Guilds of London Institute courses provided a considerable amount of training at that time. This was especially true of the City and Guilds of London Institute Further Education teachers course (CGLI 730) that had attracted some 3,000 candidates in 1975 and 1976. About half of those were tutors in branches of education outside further and adult education, notably the health service professions, Her Majesty's Forces and industry. Nursing certainly took advantage of this course for many years, although the Panel of Assessors for District Nursing withdrew recognition of it as a qualifying route for practical work teachers since it tended to be further education orientated rather than specifically orientated towards the professional clinical situation. Nevertheless, this course did attract 700 from the ranks of the part-time staff of further and adult education, but it was recognized that it is predominately a further education course, and the City and Guilds of London Institute subsequently devised a new course (CGLI 942) that was piloted in London in 1982.

The Advisory Committee's second report focused upon the East Midlands Regional scheme and noted that this was already being regarded as a model upon which the North West Region was considering constructing its own training programme. Finally, the Committee recommended that there should be a coherent scheme of initial training for all teachers working at post-school level which should lead to the award of Certificate of Education (Further Education) and to qualified teacher status, although this was more fully developed in a subsequent report.

The Haycocks Committee then went on to outline its proposal for this scheme, which was a three-stage scheme similar to the East Midlands scheme. The first stage, it was recommended, should be widely available, as an induction, and should preferably be undertaken prior to employment. However, it was recognized that this was perhaps idealistic and so it was suggested that this initial stage might be offered during the first two terms of teaching. While this proposal appeared more realistic it had to be recognized that new teachers do find preparation time-consuming, so it might not be as realistic as it appeared. Table 11.1 records the suggested content of this initial course, which was to involve 36 hours of attendance.

Table 11.1 The recommended content for Stage I courses

- Motives and expectations of teachers and students
- Setting aims and objectives
- Introduction to learning theory
- Planning learning situations
- Introduction to teaching aids
- Introduction to lesson
- Evaluation

In addition it was suggested that new part-time teachers should have a mentor who would work closely with them.

The second stage of the recommended course was to be more advanced and involved 60 hours in the classroom and 36 hours of supervised teaching practice. This amount of supervised teaching practice certainly placed the emphasis of the course on practical teaching but there was little doubt that it was both an expensive and time-consuming recommendation. Table 11.2 specifies the subjects that were to be studied at this level.

Each of these modules required between 8 and 12 hours of attendance at lectures and seminars, etc. Initially it was considered that some of this might actually be reduced by using resource-based packages, which was clearly an interesting suggestion, although the final report did not make such a recommendation. Little distance learning material at this level had been produced, except the Open University's course, which is produced in conjunction with the Council of Europe. The draft scheme of this course was published in 1982 and its content included three booklets:

- adult learners: needs, motivations and expectations;
- adult learners: responding to need;
- a further reference booklet, containing 15 short papers on different but relevant topics.

The Stage II courses were to be pitched at about the same level as the well-established City and Guilds of the London Institute Further Education Teachers' Certificate, course 730. The revised course (City and Guilds, 1978) included the topic areas shown in Table 11.3. This course also had a supervised teaching practice, so that it approximated even more closely to the Stage II courses. While the City and Guilds actually piloted a new course (CGLI 942) at this time that was specifically orientated to Stage II of training for adult education, the curriculum for the 730 course remained substantially unaltered over the next ten years.

The third stage of this training, the Advisory Committee recommended, should lead to full certification, equivalent to a full-time first year of an undergraduate course of study, and should be provided by institutions in which 'there is a substantial nucleus of experienced staff who

Table 11.2 The recommended content for Stage II courses

- Setting objectives for teaching
- Psychology of learning in post-adolescent stages of life
- Teaching methods with post-school students
- Audio-visual aids
- Teaching specialist subjects
- Context of Further and Adult Education

Table 11.3 The recommended content of the City and Guilds Course 730

- Principles of learning
- Principles of teaching strategy
- Learning resources
- Course organization and curriculum development
- Assessment
- Communication
- The teacher's role in relation to students in further education

have themselves completed courses in advanced study in education and whose major commitment is the professional education and development of teachers at the post-school stage'. No other specific location was suggested for these courses nor was the content of the curriculum specified. However, it was stipulated that the course should take one year full-time or two years part-time to complete.

In addition, the Advisory Committee recognized the diversity of adult education and made the following recommendations for the training of full-time staff:

- new, untrained teachers entering full-time teaching in adult education should embark upon the first stage off the full-time Further Education Certificate recommended in the first Haycocks Report;
- for those trained as teachers, in sectors other than further education, a six-week part-time, conversion course;
- for part-time adult educators who have taken Stages I and II, a Stage III course leading to a Certificate in Education (FE);
- a one-year full-time, or equivalent part-time, for those who possess the Certificate in Education (FE) for those who wish to work as organizers and administrators in adult education – leading to an advanced diploma in adult education or higher degree.

Thus, it may be seen that no division between further education and adult education existed in the recommendations for initial training at all three levels and that it was only at post-certificate level that adult education was regarded as a specialism. This was one of the criticisms made by the Advisory Council for Adult and Continuing Education (1978) in its formal response to the recommendations. In addition, it criticized the Haycocks Committee for being too narrow, for trying to combine forms of training that ought to be separated and for omitting any consideration of using the university departments of adult education in initial training. These were all valid criticisms of an important but conceptually confused report and also reflects the level of concern about training in adult and further education at this period, something from which the European Council's 2002 proposals might learn.

By mid-1981, Graham *et al.* (1982:1) reported that there was considerable variation in provision both between and within Regional Advisory Council areas. They also noted that while areas had introduced Stage I schemes, fewer Councils had approved guidelines for Stage II. Stage III schemes appeared to be assuming one of two forms: either the Certificate of Education (Further Education), as recommended by the Advisory Committee on the Supply and Training of Teachers, but in other regions consideration was being given for special arrangements with universities in which a Certificate of Education (Adult Education) would be awarded. This is a confusion that, in retrospect, the Advisory Committee might have prevented had its recommendations been a little clearer, but it should be borne in mind that in the United Kingdom adult education was usually coupled with further education for administrative purposes. However, one university (Surrey) had already introduced a postgraduate certificate in the education of adults, in which the process of teaching and learning among adults was paramount, irrespective of the professional background from which the trainee teacher came, although the specific sphere of intended teaching did constitute an option within the study and it was also the area in which practical experience in teaching was gained. Thus the term 'education for adults' did overcome some of the conceptual difficulties raised by the Advisory Committee's report and the scheme at Surrey allowed for teachers of adults to be trained together irrespective of whether they came from adult, further or higher education or from the professions. In 1983, there was also a proposal by the Advisory Committee for the Supply and Education of Teachers for a Certificate in Education course for all teachers, irrespective of their background.

Higher education was rarely mentioned in the above discussions since it is usually regarded as distinct from further and adult education, although the Surrey scheme did make provision for preparation for higher education. Even so, this division had been blurred with a number of colleges being called 'colleges of further and higher education'. Indeed, some of the early proposals for Certificate in Education courses made to the Council for National Academic Awards specified that they were in further and higher education. The Council, however, did not recommend acceptance of many titles incorporating the term at that time although many students in higher education were adults, so that teachers in higher education were actually teachers of adults. Some initial training of teachers was occurring in some universities, but few moved in the direction of awarding qualifications, such as Stage I, in higher education. Nevertheless, the London Region of the Workers Educational Association, which offered a variety of part-time courses for adults including university extension classes, introduced a training scheme for its own part-time staff, which is based on the Advisory Committee's recommendations and which was recognized as a Stage I course.

Planning schemes for the first two stages of training became the responsibility of the institutions offering the courses and validation rested with the Regional Advisory Councils until their dissolution. However, the Advisory Committee on the Supply and Training of Teachers recommended that there should be some type of national forum established in order to ensure comparability and transferability. With the emergence of credit accumulation and transfer schemes this was to become a practicality.

It will be recognized that much of the preceding discussion reflected developments that occurred before a greater emphasis was placed on competency and national vocational qualifications. Even universities considered adopting a national vocational qualification approach. Consequently, the training of adult educators could not remain outside these developments, as the City and Guilds showed by undertaking pilot studies of a competence based 730 course, although at that time it did not have a National Council of Vocational Qualifications approval. However, this was the direction that training had been taking from the outset, since most of the curricula described above had been framed in terms of behavioural objectives.

In addition, Last and Chown (1993:234–236) reported that the Further Education Unit had taken it upon itself to produce 'an entirely new competence based qualification framework for the sector' which did have NCVQ approval. While they were not entirely happy with the approach, they reported that they were preparing their own curriculum for the training of adult educators that would be much more orientated to the current competency based approach. They suggested that this was in accord with some of the best practices in adult education, such as reflective learning, in a manner espoused by Schon (1983), and so it might well be asked what were considered to be the best practices of educators of adults? Many of the answers came from analyses of the roles that they were actually performing, although it might have been better to train new recruits into the role that they might play in the future, rather than the one that current practitioners were actually performing. However, there were a multitude of such lists and Campbell wrote:

> Such lists are well nigh endless, indeed tiresome – but useful to a degree. Out of this formidable, though by no means exhaustive array of analyses it is possible to identify three distinct, significant clusters of competencies marking the ideal adult educator which can be taken as generalized goals for training. The first is a conviction within the adult educator of the potentiality for growth of adults, and a strong personal commitment to adult education exemplified by the extension of his own education. The willingness to accept others' ideas, the encouragement of freedom of thought and expression is fundamental as is a dynamic rather

than a static view of the field of adult education. The second is the possession of certain skills – of writing and speaking, certainly – but also the capacity to lead groups effectively, to direct complex administrative activity, and to exercise a flair in the development of programs. Finally, the adult educator must understand the conditions under which adults learn, their motivation for learning, the nature of the community and its structure. Underlying all of these, and essential, is an understanding of oneself undergirded by a sustaining personal philosophy.

(Campbell, 1977:58)

Tough (1979:181–183) echoed many of these points in his discussion of the characteristics of the ideal helper as: warm and loving; having confidence in the learner's ability; being prepared always to enter a genuine dialogue with the learner; having a strong motivation to help; being an open and growing person. Both Campbell and Tough reflected the humanistic tradition which was prevalent in the adult education, but which was less strong in other areas of the education of adults. For instance, Gibbs and Durbridge (1976) asked Open University full-time staff tutors what they looked for in effective part-time tutors. The replies were reported under the following headings: knowledge of the subject matter; ability to handle the subject matter; general teaching skills; classroom skills; correspondence skills; social competence; academic suitability; values and work rate; administrative competence; interesting style; systematic style; understanding style; informal, flexible style. Hence, it may be seen that more emphasis was placed on teachers and their competencies by Open University staff than on the adult educator as a human being who facilitated adult learning. In the USA, Mocker and Noble (1981:45–46) sought to construct a full list of competencies, but even they warned their readers that it was neither exhaustive nor was it a blue print for training. Their 24 different competencies are that an adult educator should be able to:

- communicate effectively with learners
- develop effective working relationships with learners
- re-inforce positive attitudes towards learners
- develop a climate that will encourage learners to participate
- establish a basis for mutual respect with learners
- adjust rate of instruction to the learners' rate of progress
- adjust teaching to accommodate individual and group characteristics
- differentiate between teaching children and teaching adults
- devise instructional categories that will develop the learners' confidence
- maintain the learners' interest in classroom activities

307

- adjust a programme to respond to the changing needs of learners
- use classrooms and other settings that provide a comfortable learning environment
- recognize learners' potentiality for growth
- place learners at their instructional level
- summarize and review the main points of a lesson or demonstration
- participate in a self-evaluation of teaching effectiveness
- provide continuous feedback to the learners on their educational progress
- select those components of a subject area that are essential to learners
- coordinate and supervise classroom activities
- determine those principles of learning that apply to adults
- demonstrate belief in innovation and experimentation by willingness to try new approaches in the classroom
- plan independent study with learners
- apply knowledge of material and procedures gained from other teachers
- relate classroom activities to the experience of learners.

At first sight this list appears full and exhaustive and yet on closer scrutiny there are points with which some adult educators may wish to dispute. Indeed, this would no doubt be the case with any such list, however long it might be. The values of the person who constructs such an inventory must always be apparent, so that no such list could provide an undisputed basis for devising a curriculum of training. If many lists were consulted, it might be possible to distil out the common factors that might provide something of a foundation, but without an agreed theoretical perspective this approach still fails to provide a problem-free approach.

It may thus be seen that attempts to devise a list of competencies for educators of adults has not been successful in the past, and there is no reason why it should be so in the future. Nevertheless, it is not surprising when the current emphasis is on performativity and competence that we should have discussed the concept of practical knowledge. However, there is a major difference between competence and role, perhaps the curriculum should be constructed on the roles that educators might be required to perform; the issues about competence might be discussed in and across the different roles.

Having traced these historical developments through the 1970s and 1980s we are now in a position to recognize the more recent developments in the professional preparation of post-school educators.

Recent developments in the professional preparation of educators in both adult education and lifelong learning

Three other developments occurred during the above period: the study of adult and further education at postgraduate level; the increasing dominance of the market with education gradually being seen as a marketable commodity; modularization. All of these are reflected in the research reported by Harrop and Woodcock (1992). They surveyed all the universities mentioned in the 1988–9 National Institute of Adult Continuing Education handbook offering courses in the education of adults and found that 43 per cent were completely structured; 52 per cent were core courses with options; only Liverpool's course was completely free choice. Harrop and Woodcock then asked all the Liverpool students enrolled between 1988 and 1990 which modules they regarded as essential core modules and they compared the results with the actual registrations. There was considerable dissimilarity which illustrated that the learning market was not, and could not, be entirely free since part-time students were constrained by the demands of their work, the time at which modules were offered and even the modules' availability. The researchers thus illustrated some of both the strengths and the weaknesses of modularization and of the marketing of educational courses.

Only when courses were offered at a distance like, for instance, the University of Surrey's MSc in Educational Studies in the late 1980s and the more recent Open University's Post Graduate Certificate of Education could freedom of choice become more of a reality. One other effect of offering these courses at a distance was that the market for them became to the English-speaking world, in other words the globalization of the study of the education of adults began. Even so, colleges of further education still offer some certificate courses on a part-time – usually evening – basis, such as the City and Guilds 730 and 7307, which are often advertised as taking a nationally recognized step in getting qualified and gaining a Certificate of Education – which is generally regarded as equivalent to successful completion of the first year of an undergraduate degree. With the introduction of foundation degrees (two-year degrees) as an access route for teaching assistants in schools into the BEd, it might be surmised that it will not be long before a similar route will occur for educators of adults, possibly through foundation degrees developed by some of the large corporations, who are already developing such degrees in other areas of specialism, for their human resource and development staff.

Now many universities and colleges offer modular degree courses both in preparing students to teach in adult, further and professional education, such as undergraduate degrees and postgraduate certificates, and on a part-time basis both taught postgraduate degrees (Masters and Doctorates) and doctoral research programmes. However, a significant change has now occurred – the courses and research may not only be in teaching and learning, but in a variety of the specialist 18 roles cited in the first section of this chapter. Indeed, one of the major changes that has occurred has been the vast increase in the number of postgraduate courses on offer in the various sectors of the education of adults. The Open University, for instance, offers courses of the practice and study of distance education, the Kennedy Report (1997) implied the need for greater training in educational counselling and guidance, there are now courses in teaching and learning in higher education, educational management, and so on. The segments of the original occupations are coming apart, becoming new occupations in their own right and beginning to professionalize, as Bucher and Strauss suggested.

However, there has been considerable resistance in higher education to the introduction of pre-service or in-service preparation for teaching and, indeed, when the *National Committee of Inquiry into Higher Education* (Dearing, 1997) reported, it focused on the need for higher education to professionalize. Among its recommendations was:

> We recommend that the representative bodies, in consultation with the Funding Bodies, should immediately establish a professional Institute for Learning and Teaching in Higher Education. The functions of the Institute would be to accredit programmes of training for higher education teachers; to commission research into learning and teaching practices; and to stimulate innovation.
>
> (Dearing, 1997, Recommendation 14)

It was recommended that all lecturers should, during their probationary period, be expected to become a member of the Institute as 'higher education teaching needs to have higher status and be regarded as a profession of standing' (para 14.28). The Institute would be expected to accredit programmes of teacher training for higher education. The Report not only recommended that these qualifications should be gained during the probationary period but that this should be followed by appropriate in-service training as academics' careers progressed, which should be recognized by the award of a Fellowship. Universities have also been encouraged to establish their own Centres for Teaching and Learning, which some have done. However this is also happening elsewhere in the world: the University of Singapore, for instance, has established a centre which has already run two international conferences on teaching and learning in higher education (Wang *et al.*, 2000, 2002).

In a sense these recommendations almost premised the separation of teaching and research as university academic responsibilities, something that universities have long resisted but, as I argued elsewhere (Jarvis, 1983a), it is difficult to straddle two professions. Consequently, the Institute's development has been slow since many university staff have tended to ignore, or are unaware of, its existence. Nevertheless we can see how the Dearing Committee returned to the issue of professionalization in its consideration of teaching in higher education and that the roles of teaching and research are themselves being separated in this professionalization process.

In 2003 the government's White Paper *The Future of Higher Education* (DfES) returned to the subject of professionalism yet again:

> At present, there are no nationally recognized professional standards for teachers in higher education; and many of those who teach have never received any training to do so. In order that teaching in higher education is treated seriously as a profession in its own right, and that teachers are given the skills that they need, we expect that national professional standards will be agreed by 2004–5, through the proposed new teaching quality academy, . . .
>
> (para 4.14)

These standards are to be competence based and, as from 2006, the government expects all new teaching staff to obtain a teaching qualification. As a carrot, the government will ask the Higher Education Funding Council for England to make more funding available 'to those institutions that can demonstrate that it will be spent on rewards for their best teaching staff' (para 4.23). Indeed, those departments that produce quality teaching will be declared centres of excellence (para. 4.28). The roles of teaching and research have now been completely divided, since we are also seeing the development of Masters degrees in research being supported by research councils.

The rationale for this emphasis on good teaching is clearly outlined in the White Paper:

> All students have the right to good teaching, and some may not be able to exercise their choices as easily as others – perhaps because they want to study a very specialized course, or because they want to live at home. So as well as making sure that students can make well-informed choices, we must guarantee good-quality teaching for everybody. This means being clearer about the teaching and learning practices and students and governments, as the principle funders, have the right to expect from all higher education providers. All providers should set down their expectations of teachers with reference to national professional standards; should ensure that staff are trained to teach and continue to develop professionally; should have effective quality assurance systems and

robust degree standards; and should value good teaching and reward good teachers.

(para 4.13)

Despite a confusion of logic in respect to choice of courses in the above quotation, it is clear that the professionalization of teaching is very much part of the government's agenda. Reward for good teaching has been practised in some higher education institutions in the USA for some time. For instance, I attended an award ceremony for good teaching at the University of Maryland in the mid-1980s and it is interesting that my memorandum to my own university commending the practice on my return did not even merit a reply!

However, it is also clear from the above quotation that the market philosophy is the dominant driving force: the government and the students are the customers, the universities the retailers and the staff are the sales assistants and they need to be proficient and efficient in their provision. It is ironic that it is the market that can drive the universities to professionalize their teaching in the UK, but perhaps this was also the driving force in the USA.

Conclusion

The theme running through this chapter has been that educating adults might be conceptualized as an occupation that is continually in process of professionalization. However, the role has never been a single, homogeneous 'whole' but a variety of different roles that have been held together at a moment in history. As the demands of the role have become greater it has been impossible for the segments to remain together so that we have witnessed segmentation, the creation of new occupations and the generation of a multitude of opportunities for professional preparation and development of educators in all the new occupations formed. Now teaching is being regarded as a single role, but the Open University is already offering courses in the preparation and development of distance educators, so that teaching itself is subdividing. The wheel is continually re-inventing itself and in each instance the customers are becoming a more clearly defined target, and the process will no doubt continue for some time to come.

12

THE PROVISION OF ADULT EDUCATION AND LIFELONG LEARNING IN THE UNITED KINGDOM

In one of the volumes of the 1980 handbook of the Adult Education Association of the United States (to be succeeded by the American Association of Adult and Continuing Education) Knowles (1980c) and Griffiths (1980) both raised the issues of how adult education should be coordinated. Griffiths (1980:113) maintained that:

> Coordination may prove to be the missing ingredient in forging an integrated and efficient system of lifelong education that will attract and serve millions of adults who presently cannot find programs that offer a means of achieving more satisfying and rewarding lives.

In contrast, Knowles (1980c:39–40) insightfully predicted:

> Several current trends seem to augur a period of major change in the education system in the near future. The most potent of these is lifelong education, based on the notion that in a world of accelerating change, learning must be a continuing process from birth to death, and that therefore society must provide educational resources and services throughout the lifespan. A related trend is self-directed learning, based on the notion that it is no longer sufficient for individuals to be taught what others already know, but they must acquire the skills of self-directed inquiry so that they can discover new knowledge continuously. A third trend is toward the unity of education, work and life, based on the notion that learning is most efficient when it is related to and integrated with working and living. When combined, these three trends predict a new kind of educational system that would bring all the institutions of society into a consortium to provide continuous or recurrent learning experiences for self-directed inquirers throughout their life-span. The days of separate institutions for elementary, secondary, higher and adult education seem to be numbered.

313

While Knowles did not quite envisage the market being this mechanism, he was concerned that too much centralized control would inhibit the flexibility that would allow adult education and lifelong learning institutions to respond to all the demands that the changing world places upon them. Significantly, the development of adult education and lifelong learning reflects something of the movement from Griffiths to Knowles.

For instance, since the 1944 Education Act it has been the duty of the Secretary of State for education

> to promote the education of the people of England and Wales and the progressive development of institutions devoted to that purpose, and to secure effective execution by local authorities, under his control and direction, of the national policy of providing a varied and comprehensive educational service in every area.
>
> (cited from the Russell Report, 1973:25)

Later in the same Act of Parliament, the requirements are specified:

> Section 4.1: Subject as hereinafter provided, it shall be the duty of every local education authority to secure the provision for their area of adequate facilities for further education, that is to say:
>
> a   full-time and part-time education for persons over compulsory school age; and
> b   leisure time occupation, in such organised cultural training and recreative activities as are suited to their requirements, for any persons over compulsory school age who are able and willing to profit by the facilities provided for that purpose.
>
> (cited from Stock, 1982:12)

The precise meaning of the words of the above Act were disputed in the 1980s, when there were considerable financial restrictions placed on the provision of adult education locally. Nevertheless, it is clear that since the 1944 Education Act it has been a duty of every local education authority in the United Kingdom to make provision for lifelong education, but it will be recognized immediately that the educational model implicit in this Act is a front-end model, and that no consideration was given to the idea of either an integrated service or a learning region. Even so, the vision of the 1944 Act was long term and idealistic and this is as significant as other parts, such as the structure of initial education, of this most influential statute. During the prosperous years of the late 1950s, 1960s and 1970s there was a considerable expansion in the provision of education for adults. Yet this branch of education remained marginal although contemporary changes have now mainstreamed it and it has become a commodity in the market place as the government recognizes partnerships of providers. There are many problems in having an educational market, not the least being that the poorer people can ill-afford the opportunities that education beyond schooling offers and those with minority interests will not necessarily find what they seek in a market that caters for majorities. In addition, the market has no place for welfare or moral concern and so the ethos of many educational institutions is undergoing rapid change, dashing the ideals of those who framed the 1944 Act and who anticipated that it would 'contribute towards the spiritual, moral, mental and physical development of the community by securing that efficient education ... to meet the needs of the population of their area' (1944 Education Act: Section 7).

In contrast to the forces inhibiting the provision of low-cost liberal adult education the creation of the learning society has meant that business and industry may now actually be the biggest single provider of education beyond school in the UK, and in other countries of the Western world. Indeed, it might be argued that education has become the 'handmaiden of industry' (Kerr *et al.*, 1973) and that educational providers are restructuring their provision to meet this new demand. At the same time, adult educational providers are striving to retain a liberal adult education programme. Nevertheless it would be contrary to the ideals of the 1944 Education Act and to the nature of education itself if the whole person were not taken into consideration in the provision of continuing education in the future. The purpose of this chapter is to examine the provision made for, and developments in, lifelong learning and some of the organizations that support the service in the United Kingdom.

Sectors of lifelong learning provision

There are three main sectors of provision of lifelong learning in the UK: the State, the non-governmental organizations (NGOs), and business and industry, but the World Wide Web constitutes a major resource for each of them and also for self-directed learning. Each of these four will be examined in turn.

The State

In all the European policy documents on lifelong learning (1995, 2000, 2001a), it is seemingly assumed that the State is the major provider of lifelong learning and is free to set its own policies about provision. However, this was disputed at the ASEM (Asean Europe Meeting, 2002) and the European Presidency conferences on lifelong learning (Jarvis, 2002a, 2002b) in which it was argued that business and industry were not only major players in this provision in their own right but that they also

315

exercised considerable influence over the policies of individual states. This it does in two distinct ways: first of all by being involved in many of the policy making bodies but, second, by being a major sponsor of students for part-time study in the learning market. It is not the intention here, however, to rehearse these arguments although it is important to bear them in mind in all discussions about policy and provision of adult education and lifelong learning in the United Kingdom.

There are two major State providers of educational opportunities: the local educational authorities (LEAs) and the universities.

The local education authorities

It will be recognized that the place of these authorities is becoming less influential in modern Britain. Indeed, the LEAs role in education beyond school was further curtailed when the government took the control of Further Education from them and created a Further Education Funding Council to administer the total funding of this sector of education – it is now administered by local Learning and Skills Agencies. Even some of the activities of the traditional liberal adult education institutes, which still remain within the jurisdiction of the local authorities, are funded from the Further Education budget.

The liberal adult education service has remained partly as the responsibility of the local authorities; whether it is administered as a separate service or as part of a broader one depends upon the specific authority. For instance, some authorities have endeavoured to retain a free standing adult education service; some within further education and others have combined it with the school service and created community colleges; while others have combined it with other services, such as the Youth Service, and called it continuing education. However, for the most part it is now run as part of the outreach service of colleges of further education, and in almost all instances it is administered as part of the FE budget.

Separate institutions of adult education tend to have a centre, with a small full-time staff, and perhaps a small amount of prime use accommodation. The institutes use classrooms from local schools and colleges on an evening and, occasionally, a day-time basis. Even if the base for adult education is the local College of Further Education, the same type of arrangements obtain. The curriculum of adult education tends to be mainly based upon leisure time and hobby activities, although more of them are vocationally orientated and accredited than was previously the case. Perhaps the leisure nature of adult education is one of the reasons why it has remained a low status marginal activity. The colleges of further education run large vocational programmes for adults, both in and out of work.

While many adult education institutes were formed after the 1944 Education Act, Kelly stated that:

> The tradition of the non-residential centre can be traced back to the mechanics' institutes and working men's colleges of the nineteenth century, but few of these survived as educational institutions into the twentieth century. It was the Educational Settlements Associations (from 1946 the Educational Centres Association) which took the lead in developing the modem movement and at the same time provided a link with the historic past.
>
> (Kelly, 1970:383–384)

Perhaps Kelly underplayed the degree of continuity between the mechanics' institutes and the contemporary adult education institutes, as Devereux (1982) suggested for London. However, discussion upon this point will be pursued no further here, since historical analysis is beyond the scope of this study. Nevertheless, it may be seen that the history of adult education has been one in which institutes, rather than schools or colleges, have been the location of the education offered.

Perhaps the most well known of all the adult education provision made by local education authorities were the community colleges, associated with the name of Henry Morris. Morris, who was chief education officer for Cambridgeshire, had a passionate belief in lifelong education and an interest in architecture. He had a vision of the educational institution becoming the centre of the village community in almost the same manner as the ecclesiastical institution had been in a bygone age. Morris (1956, cited in Fletcher and Thompson, 1980:16) claimed 'that the centre of gravity in education and the culture it transmits should be in that part which provides for youth and maturity. ... Our main means to this end is to group our local communities round their colleges and secondary schools.' Under his direction, in the 1930s, the first four village colleges were opened and, after the Second World War, other colleges were opened in Cambridgeshire and elsewhere. The village college incorporated the village hall, adult classrooms, rooms for other public meetings and organizations and the secondary school. Fairbairn (1971) actually provided a plan of the Countesthorpe school which had a community education department within a comprehensive school. The idea of utilizing a large comprehensive school as the basis for a community school has subsequently been adopted in a number of places, such as the Sutton Centre in Nottinghamshire (Wilson, 1980), the Abraham Moss Centre in Manchester, and the model has been copied in Grenoble in France. There appears to be tremendous advantages in providing all the community facilities on one campus (see Fletcher's [n.d.] study of the Sutton Centre).

317

Less adventurous and expensive experiments in community colleges were started by other local education authorities, and in these instances they merely designated one portion of a local secondary school for work with adults, employed one or more members of staff with some form of adult education specialism, and called it a community college. These colleges have clearly been useful in rural areas where it would not be financially viable to run a free-standing adult education institute.

The universities

In 1867, James Stuart, who was a fellow of Trinity College, Cambridge, delivered a course of lectures in various cities organized by the North of England Council for Providing Higher Education for Women, and this is generally regarded as the start of the university extension movement (Kelly, 1970:219). The movement was actually sanctioned by the University of Cambridge in 1873 with the first course commencing in Derby on the 8th October of that year. Thereafter, the universities of Oxford and London offered classes and by 1983 there were twenty-five universities in England and Wales having a department with extramural responsibility and providing a university extension service in their regions. These universities had the designation of Responsible Body, which entitled them to receive a grant from the Department of Education and Science towards the cost of organizing adult education classes of a university standard in their designated area. This was the only aspect of the normal work of a university that was then open to the scrutiny of Her Majesty's Inspectorate.

However, when the Responsible Body status was abolished all universities were encouraged to provide continuing education for adults, including those which were formerly polytechnics and which only received their university status in the early 1990s. For a while during the late 1980s and 1990s universities were expected to run only certificated courses unless they were self-funding, although the government did change its policies a little about non-certificated courses towards the end of the decade. In one sense this was advantageous to adult education since it helped in mainstreaming the provision for education for adults in universities, but it has a number of major disadvantages including the fact that the liberal adult education as learning for learning's sake was subsumed and those who could not afford to pay for such courses were disadvantaged. Another disadvantage was that many older adults, who attended liberal adult education classes, simply did not see the need for certification.

However, another major change that occurred during this period was the growth in continuing professional education offered by the universities. The traditional universities were slow to move in this direction and it might be argued that only the reduction in government funding that occurred from 1981 onwards forced the universities to innovate with their programmes and regard teaching and research as essential income-generating activities. Now most universities have extensive programmes of part-time masters degrees and doctorates (both taught and research) although the traditional universities emphasize research to a greater extent than do the former polytechnics. Much of this activity is also undertaken in conjunction with large employing organizations.

From the outset the polytechnics and colleges of higher education frequently provided both vocational and advanced courses in general education for adults. There was considerable debate during the 1980s about the extent to which polytechnics should play similar roles to universities or whether they should retain the function for which they were originally established – to provide opportunities for adults to follow work related education at an advanced level on either a full-time or a part-time basis. If the polytechnics and colleges of higher education were actually able to provide this service they would have had the means of creating a lifelong system of education, and Wood (1982:911) indicated that adult continuing education, at least, was being seriously considered by many of these institutions. Despite these considerations the pressure to respond to the demands of the young adults and to concentrate resources on first degree work resulted in much of the work of such institutions becoming similar to university-type undergraduate education.

By the early 1990s it was clear that the government intended to change the status of the polytechnics and some of the colleges of further and higher education and it eventually created a national system of higher education with most of the institutions having the title of 'university', although the newer ones do not have separate charters. The former polytechnics, whilst rightly aspiring to include research in their overall programmes have found this difficult because of the lack of a research culture and the heavy teaching load of academic staff. It is clear, however, that by the 1990s universities have all, to some extent or other, orientated their programmes towards lifelong learning, although resistance is still displayed in some of the more traditional ones.

That lifelong learning has become the focus of higher education in the new learning market has been one of the driving forces for the improvement of university teaching, as we noted in the previous chapter, and this in turn has meant that the education of adults is being recognized as a field of study in its own right.

Throughout the twentieth century there were two notable exceptions to the failure of universities to respond to the demand for education at an advanced level by adults. Birkbeck College, a constituent college of the University of London, has been concerned exclusively with adult students. This college is named after Dr George Birkbeck who was professor of natural philosophy at Anderson's Institute in Glasgow when he offered courses of lectures to adults in that city at the start of the nineteenth century and who later moved to London. Birkbeck College has offered a wide range of courses, including part-time masters degree programmes, for mature students for many years. The University of London has also offered part-time undergraduate level study at Goldsmiths' College. In addition, it has also provided the opportunity for part-time mature students to take external degrees and diplomas.

In the 1970s, under the then Labour government, the education of adults in universities received a major boost with the establishment of the Open University. This was funded directly by the Department of Education and Science and offered a range of courses at undergraduate level, a smaller amount of postgraduate work and a programme of short courses. The undergraduate programme was modular in structure, with each module being equivalent to a year's part-time study. In addition, there were some half credit courses but they also spanned a year's study. Students were expected to accumulate six credits for the award of a degree and eight for an honours. However, this has recently changed to bring the Open University into line with the Credit Accumulation and Transfer scheme adopted by the other universities that requires students to complete only six modules for an honours, although some of the modules need to be passed at this level. The Open University also introduced a taught higher degree (B.Phil) and a small research degree programme – which has now expanded. Some of the Open University's undergraduate courses may be studied by associate students who are not registered for a degree and who may have no intention of registering for one. In addition, the Open University offers a programme of short courses in both continuing and community education. After a decade of existence the Open University began to offer courses in adult education itself, with both tutor training courses and a third level, half credit course in education for adults, which commenced in 1984. After a quarter of a century the Open University began to expand its activities throughout the world and it came to regard itself as one of the mega-universities, indicating the tremendous need adults experience for more education and also demonstrating one of the strengths of having an entrepreneurial attitude to distance education. During the first quarter of a century there were major changes in the functioning of the Open University: first, its funding ceased to be a separate grant from the government and it became funded in the same manner as other universities, indicating that distance education had itself been accepted into mainstream higher education; second, its activities were extended to include an increasing number of vocational courses and business and industry began to play a larger role in its activities.

Distance teaching in its present form, especially that employed by the Open University using the media as an integral part of the course design, has now become widely accepted, and it is beginning to occupy a more significant place in the programmes of a considerable number of universities, including the University for Industry. While the Open University pioneered the idea of distance learning undergraduate programmes, other countries in the world have rapidly developed similar versions, as Rumble and Harry (1982) demonstrated. With the advent of advanced technology new forms of distance education began to appear, so that cable networks are being used, computer link-ups are common, teleconferencing is occurring and, more recently, interactive compact video disks are being seen as developments that will affect the provision of education for adults at university level.

As the idea of lifelong learning develops it is being recognized that the rigid division between further and higher education is antiquated in many ways. Some colleges of further education are becoming colleges of further and higher education, so that adults can study to degree level in such colleges, although the courses are accredited by universities and the award of the degree is made by the certificating university. In some instances, colleges of further and higher education have entered liaisons with their local universities so that they can offer, under franchise, parts of their degree courses; one common arrangement is for the college to offer the first year of an undergraduate degree course and then the students attend university for the final two years. This movement illustrates the fact that the first degree is systematically being downgraded and the taught masters degree is replacing it as the necessary stage to have been achieved by people in the professions, etc. However, there is now another movement occurring as some universities and colleges of further education are examining the possibility of merging and, therefore, of creating lifelong education institutions. This might also be seen as a stage in the creation of the learning region, but as we see lifelong education institutions develop and lifelong learning develop we do well to recall that Illich and Verne (1976) warned of the dangers of too much institutionalization of lifelong education. They may well have overstated their case but at least it does point to the need to be circumspect about the developments that are occurring.

The non-governmental and other organizations

Having examined the two major statutory sectors of provision of adult education and lifelong learning, it is now necessary to turn our attention to the NGOS, a wide variety of which have traditionally provided education to adults.

Churches

The Christian churches in Britain were amongst the earliest organizations to establish adult education opportunities. The adult school movement (Hall, 1985; Rowntree and Binns, 1903[1986]) has been well documented in histories of adult education. What is less well known is that the very first PhD in adult education was entitled *Spiritual Values in Adult Education* and was awarded in 1925 (Yeaxlee, 1925), many years before other doctorates in the subject were awarded. In recent years, however, the Christian churches have played a less significant role in the education of adults and, as the world has become more secular, the churches have become more introverted. Nevertheless, there are still adult education activities within the churches – most Anglican dioceses have an adult education officer and other denominations also have individuals and departments responsible for adult education activities, with the Methodist Church having its own distance education department. However, with few exceptions local churches do not seem to offer adult education activities to the wider society.

Within the churches another division in adult education is appearing, reflecting the global society within which we live – a distinction is being drawn between adult religious education and adult Christian education. Adult religious education can have two separate meanings – first, education about the religions of the world or even about religion in general whereas adult Christian education is more about education in the Christian faith, and this was traditionally called lay training. More recently a movement has emerged within the churches called *Alpha*, which claims to offer learners answers to questions surrounding the meaning of life, and would perhaps regard itself as an adult religious education activity. However, any examination of the movements publication's would suggest that it is actually an evangelical activity appearing in the guise of an educational movement and this gives rise to major conceptual questions about the nature of education itself – a problem overcome by the use of the term 'adult learning'. The conceptual question is actually about the nature of education itself and the aim to convert people is not educational but may be considered by some to be indoctrinational. However, there are nice conceptual points here, that we will not pursue, like, for instance whether trying to make learners into entrepreneurs falls into the same category of debate! Some research has been conducted into this movement; one piece of which is being conducted at doctoral level at the University of Surrey, which should be completed within a few months of this book being finished. Other adult Christian education activities are occurring at the University of Durham where a centre devoted to it exists. In addition, there has been a growth in doctoral research both in adult Christian and adult Jewish education in the United Kingdom in recent years.

Independent education organizations

There are a number of independent organizations offering a variety of educational services to adults, e.g. correspondence colleges, conference centres, language schools and commercial schools. Correspondence colleges offer courses in a variety of areas, especially in the sphere of the General Certificate of Secondary Education, but it is difficult to ascertain the number of adult students enrolling with these colleges each year. The private language schools are flourishing at the time of writing since English as a foreign language is becoming increasingly important for foreign nationals who wish to reside in the United Kingdom and because it is used so widely in international trade and commerce. It would be difficult to describe all the different types of education offered by these various independent organizations, indeed it is a study in itself, but their existence is evidence of the demand for education that exists and which is often met in an open market situation.

Residential colleges

There are basically two types of residential college: those that run long courses lasting about an academic year or more and those that organize mostly short courses. There are currently nine of the long-term colleges, Ruskin College being the oldest while Northern College was founded more recently in 1977. The other seven are: Coleg Harlech, Co-operative College, Fircroft, Hillcroft, Newbattle Abbey, Plater and Woodbrooke. All the aforementioned colleges offer courses for mature students of both sexes, with the exception of Hillcroft which is for female students only. Two of these colleges have a religious foundation: Plater being a college of the Church of Rome and Woodbrooke being organized by the Society of Friends. Many of the students who attend these colleges receive grant aid, although some attend on scholarships awarded by the Trades Union Movement, this being especially true for some attending Ruskin and Northern colleges. Frequently the courses studied by students at these colleges lead to an award of a diploma, validated by a university, and while these courses are entities in their own right, they also provide sufficient qualification to enable their holders to proceed to a university in order to read for a degree.

Apart from these nine long-term residential colleges there were, according to Legge (1982), about fifty short-term residential colleges that organize short, work-related courses. Often these courses are organized by the college in conjunction with specific companies for their employees and run during the weekdays, while at the weekend they run liberal adult education courses for the general public. Some of these colleges are owned by universities, others by local education authorities, whilst some are private enterprises. Many employ a full-time principal, or warden, but use specialist part-time staff on the specific courses that are organized.

University of the Third Age

The University of the Third Age was founded in Toulouse, in France, in 1974 and really commenced in the United Kingdom in the early 1980s. It is not a university in the technical sense and it has no campus. It is a rapidly growing voluntary association, or rather an association of associations since local associations are independent. The University of the Third Age provides a non-formal system of adult education to its members. It adopts the principle that 'anybody can teach and anybody can learn', and its courses are organized locally and are not certificated. Members pay an annual fee in order to join and they can then attend classes organized by the association. The concept of the University of the Third Age has now extended throughout the world, with there being an international movement and international visits.

However, there are two quite distinct types of U3A organization, with those in continental Europe being a little more formal and more closely associated with their local universities, so that they might almost be regarded as extensions of the university into the community although they have their own local and independent administrations.

The Workers' Education Association

This was founded in 1903 by Albert Mansbridge as the Association to Promote the Higher Education of Working Men, but was soon renamed, the Workers' Educational Association. It had Responsible Body status from the Department of Education and Science and after the Russell Report (1973) the Association stressed its work with industry and the socially disadvantaged, in accordance with the recommendations made in the Report. The Association is a national voluntary body, divided into 17 districts in England and Wales, plus a further three in Scotland and one in Northern Ireland. Each has its own full-time secretary and a few full-time tutor organizers who both teach on the programme and are involved in its development.

However, each local branch is autonomous, so that the members' interests constitute one of the basic criteria for the content of the programme for any one year. Often this programme is arranged in conjunction with a local university or education authority provider, so that in such instances duplication should not occur. While it is the members of the local branches who contribute to the programme planning, each branch offers its courses to the general public so that it depends on the extent to which members are aware of local interests as to whether the classes actually attract many non-members of the association. Since most branches do not have their own premises, each course is usually offered in premises hired by the association and it is often the same set of premises as the other providers use, e.g. a local school. During the funding crises of the late 1980s the existence of the WEA was threatened but it managed to survive. Even so, its existence as a large voluntary organization depending on financial support is fairly precarious in the learning market.

Women's Institute

The Women's Institute was mentioned previously and it is one of the three major providers of education for women, the others being the Townswomen's Guilds and the women's clubs. The Women's Institute receives a grant towards its educational activities and it has also cooperated with the Open University in mounting one of the latter's courses. The Women's Institute has its own residential college, Denman College, near Oxford.

Business and industry

When the first edition of this book was first written business and industry was beginning to develop its own training departments and schools as the knowledge society was dawning. Over the past twenty years the growth and development of the provision made by the corporate sector to education has been immense and at the start of the twenty-first century more adults, especially males, pursue lifelong learning for work-related reasons than for any other reason. This has become the largest post-school educational sector.

Currently, it is very hard to document the time when this sector 'took off', but there has been vocationally orientated further education offered through private colleges, such as Pitmans, for many decades. However, it does appear that in the 1960s and 1970s there was some development. Much of this occurred initially in the USA, where by 1985 Eurich had discovered 18 corporate institutions training schools offering courses leading to academic qualifications at associate, bachelors, masters and doctoral level – the earliest award was offered as early as 1945. She (1985:97) wrote:

> All 18 corporate institutions operate what may be called an 'open admissions' policy. They are quite literally open to all qualified persons *outside* the sponsoring corporation.
>
> (*Italics* in original)

Not only was human resource development growing but the corporate university was being born; she actually discovered about 400 companies that had their own learning centres. By 1990, Carnivale *et al.* (1990a, 1990b) estimated that about $210 billion was spent annually on training in the USA, but this was something of an estimate, since Laurent Technologies (1996) estimated that $52.2 billion was being spent on corporate universities and Meister (1998) suggested that by the year 2000 there would be 2,000 corporate universities in the USA.

Such statistics are harder to find for the UK, but the development of the British Aerospace Virtual University and the National Health Service University indicates that the same movement is occurring in the UK. Indeed, it is a worldwide phenomenon and when I was in Singapore in the year 2000 I saw advertisements for the first conference of Asian Corporate Universities. The first Vice-Chancellor of the British Aerospace University actually wrote about these institutions:

> Traditional universities are no longer the dominant players in the creation and communication of knowledge, especially in cyberspace. Just-in-case education has moved to just-in-time and just-for-you, as self-managed computer-based learning plays an increasing and natural role for individuals and families. What to teach, how to learn and issues of quality are topical again. Plato.com has arrived.
>
> (Kenny-Wallace, 2000:61)

Elsewhere I (Jarvis, 2001b) have argued that a great deal of what is offered through these institutions is not yet at higher education level, but at the level of further education, but this might easily change as the British government seems to be warming to corporate universities being allowed to award their own degrees, provided that they gain sufficient recognition.

At the same time, business and industry still releases many staff to attend the vocationally orientated courses in both Further and Higher education in the United Kingdom, sponsors professorial chairs and commissions research into its own education and training programmes. However, Jarvis et al. (1997) discovered a number of companies in the City of London who were unwilling to support their own employees undertaking liberal adult education in case in prevented them from undertaking the study programme that they wanted for their employees.

Some developments in lifelong learning in the UK

Naturally not all developments can be discussed here but, anecdotally, there has been a greater emphasis in the caring professions of the professionals trying to teach their patients and clients in informal and non-formal ways how to care for themselves better. This might be considered as one of the signs of the learning society; it also results in greater responsibility being placed on individuals to look after themselves more, and this is certainly one of the hidden benefits of learning. Currently, there is research being undertaken on the hidden benefits and clearly once they have been researched then they will be hidden no longer. There have been a series of reports published on this research, including:

- the benefits from further education perceived by practitioners – esteem, efficiency, independence of thought and social integration (Preston and Hammond, 2002);
- family learning (Brassett-Grundy, 2002) and family formation and dissolution (Blackwell and Bynner, 2002);
- adaptation and change, family lives and health (Schuler *et al.*, 2002);
- social benefits, such as crime (Feinstein, 2002a) and health (Feinstein, 2002b).

This research can be useful and important in policy formation. The other side of this coin, however, might be that as welfare funding becomes even tighter, the State then withdraws its services from those whom it considers to be irresponsible. Nevertheless this research does point to the existential nature of human learning and in this sense raises significant questions about our understanding of the place of learning in human being. Amongst other developments there has been: greater access to education; adult basic education; educational guidance; education and the third and fourth ages; University for Industry.

Access

In the 1960s there were a number of educational developments that enabled individuals to use education to rethink their lives and careers (e.g. Hutchinson and Hutchinson, 1978). There were two other developments that led to ACCESS courses. The first was the special provision made for members of deprived groups, including ethnic minorities, to study for entry into the professions. But the major influence was the development of the Open College networks – first, from Nelson and Colne College in conjunction with institutions of higher education in the north-west of England, especially what was then called Preston Polytechnic in 1975. The idea behind the courses run by Nelson and Colne College was to prepare adults to enter higher education and for them to bypass the General School Certificate in Education (Advanced Level) by being guaranteed entry to an institution of higher education if they were successful in the courses being studied. These types of arrangements proliferated and a number of Open College networks appeared throughout the United Kingdom. Davies and Robertson elaborated the basic principles of Open Colleges; they should:

- be genuinely open;
- set no limit for individuals' personal or intellectual growth;

- receive and validate courses meeting community needs;
- offer credit for courses;
- offer courses at different levels;
- be democratic and federal.
- initiate educational developments and promote and market courses throughout the area of its operation;
- link post-16 education with higher education.

(Davies and Robertson, 1986:109–110)

By the early 1990s the Open College Network had become widespread and the Unit for the Development of Adult Continuing Education (UDACE) published a handbook of good practice which contained some seventy examples drawn from across the country (Mager, 1991). Currently there is the National Open College Network (NOCN), which both represents and insures the quality of those networks which it licenses, and there are over 3,500 organizations associated with it including adult and community education centres, higher education institutions, trades unions and employers, local education authorities and training organizations. NOCN is a fully integrated service of accreditation and qualifications, thereby ensuring that access is both of high quality and flexible.

Adult basic education

Despite all of the developments in the education of adults it must be recognized that it is not that many years ago that the prevalence of adult illiteracy in the United Kingdom, thought to have been eradicated by the introduction of compulsory education, was first recognized. Indeed, Cardy and Wells (1981:5) pointed out that provision to cope with adult illiteracy only began in 1975 in the UK. This was initially organized by the Adult Literacy Resource Agency, established as a specialist division initially under the auspices of the National Institute of Adult Education. This agency disbursed grants from central government to the local education authorities in order to stimulate an awareness of the problem. As a result of the British Broadcasting Corporation's involvement in the field with the television programme On the Move, the demand for basic education grew enormously, so that from 1 April 1980 the government established the Adult Literacy and Basic Skills Unit (ALBSU), as an agency of the National Institute of Adult Education, with an initial grant for a period of three years and with a remit to develop:

> provision designed to improve the standards of proficiency for adults, whose first or second language is English, in the area of literacy, numeracy, and those related basic communication and

coping skills without which people are impeded from applying or being considered for employment.

(ALBSU, n.d.: para 1.1)

Both numeracy and life skills were included in this remit, which made it far broader than the original area of concern. The remit was in accordance with the recommendations of the Advisory Council for Adult and Continuing Education (1979b) which also specified that adult basic education should include language, number and life skills. Among the other recommendations of this report were that the Department of Education and Science and the Welsh Office should establish a strategic plan for adult basic education over the next decade and that an Adult Basic Education Unit should be established. Even so, it appealed that the increased provision of adult basic education should not be made at the expense of other adult and further education provision. It was also quite significant that the New Training Initiative, which was initiated by central government and funded by the then Manpower Services Commission, included some of the main aspects of adult basic education within its recommended curriculum. In addition, the Advisory Council for Adult and Continuing Education recommended that it should be included in courses for the unemployed (ACACE, 1982d). Little *et al.* (1982) noted that, while adult education provision for the black communities in the United Kingdom tended not to consider their needs very adequately, adult basic education was still needed by many of them.

Thereafter, adult basic education has mushroomed and a multitude of different approaches have been employed, all of which were tremendously important and many very innovative. Amongst them, English as a Second Language became important in a multicultural society. Gurnah (1992) pointed out, for instance, that illiterate migrants coming from some Third World societies live perfectly adequate lives in their own countries, but on coming to England they discover that literacy 'especially English, assumes an importance entirely out of proportion to what they would consider to be the key issues of their lives, (1992:196). In an edition of *Adults Learning* devoted to adult basic education in the city of Sheffield, the significance of, and innovations in, adult literacy were fully discussed, involving the use of literacy assistants, the cooperation of higher education, involvement of the local community and the local education authority.

Literacy, however, was only one element in these new developments. Rodd (1992) recorded how another scheme sought to involve employers in 'workplace basic skills training'. At that time, it gained little support from some employers unless they focused their work, not on the human benefits of learning, but on the likelihood of increased productivity and harmonious labour relations. Rodd went on to point out that there was a danger that 'the narrow and short-term interests of training providers, increasingly dependent on outcome-related funding, will define the nature of literacy provision, (1992:56). Other schemes, however, did demonstrate that some employers were examining ways of maximizing their work forces' potential through educational projects; Hughes and Mayo (1991), for instance, described how the city of Oxford initiated a project with Ruskin College, whereby the course centred on individual staffs' perceived needs rather than on the training that the employers considered necessary.

While workplace learning was an important part of adult basic education, it was clear that many individuals who received training did not find it stimulating nor even worth their time. Payne (1993:275), writing about the University of Leeds project, recorded how 38 per cent of non-manual and 44 per cent of manual workers considered their training to be poor or unsatisfactory, as opposed to 17 per cent of manual and 23 per cent of non-manual workers who described their training as good or excellent. He showed how many people had educational aspirations that went far beyond the workplace. However, Sargant and Aldridge (2002) still point to the persistent minority of non-learners!

Adult basic education became a very important element in the education of adults and for many years the Adult Learning and Basic Skills Unit received funding as a separate organization responsible for this work. More recently, this has become the Basic Skills Agency having an even wider remit. In addition, the Agency now has a resource centre offering information and is based in the Institute of Education at the University of London. However, basic skills have themselves expanded from just literacy as society has become even more complex.

Educational guidance services for adults

As the amount of provision of education for adults increased, so there has been an increasing need to provide a guidance and counselling service to assist those who needed both to find their way around all that was offered and also to discover the best route for those seeking more education to achieve their goals. These local services began in the 1970s in an uncoordinated manner, with one of the first being started in Northern Ireland in 1967. This initiative grew rapidly and in the 1980s a Standing Conference of Associations for Guidance in Educational Settings (SCAGES) was established. By the time that the NIACE Yearbook for 1993–4 was published, the term 'learning guidance' was being used, and as the Yearbook pointed out this service was still locally organized:

> In some areas provision is made primarily through the local careers service, in others through free-standing educational guidance services for adults, Training and Enterprise Councils are

developing an increasingly visible co-ordinating role through such initiatives as the 'Gateways to Learning' scheme.

(NIACE Yearbook, 1993–4:75)

The Careers Service in the United Kingdom, as a result of the 1993 Trades Union Reform and Employment Act, came under the responsibility of the Secretary of State for Employment and these agencies were re-organized. Now there is a National Advisory Council for Careers and Educational Guidance, commonly called the Guidance Council, concerned with information, advice and guidance about learning and work for all adults and young people.

One of the other early innovations in guidance was the establishment of the Careers Research and Advisory Centre (CRAC) in 1964. This was established as an independent educational charity which, since 1975, has sponsored the National Institute for Careers Education and Counselling (NICEC). This is a professional organization which seeks to develop theory as a result of seminars and research, inform policy at every level and to improve practice. It also offers guidance to practitioners including briefing papers such as *Adult Guidance in Community Settings* (NICEC) on the World Wide Web.

Significantly, one of the aims of LearnDirect which is organized under the auspices of the University for Industry is to offer a national learning advice service about the over 500,000 courses on its database via telephone and web-site facilities. It calls itself a 'Yellow Pages' for learning.

Pre- and post-retirement education

Pre-retirement education has been among the most rapidly expanding areas of education for adults in the United Kingdom in the latter half of the twentieth century, and Coleman claimed that:

> The foundations of the pre-retirement education movement in the United Kingdom were laid during the years 1955–1959, in Scotland by the efforts of the late Dr Andrew Hood when he was Lord Provost of Glasgow; and in England and Wales through the work of the late Mr W.A. Sanderson, secretary of the Gulbenkian Foundation.
>
> (Coleman, 1982:7)

Initially a great deal of pre-retirement education was organized by local authority adult education provision, although industry and commerce also mounted its own courses. However, many of the courses appear to be rather instrumental and it was argued elsewhere that they should include a much greater emphasis upon individuals and their own perspectives

upon their approaching retirement (Jarvis, 1980). Curriculum development was clearly a very important issue in this form of education, and
Coleman (1982:60–72) recorded a course which he conducted during his
own research. This was a useful inclusion since it both demonstrated an
educator of adults at work and showed the type of content that the
participants themselves considered they needed.

One of Coleman's recommendations was that: the Department of Education and Science along with the industrial and voluntary sector should
support the establishment of a national organization which shall be recognized as the focus for pre-retirement education in England and Wales
(1982:95–96). In an important post-script to the research the chairman of
the Pre-Retirement Association wrote, 'that the Department of Education
and Science was recognising the Pre-Retirement Association as the appropriate national body. Funds were being made available on an initial three
year basis, to enable the PRA to create an educational development
group' (cited in Coleman, 1982:99). Hence, it may be seen that this was
another area in the education of adults which central government had
viewed as significant enough to invest monies. However, this support was
not continued through the following decade and, as the recession of the
late 1980s developed, many industrial companies which had previously
organized their own courses, often through their Welfare Departments,
ceased to run courses.

Even so, not all pre-retirement courses were successful, as Phillipson
and Strang (1983) showed very clearly in their in-depth study; they
(1983:184) demonstrated that not all courses created a more carefully
planned retirement and that many courses addressed issues relevant to
only one group of employees, usually management. However, they also
pointed out that these courses often came too late for many of the
participants and that there was a case for mid-life planning courses, so
they (1983:215–221) arranged an experimental one in which they
demonstrated that individuals had already begun to plan for retirement in
mid-life and that there is a case for offering planning support at a much
earlier age. This is still an issue with which the Pre-Retirement Association
of Great Britain (PRA) was concerned and it started courses on mid-life
planning.

The PRA has both run pre-retirement courses and also been concerned
with the standard of tutoring on other similar courses. It initially started
training tutors for pre-retirement courses and now organizes a part-time
masters degree course, validated by the University of Surrey, for tutors in
mid-life pre-retirement education.

By contrast to education before retirement, the education of the
elderly after retirement has also gained an important place in the education of adults, which is not surprising since the population of retired
people has grown so rapidly in recent years. Indeed, Glendenning

(1985:7) pointed out that in the United Kingdom there were approximately 2.4 million elderly by 1901 and in 1991 that figure had increased to 9.9 million. Similarly, there were 3.1 million who lived beyond 65 years in 1900 in the USA but by the year 2000 there were 32 million. There is, therefore, a large potential market into which the education for adults might expand, as the U3A illustrates. Even so, it has to be recognized that older people have less educational capital to bring to future education, and there is a strong relationship between the amount of previous learning and enrolling on future courses. However, the fact that the next generation has more learning might suggest that education for elders will continue to expand in the coming generations. In America the elderly have been attending university summer schools and Zimmerman (1979) recorded the enthusiasm with which they tackled their studies. But the education of the elderly does not have to carry a university label to be popular; some holiday camps are now filled in out-of-season times with elderly adults seeking to learn. Additionally, some holiday complexes and hotels are offering hobby and skills holidays and weeks that, outside of the school holiday period, are filled with seniors. Thus, we see another element in the education of adults emerging. At the same time, Sargant and Aldridge (2002:22ff.) still record that there is a lower proportion of those in the over 65 years age group who regard themselves as learners than in any other.

In the past few years there has been considerable research into learning in later life (Jarvis, 2001a), with a wider recognition of the benefits of learning throughout the whole of life, as we also illustrated above with reference to the wider benefits of learning research which is still being conducted at the time of writing.

Self-directed learning, the media and the World Wide Web

The history of adult education and lifelong learning is full of stories of autodidacts who, having learned to read, spent the whole of their lives reading and studying, often these self-directed learners became political and social activists. Reading rooms and libraries were established, where these learners were able to control and develop their own learning. Now the World Wide Web is the world's largest, easily accessible library – a tremendous resource for learning. However, the Web is notably different from the library in as much as anybody can open a website and produce materials and make their own material widely available. Now there is not even a cursory check to insure that the material is accurate, and so on. Consequently, it becomes even more important for self-directed learners using the Web to approach their reading in a critical frame of mind and to be prepared to reject anything that does not ring true to them.

The UK government has also entered into a partnership with the private sector to use distance and self-directed learning to help individuals develop their skills and improve their career prospects through the University for Industry. Created in 1998, it started LearnDirect in October 2000, which is planned to have as significant an impact on the post-16 sector as the Open University had on adult learning. It will develop e-learning to endeavour to reach those learners who persistently fall beyond the reach of traditional education, as well as others who need to improve their skills in order to bolster their career opportunities. Its organizational target group is small and medium sized enterprises (SMEs) who traditionally find it difficult to sponsor their employees for continuing education and training, and aimed to reach 12,000 by 2001–2. Additionally, it is prepared to tailor courses for specific situations. It plans to develop both on-line facilities and have 1,600 centres offering its services. Its aim is to reach one millions learners by 2005 through its many partners.

By contrast, it is probably true to claim that the other largest providers of information in the United Kingdom are the media, and it might be claimed that they constitute a major element in the education of adults in the country. Obviously the tabloid newspapers offer little in the way of systematic education for their readers but they do constitute a source of information regularly provided for many people. Unlike these, the so-called 'quality press', and many local newspapers offer regular financial and legal columns, systematic analyses of the current political and economic situation, and even columns about architecture and antiques. Indeed, Rogers and Groombridge (1976:171) recorded how some educational courses have been offered through the newspapers. Radio and television, likewise, provide a similar service to their listeners and viewers and these have certainly become a major instrument in the transmission of culture. The Open University has used both in a much more systematic manner than any other educational institution in the United Kingdom, but in other parts of the world they are also used for this purpose, (e.g. Moemeka, 1981) and with the growth of local radio in the United Kingdom these media, apart from when they are employed in a more systematic manner, raise a conceptual issue – do they actually provide education as opposed to being media through which learning occurs? Obviously they are the latter, but are they also the former? For somebody following a series of documentary programmes or who reads regularly the analysis of the contemporary political scene, for instance, they provide the material for a planned series of learning episodes on a self-directed basis. Whether it is the editor or the viewer/listener/reader who is the planner is irrelevant; the fact remains that they may be planned and systematic, so that they constitute the basis of a curriculum.

Professional journals and magazines also constitute a medium through which education occurs. Indeed, there are a number of plans for universities to run their continuing professional education degree courses using these professional journals as a distance teaching medium. Naturally, the universities and colleges will not publish their whole course in the journals, but this is indicative of the way that both continuing professional education and distance education are developing.

In addition, with the improvement in communications, there has been a considerable expansion of interest in education for adults worldwide, with book series examining international issues and the *International Journal of Lifelong Education* focusing entirely on this sphere of activity. In addition, the International Council of Adult Education has continued to play a major role, especially in seeking to link the less developed countries with those which are more wealthy and has produced the journal *Convergence*. Other professional journals include *Studies in the Education of Adults* in the UK, *Adult Education Quarterly* in the USA, *Lifelong Learning in Europe* from Finland, *Adult Education and Development* from Germany, and the *International Review of Education* from the UNESCO Institute of Education in Hamburg.

Having examined some of the recent trends in the education of adults, the main organizations and associations in the field will now be considered.

Organizations involved in lifelong learning and adult education

In this final section we shall look briefly at a few of the main organizations involved in adult education and lifelong learning in the UK: namely, the Educational Centres Association, the National Institute of Adult Continuing Education, the Standing Conference of University Teaching and Research in the Education of Adults and the Universities Council for Adult and Continuing Education. Finally we shall mention a number of the relevant leading European associations.

The Educational Centres Association

This association was established in 1947 as a result of a decision of the Educational Settlements Association to change its name and to broaden its membership (Allaway, 1977:41–42); it is a national, voluntary body which seeks to represent all those centres which cater specifically for the education of adults. Allaway (1977:106) estimated that one-third of all adult education centres were in membership with the association in the mid-1970s and, in addition, there is also a category of individual membership. Since the association grew out of the Educational Settlements Association, it is hardly surprising that it has a democratic philosophy and seeks to support the educational centres in a national context. Like other associations, it organizes conferences for its members and also seeks to disseminate information about adult education as widely as possible, but in the light of the rapid changes in recent years it is no longer such a major player in adult education and lifelong learning as it was in the past.

The National Institute of Adult Continuing Education (NIACE)

NIACE is the major player amongst the NGOs in the fields of adult education and lifelong learning in England and Wales, and it is probably the largest national NGO concerned with adult learning throughout Europe. It was formerly the National Foundation of Adult Education, which was started in 1946. In 1949 this new body merged with a much older one, the British Institute of Adult Education (established in 1921), to become the National Institute of Adult Education. However, the term 'national' is a little misleading because it refers only to England and Wales, since Scotland had its own Institute and Northern Ireland its own National Association. The National Institute of Adult Education (NIAE), which changed its title to the National Institute of Adult Continuing Education to keep abreast with the changes that were happening at this period, was originally located in London but is currently based in Leicester. The Institute has a professional staff and its strategic plan is to 'support an increase in the total numbers of adults engaged in formal and informal learning in England and Wales: and at the same time to take positive action to improve opportunities and widen access to learning opportunities for those communities under-represented in current provision'. Its website suggests that it does this through:

- advocacy to national and local government, funding bodies, industry and providers of education and training;
- collaboration with providers across all sectors of post-compulsory education and training; and through fostering progression routes for adults seeking to develop pathways as learners;
- a commitment to supporting evaluation and monitoring and to a high quality of service;
- securing informed debate – through research, enquiry, publication and through arranging seminars and conferences;
- effective networking – to ensure that lessons learned in one part of the system can be drawn on elsewhere;
- ensuring that the best international practice is available to its members and users;
- a commitment to being itself a well-managed learning organization.

In contemporary society, NIACE certainly performs all of these functions, as well as having its own list of publications and being associated with the journal *Studies in the Education of Adults*.

Standing Conference on University Teaching and Research in the Education of Adults (SCUTREA)

It was established nearly thirty years ago and assumes the role of a professional association: universities which have either a teaching or a research function, or both, in the education of adults may have membership. In addition, individuals who are actively involved in university teaching or research in this field might apply for individual membership. Like the other bodies mentioned, this organization runs a very successful annual conference and it has also established a number of working groups in various disciplines in order to bring together academics who have interests in specific areas of the education of adults, such as the sociology of the education of adults, psychology of adult learning, and so on. It publishes its own newsletter SCOOP that provides a notice board for its members.

Universities Association for Continuing Education (UACE)

Prior to 1947 the universities liaised with each other through the Universities Extra-Mural Consultative Committee, but, in that year, the Universities Council for Adult Education was formed. During the 1980s this association changed from a group concerned with extramural liberal adult education to the wider remit of university education for adults, and universities not having a major extramural function were able to join. With the creation of the new universities, Universities Council for Adult Continuing Education (UCACE) expanded once again. The polytechnics actually had their own association (Polytechnic Association for Continuing Education, PACE) and so when the two associations merged, the new title adopted was the Universities Association for Continuing Education. This association serves as an advocate for university continuing education, conducts its own research and provides a focal point for policy discussions about research and teaching in university continuing education. Now its membership can be institutional, associate, international and individual and most institutions of higher education in the UK are involved in it (Scotland and Wales also have active committees).

Relevant European associations

There are three relevant European associations that should be mentioned here: the European Association for the Education of Adults (EAEA), the European Society for Research into the Education of Adults (ESREA) and the European Network for Continuing Education (EUCEN). The first is an association of the national associations for adult education having its main office in Brussels, the second is a professional association of academics holding European conference and organizing a number of Europe-wide networks, and its secretariat has been at the University of Leiden since its foundation in 1991, and the third is a network of universities involved in continuing education and it holds two conferences each year in different venues throughout Europe.

Conclusion

This chapter has endeavoured to provide an overview of a most rapidly changing field of study, lifelong learning in the United Kingdom – a country that in many ways has pioneered many of the innovations in adult education and lifelong learning in recent years. As the UK is now part of the wider European community, it would be fair to say that the United Kingdom has a great deal to teach other Member States, but at the same time there are many developments elsewhere in Europe from which UK adult learning will benefit. The European Commission fosters this inter-change with many of its programmes – from Grundtvig to Socrates, and so on – and also a conference on lifelong learning with every change of the European Presidency in which policy makers and some academics are enabled to exchange ideas and report developments. We can confidently expect, therefore, to see the European dimensions of lifelong learning develop rapidly in the coming years in each country of the Union.

SELECTED FURTHER READING

(These books are listed by chapter in order of publication date)
Two readings cover a great deal of the content of this book:

Twentieth Century Thinkers in Adult and Continuing Education, ed. P. Jarvis
(2nd Edition) (2001)
This book is a study of the writings of some of the most influential writers
in the twentieth century on adult and continuing education.

Adult and Continuing Education: Major Themes in Education, ed. P. Jarvis with
C. Griffin (5 vols) (2003)

These five volumes present a picture of the whole field of adult and
continuing education from the time of the Enlightenment to the end of
the twentieth century and contain 164 extracts from original texts, plus
editorial comment in each section.

1 Towards a rationale for the provision of learning opportunities for adults

Education and Democracy, J. Dewey (1916)
This is a classical study in the field of education that should be read by all
who are involved in the education of adults because Dewey grapples with
many of the problems that concern them. In a sense, this book contains
the foundations of a philosophy of lifelong education.

An Introduction to Lifelong Education, P. Lengrand (1975)
The author of this book has been at the forefront of the movement to
promote lifelong education in Europe. It is an easy book to read but it
raises quite succinctly many important issues.

ACACE Report: Adults: Their Educational Experience and Needs (1982)
The report contains data from a national survey of 2,460 interviews
in England and Wales and is based upon the idea of participation in

continuing education rather than adult education. It is a very important research report about adult and continuing education, and a precursor to those conducted by NIACE (see Sargant, 1990, Sargant *et al.*, 1997 and Sargant and Aldridge – 2 vols 2002) and the National Adult Learning surveys of 1997 and 2001 (Beinart and Smith, 1998 and La Valle and Blake, 2001).

Adult Education: Evolution and Achievements in a Developing Field of Study, J. Peters, P. Jarvis and Associates (1991)
This book was commissioned by the Commission of Professors of Adult Education to the American Association for Adult and Continuing Education. It contains chapters by some of the leading authors in America, and four from non-North American scholars. It is a 'state of the art' book covering many of the major areas of the field.

Globalization, Z. Bauman (1998)
This book examines clearly the human consequences of globalization and demonstrates some of the ways in which society has broken down and is losing its welfare concerns

An International Dictionary of Adult and Continuing Education, P. Jarvis (2nd Edn) (1999)
This is a thorough introduction to many of the major concepts in the field. It contains over 3500 references and provides a background against which adult and continuing education may be studied.

What is Globalization? U. Beck (2000)
A clear sociological introduction to the process illustrating both its threats and opportunities. It is an important introduction to understanding the process.

Differing Visions of the Learning Society, ed. F. Coffield (2 vols) (2000)
These two volumes contains 13 research reports and two essays: the former are reports from the ESRC research project into the learning society and the latter are introductions by the editor. They cover a wide range of material and provide an excellent picture of a wide variety of activities in contemporary society.

Handbook of Adult and Continuing Education, eds A. Wilson and B. Hayes (2000)
The American Association of Adult and Continuing Education has published a handbook, or series of books, at various intervals since 1934. This is the latest. It contains 42 chapters which provide an overview of the situation in the United States. It is a valuable introduction to under-

standing the developments in adult education in the USA at the present time.

The Age of Learning, ed. P. Jarvis (2001)
This book contains 18 chapters covering a wide variety of developments in lifelong education in the contemporary learning society – from policies to practices.

2 From adult education to lifelong learning: a conceptual framework

Learning to Be, E. Faure (1972)
UNESCO's important report on lifelong education. This is a very import-ant document and one with which all who are involved in the education of adults, especially in the vocational sphere, should be familiar.

Recurrent Education: A Strategy for Lifelong Education, OECD (1973)
This is a clear statement of OECD's policy on recurrent education in the 1970s. The report discusses the concept, sees the scene of recurrent edu-cation and highlights important points.

Foundations of Lifelong Education, ed. R.H. Dave (1976)
This book consists of eight papers, by seven authors, on lifelong educa-tion. Each is written from the perspective of a different academic discip-line and provides a wealth of ideas about lifelong education.

Adult Education and Community Action, T. Lovett, C. Clarke and A. Kilmur-ray (1983)
This book records Lovett's work in Northern Ireland and provides a theo-retical perspective on community education. It raises significant issues about the relationship between community education and community action.

Effective Continuing Education for Professionals, R. Cervero (1988)
The main aim of this book is to identify the chief elements of effective practice for continuing professional education practitioners. It is a prac-tical book raising issues which are relevant to all areas of continuing pro-fessional education.

The Long Haul, M. Horton (1990)
This is Horton's autobiography, the writing of which was assisted by Judith and Herbert Kohl. It is an exciting story of radical adult education, written in a direct and non-theoretical manner. An excellent introduction both to Highlander and to radical adult education.

Lifelong Learning and the New Educational Order, J. Field (2000)
A nice introduction to lifelong learning in society raising some significant questions.

3 The adult learner and adult learning

How Adults Learn, J.R. Kidd (1973) (revised edn)
Written by one of the most well-known of all adult educators, this is a thorough, interesting and readable book. It displays a humanistic approach to adult learning and reflects both the scholarship and the commitment of its author.

Adults Learning, J. Rogers (1977) (2nd edn)
Perhaps the most well-known book on this topic in the United Kingdom, published as a paperback and easily obtainable, this book is well written, easy to read and full of good material. However, the topics covered are wider than adults learning and much of the book is in fact about teaching adults.

The Reflective Practitioner, D. Schon (1983)
This book has become a classic, catching the mood of contemporary theory. It is perhaps the most frequently cited book on learning in professional practice and it contains the basis of a theory of reflective learning.

Experiential Learning, D.A. Kolb (1984)
This book draws together many of Kolb's thoughts and contains a full account of both his learning cycle and also of the work that he has undertaken on learning styles.

The Experience of Learning, eds F. Marton *et al.* (1984)
This book provides a clear analysis of learning and learning style, written by a variety of authors from the UK and Scandinavia. It is a good academic study and should be read by anybody seeking to develop a theoretic understanding of learning. Most of the research reported, however, has been conducted within a higher education setting.

Adults Learning in the Social Context, P. Jarvis (1987)
This book contains the full discussion of the theory of learning presented in this chapter, including the research methodology. The book offers a social science theory of learning rather than a psychological one.

Psychology and Adult Learning, M. Tennant (1988)
This is a careful and good introduction to the psychological literature and its relationship to adult learning. It offers a clear and critical analysis of some of the major schools of psychology.

Womens' Ways of Knowing, M.F. Belenky, B.L. Clinchy, N.R. Goldberger and J.M. Tarule (1986)
A classic women's study in which the authors outline different ways of knowing and relate this to the wider context. While the book examines women, the ways of knowing are as relevant to men.

Access to Education for Non-participant Adults, V. McGivney (1990)
This is an excellent introduction to the study of participation and one of the few studies which endeavours to examine why specific groups of adults do not enrol in education after school.

Learning and Leisure, N. Sargant (1990)
This is a research report about 4,608 adults' learning and leisure habits. This report updates the research cited in the previous two examples, showing how many people are, or have been, involved in education. In addition, it also reveals some findings about adult leisure time preoccupations. It is clearly written, atheoretical, but an important survey which provided significant information about adult participation. It was a timely report and one which is still worthy of study.

Learning in Adulthood, S. Merriam and R. Caffarella (1991)
This book offers a comprehensive guide to adult learning literature, from an American perspective. It is clear and thorough, and for anybody wishing to get to know developments in America, this book provides a helpful introduction.

Paradoxes of Learning, P. Jarvis (1992)
This book is a development upon *Adult Learning in the Social Context.* Written from both a social and an existentialist perspective, the book explores learning within a variety of social situations.

Learning: the Treasure Within, J. Delors (chair) UNESCO (1996)
A follow-up to the *Faure Report* in which contemporary theorizing about learning is contextualized in this report to UNESCO. It is an excellent, humanistic policy document about learning.

Supporting Lifelong Learning (3 vols) (2002) London: RoutledgeFalmer
These are the three volumes of the Open University Course E845 which is an MA course. It brings together a wide variety of readings from the UK, USA and elsewhere in the world, most of which have been covered elsewhere – a thorough introduction to the field. Vol 1 *Perspectives on Learning* (ed. Harrison *et al.*); Vol 2 *Organising Learning* (ed. Reeve *et al.*) and Vol 3 *Making Policy Work* (ed. Edwards *et al.*)

The Three Dimensions of Learning, K. Illeris (2002)
This is a thoroughly researched book looking at the work of contemporary scholars and making an original contribution to learning theory

The Theory and Practice of Learning, P. Jarvis, J. Holford and C. Griffin (2nd edn) (2003)
A basic textbook and introduction to all the major theories of learning in 14 chapters.

4 Adults learning – some theorists' perspectives

Pedagogy of the Oppressed, P. Freire (1972)
This is Freire's classic book which all who are interested in the theory of the education for adults should read. It summarizes his radical humanistic position, in which he sees education as a way of humanizing the world. In addition, it contains clear statements of his analysis of education into two types – banking and problem posing.

Cultural Action for Freedom, P. Freire (1972)
This short book encapsulates many of Freire's most significant ideas. The book is difficult to read, unless the reader has a sociological background, but the ideas that Freire discusses are very important and they repay the hard work of careful study.

The Conditions of Learning, R.M. Gagné (3rd edn) (1977)
This is an important study in which Gagné explores aspects of learning, including those discussed in the previous chapters. While it is not about adult education, or specifically about adult learning, much of what he has written is relevant to adult and continuing education.

The Modern Practice of Adult Education, M. Knowles (1980) (revised and updated)
This is a large book in which Knowles offers a guide to the theory and practice of adult education. Knowles has been a prolific author and this book contains many of his mature ideas. This edition is important since it includes his response to the andragogy–pedagogy debate that the publication of the first edition of this book stimulated.

Using Learning Contracts, M.S. Knowles (1986)
In this text Knowles shows how he has extended his theory of andragogy to incorporate the use of learning contracts. It is a useful book about how Knowles has used self-directed learning and learning contracts and there are practical examples. It is a useful book for anybody who uses, or wants

to use, contracts in teaching and learning. Knowles advocates written contracts, although some might feel that this is too formal.

Learning to Question, P. Freire and A. Faundez (1989)
This book is one of the lesser known talking books which Freire has prepared in which the two authors engage in discussion about learning through problem posing. It shows very clearly that Freire's understanding of this approach to learning is a Socratic approach to teaching.

The Making of an Adult Educator, M.S. Knowles (1989)
Knowles has had a considerable effect on the development of adult education and while the level of theory has developed so that his work is no longer at the centre, this is an interesting autobiographical sketch of the man and his work.

We Make the Road by Walking, M. Horton and P. Freire (1990)
This is a wonderful book of dialogues between Horton and Freire that records a meeting that they had at Highlander – it was both audio- and video-taped. The philosophies of both men are clearly seen in these biographical records.

Transformative Dimensions of Adult Learning, J. Mezirow (1991)
After many papers published in a variety of journals, Mezirow finally published a full-length book about his theory of transformative learning. This is a full book, tersely written in places, in which he attempted to incorporate a great deal of information. It is an important book for theorists of adult education but there is a sense in which he still needs to publish a book in which he brings together all of the papers he has written about this subject.

Freedom to Learn, C. Rogers and H.F. Freiberg (3rd edn) (1994)
This is a thorough revision of his *Freedom to Learn* in which Rogers presented his ideas about experiential learning. The original has become a classic and this is an important updating of his ideas about the excitement of learning and, even more significantly, his existentialist philosophy of education – one which many traditionalists find extremely difficult to accept. However, the third edition contains some material that is more school based and, I think, it loses by the additions.

5 Teaching adults

The Management of Learning, I.K. Davies (1971)
A very thorough book, useful to anyone who teaches in post-compulsory education, whether their area is cognitive or skill based. It is both a guide

through the literature and handbook on how to teach, even though it is now a little dated. The book has a behavioural bias, but is useful to teachers working within an institutional setting.

Helping Others Learn, P.A. McLagan (revised edn) (1978)
A handbook, not mentioned in the chapter, in which the author guides readers through the techniques of teaching adults – a simple but useful little book.

Teaching Adults, A. Rogers (1986)
This book is directed specifically to adult education, containing chapters on both teaching and learning. It is clearly written and a useful introduction; it contains some useful exercises which can help an inexperienced teacher.

The Craft of Teaching, K.E. Elbe (2nd edn) (1988)
This is a book aimed at teaching in higher education rather than adults, but there are relevant aspects which adult educators might find useful.

Adults Learning, J. Rogers (3rd edn) (1989)
Despite its title, this book is a well-written basic introduction to teaching adults. It is descriptive and realistic, covering most of the essential elements in teaching adults. The book has become one of the most well-known texts in this area and, as a relatively cheap paperback, it is good value for any teacher of adults.

The Skillful Teacher, S. Brookfield (1990)
This is a rather personalized approach to teaching, in which the author describes how he plays the role of teacher of adults. In common with many of Brookfield's books, there is a relatively good bibliography.

Workshops that Work, eds. T. Bourner, V. Martin and P. Race (1993)
This is a simple 'how-to' book which outlines 100 different ideas for designing practical teaching sessions and workshops. It is not meant to be critical or theoretical in any way and so it includes theoretical ideas that are in need of debate, but many of the suggestions are very practical and workable.

Becoming a Critically Reflective Teacher, S. Brookfield (1995)
This is about teaching in higher education – it is informative, insightful and experiential. There is a lot of worthwhile material here for anybody teaching adults.

The Courage to Teach, P.J. Palmer (1998)
Perhaps the most moving and profound book about teaching that I have ever read. This shows teaching at its very best and also displays something

about the quality of the person who wrote it. It is personal and challenging.

Pedagogy of Freedom, P. Freire (1998)
This is Freire at his best; here in a posthumous book we revisit Freire and we rediscover his philosophy. Perhaps this is a book that is as challenging as anything Freire wrote in his later years – for him teaching is a human and a democratic process.

6 Some theoretical perspectives on teaching adults

Experience and Education, I. Dewey (1938)
This is a short book, written after Dewey's experiences with progressive education. It is orientated towards initial education, but both the philosophy and many of the ideas are most appropriate to the education of adults.

Towards a Theory of Instruction, J. Bruner (1968)
This is a well-known study of teaching which, while it is especially appropriate for teaching school children, has a number of points that adult educators might wish to consider. This is especially true in the way that Bruner sees instruction within his wider philosophical perspective.

Deschooling Society, I. Illich (1973)
This is one of Illich's many books on a variety of subjects which focus upon his concerns about professionalization and institutionalization. He has clearly a part to play in making educators critically aware of the process in which they are engaged and some of the solutions that he poses are significant for branches of adult education such as community education. It is wise to see Illich's work as a whole rather than merely regarding him as an idealistic critic of schooling.

Ethics and the Education of Adults in Later Modern Society, P. Jarvis (1997)
This book explores the basis of ethics as a discipline and applies some of the discussion to teaching. It is a book influenced by existentialists such as Martin Buber and E. Levinas and one of the only books that examines the teaching of adults from an ethical standpoint.

7 Distance education

Learning at the Back Door, C. Wedemeyer (1981)
This book starts from the premise that all people are learners and that the educational institutions have not always catered for all of these needs – hence, learning at the back door. It suggests that with the development of

new technologies, learning opportunities are now open throughout the lifespan. An optimistic book.

Distance Education: International Perspectives, eds D. Stewart, D. Keegan and B. Holmberg (1984)
This is a poorly produced book but provides an excellent overview of the field, with extracts from the writings of many of the major early writers on the subject.

Theory and Practice of Distance Education, B. Holmberg (1989)
This is an excellent introduction to many of the issues about distance education. It is practical and introduces the reader to Holmberg's own attempts to make distance education a two-way interpersonal communication.

Foundations of Distance Education, D. Keegan (2nd edn) (1990)
This is a comprehensive introduction into theoretical perspectives on distance education; it introduces readers to the main thinkers and provides clear insights into their work. Additionally, the book provides some practical points about planning distance education systems, although it does not enter into the minutiae of the issues involved in preparing distance education texts.

Theoretical Principles of Distance Education, ed. D. Keegan (1993)
This is a comprehensive introduction to the theory of distance education, written by scholars from an international perspective.

Distance Education in Transition, O. Peters (2002)
Otto Peters has always been one of the leading theorists in distance education and in his new book he develops his ideas into the realm of e-learning. An important study.

8 Assessing and evaluating

Assessing Students How shall we know them? D. Rowntree (1977)
One of the classic books on this topic and which it is hard to surpass even now – it is well written, clear and humanistic.

9 Curriculum theory and programme planning

Developing Programs in Adult Education, E. Boone (1985)
This is a comprehensive coverage of the American literature, providing both a basic theory and a practical understanding of programme design.

Curriculum Models in Adult Education, M. Langenbach (1988)
This is a textbook covering a wide variety of curriculum models, mostly from American sources although there is a discussion of Paulo Freire's approach to adult literacy. In a sense, this book is more than just curriculum theory since it introduces the reader to a selection of North American thinkers and their approaches to the education of adults.

Planning Responsibly for Adult Education, R. Cervero and A. Wilson (1994)
This is an excellent introduction to American thinking about programme planning; it is realistic and includes the discussion about power, politics and funding. It is relevant beyond the American scene.

10 Practice, theory and research

Adult Education as Theory, Practice and Research, R. Usher and I. Bryant (1989)
As university adult educators began to undertake more research, it became important to consider the relationship of theory and practice to each other and to research. This book is an excellent study of this interrelationship.

Handbook of Qualitative Research, eds N.K. Denzin and Y.S. Lincoln (1994)
A very comprehensive introduction to qualitative research containing 35 chapters covering almost every aspect of qualitative research. Any educational researcher will find this book invaluable.

The Practitioner Researcher, P. Jarvis (1999)
A small basic book which uses experiential learning theory to question the relationship between theory and practice and also to demonstrate a relationship between research and learning.

11 The professional preparation of teachers of adults

Training for Adult Education, K.T. Elsdon (1975)
This book, now a little dated because of the recent rapid developments in training, remains the only one published in the United Kingdom that seeks to explore the rationale for, and provides a number of models of, training. Therefore, it is an important book to read for anyone concerned to place training in a broad, historical and theoretical, framework.

Training of Adult Educators in East Europe, ed. J. Kulich (1977)
One of a series of monographs published by the University of British Columbia, providing a description of the training programmes for adult

education being organized in Eastern European societies. It is an interesting study, especially for those interested in comparative education.

Preparing Educators of Adults, S.M. Grabowski *et al.* (1981)
One of the series of studies produced by the Adult Education Association of the United States of America, containing chapters on different aspects of training in America. This book is thorough and most interesting to read.

Training Educators of Adults, ed. S. Brookfield (1988)
This is a book containing some of the most important essays written in American adult education about the way in which the training of adult educators has developed in America. For anyone interested in the development of training, this is an important book.

Training Adult Educators in Western Europe, ed. P. Jarvis and A. Chadwick (1991)
This book contains chapters by 16 adult educators about the development of training in different countries in Western Europe – but it remains the only full account of the preparation of adult educators in these countries and constitutes data for any study of developments in this area, although it is a trifle dated now.

12 The provision of adult education and lifelong learning in the United Kingdom

The Learning University, C. Duke (1992)
This book suggests ways in which universities are developing in the latter part of the twentieth century: much of which impinge upon the manner in which the education of adults will develop. A good introduction to current thinking.

A Map to the End of Time, R. Manheimer (1999)
This is a challenging and stimulating philosophy of seniors' learning. Manheimer is both a philosopher and an educator of third-agers and there is a great deal of experience here about which all those involved in adult education should be aware.

Learning in Later Life, P. Jarvis (2001)
This is an introductory text examining a wide range of literature about learning in later life – it was written for all who work with older people, both educators and carers.

BIBLIOGRAPHY

Adult Learning Australia (updated 23rd Jan 2003) *Learning Towns and Learning Cities*, http://www.ala.asn.au/cities.html

Adult Literacy and Basic Skills Unit (n.d.) *Guidelines for Special Development Projects*, London: Adult Literacy and Basic Skills Unit.

Advisory Council for Adult and Continuing Education (1978) *The Training of Adult Education and Part Time Further Education Teachers – a Formal Response from the Advisory Council for Adult and Continuing Education*, Leicester: ACACE.

—— (1979a) *Towards Continuing Education*, Leicester: ACACE.

—— (1979b) *A Strategy for the Basic Education of Adults*, Leicester: ACACE.

—— (1979c) *Links to Learning*, Leicester: ACACE.

—— (1980) *Regional Provision for the Training of Part Time Adult Education Staff*, Leicester: ACACE.

—— (1981) *Protecting the Future for Adult Education*, Leicester: ACACE.

—— (1982a) *Continuing Education From Policies to Practice*, Leicester: ACACE.

—— (1982b) *Adults: Their Educational Experience and Needs*, Leicester: ACACE.

—— (1982c) *Prime Use Accommodation for Adult Education*, Leicester: ACACE.

—— (1982d) *Education for Unemployed Adults*, Leicester: ACACE.

—— (1982e) *The Case for a National Development Body for Continuing Education in England and Wales*, Leicester: ACACE.

Alford, H.I. (ed.) (1980) *Power and Conflict in Continuing Education*, Belmont, California: Wadsworth Publishing Co.

Allaway, A. (1977) *The Educational Centres Movement, 1909–1977*, NIAE in association with the Educational Centres Association.

Allman, P. (1982) 'New perspectives on the adult: An argument for lifelong education', *International Journal of Lifelong Education* 1(1).

—— (1984) 'Self help learning and its relation to learning and development in later life', in Midwinter, E. (ed.) *Mutual Aid Universities*, London: Croom Helm.

Apps, J.W. (1979) *Problems in Continuing Education*, New York: McGraw Hill Book Co.

Apter, M. (1989) 'Negativism and the Sense of Identity', in Breakwell, G. (ed.) *Threatened Identities*, London: Wiley.

Argyle, M. (1974) *The Social Psychology of Work*, Harmondsworth: Penguin.

Argyris, C. and Schon, D. (1974) *Theory in Practice: Increasing Professional Effectiveness*, San Francisco: Jossey Bass.

—— (1978) *Organizational Learning: A Theory of Action Perspective*, Reading, Mass: Addison-Wesley.

351

Aristotle (1925) *Nichomachean Ethics* (trans. Davis Ross), Oxford: Oxford University Press.

Armstrong, P.F. (1982) 'The "needs meeting" ideology in liberal adult education', *International Journal of Lifelong Education* 1 (4).

Aronowitz, A. (2000) *The Knowledge Factory*, Boston: Beacon Press.

ASEM (2002) *Lifelong Learning in ASEM Countries: The Way Forward*, Copenhagen: Ministry of Education.

Aslanian, C.B. and Brickell, H.H. (1980) 'Americans in transition: life changes and reasons for adult learning', in *Future Directions for a Framing Society*, New York: College Board.

Ausubel, D.E., Novak, I.S. and Hanesian, E. (1978) *Educational Psychology: A Cognitive View*, New York: Holt, Rinehart and Winston.

Bandura, A. (1969) *Principles of Behaviour Modification*, New York: Holt, Rinehart and Winston.

—— (1973) *Aggression: a Social Learning Analysis*, Englewood Cliffs N.J: Prentice Hall.

Barlow, S. (1991) 'Impossible dream: why doesn't mentorship work in UK nurse education', *Nursing Times* 87, 78 *Bibliography*.

Baskett, M. and Marsick, V. (eds) (1992) *Professionals' Ways of Knowing: New Findings on How to Improve Professional Education*, San Francisco: Jossey Bass.

Bauman, Z. (1987) *Legislators and Interpreters*, Cambridge: Polity Press.

—— (1992) *Intimations of Post-Modernity*, London: Routledge.

—— (1998) *Globalization*, Cambridge: Polity.

—— (1999) *In Search of Politics*, Cambridge: Polity.

—— (2002) *Society under Siege*, Cambridge: Polity.

Beard, R. (1976) (3rd edn) *Teaching and Learning in Higher Education*, Harmondsworth: Penguin.

Beck, U. (1992) *Risk Society*, London: Sage.

—— (1994) 'The reinvention of politics', in Beck, U., Giddens, A. and Lash, S. (eds) *Reflexive Modernization*, Cambridge: Polity.

—— (2000) *What is Globalization?*, Cambridge: Polity.

Beinart, S. and Smith, P. (1998) *The National Learning Survey, 1997*, London: Department for Education and Science.

Beisgen, B. and Kraitchman, M. (2003) *Seniors Centers: Opportunities for Successful Aging*, New York: Springer.

Belbin, C. and Belbin, R.M. (1972) *Problems in Adult Retraining*, London: Heinemann.

Belenky, M., Clinchy, B., Goldberger, N. and Tarule, J. (1986) *Women's Ways of Knowing*, New York: Basic Books.

Berger, P.L. (1974) *Pyramids of Sacrifice*, Harmondsworth: Pelican.

Berger, P.L. and Luckmann, T. (1966) *The Social Construction of Reality*, London: Penguin.

Bergevin, P., Morris, D. and Smith, R.M. (1963) *Adult Education Procedures*, New York: Seabury Press.

Bestwick, D. and Chadwick, A. (1977) 'A co-operative training scheme for part-time teachers of adults', in *Adult Education* 50 (4). Leicester: NIAE.

Bines, H. (1992) 'Issues in course design', in Bines, H. and Watson, D. (eds) *Developing Professional Education*, Buckingham: SRHE and Open University Press.

Blackwell, L. and Bynner, J. (2002) *Learning, Family Formation and Dissolution*,

London: Institute of Education, Centre for Research on the Wider Benefits of Learning.

Bligh, D.A. (1971) *What's the Use of Lectures?* Exeter: D.A. and B. Hugh, Briar House.

Bloom, B. (ed.) (1956) *Taxonomy of Educational Objectives – Book I The Cognitive Domain*, London: Longman.

Boone, E. (1985) *Developing Programs in Adult Education*, Englewood Cliffs, New Jersey: Prentice Hall.

Borger, R. and Seaborne, A.E.M. (1966) *The Psychology of Learning*, Harmondsworth: Penguin.

Boshier, R. (1980) *Towards a Learning Society*, Vancouver: Learning Press.

Bottomore, T. and Reubel, M. (eds) (1963) *Selected Writings in Sociology and Social Theory*, Harmondsworth: Pelican Books.

Boud, D. and Bridge, W. (1974) *Keller Plan: A Case Study in Individualized Learning*, Institute of Educational Technology, University of Surrey.

Boud, D. and Miller, N. (eds) (1996) *Working with Experience*, London: Routledge.

Boud, D.J., Bridge, W.A. and Willoughby, L. (1975) 'P.S.I. now – a review of progress and problems', *Journal of Educational Technology* 6 (2).

Boud, D., Keogh, R. and Walker, D. (eds) (1983) *Reflection: Turning Experience into Learning*, London: Kogan Page.

Bourdieu, P. (1973) 'Cultural reproduction and social reproduction', in Brown, M. (ed.) *Knowledge, Education and Social Change*, London: Tavistock.

Bourdieu, P. and Passeron, J.-C. (1977) *Reproduction in Education, Society and Culture*, London: Sage.

—— (1994) 'Language and the teaching situation', in Bourdieu, P., Passeron, J.-C. and Saint Martin, M. (eds) *Academic Discourses*, Cambridge: Polity.

Bourner, T., Martin, V. and Race, P. (eds) (1993) *Workshops that Work*, Maidenhead: McGraw Hill.

Bowles, S. and Gintis, H. (1976) *Schooling in Capitalist America*, London: Routledge and Kegan Paul.

Boyle, C. (1982) 'Reflections on recurrent education', *International Journal of Lifelong Education* 1 (1).

Bradshaw, J. (1977) 'The concept of social need', in Fitzgerald, M., Malmos, P., Muncie, J. and Zeldin, D. (eds) *Welfare in Action*, London: Routledge and Kegan Paul/OUP.

Brassett-Grundy, A. (2002) *Parental Perspectives on Family Learning*, London: Institute of Education, Centre for Research on the Wider Benefits of Learning.

Bright, B. (ed.) (1989) *Theory and Practice in the Study of Adult Education*, London: Routledge.

Brinkerhoff, R. (1987) *Achieving Results from Training*, San Francisco: Jossey Bass.

Brockett, R. and Hiemstra, R. (1991) *Self-Direction in Adult Learning*, London: Routledge.

Brookfield, S. (ed.) (1988) *Training Educators of Adults*, London: Routledge.

—— (1990) *The Skillful Teacher*, San Francisco: Jossey Bass.

—— (1995) *Becoming a Critically Reflective Teacher*, San Francisco: Jossey Bass.

Brown, G. and Atkins, M. (1988) *Effective Teaching in Higher Education*, London: Methuen.

Brown, H. (ed.) (1973) *Knowledge, Education and Social Change*, London: Tavistock.

Brown, V. (1992) 'The emergence of the economy', in Hall, S. and Gieben, B. (eds) *Formations of Modernity*, Cambridge: Polity Press.

Brundage, D.H. and Mackeracher, D. (1980) *Adult Learning Principles and their Application to Program Planning*, Toronto: The Ontario Institute for Studies in Education.

Bruner, J.S. (1968) *Towards a Theory of Instruction*, New York: W.W. Norton and Co.

—— (1979) *On Knowing*, Cambridge, Mass.: Belknap Press of Harvard University Press.

Bryant, I. (1983) 'Paid educational leave in Scotland', *International Journal of Life-long Education* 2 (1).

Buber, M. (1959) *I and Thou*, Edinburgh: T&T Clark.

—— (1961) *Between Man and Man*, London: Fontana.

Bucher, R. and Strauss, A. (1966) 'Professional associations and the process of segmentation', in Vollmer, H. and Mills, D. (eds) *Professionaliation*, Englewood Cliffs NJ: Prentice Hall.

Burgess, P.D. (1974) *The Educational Orientations of Adult Participants in Group Educational Activities*, Unpublished doctoral thesis, University of Chicago.

Caffarella, R. (1988) 'Ethical issues in the teaching of adults', in Brockett, R. (ed.) *Ethical Issues in Adult Education*, New York: Teachers' College, Columbia University.

Caldwell, P.A. (1981) 'Preservice training for instructors of adults', in Grabowski, S. *et al.* (eds) *Preparing Educators of Adults*, San Francisco: Jossey Bass.

Campbell, C. (1987) *The Romantic Ethic and the Spirit of Modern Consumerism*, Oxford: Blackwell.

Campbell, D.D. (1977) *Adult Education as a Field of Study and Practice*, Vancouver: Centre for Continuing Education, University of British Columbia.

Candy, P.C. (1981) *Mirrors of the Mind*, Manchester Monographs 16, Department of Adult and Higher Education, University of Manchester.

—— (1991) *Self Direction for Lifelong Learning*, San Francisco: Jossey Bass.

Cantor, L.M. (1974) *Recurrent Education – Policy and Developments in OECD Member Countries; United Kingdom*, Paris: OECD.

Caplow, T. (1954) *The Sociology of Work*, Minneapolis: University of Minnesota Press.

Cardy, E. and Wells, A. (1981) *Adult Literacy Unit: Development Projects 1978–80*, London: Adult Literacy and Basic Skills Unit.

Carlton, S. and Soulsby, J. (1999) *Learning to Grow Older and Bolder*, Leicester: NIACE.

Carnivale, A., Gainer, L. and Villet, J. (1990a) *Training in America*, San Francisco: Jossey Bass.

—— (1990b) *Training the Technical Workforce*, San Francisco: Jossey Bass.

Carp, A., Peterson, R. and Roelfs, P. (1974) 'Adult learning interests and experiences', cited in Cross, K. (ed.) (1981) *Adults as Learners*, San Francisco: Jossey Bass.

Carr, W. and Kemmis, S. (1986) *Becoming Critical*, London: Falmer.

Casner-Lotto, J. and Associates (1988) *Successful Training Strategies*, San Francisco: Jossey Bass.

Castells, M. (1996) *The Rise of the Network Society*, Oxford: Blackwell (Vol. 1 of *The Information Age: Economy, Society and Culture*).

Cervero, R. (1988) *Effective Continuing Education for Professionals*, San Francisco: Jossey Bass.

—— (1991) 'Relationships between theory and practice', in Peters, J., Jarvis, P. and Associates (eds) *Adult Education: Evolution and Achievements in a Developing Field of Study*, San Francisco: Jossey Bass.

Cervero, R. and Wilson, A. (1994) *Planning Responsibly for Adult Education*, San Francisco: Jossey Bass.

Chadwick, A.F. (1980) *The Role of the Museum and Art Gallery in Community Education*, Department of Adult Education, University of Nottingham.

Charnley, A., Osborn, M. and Withnall, A. (1980) *Review of Existing Research in Adult and Continuing Education: Vol. 1 – Mature Students*, Leicester: NIAE.

Child, D. (1977) (2nd edn) *Psychology and the Teacher*, London: Holt, Rinehart and Winston.

—— (1981) (3rd edn) *Psychology and the Teacher*, New York: Holt, Rinehart and Winston.

Child, J. (1977) *Organizations: A Guide to Problems and Practice*, London: Harper and Row.

City and Guilds of London Institute (1978) *730 Further Education Teachers' Certificate*, London: CULl.

Clark, C. (1990) 'The teacher and the taught: moral transactions in the classroom', in Goodlad, J.L., Soder, R. and Sirontik, K.A. (eds) *The Moral Dimensions of Teaching*, San Francisco: Jossey Bass.

Coates, K. and Silburn, R. (1967) *St Ann's: Poverty, Deprivation and Morale in a Nottingham Community*, Department of Adult Education, University of Nottingham.

Coffield, F. (ed.) (2000) *Differing Visions of a Learning Society*, Bristol: Polity (2 vols).

Cohen, N. (2002) 'One way to get very rich', *Observer*, London, 24th February,

Coleman, A. (1982) *Preparation for Retirement in England and Wales*, Leicester: NIAE.

Coleman, J. (1990) *Foundations of Social Theory*, Cambridge, Mass: Belknap Press of the Harvard University Press.

Collins *Dictionary of the English Language* (1979) London and Glasgow: Collins.

Collins, M. (ed.) (1995) *The Canmore Proceedings*, Saskatchewan: University of Saskatchewan.

Coombs, P. and Ahmed, M. (1974) *Attacking Rural Poverty*, Baltimore: Johns Hopkins University Press.

Cooper, D. (1983) *Authenticity and Learning: Nietzsche's Educational Philosophy*, London: Routledge.

Council on the Continuing Education Unit (1984) *Principles of Good Practice in Continuing Education*, Maryland, USA: CCEU.

Courtney, S. (1981) 'The factors affecting participation in adult education: an analysis of some literature', *Studies in Adult Education* 13 (2).

Cox, R. and Pascall, G. (1994) 'Individualism, self-evaluation and self-fulfilment in the experience of mature women students', *International Journal of Lifelong Education* 13 (2): 159–173.

Crane, J.M. (1982) '*Individualized learning: an analysis of the theoretical principles with illuminative references from the experientially-evolved practices of an individualized learning system developed in an adult basic academic upgrading programme*', unpublished MSc dissertation, University of Surrey.

Cross, K.P. (1981) *Adults as Learners*, San Francisco: Jossey Bass.

Cussack, S. (1996) Developing a Lifelong Learning Program: empowering seniors in lifelong learning, *Educational Gerontology* 21 (4): 305–320.

Dadswell, G. (1978) 'The adult independent learner and public libraries', in *Adult Education* 51 (1), Leicester: NIAE.

Dahlgren, O.-L. (1984) 'Outcomes of learning', in Marton, F. *et al.* (1984) *The Experience of Learning*, Edinburgh: Scottish Academic Press.

Dale, S.M. (1980) 'Another way forward for adult learners: the public library and independent study', *Studies in Adult Education* 12 (1).

Dale, S. and Carty, J. (1985) *Finding Out about Continuing Education*, Milton Keynes: Open University Press.

Daloz, L. (1986) *Effective Teaching and Mentoring*, San Francisco: Jossey Bass.

Danaher, G., Schirato, T. and Webb, J. (2000) *Understanding Foucault*, London: Sage.

Daniel, J. (1996) *Mega-Universities and Knowledge Media*, London: Kogan Page.

Dave, R.H. (ed.) (1976) *Foundations of Lifelong Education*, Oxford: Pergamon Press (for UNESCO Institute for Education).

Davies, D. and Robertson, D. (1986) 'Open college – towards a new view of adult education', *Adult Education* 59 (2): 106–114.

Davies, I.K. (1971) *The Management of Learning*, London: McGraw Hill Book Co.

—— (1976) *Objectives in Curriculum Design*, London: McGraw Hill Book Co.

Day, C. and Baskett, H.K. (1982) 'Discrepancies between intentions and practice: Re-examining some basic assumptions about adult and continuing professional education', *International Journal of Lifelong Education* 1 (2).

de Wit, P. (1992) *Quality Assurance in University Continuing Vocational Education*, London: HMSO.

—— (1993) *Approaches to Good Practice in Quality Assurance in University Continuing Education*, Universities Association for Continuing Education Working Paper 3, University of Birmingham.

Dearden, R.F. (1972) '"Needs" in education', in Dearden, R.F., Hirst, P.H. and Peters, R.S. (eds) *A Critique of Current Educational Aims (Part I of Education and the Development of Reason)*, London: Routledge and Kegan Paul.

Dearden, R.F., Hirst, P.H. and Peters, R.S. (eds) (1972) *A Critique of Current Educational Aims (Part I of Education and the Development of Reason)*, London: Routledge and Kegan Paul.

Dearing, R. (Chair) (1997) *Higher Education in the Learning Society*, Norwich: HMSO.

Delors, J. (Chair) (1996) *Learning the Treasure Within*, Paris: UNESCO.

Denzin, N. and Lincoln, Y. (eds) (1994) *Handbook of Qualitative Research*, Thousand Oaks: Sage.

DfEE (1998) *The Age of Learning*, London: Department for Education and Employment.

DfES (2003) *The Future of Higher Education*, CM 5735, Norwich: HMSO.

Devereux, W. (1982) *Adult Education in Inner London 1870–1980*, London: Shepheard-Welwyn/ILEA.

Dewey, J. (1916) *Education and Democracy*, New York: The Free Press.

—— (1938) *Experience and Education*, London: Collier Macmillan.

—— (ed.) (1958) *Experience and Nature*, New York: Dover Publications.

Directorate-General for Education and Culture (2002) *Education and Training in Europe: diverse systems, shared goals for 2010*, Brussels: European Commission.

Dohman, G. (1996) *Lifelong Learning: Guidelines for a modern education policy*, Bonn: Federal Ministry of Education, Science, Research and Technology.

Dovey, K. and Onyx, J. (2001) 'Generating social capital at the workplace: a South African case of inside-out social renewal', *International Journal of Lifelong Education* 20: 151–168.

Draves, W. (1979) 'The free university network', *Lifelong Learning – The Adult Years* 3 (4).

—— (1980) *The Free University – a Model for Lifelong Learning*, Chicago: Association Press.

Duke, C. (1992) *The Learning University*, Buckingham: Open University Press in association with Society for Research in Higher Education.

Durkheim, E. (1933) *The Division of Labor in Society*, New York: Free Press.

—— (1956) *Education and Sociology* (trans. S.D. Fox), New York: The Free Press.

Edwards, R., Small, N. and Tait, A. (eds) (2002) *Supporting Lifelong Learning (vol 3) – Making Policy Work*, London: RoutledgeFalmer.

Eisner, E.W. (1969) 'Instructional and expressive educational objectives', in Popham, W.J., Eisner, E.W., Sullivan, H.J. and Tyler, L.L. (eds) *Instructional Objectives*, Chicago: Rand McNally.

Elbe, K. (1988) (2nd edn) *The Craft of Teaching*, San Francisco: Jossey Bass.

Elias, J.L. (1979) 'Andragogy revisited', *Adult Education* 29: 252–256.

Elias, J.L. and Merriam, S. (1980) *Philosophical Foundations of Adult Education*, Florida: Krieger.

Elsdon, K.T. (1970) 'The East Midlands Scheme', *Adult Education* 46 (4), Leicester: NIAE.

—— (1975) *Training for Adult Education*, Department of Adult Education, University of Nottingham in conjunction with NIAE.

Elsey, B. (1986) *Social Theory Perspectives on Adult Education*, Department of Adult Education, University of Nottingham.

Engestrom, Y. (1987) *Learning by Expanding*, Helsinki: Orienta-Konsultit Oy.

—— (1990) *Learning, Working and Imagining*, Helsinki: Orienta-Konsultit Oy.

Entwistle, N. (1981) *Styles of Learning and Teaching*, Chichester: John Wiley.

Eraut, M. (1994) *Developing Professional Knowledge and Competence*, London: Falmer.

Eurich, N. (1985) *Corporate Classrooms*, Princeton, New Jersey: Carnegie Foundation for the Advancement of Teaching.

European Commission (1995) *Teaching and Learning: Towards the Learning Society*, Brussels: European Commission.

—— (2000) *A Memorandum on Lifelong Learning*, Brussels: European Commission, SEC(2000) 1832.

—— (2001a) *Making a European Area of Lifelong Learning a Reality*, Brussels: European Commission, COM (2001) 678 final.

—— (2001b) *The Concrete Future Objectives of Education Systems*, Brussels: E.C. COM(2001) 59 final.

—— (2002) *Education and Training in Europe: diverse systems, shared goals for 2010*, Brussels: European Communities.

—— (2003) *Investing Efficiently in Education and Training: an Imperative for Europe*, Brussels: E.C. COM(2002) 779 final.

Fairbairn, A.N. (1971) *The Leicestershire Community Colleges*, London: NIAE.

—— (1978) *The Leicestershire Community Colleges and Centres*, Department of Adult Education, University of Nottingham.

Faure, E. (1972) *Learning to Be*, Paris: UNESCO.

Feigenbaum, E. and McCorduck, P. (1984) *The Fifth Generation*, New York: Signet.

Feinstein, L. (2002a) *Quantitative Estimates in the Social Benefits of Learning, 1: Crime*, London: Institute of Education, Centre for Research on the Wider Benefits of Learning.

—— (2002b) *Quantitative Benefits of the Social Benefits of Learning, 2: Health*, London: Institute of Education, Centre for Research on the Wider Benefits of Learning.

Field, J. (2002) *Lifelong Learning and the New Social Order*, Stoke: Trentham.

Finch, J. (1984) *Education as Social Policy*, London: Longman.

Fletcher, C. (1980a) 'The theory of community education and its relation to adult education', in Thompson, J.L. (ed.) *Adult Education for a Change*, London: Heinemann.

—— (1980b) 'Community studies as practical adult education', *Adult Education* 53 (2), Leicester: NIAE.

—— (1982) 'Adults in a community education centre', *International Journal of Lifelong Education* 1 (3).

—— (n.d.) *The Challenges of Community Education*, Department of Adult Education, University of Nottingham.

Fletcher, C. and Thompson, N. (1980) *Issues in Community Education*, Lewes: Falmer Press.

Flude, R.A. (1978) 'A course in rural community action', *Adult Education* 51(3), Leicester: NIAE.

Flude, R. and Parrott, A. (1979) *Education and the Challenge of Change – a Recurrent Education Strategy for Britain*, Milton Keynes: Open University Press.

Fordham, P., Poulton, G. and Randle, L. (1979) *Learning Networks in Adult Education*, London: Routledge and Kegan Paul.

Fowler, J. (1981) *Stages of Faith*, New York: Harper & Row.

Fraser, W. (1995) *Learning from Experience*, Leicester: NIACE.

Freire, P. (1971) 'A few notions about the word "concientization"', *Hard Cheese* No. 1. Reprinted in Dale, R., Esland, U. and MacDonald, M. (eds) *Schooling and Capitalism* (1976), London: Routledge and Kegan Paul/Open University Press.

—— (1972a) *Cultural Action for Freedom*, Harmondsworth: Penguin.

—— (1972b) *Pedagogy of the Oppressed* (trans. M.B. Ramer), Harmondsworth: Penguin.

—— (1973a) *Education for Critical Consciousness*, London: Sheed and Ward. Reprinted under the title *Education: the Practice of Freedom*, London: Writers and Readers Publishing Cooperative.

—— (1973b) 'Education, liberation and the Church', *Study Encounter* 9 (1).

—— (1973c) 'By learning they can teach', *Convergence* 6 (1).

—— (1978) *Pedagogy in Process. The Letters to Guinea-Bissau*, London: Writers and Readers Publishing Cooperative.

—— (1985) *The Politics of Education*, London: Macmillan.

—— (1996) *Pedagogy of Hope*, New York: Continuum.

—— (ed) (1997) *Mentoring the Mentor*, New York: Peter Lang.

—— (1998) *Pedagogy of Freedom*, Lanham: Rowman and Littlefield.

Freire, P. and Faundez, A. (1989) *Learning to Question: a Pedagogy of Liberation*, Geneva World Council of Churches.

Freire, P. and Macedo, D. (1987) *Literacy: Rending the Word and the World*, London: Routledge.

Freire, P. and Shor, I. (1987) *A Pedagogy for Liberation*, London: Macmillan.

Fryer R (Chair) (1997) *Learning for the Twenty First Century*, London: Department for Education and Employment.

—— (1998) *Creating Learning Cultures*, London: Department for Education and Employment.

Further Education Unit (1989) *Supporting Quality in YTS*, London: FEU.

—— (1992) *Quality Education and Training for the Adult Unemployed*, London: FEU.

Gagné, R.M. (1977) (3rd edn) *The Conditions of Learning*, New York: Holt, Rinehart and Winston.

Gagné, R.M., Briggs, L. and Wager, W. (1992) (4th edn) *Principles of Instructional Design*, Fort Worth: Harcourt Brace Jovanovich.

Gardner, H. (1983) *Frames of Mind*, New York: Basic Books.

—— (1999) *Intelligence Reframed*, Basic Books: New York.

Garrison, R. and Shale, D. (eds) (1990) *Education at a Distance*, Malabar, Florida: Krieger.

Gibbons, M., Limoges, C., Nowotney, H., Schwartzman, S., Scott, P. and Trow, M. (1994) *The New Production of Knowledge*, London: Sage.

Gibbs, G. (1981) *Teaching Students to Learn*, Milton Keynes: Open University Press.

Gibbs, G. and Durbridge, N. (1976) 'Characteristics of Open University tutors (Part 2): Tutors in action', *Teaching at a Distance* (7), Milton Keynes: Open University.

Giddens, A. (1990) *The Consequences of Modernity*, Cambridge: Polity Press.

—— (1991) *Modernity and Self-Identity*, Cambridge: Polity.

Giles, H.H., McCutcheon, S.P. and Zechriel, A.N. (1942) *Exploring the Curriculum*, New York: Harper.

Glendenning, F. (ed.) (1985) *Educational Gerontology: International Perspectives*, London: Croom Helm.

Glendenning, F. and Percy, K. (eds) (1990) *Ageing, Education and Society*, Association for Educational Gerontology, University of Keele, Staffs.

Goleman, D. (1998) *Working with Emotional Intelligence*, New York: Bantam Books.

Gould, A. (1979) *Towards Equality of Occupational Opportunity*, Association of Recurrent Education. Discussion Paper 5, Centre for Research into Education for Adults, University of Nottingham.

Grabowski, S.H. *et al.* (1981) *Preparing Educators of Adults*, San Francisco: Jossey Bass.

Graham, T.B., Dames, J.H., Sullivan, T., Harris, P. and Baum, FE. (1982) *The Training of Part-Time Teachers of Adults*, Department of Adult Education, University of Nottingham.

Greenfield, S. (1999) 'Soul, brain and mind', in Crabbe, J. (ed.) *From Soul to Self*, London: Routledge.

Greenwood, E. (1957) 'Attributes of a profession', *Social Work* 2: 44–55.

Griffin, C. (1978) *Recurrent and Continuing Education – a Curriculum Model Approach*, Association of Recurrent Education, School of Education, University of Nottingham.

—— (1979) 'Continuing education and the adult curriculum', *Adult Education* 52 (2), Leicester: NIAE.

—— (1982) 'Curriculum analysis of adult and lifelong education', *International Journal of Lifelong Education* 1 (2).

—— (1987) *Adult Education as Social Policy*, London: Croom Helm.

—— (1999a) 'Lifelong learning and social democracy', in *International Journal of Lifelong Education* 18 (5): 329–342.

—— (1999b) 'Social learning and welfare reform', in *International Journal of Life-long Education* 18 (5): 431–452.

Griffith, S.W. (1980) 'Coordination of personnel, programs and services', in Peters, J. and Associates (eds) *Building an Effective Adult Education Enterprise*, San Francisco: Jossey Bass, (Chapter 4).

Groombridge, B. (1972) *Television and the People*, Harmondsworth: Penguin.

Gross, R. (1977) *The Lifelong Learner*, New York: Touchstone Books, Simon and Schuster.

Grossman, M. and Kaestner, R. (1997) 'Effects of education on health', in Behrman, J. and Sracey, N. (eds) *The Social Benefits of Education*, Ann Arbor: University of Michigan Press.

Gurnah, A. (1992) 'Editorial', *Adults Learning* 3 (8).

Habermas, J. (1972) *Knowledge and Human Interests*, London: Heinemann.

Hall, A. (1985) *The Adult School Movement in the Twentieth Century*, Nottingham: University of Nottingham, Department of Adult Education.

Hall, C. (1954) *A Primer of Freudian Psychology*, New York: Mentor Books.

Hallenbeck, W.C. (1948) 'Training adult educators', in Ely, M. (ed.) *Handbook of Adult Education in the United States*, Center for Adult Education. Republished in Brookfield, S. (ed.) (1988) *Training Educators of Adults*, London: Routledge.

Halmos, P. (1978) 'The concept of social problem', *Social Work and Community Course DE206*, Block 1, Milton Keynes: Open University Press.

Handley, J. (1981) 'An investigation into the training needs of part-time tutors, with particular reference to the development of courses at ACSTT Stage II level', unpublished MSc dissertation, University of Surrey.

Hargreaves, A. (2003) *Teaching in the Knowledge Society*, Maidenhead: Open University Press.

Hargreaves, P. and Jarvis, P. (2000) *The Human Resource Development Handbook*, London: Kogan Page (revised edition).

Harper, K. (1982) 'Colleges warned against "politics" in YOP courses', *Guardian* 29 November, p. 22.

Harre, R. (1998) *The Singular Self*, London: Sage.

Harrison, R., Reeve, F., Hanson, A. and Clarke, J. (eds) *Supporting Lifelong Learning (vol 1) – Perspectives on Learning*, London: RoutledgeFalmer.

Harrop, S. and Woodcock, G. (1992) 'Issues in the construction of a modular curriculum for university professional adult education courses', *Studies in the Education of Adults* 24 (1): 86–94.

Hartree, A. (1984) 'Malcolm Knowles' theory of andragogy: a critique', *International Journal of Lifelong Education* 3 (3): 203–210.

Harvey, D. (1990) *The Condition of Postmodernism*, Oxford: Blackwell.

Haycocks, J.N. (1978) *The Training of Adult Education and Part-Time Further Education Teachers*, Advisory Committee on the Supply and Training of Teachers, London.

Hegarty, T.B. (1976) 'Education for the legal profession', in Turner, J.R. and Rushton, I. (eds) *Education for the Professions*, Manchester: Manchester University Press.

Held, D., McGrew A., Goldblatt, D. and Perraton, J. (1999) *Global Transformations*, Cambridge: Polity.

Heller, A. (1984) *Everyday Life*, London: Routledge and Kegan Paul.

—— (1988) *General Ethics*, Oxford: Blackwell.

Henry, J. (1989) 'Meaning and practice in experiential learning', in Weil, S. and McGill, I. (eds) *Making Sense of Experiential Learning*, Buckingham: Open University Press in association with SRHE.

—— (1992) 'Creativity, capability and experiential learning', in Mulligan, J. and Griffin, C. (eds) *Empowerment through Experiential Learning*, London: Kogan Page: 187–196.

Her Majesty's Stationary Office (1998) *Learning Towns and Learning Cities*, London HMSO.

Hermann, U. and Keynon, R. (1987) *Competency Based Vocational Education*, London: Further Education Unit.

Hetherington, J. (1980) 'Professionalism and part-time staff in adult education', *Adult Education* 52 (5), Leicester: NIAE.

Hilgard, E.R. and Atkinson, R.C. (1967) (4th edn) *Introduction to Psychology*, New York: Harcourt, Brace and World, Inc.

—— (1979) (7th edn) *Introduction to Psychology*, New York: Harcourt Brace Jovanovich.

Hirst, P.H. and Peters, R.S. (1970) *The Logic of Education*, London: Routledge and Kegan Paul.

Holmberg, B. (1960) *On Methods of Teaching by Correspondence*, Lund: Gleerup.

—— (1981) *Status and Trends of Distance Education*, London: Kogan Page.

—— (1989) *Theory and Practice of Distance Education*, London: Routledge.

Hopper, E. and Osborn, M. (1975) *Adult Students: Education, Selection and Social Control*, London: Frances Pinter.

Horton, M. and Freire, P. (1990) 'We make the road by walking', in Bell, B., Gaventa, J. and Peters, J. (eds) *We Make the Road by Walking*, Philadelphia: Temple University Press.

Horton, M. with J. and H. Kohl (1990) *The Long Haul*, New York: Anchor Books.

Hostler, J. (1977) 'The education of adults', *Studies in Adult Education* 9 (1). Leicester: NIAE.

Houghton, V. (1974) 'Recurrent education: a plea for lifelong learning', in Houghton, V. and Richardson, K. (eds) *Recurrent Education: A Plea for Lifelong Learning*, London: Ward Lock Educational/Association of Recurrent Education.

Houghton, V. and Richardson, K. (eds) (1974) *Recurrent Education: A Plea for Lifelong Learning*, London: Ward Lock Educational Association of Recurrent Education.

Houle, C.O. (1960) 'The education of adult educational leaders', in Knowles, M. (ed.) *Handbook of Adult Education in the United States*, Washington, DC: Adult Education Convention of the USA.

—— (1961) *The Inquiring Mind*, Madison: University of Wisconsin Press. Republished as a second edition in 1988 by The Oklahoma Research Center for Continuing and Professional Higher Education, University of Oklahoma.

—— (1964) 'The emergence of graduate study in adult education', in Jensen, U., Liveright, A.A. and Hallenbeck, W. (eds) *Adult Education: Outlines of an Emerging Field of University Study*, Washington, DC: Adult Education Association of the USA.

—— (1972) *The Design of Education*, San Francisco: Jossey Bass.

—— (1979) 'Motivation and participation with special reference to non-traditional forms of study', OECD 1977, Vol 3.

—— (1980) *Continuing Learning in the Professions*, San Francisco: Jossey Bass.

Houston, R.P., Bee, H., Hatfield, E. and Rimm, D.C. (1979) *Invitation to Psychology*, New York: Academic Press.

Hoy, J.D. (1933) 'An enquiry as to interests and motives for study among adult evening students', *British Journal of Educational Psychology* 3 (1).

Hughes, K. and Mayo, M. (1991) 'Opening up personal development', *Adults Learning* 3 (4).

Hughes, M. (1977) 'Adult education on the cheap: an extension of adult education provision into the school classroom', *Adult Education* 50 (4), Leicester: NIAE.

Husen, T. (1974) *The Learning Society*, London: Methuen.

Husserl, E. (ed.) (1973) *Experience and Judgment*, London: Routledge and Kegan Paul.

Hutchins, R.M. (1968) *The Learning Society*, Harmondsworth: Penguin.

Hutchinson, E. and Hutchinson, E.M. (1978) *Learning Later*, London: Routledge and Kegan Paul.

Hutchinson, E.M. (ed.) (1970) 'Adult education – adequacy of provision', *Adult Education* 42 (6), Leicester: NIAE.

Illeris, K. (2002) *The Three Dimensions of Learning*, Roskilde: Roskilde University Press.

Illich, I. (1973a) *Deschooling Society*, Harmondsworth: Penguin.

—— (1973b) *After Deschooling, What?* London: Writers and Readers Publishing Cooperative.

—— (1977) 'Disabling professions', in Illich, I., Zola, I.K., McKnight, J., Caplan, J. and Shanken, R. (eds) *Disabling Professions*, London: Marion Boyars.

Illich, I. and Verne, E. (1976) *Imprisoned in a Global Classroom*, London: Writers and Readers Publishing Cooperative.

Illich, I., Zola, I.K., McKnight, J., Caplan, J. and Shanken, R. (eds) (1977) *Disabling Professions*, London: Marion Boyars.

Jarvis, P. (1977) *Protestant Ministers: Job Satisfaction and Role Strain in the Bureaucratic Organisation of the Church*, Unpublished PhD thesis, Birmingham: University of Aston.

—— (1978a) 'Students' learning and tutors' marking', *Teaching at a Distance No. 13*, Milton Keynes: Open University Press.

—— (1978b) 'Knowledge and the curriculum in adult education: a sociological approach', *Adult Education* 51(4), Leicester: NIAE.

—— (1980) 'Pre-retirement education: design and analysis', *Adult Education* 53 (1), Leicester: NIAE.

—— (1981) 'The Open University unit: andragogy or pedagogy?', *Teaching at a Distance No. 20*, Milton Keynes: Open University Press.

—— (1982a) 'What's the value of adult education?' *Adult Education* 54 (4), Leicester: NIAE.

—— (1982b) *Adult Education in a Small Centre: a Case Study in the Village of Lingfield*, Department of Adult Education, University of Surrey.

—— (1983a) *Professional Education*, London: Croom Helm.

—— (1983b) 'Education and the elderly', *Adult Education* 55 (4), Leicester: NIAE.

—— (1983c) 'The lifelong religious development of the individual and the place of adult education', *Lifelong Learning: The Adult Years* 6 (9).

—— (1984) 'Andragogy: a sign of the times, *Studies in the Education of Adults* 16: 32–38.

—— (1985) *The Sociology of Adult and Continuing Education*, London: Croom Helm.

—— (1986) *Sociological Perspectives on Lifelong Learning and Lifelong Education*, Athens, USA: University of Georgia, Department of Adult Education.

—— (1987) *Adult Learning in the Social Context*, London: Croom Helm.

—— (1990) *International Dictionary of Adult and Continuing Education*, London: Routledge.

—— (1992) *Paradoxes of Learning*, San Francisco: Jossey Bass.

—— (1993a) *Adult Education and the State*, London: Routledge.

—— (1993b) 'Pedagogy, andragogy and professional education', paper presented at the International Conference on the Training of Adult Educators, Wadham College, Oxford.

—— (1994) 'Learning practical knowledge', *Journal of Further and Higher Education* 1: 31–43.

—— (1996) 'The public recognition of lifetime learning', *Lifelong Learning in Europe* 1 (96): 10–17.

—— (1997) *Ethics and the Education of Adults in Late Modern Society*, Leicester: NIACE.

—— (1999a) *The Practitioner Researcher*, San Francisco: Jossey Bass.

—— (1999b) *International Dictionary of Adult and Continuing Education*, London: Kogan Page (2nd edn).

—— (2001a) *Learning in Later Life*, London: Kogan Page.

—— (2001b) *Universities and Corporate Universities*, London: Kogan Page.

—— (2002a) *Learning from Experience*, Unpublished paper presented at the Danish Pedagogical University, as the opening of the academic year lecture (Sept).

—— (2002b) *Lifelong Learning, Governance and Active Citizenship*, unpublished lecture delivered at the ASEM Conference, Copenhagen.

—— (2002c) *The Implications of Lifelong Learning for Lifewide Learning*, unpublished lecture delivered to the European Union Presidency Conference on Lifelong Learning: Copenhagen.

—— (ed.) (1988) *Britain: Policy and Practice in Continuing Education*, San Francisco: Jossey Bass.

—— (ed) (2001) *Twentieth Century Thinkers in Adult and Continuing Education*, (2nd edn), London: Kogan Page.

—— (ed) (2001a) *The Age of Learning*, London: Kogan Page.

—— (ed) (2002) *The Theory and Practice of Teaching*, London: Kogan Page.

Jarvis, P. and Walker, J. (1997) 'When the process becomes the product: Summer Universities for elders', *Education and Ageing* 12: 60–68.

Jarvis, P., Holford, J., Griffin, C. and Dubelaar, J. (1997) *Towards a Learning City*, London: Corporation of the City of London Education Department (2nd edn, 2003).

Jarvis, P., Holford, J. and Griffin, C. (1999) *Theory and Practice of Learning*, London: Kogan Page (2nd edn, 2003).

Jarvis, P. and Chadwick, A. (eds) (1991) *Training Adult Educators in Western Europe*, London: Routledge.

Jarvis, P. and Walters, N. (eds) (1993) *Adult Education and Theological Interpretations*, Malabar, Florida: Krieger.

Jarvis, P. with Griffin, C. (ed.) (2003) *Adult and Continuing Education: Major Themes in Education*, (5 vols), London: Routledge.

Jayagopal, R. (1990) *Human Resource Development: conceptual analysis and strategies*, New Delhi: Sterling Publishers.

Jennings, B. (ed.) (n.d.) *Community Colleges in England and Wales*, Leicester: NIAE.

Jensen, G., Liveright, A.A. and Hallenbeck, W. (eds) (1964) *Adult Education: Outlines of an Emerging Field of University Study*, Washington DC: Adult Education Association of the USA.

Jessup, F.W. (ed.) (1969) *Lifelong Learning – A Symposium on Continuing Education*, Oxford: Pergamon Press.

Johnstone, J.W.C. and Rivera, R.J. (1965) *Volunteers for Learning*, Chicago: Aldine Publishing.

Joll, J. (1977) *Gramsci*, Glasgow: Fontana/Collins.

Kagan, I. (1971) 'Developmental studies in reflection and analysis', in Kidd, A.H. and Rivoire, I.E. (eds) *Perceptual Development in Children*, New York: International Universities Press. Reprinted in Cashdow, A. and Whitehead, I. (eds) (1971) *Personality, Growth and Learning*, London: Longman.

Kallen, D. (1979) 'Recurrent education and lifelong learning: definitions and distinctions', in Schuller, T. and Megarry, I. (eds) *World Yearbook on Education 1979: Recurrent Education and Lifelong Learning*, London: Kogan Page.

Katz, R. and Associates (1999) *Dancing with the Devil*, San Francisco: Jossey Bass.

Keddie, N. (1980) 'Adult education: an ideology individualism', in Thompson, I.C. (ed.) *Adult Education for a Change*, London: Heinemann.

Keegan, D. (1990) *Foundations of Distance Education*, London: Routledge.

—— (ed.) (1993) *Theoretical Principles of Distance Education*, London: Routledge.

Keller, E.S. (1968) 'Good-bye, Teacher . . .', *Journal of Applied Behaviour Analysis* 1.

Kellner, D. (1989) *Jean Baudrillard: From Marxism to Postmodernism and Beyond*, Cambridge: Polity Press.

Kelly, A.V. (1977) *The Curriculum: Theory and Practice*, London: Harper and Row.

Kelly, G.A. (1955) *The Psychology of Personal Constructs*, New York: Norton.

Kelly, T. (1970) (3rd edn 1990) *A History of Adult Education in Great Britain*, Liverpool: Liverpool University Press.

Kennedy, H. (1997) (Chair) *Learning Works*, Coventry: Further Education Funding Council.

Kenny-Wallace, G. (2000) 'Plato.com: The role and impact of the corporate universities in the third millennium', in Scott, P. (ed.) *Higher Education Reformed*, London: Falmer.

Kerr, C., Dunlop, J., Harbinson, F. and Myers, C. (1973) *Industrialism and Industrial Man* (2nd edn), Harmondsworth: Penguin.

Kett, J. (1994) *The Pursuit of Knowledge Under Difficulties*, Stanford: Stanford University Press.

Kidd, J.R. (1973) *How Adults Learn*, Chicago: Association Press.

Killeen, J. and Bird, M. (1981) *Education and Work*, Leicester: National Institute of Adult Education.

Kirkwood, C. (1978) 'Adult education and the concept of community', *Adult Education* 51(3), Leicester: NIAE.

Kirkwood, G. and Kirkwood, C. (1989) *Living Adult Education*, Milton Keynes: Open University Press.

Knapper, C.K. and Cropley, A.J. (1985) *Lifelong Learning and Higher Education*, London: Croom Helm.

Knowles, M.S. (1978) (2nd edn) *The Adult Learner: A Neglected Species*, Houston: Gulf Publishing Co.

—— (1979) 'Andragogy revisited II', *Adult Education* 3: 52–53, Washington DC.

—— (1980a) *The Modern Practice of Adult Education*, Chicago: Association Press.

—— (1980b) 'The growth and development of adult education', in Peters, I. and Associates (eds) *Building an Effective Adult Education*, San Francisco: Jossey Bass.

—— (1986) *Using Learning Contracts*, San Francisco: Jossey Bass.

—— (1989) *The Making of an Adult Educator*, San Francisco: Jossey Bass.

Knowles, M. and Associates (1984) *Andragogy in Action*, San Francisco: Jossey Bass.

Knox, A.B. (1977) *Adult Development and Learning*, San Francisco: Jossey Bass.

Knudson, R.S. (1979) 'Andragogy revisted: Humanagogy anyone?', *Adult Education* 29: 261–264, Washington DC.

Kohlberg, L. (1981) *The Philosophy of Moral Development Vol. 1 – Essays in Moral Development*, San Francisco: Harper.

Köhler, W. (1947) *Gestalt Psychology*, New York: Liveright Publishing Corporation.

Kolb, D. (1984) *Experiential Learning*, Englewood Cliffs, New Jersey: Prentice Hall.

Kolb, D.A. and Fry, R. (1975) 'Towards an applied theory of experiential learning', in Cooper, C.L. (eds) *Theories of Group Processes*, London: John Wiley and Sons.

Korten, D. (1995) *When Corporations Rule the World*, London: Earthscan.

Krech, D., Crutchfield, R.S. and Ballachery, E.L. (1962) *Individual in Society*, New York: McGraw Hill.

Kulich, J. (1977) *Training of Adult Educators in East Europe*, Vancouver, University of British Columbia: Centre for Continuing Education.

—— (1982) 'Lifelong education and the universities: a Canadian perspective', *International Journal of Lifelong Education* 1 (2).

Kumar, K. (1978) *Prophecy and Progress*, Harmondsworth: Penguin.

Kwan, C.-Y. (2000) 'Problem-based learning in medical education: from McMaster to Asia Pacific Region', in Wang, C. *et al.* (eds) *Teaching and Learning in Higher Education Symposium*, Singapore: National University of Singapore: 135–142.

Label, I. (1978) 'Beyond andragogy to gerogogy', *Lifelong Learning: The Adult Years* 1.

Labouvie-Vief, G. (1978) 'Models of cognitive functioning in the old adult: Research needs in educational gerontology', in Sherron, R.H. and Lumsdon, D.B. (eds) *Introduction to Educational Gerontology*, Washington DC: Hemisphere Publishing Co.

Lacey, A.R. (1989) *Bergson*, London: Routledge.

Langenbach, M. (1988) *Curriculum Models in Adult Education*, Malabar, Florida: Krieger.

Last, I. and Chown, A. (1993) 'Teacher training in adult education', *Adults Learning* 4 (9): 234–236.

La Valle, I. and Blake, M. (2001) *National Adult Learning Survey 2001*, London: Dept for Education and Skills.

Lawson, K.H. (1975) *Philosophical Concepts and Values in Adult Education*, Department of Adult Education, University of Nottingham. Reprinted in a 2nd edition and published by the Open University Press.

—— (1977) 'Community education: a critical assessment', *Adult Education* 50 (1), Leicester: NIAE.

—— (1982) 'Lifelong education: concept or policy?', *International Journal of Lifelong Education* 1 (2).

Lawton, D. (1973) *Social Change, Educational Theory and Curriculum Planning*, London: Hodder and Stoughton.

Learmouth, J. assisted by Maidments, L. (eds) (1993) *Teaching and Learning in Cities*, Whitbread Educational Partnership Paper.

Learning City Network, *LCN eNews*, published regularly, Nottingham.

—— (2000) *LCN Conference Report*, LCN: Nottingham.

Learning Towns and Cities, *The Toolkit – Practice, Progress and Value.*

Legge, D. (1968) 'Training adult educators in the United Kingdom', *Convergence* 1 (1).

—— (1971a) 'The use of the talk in adult classes', in Stephens, M.D. and Roderick, G.W. (eds) *Teaching Techniques in Adult Education*, Newton Abbot: David and Charles.

—— (1971b) 'Discussion methods', in Stephens, M.D. and Roderick, G.W. (eds) *Teaching Techniques in Adult Education*, Newton Abbot: David and Charles.

—— (1981) 'The training of teachers of adults', in Harvey, B., Dames, I., Jones, D. and Wallis, I. (eds) *Policy and Research in Adult Education*, Department of Adult Education, University of Nottingham.

—— (1982) *The Education of Adults in Britain*, Milton Keynes: The Open University Press.

—— (1991) 'Educators of adults in England and Wales', in Jarvis, P. and Chadwick, A. (eds) *Training Adult Educators in Western Europe*, London: Routledge.

Lengrand, P. (1975) *An Introduction to Lifelong Education*, London: Croom Helm.

Lester-Smith, W.O. (1966) *Education – An Introductory Survey*, Harmondsworth: Penguin.

Levinas, E. (1991) *Totality and Infinity* (trans. A. Lingis), Dordrecht: Kluwer.

Leytham, G. (1971) 'The principles of programmed learning', in Stephens, M.D. and Roderick, G.W. (eds) *Teaching Techniques in Adult Education*, Newton Abbot: David and Charles.

Light, G. and Cox, R. (2001) *Learning and Teaching in Higher Education*, London: Paul Chapman.

Lindeman, E. (1961; first published 1926) *The Meaning of Adult Education*, Montreal: Harvester House.

—— (1988) 'Preparing leaders in adult education' (speech given to Pennsylvania Association for Adult Education, 18th November). Published in Brookfield, S. (ed.) *Training Educators of Adults*, London: Routledge.

Lippitt, R. and White, R.K. (1958) 'An experimental study of leadership and group life', in Maccoby, E.E., Newcomb, T.M. and Hartley, E.L. (eds) *Readings in Social Psychology*, New York: Holt.

Little, A., Willey, R. and Gundara, I. (1982) *Adult Education and the Black Communities*, Leicester: ACACE.

London, J. (1973) 'Reflections upon the relevance of Paulo Freire for American Adult Education', *Convergence* 6 (1).

Long, H. and Associates (1988) *Self-Directed Learning: Application and Theory*, University of Georgia: Dept of Adult Education.

—— (1993) *Emerging Perspectives of Self-Directed Learning*, University of Oklahoma: Research Centre for Continuing and Professional Higher Education.

—— (1997) *Expanding Horizons in Self-Directed Learning*, University of Oklahoma: College of Education.

—— (1998) *Developing Paradigms for Self-Directed Learning*, University of Oklahoma: College of Education.

Long, H. and Lord, C. (eds) (1978) *The Continuing Education Credit Unit: Concept, Issues and Use*, Georgia, USA: University of Georgia Centre for Continuing Education.

Longworth, N. (1999) *Making Lifelong Learning Work: Learning Cities for a Learning Century*, London: Kogan Page.

Lovell, B.R. (1980) *Adults Learning*, London: Croom Helm.

Lovett, T. (1975) *Adult Education, Community Development and the Working Class*, London: Ward Lock Educational.

—— (1980) 'Adult education and community action', in Thompson, J.L. (ed.) *Adult Education for a Change*, London: Heinemann.

Lovett, T., Clarke, C. and Kilmurray, A. (1983) *Adult Education and Community Action*, London: Croom Helm.

Lucent Technologies (1996) *Distance Education: the Vision*, www.lucent.com/cedl/

Luckmann, T. (1967) *The Invisible Religion*, London: Collier-Macmillan.

Lukes, S. (1981) 'Fact and theory in the social sciences', in Potter, D. *et al.* (eds) *Society and the Social Sciences*, London: Open University Press in association with Routledge and Kegan Paul.

Lyotard, J.-F. (1984) *The Postmodern Condition*, Manchester: University of Manchester Press.

McAdam, S.D. (2001) *The Person*, Fort Worth: Harcourt.

Macfarlane, T. (1978) 'Curriculum innovation in adult literacy: the cost of insularity', *Studies in Adult Education* 10 (2).

McGivney, V. (1990) *Access to Education for Non-Participant Adults*, Leicester: NIACE.

McGregor, D. (1960) *The Human Side of Enterprise*, New York: McGraw Hill.

McIntosh, N. (1974) 'The Open University student', in Tunstall, I. (ed.) *The Open University Opens*, London: Routledge and Kegan Paul.

—— (1979) 'To make continuing education a reality', *Oxford Review of Education* 5 (2) and republished by ACACE, Leicester.

McKenzie, L. (1977) 'The issue of andragogy', *Adult Education* 27: 225–229, Washington DC.

—— (1979) 'Andragogy revisited: Response to Elias', *Adult Education* 29: 256–261, Washington DC.

McLagan, P.A. (1978) *Helping Others Learn*, Massachusetts: Addison-Wesley.

MacMurray, J. (1961) *Persons in Relation*, New Jersey: Humanities Press Ltd.

McNiff, J. (1988) *Action Research: Principles and Practice*, London: Routledge.

Mace, I. and Yarnit, M. (eds) (1987) *Time Off to Learn*, London: Methuen.

Mager, C. (1991) 'Open college networks', *Adults Learning* 3 (4): 97–98.

Manheimer, R. (1999) *A Map to the End of Time*, New York: W.W. Norton.

Mannings, R. (1986) *The Incidental Learning Research Project*, Bristol Folk House: Adult Education Centre.

Marcuse, H. (1964) *One Dimensional Man*, reprinted in 1986 by ARK paperbacks, London.

Marsick, V. (ed.) (1987) *Learning in the Workplace*, London: Croom Helm.

Martin, B. (1981) *A Sociology of Contemporary Cultural Change*, Oxford: Basil Blackwell.

Martin, L.C. (1981) 'A survey of the training needs of part-time tutors in a region', *Studies in Adult Education* 13 (2).

Martin, P. (1999) *Art Teachers in Contemporary Adult Education*, unpublished PhD thesis, Guildford: University of Surrey.

Marton, F. and Booth, S. (1997) *Learning and Awareness*, New Jersey: Lawrence Erlbaum Associates.

Marton, F., Hounsell, D. and Entwistle, N. (1984) *The Experience of Learning*, Edinburgh: Scottish Academic Press.

Maslow, A.H. (1968) (2nd edn) *Towards a Psychology of Being*, New York: D. Van Nostrand Company.

Mee, G. (1980) *Organisation for Adult Education*, London: Longman.

Mee, G. and Wiltshire, H. (1978) *Structure and Performance in Adult Education*, London: Longman.

Meister, L. (1998) *Corporate Universities*, New York: McGraw-Hill (2nd edn).

Merriam, S. and Caffarella, R. (1991) *Learning in Adulthood*, San Francisco: Jossey Bass.

Mezirow, J. (1977) 'Perspective transformation', *Studies in Adult Education* 9 (2).

—— (1981) 'A critical theory of adult learning and education', *Adult Education* 32 (1), Washington DC.

—— (1991) *Transformative Dimensions of Adult Learning*, San Francisco: Jossey Bass.

Mezirow, J. and Associates (1990) *Fostering Critical Reflection in Adulthood*, San Francisco: Jossey Bass.

—— (2000) *Learning as Transformation*, San Francisco: Jossey Bass.

Midwinter, F. (1975) *Education and the Community*, London: Allen and Unwin.

—— (ed.) (1984) *Mutual Aid Universities*, London: Croom Helm.

Mill, J.S. (1962) 'On liberty' (1st edn, 1859). Reprinted in *Utilitarianism*, London: Fontana Library Collins.

Miller, N. and Boud, D. (1996) 'Animating learning from experience', in Boud, D. and Miller, N. (eds) *Working with Experience*, London: Routledge.

Mocker, D.W. and Noble, F. (1981) 'Training part-time instructional staff', in Grabowski, S. *et al.* (eds) *Preparing Educators of Adults*, San Francisco: Jossey Bass.

Moemeka, A.A. (1981) *Local Radio – Community Education for Development*, Zaria, Nigeria: Ahmodu Bello University Press.

Monbiot, G. (2000) *The Captive State*, London: MacMillan.

Morris, H. (1956) 'Architecture, humanism and the local community', paper read at RJBA on 15 May, and published in Fletcher, C. and Thompson, N. (eds) (1980) *Issues in Community Education*, Lewes: Falmer Press.

Morrison, J. and Meister, J. (2002) 'e-Learning in the Corporate University: an Interview with Jeanne Meister', in *Commentary* http://ts.mivu.org/default. asp?show=article&id=888

Morstain, B.R. and Smart, J.C. (1974) 'Reasons for participation in adult education courses: a multivariate analysis of group difference', *Adult Education* 24 (2), Washington DC.

Muller, D. and Funnell, P. (1991) (eds) *Delivering Quality in Vocational Education*, London: Kogan Page.

Murgatroyd, S. and Morgan, C. (1993) *Total Quality Management and the School*, Milton Keynes: Open University Press.

Murray, M. with Owen, M. (1991) *Beyond the Myths and Magic of Mentoring*, San Francisco: Jossey Bass.

Murray, R. (2002) *How to Write a Thesis*, Maidenhead: Open University Press.

Newman, M. (1973) *Adult Education and Community Action*, London: Writers and Readers Publishing Co-operative.

—— (1979) *The Poor Cousin*, London: Allen and Unwin.

NIACE (1993a) *Yearbook of Adult Continuing Education 1993–4*, Leicester: NIACE.

NICEC (n.d.) *Adult Guidance in Community Settings* http://www.gla.ac.uk/avg/en/avgrd2_2.htm

Nyiri, I. (1988) 'Tradition and practical knowledge', in Nyiri, I. and Smith, B. (eds) *Practical Knowledge: Outlines of a Theory of Traditions and Skills*, London: Croom Helm.

Nyiri, I. and Smith, B. (eds) (1988) *Practical Knowledge: Outlines of a Theory of Traditions and Skills*, London: Croom Helm.

O'Neill, C. (2003) *Learning to be Me*, unpublished PhD thesis, Guildford, UK: University of Surrey.

Oakeshott, M. (1933) *Experience and its Modes*, Cambridge: Cambridge University Press.

—— (1991) *Educational Guidance for Adults: Identifying Competences*, London: FEU.

Organization for Economic Cooperation and Development (1973) *Recurrent Education: a Strategy for Lifelong Learning*, Paris: OECD.

—— (1975) *Lifelong Education: Trends and Issues*, Paris: OECD.

—— (1977) *Learning Opportunities for Adults* (2 vols), Paris: OECD.

—— (1979) *Learning Opportunities for Adults* (2 vols), Paris: OECD.

—— (1996) *Lifelong Learning for All*, Paris: OECD.

—— (2001) *Cities and Regions in the New Learning Economy*, Paris: OECD.

Overstreet, H. and Overstreet, B. (1941) 'The making of the makers', in Overstreet, H. and Overstreet, B. (eds) *Leaders for Adult Education*, New York: American Association of Adult Education.

Palmer, P.J. (1998) *The Courage to Teach*, San Francisco: Jossey Bass.

Parker, S. (1976) *The Sociology of Leisure*, London: Allen and Unwin.

Parsons, T. (1994) *Quality Improvement in Education; case studies in schools, colleges and universities*, London: Fulton.

Paterson, R.W.K. (1979) *Values, Education and the Adult*, London: Routledge and Kegan Paul.

Pavlov, I.P. (1927) *Conditioned Reflexes*, New York: Oxford University Press.

Payne, J. (1993) 'Too little of a good thing', *Adults Learning* 4 (10).

Pedler, M., Burgoyne, J. and Boydell, T. (1997) *The Learning Company*, London: MacGraw-Hill (2nd edn).

Peers, R. (1958) *Adult Education – A Comparative Perspective*, London: Routledge and Kegan Paul.

Peters, J.M. and Gordon, S. (1974) *Adult Learning Projects: A Study of Adult Learning in Urban and Rural Tennessee*, Knoxville: University of Tennessee.

Peters, J. and Associates (1980) *Building an Effective Adult Education Enterprise*, San Francisco: Jossey Bass.

Peters, J., Jarvis, P. and Associates (1991) *Adult Education: Evolution and Achievements in a Developing Field of Study*, San Francisco: Jossey Bass.

Peters, O. (1984) 'Distance teaching and industrial production: a comparative interpretation in outline', in Sewart, D., Keegan, D. and Hohmberg, B. (eds) *Distance Education: international perspectives*, London: Croom Helm.

—— (1998) *Learning and Teaching in Distance Education*, London: Kogan Page.

—— (2002) *Distance Education in Transition*, Oldenburg: Biblioteks und Informationssystems der Universitat Oldenburg.

Peters, R.S. (1966) *Ethics and Education*, London: Allen and Unwin.

—— (1972) 'Education and the educated Man', in Dearden, D.F., Hirst, P.H. and Peters, R.S. (eds) *A Critique of Current Educational Aims (Part I of Education and the Development of Reason)*, London: Routledge and Kegan Paul.

Peterson, R.E. *et al.* (1979) *Lifelong Learning in America*, San Francisco: Jossey Bass.

Peterson, S. (1989) 'Reducing student attrition', in Weil, S. and McGill, I. (eds) *Making Sense of Experiential Learning*, Buckingham: SRHE and Open University Press.

Phillipson, C. and Strang, P. (1983) *The Impact of Pre-Retirement Education*, University of Keele, Department of Adult Education.

Piaget, J. (1929) *The Child's Conception of the World*, London: Routledge and Kegan Paul.

Polanyi, M. (1967) *The Tacit Dimension*, London: Routledge and Kegan Paul.

Poole, R. (1990) *Morality and Modernity*, London: Routledge.

Popham, W.J., Eisner, E.W., Sullivan, H.J. and Tyler, L.L. (1969) *Instructional Objectives*, Chicago: Rand McNally.

Poster, C. and Kruger, A. (eds) (1990) *Community Education in the Western World*, London: Routledge.

Poster, M. (ed.) (1988) *Jean Baudrillard: Selected Writings*, Cambridge: Polity Press.

Pratt, D. and Associates (1998) *Five Different Approaches to Teaching in Adult and Higher Education*, Malabar, Florida: Krieger.

Press Release (Nov 2002) *Ireland to become a Nation of 'Learning Cities and Learning Counties'*, http://www.dublincity.ie/profile/pressr/201119.htm

Preston, J. and Hammond, C. (2002) *The Wider Benefits of Further Education: Practitioner Views*, London: Institute of Education, Centre for Research on the Wider Benefits of Learning.

Putnam, R. (2000) *Bowling Alone*, New York: Simon and Schuster.

Ranson, S. (1994) *Towards the Learning Society*, Cassell: London.

Redmann, D. (ed.) (2000) *Defining the Cutting Edge*, Academy of Human Resource Development.

Reeve, F., Cartwright, M. and Edwards, R. (eds) (2002) *Supporting Lifelong Learning (vol 2) – Organising Learning*, London: RoutledgeFalmer.

Richardson, M. (ed.) (1979) *Preparing to Study*, Milton Keynes: Open University Press.

Riegel, K. (1973) 'Dialectic operations: The final period of cognitive development', *Human Development* 16 (3).

—— (1979) *Foundations of Dialectic Psychology*, London: Academic Press.

Riesman, D. (1950) *The Lonely Crowd: A Study of Changing American Character*, New Haven: Yale University Press.

Robertson, R. (1995) 'Glocalisation', in Featherstone, M., Lash, S. and Robertson, R. (eds) *Global Modernities*, London: Sage.

Rodd, M. (1992) 'Change for the better? Recent developments in adult literacy', *Adults Learning* 4 (2).

Roderick, G.W., Bell, J., Dickenson, R., Turner, R. and Wellings, A. (1981) *Mature Students in Further and Higher Education*, Division of Continuing Education, University of Sheffield.

Rogers, A. (ed.) (1976) *The Spirit and the Form*, University of Nottingham, Department of Adult Education.

—— (1986) *Teaching Adults*, Milton Keynes: Open University Press.

Rogers, C.R. (1969) *Freedom to Learn*, Columbus, Ohio: Charles F. Merrill Publishing Co.

—— (1983) *Freedom to Learn for the 80's*, New York: Merrill-Macmillan.

—— and Freiberg, H.J. (1994) *Freedom to Learn*, New York: Merrill (3rd edn).

Rogers, J. (ed.) (1973) *Adults in Education*, London: British Broadcasting Corporation.

—— (1977) (2nd edn) *Adults Learning*, Milton Keynes: Open University Press.

—— (1989) (3rd edn) *Adults Learning*, Milton Keynes: Open University Press.

Rogers, J. and Groombridge, B. (1976) *Right to Learn*, London: Arrow Books.

Rorty, R. (1982) *Consequences of Pragmatism*, New York: HarvesterWheatsheaf.

Rowntree, D. (1977) *Assessing Students – How shall we know them?*, London: Harper and Row.

Rowntree, J. and Bins, H. (1986[1903]) *History of the Adult School Movement*, Nottingham: University of Nottingham, Department of Adult Education.

Rumble, G. (1982) *The Open University of the United Kingdom*, Milton Keynes: Distance Education Research Group, The Open University.

Rumble, G. and Harry, K. (1982) *The Distance Teaching Universities*, London: Croom Helm.

Russell, L. (1973) *Adult Education: A Plan for Development*, London: Her Majesty's Stationery Office.

Ryle, G. (1963) *The Concept of Mind*, London: Peregrine Books.

Sargant, N. (1990) *Learning and Leisure*, Leicester: NIACE.

Sargant, N. and Aldridge, F. (2002) *Adult Learning and Social Division*, Leicester: NIACE (2 vols).

Sargant, N. with Field, J., Francis, H., Schuller, T. and Tuckett, A. (1997) *The Learning Divide*, Leicester: NIACE.

Scheler, M. (1926) *Die Wissens former and die Gessellschaft*, Leipzig: Der NeueGuist Verlag.

—— (1980) *Problems of Sociology of Knowledge* (trans. M.S. Frings), London: Routledge and Kegan Paul.

Schon, D.A. (1973) *Beyond the Stable State*, Harmondsworth: Penguin.

—— (1983) *The Reflective Practitioner*, New York: Basic Books.

—— (1987) *Educating the Reflective Practitioner*, San Francisco: Jossey Bass.

Schuler, T. and Megarry, I. (eds) (1979) *World Yearbook on Education 1979: Recurrent Education and Lifelong Learning*, London: Kogan Page.

Schuler, T., Brassett-Grundy, A., Green, A., Hammond, C. and Preston, C. (2002) *Learning, Continuity and Change in Adult Life*, London: Institute of Education, Centre for Research on the Wider Benefits of Learning.

Schultz, T. (1961) *Investment in Human Capital*, Basingstoke: MacMillan, cited from Jarvis, P. with Griffin, C. (ed.) (2003) *Adult and Continuing Education: Major Themes in Education* (vol 5), London: Routledge.

Schutz, A. (1972) (US edition 1967) *The Phenomenology of the Social World*, London: Heinneman.

Schutz, A. and Luckmann, T. (1974) *The Structures of the Life World*, London: Heinemann.

Senge, P. (1990) *The Fifth Discipline*, New York: Doubleday.

Sheridan, A. (1980) *Faucoult: The Will to Truth*, London: Tavistock.

Shilling, C. (1993) *The Body and Social Theory*, London: Sage.

Sidwell, D. (1980) 'A survey of modern language classes', *Adult Education* 52 (5), Leicester: NIAE.

Skinner, B.F. (1951) 'How to teach animals', *Scientific American* 185 (6).

—— (1968) *The Technology of Teaching*, New York: Appleton Century Crofts.

—— (1971) *Beyond Freedom and Dignity*, Harmondsworth: Penguin.

Sless, D. (1981) *Learning and Visual Communication*, London: Croom Helm.

Smith, A.L. (1919) 'Adult Education Committee Final Report', reprinted in 'The 1919 Report', Department of Adult Education, University of Nottingham.

Smith, G. (1993) 'BTEC, GNVQs and other developments in vocational education', *Adults Learning* 4(5), Leicester: NIACE.

Smith, J. and Spurling, J. (1999) *Lifelong Learning: Riding the Tiger*, London: Cassell.

Smith, M. (1994) *Local Education*, Buckingham: Open University Press.

Sommer, R. (1989) *Teaching Writing to Adults*, San Francisco: Jossey Bass.

Srinivasan, L. (1977) *Perspectives on Non-formal Adult Learning*, New York: World Education.

Stehr, N. (1994) *The Knowledge Society*, London: Sage.

Stephens, M.D. (1981) 'The future of continuing education', *Adult Education* 54 (2), Leicester: NIAE.

Stephens, M.D. and Roderick, G.W. (eds) (1971) *Teaching Techniques in Adult Education*, Newton Abbot: David and Charles.

Sternberg, R. (1997) *Thinking Styles*, Cambridge: Cambridge University Press.

Stewart, D., Keegan, D. and Holmberg, B. (eds) (1984) *Distance Education: International Perspectives*, London: Routledge.

Stock, A. (1971) 'Role playing and simulation techniques', in Stephens, M.D. and Roderick, U.W. (eds) *Teaching Techniques in Adult Education*, Newton Abbot: David and Charles.

—— (1982) *Adult Education in the United Kingdom*, Leicester: NIAE.

Surridge, R. and Bowen, J. (1977) *The Independent Learning Project: A Study of Changing Attitudes in American Public Libraries*, Public Libraries Research Group.

Taba, H. (1962) *Curriculum Development: Theory and Practice*, New York: Harcourt, Brace and World.

Taylor, C. (1991) *The Ethics of Authenticity*, Cambridge. Mass: Harvard.

Taylor, P.V. (1993) *The Texts of Paulo Freire*, London: Routledge.

Teare, R., Davies, D. and Sandelands, E. (1998) *The Virtual University*, London: Cassell.

Tennant, M. (1986) 'An evaluation of Knowles' theory of learning', *International Journal of Lifelong Education* 5 (2): 113–122.

—— (1988) *Psychology and Adult Learning*, London: Croom Helm.

Thompson, J.L. (ed.) (1980) *Adult Education for a Change*, London: Heinemann.

Thorndike, E.L. (1928) *Adult Learning*, London: Macmillan.

Tiernan, K. (1992) 'Taking credit for voluntary work', *Adults Learning* 4(2), Leicester: NIACE.

Tight, M. (1991) *Higher Education: A Part-time Perspective*, Buckingham: Society for Research into Higher Education in association with Open University Press.

Toennies, F. (1957) *Community and Society* (trans. C.P. Loomis), Michigan: Michigan State University Press. Published in the United Kingdom as *Community and Association* by Routledge and Kegan Paul, London.

Tough, A. (1979) (2nd edn) *The Adult's Learning Projects*, Toronto: Ontario Institute for Studies in Education.

Tuijnman, A. (1989) *Recurrent Education, Earnings and Well-being*, Stockholm: Almqvist and Wiksell International.

—— and Kamp Max van der (eds) (1993) *Learning Across the Lifespan*, Oxford: Pergamon.

Tuomi, I. (1999) *Corporate Knowledge*, Helsinki: Metaxis.

Tyler, R.W. (1949) *Basic Principles of Curriculum and Instruction*, Chicago: University of Chicago Press.

Usher, R. (1989) 'Locating adult education in the practical', in Bright, B. (ed.) *Theory and Practice in the Study of Adult Education*, London: Routledge.

Usher, R. and Bryant, I. (1989) *Adult Eduction as Theory, Practice and Research*, London: Routledge.

Vaill, P. (1996) *Learning as a Way of Being*, San Francisco: Jossey Bass.

Venables, P. (1976) *Report of the Committee on Continuing Education*, Milton Keynes: Open University Press.

Verduin, J. (1980) *Curriculum Building for Adult Learning*, Carbondale: Southern Illinois University Press.

Verner, C. (with assistance from C. Booth) (1964) *Adult Education*, Washington DC: Center for Applied Research in Education, Inc.

Vygotsky, L. (1978) *Mind and Society*, Cambridge, Mass: Harvard University Press.

—— (1986) *Thought and Language*, Cambridge, Mass: MIT Press (revised and edited by A. Kozulin).

Wallerstein, I. (1974) *The Modern World System*, New York: Academic Press.

Walshok, M. (1995) *Knowledge without Boundaries*, San Francisco: Jossey Bass.

Wang, C., Mohanan, K., Pan, D. and Chee, Y. (eds) (2000) *Proceedings of the First Symposium on Teaching and Learning in Higher Education*, Singapore: National University.

Wang, C., Mohanan, K. and Pan, D. (eds) (2002) *Proceedings of the Second Symposium on Teaching and Learning in Higher Education*, Singapore: National University.

Watkins, K. and Marsick, V. (1993) *Sculpting the Learning Organization*, San Francisco: Jossey Bass.

Wedemeyer, C. (1981) *Learning at the Back Door*, Madison: The University of Wisconsin Press.

Weil, S. and McGill, I. (eds) (1989) *Making Sense of Experiential Learning*, Buckingham: Open University Press in association with SRHE.

West, C.K., Fowler, J.A. and Wolf, P.M. (1991) *Instructional design: implications from cognitive science*, Englewood Cliffs: Prentice Hall.

Westwood, S. (1980) 'Adult education and the sociology of education: an exploration', in Thompson, J.L. (ed.) *Adult Education for a Change*, London: Heinemann.

Wilensky, H.A.L. (1964) 'The professionalization of everyone?', *American Journal of Sociology* LXX: 137–158.

Wilkin, H.A. (1971) 'Psychological differentiations', *Journal of Abnormal Psychology* 1965–70 reprinted in Cashdown, A. and Whitehead, 1. (1971) *Personality, Growth and Learning*, London: Longman.

Williams, E. and Heath, A.E. (1936) *Learn and Live*, London: Methuen.

Williams, G. (1977) *Towards Lifelong Education: A New Role for Higher Education Institutes*, Paris: UNESCO.

Williams, G.L. (1980) 'Adults learning about adult learning', *Adult Education* 52 (6), Leicester: NIAE.

Wilson, A. and Hayes, B. (2000) *Handbook of Adult and Continuing Education*, San Francisco: Jossey Bass.

Wilson, S. (1980) 'The school and the community', in Fletcher, C. and Thompson, N. (eds) *Issues in Community Education*, Lewes: Falmer Press.

Wiltshire, H. (1973) 'The concepts of learning and need in adult education', *Studies in Adult Education* 5 (1). Reprinted in Rogers, A. (1976) *The Spirit and the Form*, University of Nottingham, Department of Adult Education.

—— (1976) 'The nature and uses of adult education', in Rogers, A. (ed.) *The Spirit and the Form*, University of Nottingham, Department of Adult Education.

Winch, C. (1998) *The Philosophy of Human Learning*, London: Routledge.

Wlodkowski, R. (1985) *Enhancing Adult Motivation to Learn*, San Francisco: Jossey Bass.

Wood, D. (1982) *Continuing Education in Polytechnics and Colleges*, Department of Adult Education, University of Nottingham.

Woodhall, M. (1980) *The Scope and Costs of the Education and Training of Adults in Britain*, Leicester: ACACE.

—— (1988) 'Economic and financial implications of recurrent and continuing education', in Molyneux, F., Low, G. and Fowler, G. (eds) *Learning for Life*, London: Croom Helm.

Woodley, A., Wagner, L., Slowey, M., Hamilton, M. and Foulton, O. (1987) *Choosing to Learn: Adults in Education*, Buckingham: Society for Research into Higher Education in association with Open University Press.

Workers' Education Association (1982) *The Robert Tressell Papers: Exploring 'The Ragged Trousered Philanthropists'*, obtainable from Robert Tressell Workshop, c/o Robert Tressell House, 25 Wellington Square, Hastings, East Sussex.

Yarrington, R. (1979) 'Lifelong education trends in community colleges', *Convergence* XII (1–2).

Yeaxlee, B.A. (1925) *Spiritual Values in Adult Education*, (2 Vols) London: Oxford University Press.

—— (1929) *Lifelong Education*, London: Cassell.

Young, M.F.D. (1971) 'Curricula as socially organized knowledge', in Young, M.F.D. (ed.) *Knowledge and Control*, London: Collier–Macmillan.

—— (ed.) (1971) *Knowledge and Control*, London: Collier–Macmillan.

Zimmerman, F.E. (1979) 'Elder hostel '78 at Adelphi University', *Lifelong Learning: The Adult Years* LII (3).

INDEX